Reforming the European Union

We work with leading authors to develop the
strongest educational materials in politics,
bringing cutting-edge thinking and best learning
practice to a global market.

Under a range of well-known imprints, including
Longman, we craft high quality print and
electronic publications which help readers to
understand and apply their content,
whether studying or at work.

To find out more about the complete range of our
publishing please visit us on the World Wide Web at:
www.pearsoneduc.com

Reforming the European Union – from Maastricht to Amsterdam

Edited by Philip Lynch, Nanette Neuwahl and G. Wyn Rees

An imprint of **Pearson Education**

Harlow, England · London · New York · Reading, Massachusetts · San Francisco
Toronto · Don Mills, Ontario · Sydney · Tokyo · Singapore · Hong Kong · Seoul
Taipei · Cape Town · Madrid · Mexico City · Amsterdam · Munich · Paris · Milan

Pearson Education Limited
Edinburgh Gate
Harlow
Essex CM20 2JE
England
and Associated Companies throughout the world

Visit us on the World Wide Web at:
www.pearsoneduc.com

First published 2000

ISBN 0-582 28986 6

British Library Cataloguing-in-Publication Data
A catalogue record for this book is available from the British Library

Library of Congress Cataloging-in-Publication Data
A catalog record for this book is available from the Library of Congress

Set by 7 in 10/12 pt Times
Produced by Pearson Education Asia Pte Ltd
Printed in Singapore

Contents

List of contributors

Nigel M. Healey is Professor and Head of Department of Business Studies at Manchester Metropolitan University. He has acted as an economic advisor to governments in Belarus (1995–96), Bulgaria (1994–96) and Russia (1996 to date) and has held visiting posts at a number of institutions in central and eastern Europe, the United States and south east Asia. His main research interest is monetary and exchange rate policy. His recent publications include *The Economics of the New Europe* (Routledge, 1995) and *Central Banking in Transition Economies* (Routledge, 1999).

Francis Jacobs is a member of the Secretariat of the Committee on Institutional Affairs for the European Parliament. In this capacity he was closely involved in the negotiations of the Intergovernmental Conferences during the 1990s. His publications include *The European Parliament* (3rd edn., Cartermill, 1995) (with Richard Corbett and Michael Shackleton).

Charlie Jeffery is Professor of German Politics and Deputy Director of the Institute for German Studies at the University of Birmingham. A co-editor of *Regional and Federal Studies*, he has published widely on sub-national mobilization in EU policy-making, in particular the German case. He edited *The Regional Dimension of the European Union* (Frank Cass, 1997) and is currently working on a book on the German Länder and multi-level governance in the EU.

Jeff Kenner is a Lecturer in Law and Course Leader in the International Centre for Management, Law and Industrial Relations at the University of Leicester. He has written widely on Community law and social policy and is editor of *Trends in European Social Policy* (Dartmouth, 1995).

Philip Lynch is a Lecturer in Politics and Deputy Director of the Centre for European Politics and Institutions at the University of Leicester. He is author of *The Politics of Nationhood: Sovereignty, Britishness and Conservative Politics* (Macmillan, 1999). He is co-editor of *Politics Review*.

Jörg Monar is Professor of Politics and Director of the Centre for European Politics and Institutions at the University of Leicester. He is also External Professor at the

College of Europe (Bruges and Natolin) and Chairman of the European Association of Researchers in Federalism (Tübingen). His main areas of research and publication are the external relations of the EU, EU justice and home affairs and the institutional development of the EU. He is co-editor of *European Foreign Affairs Review*.

Nanette Neuwahl is Professor of European Law at the University of Liverpool where she holds a Jean Monnet Chair of European Union Law. She has published widely in the field of European integration, being the author or co-author of a number of key articles and books. She is co-editor (with Allan Rosas) of *The European Union and Human Rights* (Martinus Nijhoff, 1995). Her main research interests include constitutional questions in European Union law and external relations.

G. Wyn Rees is Senior Lecturer in International Relations and Deputy Director of the Centre for European Politics and Institutions at the University of Leicester. His recent publications include *The Western European Union at the Crossroads: Between Trans-Atlantic Solidarity and European Integration* (Westview, 1998) and *The Enlargement of Europe* (co-authored, Manchester University Press, 1999).

David Spence is responsible for NATO affairs within the European Commission. Former Advisor at the Foreign Office Conference Centre (Wilton Park) and Head of European Training at the British Civil Service College, he joined the Commission in 1990. His responsibilities have included relations between the Commission and the Council of Ministers, secretaryship of the Task Force for German unification and coordinator of the Commission's public relations programmes on German unification and on the enlargement of the European Union. He is editor, *inter alia*, of *The European Commission* (Cartermill, 1997) (with Geoffrey Edwards) and author of various articles on European affairs.

Takis Tridimas is Professor of European Law at the University of Southampton. He was formerly référendaire at the European Court of Justice. His publications include *Public Law of the European Community* (Sweet and Maxwell, 1995) (with Evelyn Ellis), *New Directions in European Public Law* (Hart, 1998) (co-editor with Jack Beatson) and *The General Principles of EC Law* (Oxford University Press, 1999).

Martin Westlake is Head of Unit for Institutional Relations in the European Commission. He is author of *The Council of the European Union* (Cartermill, 1995) and editor of *The European Union Beyond Amsterdam: New Concepts of European Integration* (Routledge, 1998).

Robin White is Professor of Law at the University of Leicester. He has written extensively in the field of European law. He is joint editor of the *European Law Review* and the author of *EU Social Security Law* (Addison Wesley Longman, 1999).

List of abbreviations

BSE	bovine spongiform encephalopathy
CDU	Christian Democratic Union (Germany)
CEECs	countries of central and eastern Europe
CEEP	European Centre of Enterprises and Public Participation
CFSP	Common Foreign and Security Policy
CoR	Committee of the Regions
Coreper	Committee of Permanent Representatives
COSAC	Conference of European Affairs Committees
CSCE	Conference on Security and Cooperation in Europe
CSU	Christian Social Union (Germany)
DG	Directorate-General
DM	deutschmark
EC	European Community
ECB	European Central Bank
ECHR	European Convention on Human Rights
ECJ	European Court of Justice
ECOFIN	Council of Economic and Finance Ministers
Ecosoc	Economic and Social Committee
ECSC	Euorpean Coal and Steel Community
ECU	European Currency Unit
EEA	European Economic Area
EEC	European Economic Community
EFTA	European Free Trade Association
EMS	European Monetary System
EMU	Economic and Monetary Union
EP	European Parliament
EPP	European People's Party (group in EP)
EPC	European Political Cooperation
ERM	Exchange Rate Mechanism
ESCB	European System of Central Banks
ESF	European Social Fund
ETUC	European Trades Union Confederation

EU	European Union
EURATOM	European Atomic Energy Community
EuroCorps	multilateral European military force
EUROFOR	European Force
EUROMARFOR	European Maritime Force
Europol	European Police Office
FFr	French franc
G7	Group of Seven
GDP	Gross Domestic Product
IGC	Intergovernmental Conference
JET	Joint European Torus
JHA	justice and home affairs
MEP	Member of the European Parliament
NATO	North Atlantic Treaty Organization
NGO	non-governmental organization
OJ	Official Journal of the European Communities
OSCE	Organization on Security and Cooperation in Europe
PPEWU	Policy Planning and Early Warning Unit
QMV	qualified majority voting
SEA	Single European Act
SEM	Single European Market
SG	Secretariat General
SME	small and medium-sized enterprises
SPA	Agreement on Social Policy
TEU	Treaty on European Union
UEAPME	European Assocation of Craft, Small and Medium-Sized Enterprises
UK	United Kingdom
UN	United Nations
UNICE	Union of Industrial and Employers' Confederations of Europe
UPE	Union for Europe (group in EP)
WEU	Western European Union

Preface

Throughout the book when reference is made to primary EU law, the numbering of the consolidated treaty is used with any previous numbering appearing within square brackets e.g. Article 234 [ex Article 177] EC. Deviations from this guideline occur only when the meaning of a reference is clear from the context in which it is used.

The chapters by Martin Westlake, David Spence and Francis Jacobs are written in a personal capacity and therefore do not necessarily represent the views of the EU institutions of which they are members.

Introduction: the Amsterdam Treaty and reform of the European Union

Philip Lynch, Nanette A. Neuwahl and G. Wyn Rees

This book examines developments in the European Union (EU) in the 1990s, focusing on the changes brought about by the 1997 Treaty of Amsterdam. Twelve chapters, written by a range of experts – practitioners working in EU institutions and academics from the fields of politics, law and economics – provide detailed assessments of institutional reforms, policy developments and constitutional issues in the Union. Each chapter examines the key debates in the 1996–97 Intergovernmental Conference (IGC), assesses the achievements and shortcomings of the Treaty of Amsterdam, and compares its provisions with those of the 1992 Treaty on European Union (TEU) or Maastricht Treaty. The IGC and Amsterdam Treaty and the resignation of the Santer Commission are also examined in the wider context of contemporary European integration and the changing political environment of the late 1990s. The EU's road to reform is thus examined through an assessment of the pressures for and obstacles hindering reform in the post-Maastricht period.

IGCs have been held on a number of occasions in the EU's history, notably in 1985 and 1990–91. The first produced the Single European Act (SEA), the centrepiece of which was the Single European Market programme. The 1990–91 twin IGCs on Economic and Monetary Union (EMU) and Political Union resulted in the Maastricht Treaty. This created the European Union, set out a programme and timetable for EMU and created intergovernmental pillars dealing with Common Foreign and Security Policy (CFSP) and Justice and Home Affairs (JHA). The Maastricht Treaty only entered into force in November 1993, following a difficult ratification process. Yet within little over a year, preparations were under way for the next IGC.

One of the key features of the 1996–97 IGC was the comparatively long and careful preparation which preceded its official launch. Article N of the Maastricht Treaty stated that an IGC would be held in 1996 to revise a number of areas, including a possible extension of the co-decision procedure, CFSP, new titles on energy, tourism and civil protection, and the introduction of a hierarchy of Community acts. In the spring of 1995, a year before the official opening of the IGC by the Turin European Council, the main EU institutions – the Council,

European Commission, European Parliament and Court of Justice – were invited to submit reports on the functioning of the TEU. A high level Reflection Group was then established by the Union to prepare the ground for the IGC.

The relationship between the citizen and the Union, a more efficient and democratic Union and enhanced EU external action emerged as the three main areas in which the 1995 Reflection Group Report recommended progress.[1] Concern for a 'Europe close to the citizen' followed the negative experiences national governments had faced during and after the Maastricht ratification process when referendums and opinion polls pointed to a crisis of legitimacy of the European Union. The EU's 'democratic deficit' added to a perception that the Union had become remote from the interests and experiences of its citizens.

The need for reform of the decision-making processes and composition of the institutions, which were originally designed for six Member States, was another area of concern. It was widely recognized that the anticipated eastward enlargement of the Union would place even greater demands on the EU and its institutions. Without substantial institutional reform, the Union would run the risk of decision-making paralysis. The re-weighting of votes under qualified majority voting (QMV) in the Council was added to the IGC agenda following a failure to reach agreement on this matter at the 1994 Ioannina meeting of foreign ministers.

A strengthening of the external capacity of the Union was deemed necessary in the light of the shortcomings of the modest structures put in place by the Maastricht Treaty. The continued gulf between the economic influence of the EU and its politico-military weight in international affairs led Member States to advance this cause. Further encouragement was derived from the perceived inadequacies of the organization in relation to the various crises on the European continent, most notably the conflict in former Yugoslavia.

New priorities for the EU also arose in the post-Maastricht period, as a result of either their increased political salience or because of the emergence of new concerns with the ending of the Cold War. High levels of unemployment encouraged national governments to address this problem at the European level. Increased illegal immigration and the growth of organized crime have necessitated Europe-wide responses in order to deal with the problems effectively.

The publication of the Reflection Group Report did not, however, imply that an agreement on these reforms would be easily attainable. A number of governments expressed concerns about some of the proposed changes, with the British Conservative government opposing much of the reform agenda. Given the obvious difficulties of reaching a consensus, a conviction began to emerge that necessary progress could only be attained if the principle of uniformity, which had hitherto been one of the central features of the EU, was abandoned. The introduction of flexibility would enable those Member States that were willing and able to deepen integration in specific areas using the institutions and procedures of the Union, without the participation of all Member States. The extent to which this principle of flexibility, the 'agreement to disagree', should be admissible in the future became another central issue during the IGC.

One approach towards judging the results of the 1996–97 IGC process would be to evaluate it in the context of the Reflection Group's recommendations. Yet despite the fact that the Reflection Group Report had an important influence on the IGC negotiations, it related only to problems that national governments agreed could be handled in the IGC framework proper. Economic and Monetary Union had been excluded from the IGC process altogether, while other matters covered by the Maastricht Treaty were left untouched.

An IGC is not simply a one-off conference or even a series of meetings between heads of government. Rather, the IGC process consists of numerous contacts between various levels of government. Part of the process is visible to the public, but part of it remains hidden, with the views of interest groups and citizens fed into the process at various stages. Draft Treaties are produced from time to time by the Member States holding the Council Presidency, indicating the progress achieved in negotiations to date and those areas requiring further work, but there is no guarantee that these drafts will be used as a basis for further concessions. As the June 1997 Amsterdam European Council meeting illustrated, the summit meetings which form the 'end-game' of the IGC process are renowned for upsetting balances reached in earlier discussions and for disregarding the carefully drafted texts produced by specialized negotiators. A number of important issues were decided late at night when tiredness had crept in and concessions could be wrought by introducing last-minute changes. These features of the IGC process led many proponents of reform to question the EU's mechanisms for Treaty revision.

The contributors to this volume have adopted an analytical rather than prescriptive approach. There are no predetermined criteria for evaluating the outcome of the 1996–97 IGC; instead a range of standpoints is employed. The Amsterdam Treaty can thus be judged in relation to the provisions of the TEU regarding its revisions, the recommendations of the Reflection Group or the aims set out by EU leaders at the Turin European Council. A number of contributors assess the reforms according to norms such as legitimacy, democracy, justice or efficiency and comment on the internal coherence of the Treaty. Finally, the Amsterdam reforms are also located within the wider political context of the 1990s, assessing the constraints on negotiators in the 1996–97 IGC compared to the Maastricht negotiations and assessing the likely impact of the Treaty provisions on the EU.

Structure of the book

The book is divided into three parts: institutional reform, policy developments, and the Union and its citizens.

The revision of the EU's institutions and procedures was always meant to be a central element of the 1996–97 IGC, particularly given the anticipated eastward enlargement of the Union. The IGC also addressed the respective weight of the political institutions and the representation of national governments and the European citizen within them.

Part One examines the reform of the Council of the European Union, the

European Commission and the European Parliament. Although EU leaders postponed key decisions on institutional reform at the Amsterdam summit, the new Treaty nonetheless introduces a number of significant changes. Martin Westlake provides a detailed examination of the Treaty reforms which directly affect the Council, noting how the IGC discussions promoted new thinking on the functioning of the EU and revealed a number of interlinked dialectics. David Spence examines the reform of the European Commission, assessing the reform debates of the 1990s, the changes introduced by the Amsterdam Treaty and the Commission's internal reform programme. Francis Jacobs investigates the changing role of the European Parliament in the post-Maastricht reform process, its priorities and its evolving powers. Takis Tridimas assesses the Treaty reforms with regard to the European Court of Justice, examining how Amsterdam affects the jurisdiction of the Court and how it fails to address questions of organization.

Part Two provides a detailed assessment of developments in the EU's major policy areas in the 1990s. Although EMU was formally excluded from the IGC negotiations, it has been the EU's central project in the late 1990s, representing a quantum leap in the integration process. On 1 January 1999, eleven EU Member States entered Stage III of Economic and Monetary Union. Nigel Healey argues that while the economic benefits of EMU are relatively modest and predictable, the economic costs are uncertain. In a euro zone with imperfect economic integration, less well-integrated states may be disadvantaged by the 'one monetary policy fits all' rule. Fiscal policy at national and European level will be unable to take over adequately a stabilizing role, so such states may be forced to rely on wage flexibility and labour mobility to absorb asymmetric shocks. Healey examines the Maastricht provisions on EMU, the constitution of the European Central Bank and the emergence of an EMU of 'ins' and 'outs'.

Social policy had proved one of the most contentious issues at the Maastricht summit. The TEU produced a 'twin-stream' policy process in which 11 Member States adopted the Protocol and Agreement on Social Policy, without the participation of the United Kingdom. Jeff Kenner assesses the scope and effect of the Agreement on Social Policy before exploring the re-evaluation of the European Social Model signalled by the Commission's 1993 White Paper on 'Growth, Competitiveness and Employment' and 1994 White Paper on Social Policy. Kenner examines the debate over labour market flexibility and social rights, before assessing the changes introduced by the Amsterdam Treaty. Particular attention is paid to the abolition of the Social Protocol, the provisions on non-discrimination and the new title on employment.

In the Maastricht negotiations, a broad-based regional lobby led by the German Länder successfully secured an enhanced role for sub-national governments in EU decision-making. The TEU established an advisory Committee of the Regions while the principle of subsidiarity was incorporated into the Treaty in Article 3b, albeit in a form which did not explicitly extend it to the sub-national level. Charlie Jeffery assesses the political influence of the regions in the EU, noting how many of the factors which allowed for successful regional lobbying in 1990–91 had evaporated by the 1996–97 IGC.

Jörg Monar reviews the progress that has been made in the field of justice and home affairs, lauded by some as the major success story of the Amsterdam Treaty. He questions how substantive was the communitarization of third pillar activities in the Treaty and points to continuing deficits in the EU's capabilities in this field. The chapter on the Common Foreign and Security Policy by Wyn Rees traces the debates that surrounded foreign, security and defence policy from Maastricht to Amsterdam. He focuses particularly on the shortcomings of the CFSP and the extent to which its development was vulnerable both to external crises and to the evolution of partner organizations such as NATO.

Part Three of the book explores wider issues affecting the Union and its citizens. Nanette Neuwahl considers the extent to which the Treaty of Amsterdam develops further the relationship between the EU and the citizen. She argues that the momentum represented by the TEU's provision for citizenship of the Union appears to have passed and warns against the risk of raising expectations which cannot then be fulfilled. Flexibility, the concept that a number of EU Member States may be permitted to forge ahead with further integration using EU institutions without requiring the participation of states unable or unwilling to proceed, has been a central issue in debates on reform of the EU in the 1990s. Philip Lynch assesses the different ideal type models of flexible integration and the various instances of flexibility evident before and after the Maastricht Treaty. The post-Maastricht debate on flexibility is then explored, followed by a detailed analysis of the Amsterdam Treaty's provisions for closer cooperation. Finally, Robin White assesses whether the Amsterdam Treaty marks a step forward in the constitutionalization of the Union. White defends the view that there is an effective and powerful unwritten constitution for the Union. However, he believes it is too early to crystallize the evolution of that constitution by seeking to reduce it to a codified constitutional document.

In a concluding chapter, the editors draw together some of the major themes of the book. They provide an overview and assessment of developments in the EU in the 1990s, focusing in particular on the Treaty of Amsterdam, before examining the key challenges facing the Union at the beginning of the new millennium.

Endnote

1.   *The Reflection Group Report*, (1995) SN 520/95 (REFLEX 21), December, Brussels.

INSTITUTIONAL REFORM

Chapter 1

The Council

Martin Westlake

On the face of it, the Treaty of Amsterdam contained relatively few reforms directly affecting the Council. However, the preceding negotiations revealed profound currents, some touching on the very foundations of the Union and those modifications which were adopted may have considerable consequences for the Council and its working methods. This chapter will therefore address itself not only to the relevant Amsterdam Treaty amendments but to issues which were discussed but did not lead to concrete results, as well as to issues which were postponed or not addressed at all but which have since been discussed.

Article N of the Maastricht Treaty spoke blandly about examination of 'those provisions of this Treaty for which revision is provided'; the IGC was to be a '20,000 kilometre service'. But the Reflection Group proposed a detailed agenda for the IGC, which included, variously: to prepare the EU for imminent enlargement; to make the Union more relevant to its citizens; to improve the Union's efficiency and render it more democratic; and to give the Union a greater capacity for external action. All of these aims, some of them potentially conflicting (for example, democracy and efficiency) involved the Council to some degree.

The Amsterdam European Council

On what grounds should the IGC's institutional reforms be judged? By what was expected, by what was achieved, or by what, it is now generally recognized, has yet to come? Immediately after the Amsterdam European Council, most commentators felt that the IGC had failed, particularly with regard to substantive reform of the Council.[1] This chapter will show that the Treaty's reforms of the Council were not as disappointing as many argued, and that, in several areas where the IGC was unable to agree on reform, the negotiations nevertheless 'cleared the air' and set out the terms of debate. In that sense, the Amsterdam Treaty is almost as significant for its omissions as its contents.

Economic and Monetary Union

By tacit accord of the negotiating states, the Maastricht Treaty's provisions on Economic and Monetary Union (EMU) remained unchanged. Thus, although the cooperation procedure disappeared from all other parts of the Treaty on European Union (TEU) and its component treaties, it remained in the EMU Title as a reminder of just how carefully wrought was the agreement reached at Maastricht.

While the Amsterdam negotiations were nearing their conclusion, a parallel but entirely external debate was taking place about the exact rights and role of a new forum, initially dubbed the 'Euro-X', and the exact scope of this new joint mechanism for governments already in the monetary union. Awkward agreement was reached at the December 1997 Luxembourg European Council, which recognized the requirement for 'closer Community surveillance and coordination of economic policies among euro-area Member States' but also that the 'defining position of the Ecofin Council at the centre of the economic coordination and policy-making process' affirmed 'the unity and cohesion of the Community'. The agreement did not halt the debate about the Euro-X, nor could it entirely obscure the questions raised about the EU's single institutional framework, particularly with regard to the Council. This was an argument which had been waiting to happen since the TEU's draftsmen had recognized that not all Member States would be able to meet the convergence criteria at the same time and had granted an 'opt-out' facility to the UK (later joined by Denmark and Sweden).

One potentially significant consequence of the formation of the Euro-X Council relates to the Presidency of the EU Council. The UK held the Presidency in the first half of 1998 and, at special meetings on 1–2 May 1998, the Ecofin Council and a hybrid Council meeting in the composition of Heads of State or Government formally decided which Member States would proceed to full membership of monetary union on 1 January 1999. The Euro-11 met before the end of the British Presidency, on 5 June 1998, before a meeting of the full Ecofin Council. But although it was held under the (incoming) Austrian Presidency, the UK was allowed to participate in part of the meeting. The issue will not arise again until the year 2001, when an 'out' (Sweden) will again hold the Presidency of the EU. By then the issue may well have been resolved.

Some commentators drew speculative parallels with the 1997 decision of the Western European Union (WEU) Council to reorder the succession of its Presidencies so as to harmonize them as much as possible with those of the EU Council.[2] Since five EU members were not full members of the WEU, the WEU Council decided that when the Presidency of the EU was held by one of the ten WEU Member States, that same Member State would hold the WEU Presidency. In all other cases, the WEU Presidency would be held by one of its ten Member States, following the current succession of presidencies in alphabetical order (in English). Might this be a significant precedent?

In the end, the Euro-X's implications for the EU's institutional structure were not as damaging as was first feared. French attempts to strengthen the Euro-X by setting up a permanent secretariat were blocked by the German government, which feared for the independence of the European Central Bank (ECB). Instead, the secretariat would be provided by the government holding the Presidency. But, Euro-11 meetings would be prepared by all 15 Member States' representatives on the Monetary Committee together with the European Commission; the Euro-11's deliberations would always be the subject of a full report back to the Monetary Committee, and the 'prime importance of the Ecofin Council' would be 'fully respected'.[3] The earlier special arrangements of the now defunct Council of the Social Protocol had clearly established a quiet precedent.[4] Although further complications in relation to the euro's external representation were discussed at the December 1998 Vienna European Council, and although the Euro-11 Council has now met several times in its 'pure' form, the Heads of State or Government also agreed on the need for strengthened economic policy coordination both within the Euro-11 and the Ecofin Council.[5]

The Council's functioning

Qualified majority voting (QMV), which was expected to be extended to all legislative areas, was in the end extended only to five relatively insignificant areas. As a result, the combination of co-decision and unanimity remains (e.g. Article 128). The re-weighting of votes within the Council was ducked and postponed, through the device of a Treaty Protocol, to the 'date of entry into force of the first enlargement of the Union'. The issue of 'comitology' was also postponed, in this case through the device of a Declaration, though, in so doing, the Member States were following the tradition established by the Single European Act (SEA). As with the 1987 decision, it was for the Commission to come forward with a legislative proposal. This it duly did in June 1998, whereupon the proposal became the object of extended negotiations between the Council and the European Parliament (EP).

Although paragraph 3.I of the Protocol on the role of national parliaments glancingly recognized the increasingly pre-eminent role of Corepers II and I and of the Council's other preparatory bodies, the IGC effectively reasserted the basic Council methodology of filtering draft legislation upwards through appointed bodies primarily composed of national officials. The IGC failed to explore the Reflection Group's suggestion that 'consideration be given to fresh approaches to preparatory work for the Council ...' and, 'the possibility ... of replacing some stages of discussions in working parties by a written procedure'.[6]

Nor did the IGC examine the general implications for the Council's traditional working methods of the dual challenge of enlargement and new tasks. The Conference thus ducked an issue pointed up by the Council itself in its report on the functioning of the TEU: 'recent experience of the functioning of the Council confirms that the continued efficiency and consistency of its activities also depends on curbing more effectively the growing number of meetings and effectively coordinating its various formations'.[7] The Reflection Group, pointed to a 'gradual deterioration both in the organisation of the Council and its working methods'.[8]

The need for reform of the Council's mechanisms, particularly in the context of enlargement, was raised by a number of Member States, including the Benelux countries, France and Italy. In the September 1997 General Affairs Council meeting, Italy's then foreign affairs minister, Lamberto Dini, made a number of suggestions, including a call for the Council to concentrate *only* on issues ripe for a decision (strengthening the Council's preparatory bodies).[9] He also called for table rounds to be strictly controlled. These suggestions did not bear fruit, and the Belgian, French and Italian governments subsequently appended a Declaration to the Amsterdam Treaty which observed that the Treaty 'does not meet the need ... for substantial progress towards reinforcing the institutions' and considers 'that such reinforcement is an indispensable condition for the conclusion of the first accession negotiations'.

Whilst the Treaty ratification process continued in the Member States, the Council Secretariat General (SG) quietly began work on a general note regarding the Council's working methods and possible reforms. The SG referred not only to the Dini proposals but also to a number of preceding documents, including the Council's 11 May 1992 conclusions in the framework of the follow-up to Maastricht, guidelines adopted by the Council on 29 May 1995 and recommendations in the field of external relations adopted on 12 June 1995, as well as to the speech made by Jacques Poos during the July 1997 open Council debate on the Luxembourg Presidency, and a March 1998 letter from French minister Hubert Védrine to the British foreign minister, Robin Cook, during the British Presidency.

The note dealt with the Council in general, the General Affairs Council, CFSP matters and JHA matters, and made detailed recommendations relating variously to: the composition of specialized Councils; the scheduling of Council sessions and the preparation of Council agendas and proceedings; the holding of informal Council meetings; attendance at Council meetings; and continuity in exercising the Presidency. The June 1998 Cardiff European Council noted that the Council was considering the scope of improvements in its functioning and invited it to report on progress made. Although the discussion of the Council SG's suggestions/ recommendations became intertwined with a parallel debate about the role of the General Affairs Council, the foreign affairs ministers nevertheless held detailed debates in March, May, and September (Salzburg informal meeting) 1998. At its 5–6 October 1998 meeting the General Affairs Council decided on the immediate implementation of a number of these measures. A further Council SG report on streamlining the Council's effectiveness and consistency of actions appeared in 1999. The December 1998 Vienna European Council agreed on an overall political 'strategy for Europe' which included the June 1999 Cologne European Council decision to convene an IGC in 2000 to 'resolve the institutional issues left open at Amsterdam' and a review at the Helsinki European Council of the improvement of the functioning of the Council. These proposals and reforms are considered in more detail elsewhere in this chapter.

The Common Foreign and Security Policy

The Amsterdam Treaty's reforms concerning the Common Foreign and Security

Policy (CFSP) provisions are considered in detail in Chapter 9, but the main outlines are of interest to the student of Council reform.

The reworded Article 3 TEU calls on the Council and the Commission to cooperate to ensure consistency between all external policies. Article 13 TEU strengthens the European Council by conferring upon it the competence to define the principles and general guidelines of the CFSP and to decide on common strategies which are, in turn, to be defined and implemented by the Council, acting by qualified majority. If a Member State opposes such a Council decision for stated reasons of national policy, a vote is not taken but the Council may, by a qualified majority, refer the matter up to the European Council for decision by unanimity – a provision commonly described as the incorporation of the Luxembourg Compromise. Article 23 TEU also allows Member States to qualify abstentions in unanimous votes by way of a formal declaration ('constructive abstention'). A Member State thus qualifying its abstention 'shall not be obliged to apply the decision, but shall accept that the decision commits the Union'. However, if Member States representing more than a third of weighted votes qualify their abstention in this way, the decision shall not be adopted.

Article 17 TEU calls for the 'progressive framing of a common defence policy' without prejudice to WEU and NATO membership. What seemed at the time like an interesting footnote to this development was provided by the Tindemans Report on European Defence Policy, adopted by the European Parliament in May 1998. *Inter alia*, Tindemans' Report called for the creation of a council of defence ministers (European Parliament debates, 13 May 1998). This was considered a long-term possibility at best but then, on 4 November 1998, on the initiative of the Austrian Presidency, an informal meeting of EU defence ministers took place in Vienna. The meeting was unprecedented and its informal nature meant that it could do no formal business. High on the meeting's agenda was a discussion about methods of crisis management. The Austrian initiative was said to have pleased NATO, 'which feels Europe's efforts to define security policies have been stagnating. Washington, too, was said to have welcomed the initiative'.[10] It was said that the initiative, which followed hard on the heels of a British government calling for more streamlined institutional structure in this field, was a one-off, and that no similar meeting was foreseen in the near future. It nevertheless constituted a remarkable new departure in the EU's evolution.

Both a common defence policy and the eventual integration of the WEU into the EU are subject to decisions by the European Council. The European Council may establish guidelines for the WEU where the EU 'has availed itself of the WEU'. The Petersberg tasks are expressly included in those tasks that can be decided within the Treaty framework. When such a decision is taken, all Member States, including non-WEU members, may participate if they so wish, but only participating Member States will contribute to the financing. A Protocol provides for the EU and the WEU to draw up, within one year of the implementation of the Treaty, 'arrangements for enhanced cooperation between them'.

Articles 18, 26 and 27 TEU describe a new form of troika. The Presidency of the Council, representing the Union in matters falling within the CFSP and responsible for the implementation of common actions, is to be assisted by the Secretary-General of the Council ('who shall exercise the function of High Representative'), and a Commission member responsible for CFSP (Declaration 32 notes 'the desirability of bringing external relations under the responsibility of a Vice-President'). The new Article 24 TEU enables the Presidency, assisted by the Commission and subject to unanimous authorization by the Council, to negotiate or conclude agreements with other states or international organizations. The CFSP will be financed through the Community budget, with the exception of military or defence operations, or when the Council unanimously decides otherwise.

Virtually all these reforms had already been broached in the Reflection Group's Report and therefore came as something of an anticlimax. However, there was general recognition that the reforms represented slow progress.

The Treaty marked a further consolidation of the role of the European Council. A minor, but significant, innovation was the express provision for decision-making by the European Council.[11] This, in combination with the lack of an explicit dividing line between strategy and implementation measures, gave rise to fears that the new provisions could be sapped if a tendency developed to push decisions up from the Council (QMV) to the European Council (unanimity). 'For the first time the voting procedure is determined not by the substance of the decision but by the level at which it is taken.'[12]

A variation on this has been applied to the arrangements for financing EU/WEU action under the Petersberg tasks. Decisions will be unanimous, but tempered by constructive abstention. The cost of the action will be borne only by those Member States participating, critics arguing that there is 'a risk that the budgetary arrangements of constructive abstention will be misused: this decision-making procedure will allow the Member States to abstain in order not to contribute financially'.[13]

The new troika arrangement will produce greater continuity in the EU's external action, since the Council Secretary-General and the Commission Vice-President will both have considerably longer periods in office than the current troika members and should go some way towards answering Henry Kissinger's jibe about a single name and telephone number. Under Article 17 of the Council's current Rules of Procedure, the Secretary-General is appointed unanimously, and the tradition has grown of appointing Council Secretaries-General for five-year periods. In addition to becoming High Representative for the CFSP, the Secretary-General will have specific responsibility for the Policy Planning and Early Warning Unit. This is expected to be a heavyweight political and administrative position, some commentators likening it to the position of NATO Secretary-General.[14]

Declaration 6 provides for a new Policy Planning and Early Warning Unit (PPEWU) to be established within the Council Secretariat General, to be staffed with officials drawn variously from the Member States, the Council Secretariat General, the Commission, and the WEU. This will be a key element in the CFSP's future development. Since budgetary and personnel dispositions would need to be in place by the time of the Amsterdam Treaty's implementation, the Council

Secretary-General drafted informal proposals in early 1998, and parallel discussions in the Political Committee and Coreper culminated in the submission of an interim report by the British Presidency to the 30 March 1998 General Affairs Council. The report touched on such matters as composition and distribution of tasks and called on the Secretary-General to draw up reports on the reorganization of the Secretariat General.[15] These issues were again discussed at the 26 October 1998 Portschach informal European Council meeting. In a subsequent press conference the Austrian General Affairs Council President, Wolfgang Schüssel, declared that there was 'a great need for improvement in cooperation between the First and Second Pillars which will necessitate a reorganization of the Secretariat, which means that the division between external economic policy and external affairs will no longer exist, and joint regional units will be created'.[16]

The 11–12 December 1998 Vienna European Council took note of the work undertaken concerning the establishment of the PPEWU and agreed that 'the Secretary-General of the Council and High Representative for the CFSP will be appointed as soon as possible and will be a personality with a strong political profile'.[17]

At a 27 April 1998 meeting of the General Affairs Council, the Benelux countries, in contradistinction to the new provisions on 'constructive abstention', raised the problem of compatibility between CFSP and the *ad hoc* coalitions which, they argued, were increasingly formed by some Member States. Promising a working paper on the matter, the Benelux ministers argued that 'the external action of the Union and its Member States must not evolve in a way that the policy of some Member States could prevail over that of the others'. 'The existence of *ad hoc* arrangements between some Member States in areas of vital importance,' they continued, '… could in time weaken confidence in a strong CFSP'.[18]

Reduction and simplification of decision-making procedures

Once the Amsterdam Treaty was ratified, the various decision-making procedures for Community legislation were reduced to three: co-decision, assent and consultation. The one exception is Title VI on Economic and Monetary Policy, where the old cooperation procedure was retained (but can be expected to disappear at any future IGC which amends the Title). Article 251 [ex-189 B] EC will be significantly simplified. The third reading in Council will be done away with, and the procedure may be concluded in the event of agreement or of rejection by the Parliament at first reading. In terms of everyday legislative work these reforms will change little because the procedural options which have been scrapped were, in any case, only used in exceptional political cases. However, as the Parliament puts it, 'they do change the institutional symbolism and hence the institutional balance. In its legislative process, the Union is made up, more clearly than before, of two representative bodies which are equal in principle as the Union of the states and the peoples of Europe'.[19] This streamlining of the co-decision procedure goes hand in hand with an extension of the procedure to 24 new areas (not until five years after entry into force in the case of visa legislation and, in three other cases, coupled with unanimity in the Council).

The extension of QMV and the weighting of votes

The Reflection Group's Report stated that 'in the case of Community legislation a large majority in the Group is prepared to consider making QMV the general rule'. By the end of the IGC, just five points in the existing Treaty were to be subjected to QMV. In terms of new Treaty provisions, 11 new cases of QMV will be introduced. The modesty of these reforms was generally seen as a great disappointment.

Linked to the debate about the extension of QMV was the even more sensitive discussion about the re-weighting of votes in the Council. The Dutch Presidency took a strategic decision to link negotiations on re-weighting of Council votes with the composition of the Commission. In particular, it proposed that, when two new Member States joined the EU, the large Member States would give up their second Commissioner. In exchange, the votes in the Council would be re-weighted in their favour (see Box 1). The proposals tripped over a series of three problems. The first was the Belgian government's insistence on the necessary linkage between re-weighting and an extension of QMV. Second was the predilection of a large majority of the Member States for a new dual majority system but, since this would give Germany a greater demographic weight than France would be unable to accept, such proposals were stillborn. The third was the Spanish government's insistence that, were it to lose its second Commissioner, it would require equality with the four large Member States in terms of weighting of votes in the Council. At the same time, the French government insisted on a reduction in the overall number of members of the Commission as a necessary *quid pro quo*.[20]

The absence of any overall agreement led the Member States to opt for the status quo, but the 'Protocol on institutions with the prospect of enlargement of the European Union' retains the link between Commission composition and the weighting of Council votes and provides that, at the next enlargement, 'the Commission shall comprise one national of each of the Member States' provided that agreement has been reached on re-weighting of votes in the Council. The December 1998 Vienna European Council agreed that the decision should be taken at the 1999 Cologne European Council on 'how and when to tackle the institutional issues not resolved at Amsterdam'.

Enhanced cooperation and flexibility

The Amsterdam Treaty's innovatory provisions on enhanced cooperation are examined in Chapter 11. What is primarily significant is that Section V of the Treaty provides the possibility for a number of Member States – less than the full EU membership – to cooperate more closely in certain areas while using the institutional framework of the EU, with all the implications that this would have for

---

Box 1.1: The re-weighting variants considered by the IGC*

A. Dual majority voting

Two variants:
I. The current weighted majority is retained.
II. A simple majority of Member States, with each Member State having one vote.

Both these variants required that the majority should represent at least 60 per cent of the total population of the Union.

B. Re-weighting of votes
Votes are re-weighted by allocating votes to Member States in a decreasing scale subject to population size.

Two variants:

I. 12 for Germany, UK, France, Italy; 9 for Spain, Poland; 6 for the Netherlands, Romania; 5 for Greece, Czech Republic, Belgium, Hungary, Portugal; 4 for Sweden, Bulgaria, Austria; 3 for Denmark, Finland, Ireland, Slovakia, Lithuania; 2 for Luxembourg, Cyprus, Latvia, Slovenia, Estonia.
II. 25 for Germany, UK, France, Italy; 20 for Spain, Poland; 12 for the Netherlands, Romania; 10 for Greece, Czech Republic, Belgium, Hungary, Portugal; 8 for Sweden, Bulgaria, Austria; 6 for Denmark, Finland, Ireland, Slovakia, Lithuania; 3 for Luxembourg, Cyprus, Latvia, Slovenia, Estonia.

Both variants have a minimum level of about 60 per cent of the total EU population and would approximately respect the existing threshold of 71.2 per cent.

*Presidency note CONF/3888/97 of 24 April 1997 proposed to the IGC two different approaches to the re-weighting issue; dual majority voting, and re-weighting.

---

the Council and its negotiating and voting arrangements. The provisions are heavily ring-fenced in all three pillars, including bastardized versions of the Luxembourg Compromise, and it is unclear, particularly in the first pillar, whether the provisions could actually be used. Whether they were intended to be a negotiating device or a functional response to the recalcitrance of anti-integrationist Member States, the provisions have been seen as a significant 'first' in the Community's history. It is doubtful whether they will change the Council's methodology and philosophy on a day-to-day basis, although the threat of recourse to enhanced cooperation may be mooted at important moments.

Dialectics

The IGC negotiations and accompanying debates revealed a number of interlinked, or overlapping, dialectics. A first is the dialectic between democracy and efficiency.

At one level, arguments in favour of extending qualified majority voting have little to do with enhancing democracy and everything to do with enhancing the Council's decision-making capacity. This point was implicitly accepted by the negotiators of the SEA and of the Maastricht Treaty, who provided for democratic counterbalances in the form of cooperation and co-decision powers for the EP precisely in order to rectify the potentially anti-democratic consequences for the 'disenfranchised' populations of the outvoted minority states.

A second dialectic is that between symbolism and effectiveness. This is particularly apparent in debates about Council decision-making, where the emphasis on voting mechanisms and weighted votes obscures the fact that the Council very rarely votes. The UK Permanent Representative to the EU was reported as having stated that 'We never vote by QMV anyway. We always reach a consensus. We are members of a club and we are helping each other out. Voting is not the way Europe works.'[21] Formal Council decisions are at the summit of a cumulative consensual mechanism where the bulk of questions are dealt with at sub-ministerial level. Why, then, is the further extension of QMV considered so urgent? A part of the explanation can probably be gleaned from a reply Belgian prime minister Jean-Luc Dehaene gave in the Belgian Senate in July 1997.

> The weighting of votes in the Council means a revision of the Treaty: that should therefore be achieved through the accession treaty (of future Member States). This procedure is nevertheless to be avoided as a modification of Union institutions could then depend on the new members. Yet, this is the responsibility of the Fifteen alone, which means a new IGC. An IGC is not necessarily a long and difficult process: it can last half a day or a day, depending on prior agreements. In other words, Belgium's position on the re-weighting of votes will depend on the decision relating to qualified majority voting. ... Abandoning the rule of unanimity is not a concession made by the small states to the large states but is based on European interests. I would also add that the veto is more often than not used by the large states and not the small states. Extending the qualified majority also goes hand in hand with the re-weighting of votes and the representation of the large States in the Council. The discussion remains open.[22]

President Chirac presented the other end of this argument when he said 'the large countries will be careful to prevent a coalition of small countries placing them in a minority position'.[23]

A third dialectic, then, is the relationship between smaller and larger Member States and between current and future Member States. Current members, particularly the smaller states, would like to reach an agreement on weighting before the arrival of other smaller states clouds the debate and diminishes their current advantage as insiders.

A fourth, hidden dialectic is between the qualitative and quantitative aspects of EU legislative activity. After the SEA's decision-making reforms, it became common to measure the success of the new procedures through simple statistics on decision-making, particularly since a large raft of legislation (over 300 separate acts) had to be adopted within the 1986–92 period if the Single Market were to be achieved on time. Analysts of the European Parliament's new legislative role, for example, emphasized Council and Commission take-up of first- and second-reading amendments as a simple way of demonstrating its new-found influence. In the case of the Council, it was the quantity of legislation adopted. But all of the institutions have been aware of the concomitant need for legislative clarity and quality. This awareness was first explicitly recognized in the December 1992 Edinburgh European Council's conclusions, which devoted five lengthy paragraphs to the matter, followed by a June 1993 Council resolution on drafting quality.[24] Declaration 39 appended to the Amsterdam Treaty consolidates this trend by noting that 'the quality of the drafting of Community legislation is crucial if it is to be properly implemented' and by calling upon the Council, Parliament and Commission to lay down guidelines and to take 'the internal organizational measures they deem necessary to ensure that these guidelines are properly applied'. Here was implicit recognition that current methods might not always result in legislation of appropriate quality.[25] In December 1998, in anticipation of the implementation of the Amsterdam Treaty, the EP, the Council and the Commission approved an interinstitutional agreement on common guidelines for the drafting of common legislation which was composed of a number of specific recommend-ations, including discouragement of the classic Council method device of 'state-ments in the minutes'.

A fifth dialectic was revealed between representativeness and effectiveness. Even if the Council rarely votes, Member States' weighted votes are always implicit in negotiations, but it is legitimate to ask whether voting strength is the only, or the most effective, tool. The occasional public row about important decisions should not obscure the fact that the legislation produced by the Council satisfies most Member States most of the time. This, in turn, implies that the mechanisms which precede the formal decision-making level are extremely effective in adapting legislation to garner the broadest possible consensus. Underlying this is the basic tenet of the Council's negotiating method, the understanding that 'there but for the grace of God go I', whereby every effort is made to take into account the considerations of all of the Member States.

A sixth dialectic present in the debate about voting weights opposes the status quo and the acceptance of gentle decline. Analysis of the evolution of the relative strength of Member States' weighted votes shows that these have been in gentle decline, and that most adjustments to weightings (generally in anticipation or as a result of accessions) have resulted in a diminution of relative strengths.[26] The larger the Member State, the greater the decline. If this were a simple statistical indication of theoretical strength alone, the matter would remain obscure, but these declines have important knock-on consequences for Member States' abilities to block unpalatable decisions.

Until the last enlargement, Member States seemed content to acquiesce in this gentle decline. But in 1994 simmering misgivings erupted in the 'blocking minority row'. Britain, Spain and, initially, Italy argued that they could not accept a simple mechanical extension of the threshold for a blocking minority (which had remained fairly constant at around 30 per cent of total votes). Until then, two large and one smaller Member State were sufficient to form a blocking minority, but if the threshold were mechanically extended (to remain at about 30 per cent of the total vote) in a Community of sixteen, the formation of a blocking minority would have required two large and two small Member States. The dispute was settled through the 'Ioaninna Compromise', whereby if states amounting to between 23 and 26 votes were opposed to a decision, the decision would be delayed in order to enable the Council to find 'a satisfactory solution that could be adopted by at least 68 votes'.

Declaration 50 annexed to the Amsterdam Treaty extends the 'Ioannina Compromise' until the entry into force of the first enlargement. (But it is interesting to note that the Compromise has only ever been used once, by the UK, on 24–25 October 1998, in relation to monetary compensation amounts under the Common Agricultural Policy. A solution to the problem which had caused the British government to invoke the Compromise was agreed during the same Council meeting!) The way in which the blocking minority row broke in the closing stages of accession negotiations provided another powerful reason for reforming the weighting of votes in the Council before new enlargement negotiations got fully under way.

A seventh, related dialectic is the constant opposition between majority and minority rights. This is a problem common to all democracies but is becoming increasingly pronounced in the Union as successive enlargements have created a more diverse community of states. In the US Senate, all states are equally represented. In the Council of the EU, on the other hand, a state's representation depends on the type of voting procedure concerned. States have equal weight where simple majorities or unanimity are required. But under qualified majority voting a state's representation depends on what category of size it falls into. Most Member States now fall into one of four categories: large (ten votes – Germany, France, the United Kingdom, Italy); larger medium (five votes – Belgium, Greece, the Netherlands and Portugal); smaller medium (four votes – Austria, Sweden); and small (three votes – Denmark, Ireland, Finland). Moreover, voting weights are only loosely related to population size. Newly enlarged Germany wields the same number of weighted votes as France, despite having 23 million more inhabitants. In the run-up to the Amsterdam Treaty, various commentators pointed out that after the next wave of accessions, under the current system, a qualified majority of Member States could represent less than a majority of the EU's total population (in the EU 15, a qualified majority of 71 per cent of the votes can already be achieved by a coalition of Member States representing just 58 per cent of the population). Moreover, Protocol D, which links weighted voting in the Council to the number of Commissioners, refers to 'compensating those Member States which give up the possibility of nominating a second member of the Commission', implying that further 'distortions' in Member States' weighted votes might occur. Hence the various proposals floated for 'double majorities' (see Box 1.1, on page 17) – in a diverse European Union with a hybrid state chamber, defining the minority depends on the measurements used. The proponents of double majorities argued that weighted voting was a mechanical device to facilitate decision-making, and that population size was therefore a desirable double-check.[27] If proponents of double majority voting did not win the day at Amsterdam, they created a future possibility, since Article 1 of Protocol D declares that the weighting of votes in the Council should be modified 'by re-weighting of votes or by dual majority'.

A last dialectic is between simplification and complexity. During the IGC, much emphasis was put on the need for greater access to the Union's legislative and decision-making processes and on the concomitant need for simplification. At the same time, the IGC was obliged to create a large number of innovatory institutional mechanisms which will inevitably lead to greater complexity. It would be wrong to assume that these provisions were merely negotiating devices; rather, they represent the sort of transitional mechanisms to be expected in an evolutionary integration system.[28]

Malthusian predictions confounded

The genesis of the Amsterdam Treaty was accompanied by Malthusian predictions that the EU had missed out on a last chance to reform its institutions and decision-making mechanisms before *la déluge*. But these predictions may be ill-founded. In the first place, according to Protocol D, another IGC must be held one year before 'the membership of the European Union exceeds twenty'. In any case, each enlargement necessarily involves an adjustment to the weighting of votes. Moreover, there is pressure on the Member States to hold an IGC to deal with the issue of institutional reform even earlier than envisaged in Protocol D. The Commission, in its Agenda 2000 Communication, suggested that 'a new Inter-governmental Conference be convened as soon as possible after 2000 to produce a thorough reform ... (which) would, in any event, have to involve the introduction of qualified majority voting across the board'. [29]

Collapse is not imminent

Ironically, even assuming *ceteris paribus*, there is no statistical evidence to show that the Council is becoming less efficient in the strictly quantitative sense of legislation adopted/decisions taken, despite regular increases to its size. Political commentators rightly pointed to the SEA's introduction of QMV as a revolutionary constitutional innovation, but this has to be squared with the fact that in its every day life the Council rarely votes. In truth, the SEA was part of a larger trend, and the introduction of QMV both signalled and consolidated a change in mentality, a renewed political desire to get away from the stagnation of the late 1970s and early 1980s and to make progress. Seen from this point of view, QMV is not the only way of speeding up decision-making nor of rendering it more efficient. Among other important factors should be mentioned;

- the effect of Court rulings (particularly *Cassis de Dijon*, which enabled the Commission to adopt a 'new approach' to draft legislation)
- the introduction of deadlines, from overall deadlines such as '1992' and the deadlines for EMU, to the second-reading deadlines in the cooperation

procedure and the second- and third-reading deadlines for the co-decision procedure

- the creation of rafts of consensual legislation (for example, the internal market and the bulk of EMU-implementing legislation)
- rolling action programmes to tie in successive Presidencies and the steady consolidation of the practice of legislative programming
- better coordination in general, and the growing role of coordination bodies such as the Antici and Mertens Groups (Commission–Council) and the Neunreither Group (Parliament–Commission–Council).

As a result of these converging trends, the Council has become a far more efficient institution. Even in those areas where unanimity is still required, the old instinct to block indefinitely has been 'contaminated' by the new habits and the new mentality. Nevertheless, unanimity remains the bane of reformists.

Unanimity

Adopting what might be termed a 'Whig' version of the history of integration, it seems clear that the past forty years have seen the gradual erosion of a large number of sticking points thought to be at the heart of national sovereignty, for example, from direct elections to the European Parliament and the introduction of QMV to, most recently, the creation of the single currency and the ECB. These developments occurred despite the need for 'common accord' – unanimity – among the Member States. Seen from this point of view, such devices as positive abstentions in the CFSP, opt-in clauses for EMU, opt-out clauses for the Social Chapter, conventions and the *passarelle* for the third pillar, seem to serve as transitional devices to facilitate gradual erosion of adherence to the unanimity principle.

Where fundamental blockages remain through the unanimity requirement (for example, on fiscal harmonization), it is legitimate to ask whether they might not indeed *be* fundamental. But even here, if one takes the longer-term view, the integrationists have cause for optimism. In the first place, formal blockages may lead to other, more consensual and less potentially 'abrasive' forms of integration (for example, Mario Monti's initiative to use 'codes of conduct' to facilitate fiscal integration).[30] Secondly, even where formal blockages occur, methods may change, whether within or outwith the Treaty. On some thorny issues even QMV might not be attainable. For example, Lord Cockfield, when he was Commissioner responsible for the Internal Market, was fond of demonstrating the inverted bell distribution of excise duties in Europe which made it difficult to do more than encourage gradual convergence.

Last, and by no means least, unanimity is not necessarily a bad thing. It can serve as a constitutional locking device. A classic example of this was provided by the 1986 SEA, which amended the first paragraph of Article 70 (repealed by the Amsterdam Treaty) so that 'unanimity shall be required for measures which constitute a step back as regards the liberalization of capital movements'. As I have argued elsewhere, 'in the longer term, we may look more kindly upon the unanimity principle as a way of combating centrifugal forces and locking us into a quasi-fixed (though perhaps still gently evolving) constitutional settlement'.[31]

Other issues to be noted

The end of the Social Protocol

Following a change in the position of the UK on this matter by the new Labour government, the Maastricht Treaty's Social Protocol was integrated into the Community pillar, although the substantive provisions on social policy have not been fundamentally changed. The largely theoretical Council of the Social Protocol therefore becomes defunct.

The integration of the Schengen acquis and its secretariat

Protocol B annexed to the Treaty on European Union provides for the integration of the Schengen *acquis* into the framework of the European Union. Since neither the UK nor Ireland wished to participate (they may join at a later date, but only with the unanimous approval of the other Member States), the Protocol authorizes the 13 other Member States to proceed with closer cooperation. For each Schengen measure, the Council has to determine, unanimously, the appropriate legal basis, and the concrete transposition of the Schengen *acquis* into the EU framework must also be done by the Council acting unanimously. The Council must decide (by QMV) on the detailed arrangements for the integration of the Schengen Secretariat into the Secretariat General of the Council. Discussions are already under way in the Council to ensure that the necessary budgetary and personnel provisions will be in place when the Treaty is implemented.

Suspension of voting rights

Among the checks and balances brought into the Treaty to safeguard the Union's principles of liberty, democracy, respect for human rights and fundamental freedoms and the rule of law (new Article 6 TEU) with a view to enlargement is a new Article 7 TEU which enables the Council to suspend a Member State's voting rights. Under the Article's provisions, the Council, meeting in the composition of the Heads of State or Government and acting by unanimity on a proposal by one third of the Member States or by the Commission and after obtaining the assent of the European Parliament, 'may determine the existence of a serious and persistent breach' of the above principles and invite the Member State in question to submit its observations. The Council may subsequently decide, acting by a qualified majority, to suspend 'certain' rights, including the Member State's voting rights in the Council.

For the purposes of the Act, the Council would vote without taking into account the vote of the Member State concerned. Abstentions would not prevent the adoption of such provisions, and the qualified majority would be calculated as the same proportion (about 71 per cent) of the weighted votes of 'the members of the Council concerned' as laid down in Article 148(2) EC.

The Luxembourg Compromise

The pre-SEA *de facto* interpretation of the 1966 Luxembourg Compromise – that the Council should not take a decision, even if the necessary majority has been achieved, if a Member State invokes important national policy reasons – has now been incorporated *de jure* in three parts of the Treaty: the CFSP provisions on closer cooperation (Article 23 TEU), the third pillar provisions on closer cooperation (Article 40 TEU), and the EC provision (Article 11 EC). Federalist commentators saw this as part of a worrying trend towards the consolidation of intergovernmental methods.[32]

Transparency

The Conclusions of the 1992 Edinburgh European Council and the subsequent December 1993 Council decision had already laid down principles and practical arrangements for public access to Council documents.[33] The Parliament and the Commission had adopted similar arrangements. However, new Article 255 enshrines the right of access to documents in the Treaty and calls for a Council decision, to be adopted under the co-decision procedure, to lay down 'general principles and limits' within two years of the entry into force of the Amsterdam Treaty. Each institution must modify its own Rules of Procedure appropriately. In anticipation of the implementation of the Treaty, the three institutions set up a joint working party which made steady progress throughout 1998. In the meantime, the Council has continued to implement the general commitment to openness and transparency which the Edinburgh European Council gave. In January 1999, for example, an electronically accessible public register of Council documents came into being.

National parliaments

A Protocol on the role of national parliaments provides, in the context of the third pillar, for a six-week period to elapse between a legislative proposal being made available in all working languages and the date when it is placed on a Council agenda for a decision. The provision represents the second time that the Treaty's provisions, albeit a Protocol, on legislative procedures mention the national parliaments (Declaration 13 of the TEU encouraged the involvement of national parliaments, but more in relation to draft Commission legislative proposals and exchanges with the EP).

The second part of the same Protocol provides for the Conference of European Affairs Committees (COSAC) to make whatever contributions it deems appropriate 'for the attention of the institutions of the European Union, in particular on the basis of draft legal texts which representatives of governments of the Member States may decide by common accord to forward to it, in view of their subject matter'. Declaration 14 appended to the Maastricht Treaty had provided for the creation of a 'Conference of the Parliaments', but this had never met. COSAC, on the other hand, meets at least once under each Presidency, and the new protocol could lead to a direct dialogue with the Council.

The seat

A Protocol annexed to the EC Treaties settles the matter of seats for the various institutions in what is presumably a definitive way. In the case of the Council, the Protocol confirms the *status quo ante* and so the Council will meet in Luxembourg in April, June and October of each year and in Brussels at most other times. (Councils, particularly the General Affairs Council, do occasionally meet elsewhere.)

Council compositions

One of the issues addressed in the Council's 1998 internal discussions about possible reforms related to the profusion of specialized Councils – around 20 currently exist – owing to the progressive diversification of the EU's activities. According to various contemporary reports, the GAC's draft report noted the advantages of different Council compositions: they allowed close contacts to be established between national ministers responsible for particular policy areas and they encouraged ministers and national administrations to think and act in a 'European' way. But the existence of so many different compositions also led to a fragmentation of EU action and created the risk of inconsistency. It also gave rise to expectations of concrete results and a consequent profusion of 'soft' law (resolutions and conclusions, for example).

In the second half of 1998 various proposals were floated about how the number of compositions could be reduced through grouping them together in broader thematic Councils. Most notably, a 9 November 1998 Italian 'non-paper' proposed reducing the number of compositions to just eight. The December 1998 Vienna European Council endorsed the General Affairs Council's recommendation that the number of Council formations should be reduced, but without embracing any particular proposal.

Working methods

Speaking time

Various actors have pointed to the need for substantive change in working methods if the Council is successfully to meet the challenge of impending enlargement. Areas identified as requiring reform stretch from the Council's 'oral tradition' through to the role of ministers. The Parliament has pointed out that 'in a Union of 26 Member States the Council will need to sit for four hours if every minister is given only ten minutes to outline the position of his government on any particular problem'.[34] Jean-Louis Bourlanges, a noted constitutionalist and MEP, has pointed out that a Council of 26 members is almost indistinguishable from an assembly. Leaving the deeper argument about a bicameral system (with the Council as a senate or upper house) to one side, there are increasing similarities between the Council and its emerging co-legislature, the Parliament: both have had to contend with the consequences of steady growth in membership, frequent changes in legislative procedures and shifting constitutional sands; both are obliged to respect the linguistic rights of all Member State representatives at the political level and hence to contend with the disadvantages inherent in simultaneously translated debate; both are committee-based institutions, with the political level increasingly restricted to formal debate and formal decision-making.

Ministers who have made the trek to Brussels or Luxembourg could hardly be told that they should not speak, but there are a number of ways in which the problem might be at least partly addressed. One would be for Council meetings to last longer, but ministerial time is already stretched. Another would be to introduce formal mechanisms to distribute speaking time. This was the road followed by the Parliament, which carefully shares out plenary session time among the different debates and, within those debates, among the different political groups, the *rapporteurs* and draftsmen of opinions, and the representatives of the other institutions. Such a system is fair and proportionate. But it would prevent true negotiation and could reduce much debate to the formalistic reading of speeches. Interestingly, the Council's public debates have been criticized for precisely those two reasons.

In this context, a number of reforms were adopted by the 5–6 October 1998 meeting of the General Affairs Council. In particular, delegations calling for the inclusion of 'other business' items should first circulate a written exposition so that the oral presentation of such items to the Council can be kept short; the presentation to the Council by the Commission of its proposals on the latter's own initiative or at the request of a delegation is to be confined to the salient points, with the technical aspects being covered in a written communication; recourse to 'policy debates' is to be limited, taking place only when they are well prepared and not systematically in the form of round-table discussions.

Ministerial time

This problem is as old as the Council itself; but it is becoming increasingly acute.

There are ever-increasing demands on ministers' time in the domestic context, and, in the European context, fresh demands are regularly created; Association Councils, the Council of the European Economic Area, the structured dialogue with candidate countries, open debates, and so on. Sometimes, ministers are able to delegate, whether to junior ministers or their permanent representatives – Article 206 TEU even enables them to delegate to another Member State representative for voting purposes, but the political nature of much of their business frequently obliges them to be present in person. The 5–6 October 1998 General Affairs Council recognized the need for a more effective management of commitments at ministerial level with third countries. Coreper was asked to examine the Council SG's recommendation that the burden be spread between more 'actors' on behalf of the EU and that commitments to such meetings be reduced.

The general trend is clear; more and more work is squeezed into the Council day. Meetings start earlier and end later (though there is always great pressure to avoid obliging ministers to stay overnight). Informal discussions over lunch and informal Council meetings and ministerial seminars have become increasingly formalized (although the October 1998 General Affairs Council decided that any decision or operational conclusion adopted over lunch should be confirmed in the Council meeting proper). For all of these reasons the October 1998 General Affairs Council adopted the practical decisions relating to its working methods listed above and throughout this chapter. The 5–6 September 1998 Salzburg informal Council even discussed the possibility of exploiting modern technology through such mechanisms as video-conferencing. But all of these ideas could not reverse the basic trend inherent in a body which is constantly growing in size and in competences. The unavoidable tendency therefore is for the Council to delegate as much of its work as possible to its preparatory bodies, particularly Coreper, and this in itself is a phenomenon which merits attention.

Coreper

Coreper is the Council's backbone.[35] Any and every Council meeting is prepared by the stalwart denizens of Corepers II and I, and virtually every point on the agenda will have been passed in review by them, even in those areas – monetary matters for the Ecofin Council or foreign policy issues for the General Affairs Council, for example – where other preparatory bodies take a front seat role (or, at least that is still the theory to which Coreper subscribes). Each addition to the Council's and the European Council's competences and functions adds to Coreper's already extraordinary workload. But the increase in Coreper's responsibilities has given rise to two sets of questions, one structural, the other constitutional.

On the structural side, there are simple physical limits to how much the permanent representatives and their deputies are humanly able to do. A recurring suggestion has been the creation of a third Coreper, although this could lead to the sort of fragmentation which the General Affairs Council has been so eager to avoid at the Council level.

On the constitutional side, Coreper, which is composed of diplomats and civil servants, has evolved into a quasi-legislative[36] and quasi-political body, and the Council's other preparatory bodies have developed similar roles: 'the secrecy, permanence and ubiquity of Coreper have led to its members being tagged, by those who know of them at all, as the "men who really run Europe" '.[37] The Council is far from being a rubber stamp and remains the overarching political authority. Nevertheless, Coreper prides itself on only handing on to ministers those problems which are truly intractable at any lower level. At the same time, the Council's automatic reflex is to refer all dossiers down to Coreper for preparation and to delegate as much as possible, particularly where technical detail is involved. Thus, the lack of ministerial time and the growth in the role and powers of Coreper are to a considerable extent two sides of the same coin. Already, there is regular use of the device of 'false B points' by the General Affairs Council, coupled with the submission of a growing number of 'A points' to each Council.[38]

It is not clear how these problems might be resolved. At the one extreme, the Reflection Group suggested that the Council's efficiency could be enhanced through greater recourse to the written procedure. At the other, proposals to create ministers of European affairs within Member State governments are regularly made, along with suggestions that they should be Brussels-based. In January 1998, Bourlanges called for the General Affairs Council to be composed of such ministers and for it to meet on a twice-monthly basis.[39] At the June 1998 Cardiff European Council, Commission President Jacques Santer called for the creation of a 'Coordination Council' which would be composed of deputy prime ministers or ministers of state.[40] In January 1999 former Commission President Jacques Delors made similar proposals. But these were part of another debate relating to the role of the General Affairs Council.

It is perhaps important to point out in this context that, as with internal reform of the Commission, an IGC and treaty change is not necessarily needed to render the Council more efficient. In particular, significant change could be brought about through Council decisions and amendments to the Council's rules of procedure.

The role of the General Affairs Council

Rumblings about the declining role of the General Affairs Council first began during the reflection process preceding the Amsterdam IGC and were renewed during the British Presidency in the first half of 1998 when the more general context of the future of the Union began to be discussed in the perspective of imminent enlargements and of Stage III of EMU. It was decided that an informal European Council would be held in October 1998 (at Portschasch) on just this theme of the future of the EU. In parallel, there was a growing debate about the way in which the GAC had allegedly lost its pre-eminent role as a coordinating body. The debate was led by Santer who argued at the June 1998 Cardiff European Council that the General Affairs Council was too preoccupied by external relations matters and could no longer exercise its traditional coordination role and, as was seen above, that the GAC might in the future be constituted of deputy prime ministers who would travel to Brussels as often as necessary.[41] It was also reported that the foreign affairs ministers were 'wary' about the increasing importance of the Ecofin Council, and that they had become overwhelmed by and bogged down in ever-increasing representational duties.[42]

On 29 June 1998 the General Affairs Council held an informal discussion in order immediately to assert its preparatory role in relation to the informal European Council and, at the first General Affairs Council meeting under the Austrian Presidency (13 July 1998), a wide-ranging discussion raised a number of issues and a general agreement on the need to confront them. The Dutch foreign minister, Hans Van Mierlo, argued that the GAC was threatened both from above (by the 'sherpas' of the Heads of State or Government) and by the 'specialized Councils which often put the "fait accompli" before the European Union'. The General Affairs Council's 'natural role' was splitting up, he concluded.[43] A 'Gymnich'-style informal meeting of the foreign ministers was scheduled for 5–6 September 1998 in Salzburg. Wolfgang Schüssel, the Austrian foreign affairs minister, sent a questionnaire to his colleagues and the Council SG's paper on possible reforms (which had already been discussed by Coreper and the GAC in the March–May 1998 period) was polished up. [44]

The subsequent 5–6 October 1998 General Affairs Council decided that a series of measures would apply forthwith: 'horizontal' issues, such as enlargement, would be placed at the top and in a separate part of the General Affairs Council's agenda; discussions over lunch would be confined to particularly sensitive issues, with other confidential matters to be discussed in the Council chamber in very restricted session; and all meetings with third countries would take place on the second day of meetings. The clear aim was to create space on the General Affairs Council's formal agenda for its traditional coordination role. Indeed, seen in this context, all of the practical reforms implemented and/or proposed in relation to the Council's general working methods could be seen as ways of reasserting the GAC's coordinating role.

But the apparently inexorable decline of the General Affairs Council's coordination activities was connected with developments at other levels. On one hand, the Heads of State or Government had increasingly asserted their authority through the European Council, encouraged by explicit competences set out in the Maastricht and Amsterdam Treaties. On another, the creation of the euro and the start-up of Stage III of EMU radically shifted the balance between the General Affairs and Ecofin Councils. On another, Coreper's primacy as a preparatory body was being undermined. As one critical journalistic piece put it, 'How long has Coreper not been receiving the Monetary Committee papers drawn up in preparation for Ecofin Council sittings? How long has it not been receiving the papers of the Special Agriculture Committee? And are relations between Coreper and the Political Committee (which prepares CFSP decisions) still marked by mutual confidence and a spirit of cooperation?'[45] The informal Portschach summit restricted itself to requesting the General Affairs Council to come forward with detailed proposals, but ironically President Klima also announced the wish 'to strengthen the European Council's role of providing guidance and we will therefore be creating a technical infrastructure'.[46]

Conclusion: the absence of radicalism

The Council and its mechanisms and procedures have evolved organically over almost five decades. Despite the Cassandras, the institution remains a complex but highly efficient organism, and those who work in or around it are justly proud of its subtlety and its achievements. Given the Council's success, reform could only ever be gradual and cautious but, as has been seen, a number of trends may oblige the Council to evolve more rapidly than might otherwise have been the case. This is particularly true in the areas of openness and transparency, particularly when combined with the generalized use of the co-decision procedure and pressures for the Community's legislative procedures to become more open and accessible.

This chapter has shown how discussions in and around the IGC touched on a number of fundamental issues and, whether by commission or omission, highlighted a number of areas where reform has already begun or will probably be considered at a later date. At least where reform of the Council is concerned, the absence of success does not necessarily denote failure.

Endnotes

1. See European Parliament, *Report on the Amsterdam Treaty*, doc. 223.314 fin (Explanatory Memorandum), 5 November 1997, p. 50.
2. *Agence Europe*, 20 September 1997, p. 2.
3. *Agence Europe*, 3 May 1998, p. 5.
4. M. Westlake, *The Council of the European Union*, London: Cartermill, 1995, p. 283, notes: 'the development may already have had important consequences for the institutional arrangements of the Economic and Monetary Union process. In particular, the fact that British ministers and representatives were not excluded from the Council and its preparatory bodies during deliberations on Social Protocol matters may have set an important precedent for the representation of those Member States unable to make the transition to full monetary union in the "first wave" '.
5. The Council's rules of procedures have been amended to render them compatible with Stage III of EMU.
6. *Reflection Group Report*, Brussels, 5 December 1995, p. 29.
7. Council of the European Union, *Report of the Functioning of the Treaty on European Union*. Brussels, 5 April 1995, p. 12.
8. See also 'The Three Wise Men', *Report on European Institutions*, Brussels, 1979, pp. 242–9; A. Duff, 'The Report of the Three Wise Men', *Journal of Common Market Studies*, Vol. 29, No. 3, 1981.
9. *Agence Europe*, 13 September 1997, p. 14.
10. A. Nicoll, 'European Union looks at new defence dimension', *The Financial Times*, 4 November 1998.
11. Westlake, *The Council of the European Union*, pp. 29–30, examines the previous arrangements.
12. European Parliament, *Report on the Amsterdam Treaty*, p. 41.
13. European Parliament, *Report on the Amsterdam Treaty*, p. 42.
14. The Maastricht Treaty set the Commission's term of office at five years and provided for one or two Vice-Presidents (TEU Articles 158 and 161 respectively). When taken in conjunction with the Amsterdam Treaty's provisions on the appointment of the Commission and the Commission's emerging internal reforms, it is clear that the position of Vice-President responsible for external

relations will be heavyweight both in political and administrative terms.

15. *Agence Europe*, 2 April 1988, p. 2. The Council is already at work on a draft decision which would grant Council officials access to classified information in the CFSP/WEU context in line with the recommendations of Declaration 2 appended to the Amsterdam Treaty.
16. *Agence Europe*, 26–27 October 1998.
17. Already in the course of 1998 senior Council SG officials working in the CFSP field – together with Presidency representatives at official level – had begun to adopt a higher institutional profile, with frequent appearances before the Foreign Affairs Committee of the European Parliament, for example. The Parliament's Committee on the Rules of Procedure had meanwhile recommended that the future 'Mr CFSP' be given the right to speak in plenary sessions – a significant gesture.
18. *Agence Europe*, 29 April 1998, pp. 3–4.
19. European Parliament, *Report on the Treaty of Amsterdam*, p. 44.
20. See 'Weighty Matters for the European Union', *The Economist*, 1 February 1997.
21. *The Parliament Magazine*, No. 53, 7 December 1998, p. 7.
22. *Agence Europe*, 7/8 July 1997, p. 3.
23. *Agence Europe*, 4/5 May 1998, p. 5.
24. EC Bulletin, No. 12, 1992, pp. 18–20; OJ No. C 166, 17 June 1993, p. 1.
25. European Parliament, *Report on the Amsterdam Treaty*, p. 38.
26. Westlake, *The Council of the European Union*, p. 95, especially tables 3.3 and 3.4.
27. See T. Peters, 'Voting Power after the Enlargement and Options for Decision-Making in the European Union', *Aussenwirtschaft*, 51, 1996; T. Peters. 'Qualifying Influence in the European Union', *Aussenpolitik*, No. 2, 1996; T. Peters, 'Decision-Making after the EU Intergovernmental Conference', *European Law Journal*, Vol. 2, No. 3, 1996. Other indicators are possible. The European Central Bank, for example, variously uses population size, GDP, and national central banks' shares in the subscribed capital of the ECB.
28. See M. Westlake, 'The European Union's "Blind Watchmakers": The Process of Constitutional Change', in M. Westlake (ed.), *The European Union Beyond Amsterdam: New Concepts of European Integration*, London: Routledge, 1998, pp. 16–33.
29. European Commission, *Agenda 2000. Volume I: For a Stronger and Wider Union*, Luxembourg: Office for Official Publications of the European Communities, 1997, p. 6.
30. *Agence Europe*, 16 July 1998, pp. 6–7.
31. Westlake, 'The European Union's "Blind Watchmakers" ', pp. 27–8.
32. For example, Y. Devuyst, 'The Treaty of Amsterdam: An Introductory Analysis', *ECSA Review*, Volume 19, No. 3, 1997.
33. EC Bulletin No. 12, 1992, pp. 18–20; OJ No. L340, 31 December 1993, p. 43.
34. European Parliament, *Report on the Amsterdam Treaty*, p. 48.
35. Westlake, *The Council of the European Union*, pp. 285–307.
36. See E. Von Sydow, 'The Lawgivers', *The Bulletin*, Brussels, 19 June 1997.
37. 'Coreper, Europe's Managing Board', *The Economist*, 8 August 1998, p. 27. *The Economist*, 8 March 1997, p. 8, had dubbed Coreper 'the Power House'.
38. See Westlake, *The Council of the European Union*, pp. 113–14.
39. *Agence Europe*, 12–13 January 1998, p. 3.
40. *Agence Europe*, 12 June 1998.
41. See M. Turner, 'Calls grow for firmer hand on EU tiller', *European Voice*, 16–22 July 1998; L. Barber, 'Foreign ministers are being elbowed aside within the EU. Premiers and finance ministers rule the roost', *The Financial Times*, 16 July 1998; *Agence Europe*, 4 September 1998.
42. *Agence Europe*, 2 September 1998.
43. *Agence Europe*, 13–14 July 1998.
44. *Agence Europe*, 31 August–1 September 1998.
45. *Agence Europe*, 10 September 1998.
46. *Agence Europe*, 26–27 October 1998.·

Chapter 2

The European Commission

David Spence

Introduction: The pressure for reform

The resignation of the European Commission on 15 March 1999, following the
publication of a critical report by the Committee of Independent Experts on fraud,
mismanagement and nepotism in the Commission,[1] finally brought wide
recognition that its role requires redefinition. 'Finally', since proposals for reform
had been floated since the late 1970s, yet little or no practical measures had been
undertaken. Meanwhile the general crisis of legitimacy in the EU had largely
focused on the inadequacies of the Commission and the need for reform and
redefinition of its role. The Commission's new President, Romano Prodi argued in
his 4 May 1999 speech to the Euorpean Parliament that the two aspects of the
process of redefinition are: 'the definition of the institutional role of the
Commission in relation to the Council and the Parliament' and 'a clearer definition
of the relationship between politics and administration in the workings of the
Commission'.

Few would doubt the force of the argument. However, equal weight might also
be accorded to the need for internal managerial reform to encompass the
introduction of modern management practice and the avoidance of what is widely
perceived to be an administration where fraud and cronyism are all too frequent.
Prodi believes this can be achieved by clarifying the lines of responsibility between
those performing political tasks and those involved with administration. It will
remain to be seen whether solving long-standing issues relating to the
Commission's ability to perform its functions satisfactorily can be resolved simply
through the otherwise clearly desirable change in the balance between politics and
administration.

In reviewing the Commission's key roles in the interinstitutional process it is
noticeable that, despite objectively enlarged responsibility in an ever-longer list of
areas of competence, the Commission's *raison d'être* has increasingly been
questioned.[2] Despite the Commission's formal right of legislative initiative, the
Council's role in taking the political initiative has increased. One observer argues
that 'it is surprising that policy innovation is at all possible in a system where the

general rights of initiative of the Commission, as well as its executive functions, appear so tightly controlled'.[3] The situation has not been helped by the growth in importance of the European Council. Nor has the Maastricht Treaty's establishment of two intergovernmental pillars rivalling the Community pillar proven a force for clarity and efficiency in EU business. The creation of obligations for the Presidency of the Council where the Community method would have secured roles for the Commission has resulted in obstacles to efficient management of EU business. This is demonstrated by the need to review institutional matters shortly after the implementation of treaties. Both the growth in the power of the European Council and the proliferation of alternatives to the Community method have arguably signalled a decline in the role of the Commission as the motor of integration. Despite its formal role as guardian of the treaties, there has been a rising threat from those contesting the role. Despite its increased role as manager of policy, the comitology battles have underlined continuing disagreement as to purpose.[4] Despite its (first pillar) representative role abroad, its competence and leadership have been under dispute.[5]

The other Community institutions have been a source of pressure to reform. As *The Economist* put it commenting on the Court of Auditors' Report on 1997, 'The general impression given of the Commission is of an organisation with which anybody would be happy to do business. It likes spending money, it tends to botch the paperwork, and it frequently loses interest in the final result. It tries to manage too many programmes with too few resources.'[6] The EP has also increased its pressure on the Commission by using its power as part of the budgetary authority. The EP's budget committee regularly forces upon the Commission's External Service rationalization and enhanced efficiency by withholding a percentage of its administrative budget.[7] In other areas, such as reform of information policy, humanitarian aid or the Common Agricultural Policy, the main method for the EP to gain a measure of control and promote managerial change is its ability to withhold approval of the budget. At the end of 1998 the EP refused to sign off the 1996 budget because of accusations of fraud by Commission staff. The budgetary committee had set conditions including modification of the staff regulations, a draft code of behaviour with regard to the nomination of senior officials and a financial regulation mentioning the personal responsibility of Commissioners. The Court of Auditors has insisted on reform of the Commission's working methods, arguing strongly for appropriate financial control and decentralization. This led the Santer Commission to introduce the Sound and Efficient Management (SEM) initiative.[8]

The criticism of the Commission in the 1990s has been reminiscent of de Gaulle's crusade in the 1960s.[9] Reversing the integration ratchet has been a major theme and the power of the Commission the prime focus of reformers' endeavours.[10] The Commission is in the process of internal management reform parallel to the post-Amsterdam adjustment of its powers and prerogatives, the democratic legitimacy of its President, the size of its membership and its arrangements for external policy-making. The challenge of enlargement and the Amsterdam Treaty have proved a catalyst for a reform package designed to meet many diverse and long-standing challenges. When Jacques Santer took office as

Commission President, vowing to do less but do it better,[11] reform was already on the cards.[12] By the end of 1998 Santer was affirming to the EP that the Commission had proved its good faith in introducing the SEM, MAP 2000 and Tomorrow's Commission initiatives, which had introduced a far more transparent and coherent approach to reform.[13]

There was nothing new about the agenda for reform. Twenty years before, the Spierenburg Report,[14] the product of an independent review body appointed by the Commission in 1979, concluded that since 1970 there had been a decline of the Commission's influence, effectiveness and reputation and that root and branch reform was needed. The absence of practical implementation of the many reform proposals made by such official committees over the years has been striking. This must be recognized despite the fact that one 'wise man' has expressed satisfaction that his recommendations have formed part of the ongoing debate and possibly led to a gradual increase of integration.[15] Yet, the point is that nothing was seriously undertaken to remedy the many faults found with the Commission and it has continued to suffer from the effects of its decline until the 1990s. The much-vaunted 'Delors effect' – the tremendous boost in the Commission's power and status under the three Delors Commissions between 1986 and 1996[16] – did nothing to meet the need for internal reform.

This chapter reviews the evolving debate on the role of the Commission and analyses the IGC and the reform proposals set out in the Amsterdam Treaty. It then discusses the problems and prospects for the internal reform process already introduced.

Issues for institutional reform

Debates in the 1996–97 IGC focused on the formal powers of the Commission. Internal matters such as the choice of Commissioners' portfolios and administrative and managerial reform of the Commission lie outside the scope of the Treaty and were thus hardly debated during the conference. Member States' positions varied to a large extent according to traditional interests. The smaller states were keen to prevent a reduction in the Commission's powers and prerogatives and wished to enhance them. The larger states, led alternately by France, the UK and Germany, raised fundamental issues surrounding the Commission's constitutional status, concentrating particularly on the powers of the President and Vice-Presidents of the Commission, the appointment of Commissioners, their number, collegiality and the Commission's role in external relations including the CFSP. It may be too simplistic to assert that the large and the small Member States were the main cleavage or that themes based on north/south issues or the net contributors/net beneficiaries was a key to overall understanding. Yet, it is true that the smaller states were agreed in their support for maintenance of the Commission's political role, including its exclusive right of initiative in EC affairs and its role as monitor of the application of Community legislation. There were diverging views on the Commission's role in other pillars and the overall structure of power within the Commission.

The President

The lack of a clearly defined presidential role in the College has long been considered a prime weakness. It has made the College's effectiveness dependent on the personal authority of the President, himself formally only *primus inter pares* and lacking political independence and managerial control. The Spierenburg Report argued that the President-elect should be able to veto nominees, with Member States obliged to nominate a second candidate if the first proved unacceptable to the President. The Commission would benefit from greater public legitimacy if it were more dependent on an elected Parliament. It would also benefit from a stronger figurehead at a time when difficult issues such as internal reform and collegiate efficiency become more pressing.

In the IGC the Commission's ideal position was for the European Council's nominee for President to be the subject of a vote by the EP. This increased legitimacy would allow the President a freer hand in the nomination of Commissioners on the basis of a list submitted by Member States. The President would also have more say in the choice of portfolios. In a submission in May 1997, the Commission argued that the President's role in determining the membership of the Commission should be increased and that the other members should be designated by agreement between the President and the governments of the Member States. The choice could be made from a list presented by national governments. An enhanced role in the designation of Commission members, which would entail an amendment to Article 158 EC, would enable the President to achieve balance between members and their respective portfolios and tasks and balanced representation of men and women.

The Maastricht Treaty had already created a right for the EP to be consulted on the proposed Council nomination for Commission President. The quarrel within the Council over the rival merits of Belgian and Luxembourg prime ministers Dehaene and Santer in 1994 strengthened the EP's hand. It was successful in its bid to interpret its right of approval of the President of the Commission [Article 158(3) EC] as a right to a series of hearings of the newly appointed Santer's team.

The Parliament argued that the Commission President should be directly elected by the Parliament on the basis of a list submitted by the Council. The appointment of other members of the College would then be agreed jointly by the President and the Member States and then subjected to a formal vote of investiture in the EP. This would formalize the practice begun by Delors, who waited for votes of confidence from the Parliament before allowing the Commissioners to take their oaths of office at the Court of Justice. The EP's new rules of procedure state:

'Election of the Commission.

1. The President shall, after consulting the President-elect of the Commission, request the nominees proposed for the various posts of Commissioners to appear before the appropriate committees according to their prospective fields of responsibility. These hearings shall be held in public.

2. The committee shall invite the nominee to make a statement and answer questions.
3. The President-elect shall present the college of Commissioners and their programme at a sitting of Parliament which the whole Council shall be invited to attend. The statement shall be followed by a debate.
4. In order to wind up the debate, any political group may table a motion for a resolution. Rule 37 (3), (4) and (5) shall apply.
   Following the vote on the motion for a resolution, Parliament shall elect or reject the Commission by a majority of the votes cast.
   The vote shall be taken by roll call. Parliament may defer the vote until the next sitting.
5. The President shall inform the governments of the Member States of the election or rejection of the Commission.
6. In the event of portfolio changes during the Commission's term of office, the Commissioner concerned shall be invited to appear before the committees responsible for the areas of responsibility in question.'[17]

Building on Maastricht Article 158(2), which foresaw that Parliament should be consulted on the choice of President-designate and of the Commission as a whole, many in the EP argued for the right to exercise censorship of individual Commissioners. The EP currently has no authority to decide which Commissioner gets which portfolio, though it can practically veto a Commissioner from obtaining individual portfolios. The case of Padraig Flynn, vetoed by the EP from taking on responsibility for equal opportunities created a precedent. Yet, the EP's formal position in the IGC on the issue was not to press for such power. With the resignation of the Commission, the goal posts began to shift again. Prodi made clear at the Cologne European Council in June 1999 that he would expect individual Commissioners to give an undertaking to resign if he asked them to. The appointment of a Vice-President for parliamentary affairs is a symbol of Prodi's commitment to efficient relations with the Parliament.

Parliament's position in the IGC was close to that of the Commission. The Commission argued that it is and must always be collectively accountable to Parliament. Individual censure motions should be ruled out, as they would destroy collegiality. The Member States agreed, probably out of reticence to give the Parliament more powers rather than as a resolution of the issue of censure *per se*. Among the various factors that make for greater efficiency and collective responsibility, the nomination of its President and his role in the designation of the other members is by no means the least. The Commission recommended that the President, nominated by the European Council, should be formally approved by the EP, which should be given a specified period in which to give this approval. An amendment to Article 158 EC to this effect anchored the existing *de facto* situation in the Treaty and lends greater legitimacy to the President. The other idea of the EP, censorship of individual Commissioners, met with only lukewarm support during the IGC and outright opposition from Portugal. Arguably, of course, censuring the two Commissioners accused of fraud and corruption would have kept Santer's Commission otherwise intact till the end of its mandate on 4 January 2000.

Despite apparent disagreement on the detail, the IGC reached consensus easily on strengthening the role of the Commission President, which has been upgraded in four major ways:

- The President will have the right to object to the nomination of a Commissioner by a national government
- The President will have the power to allocate and reshuffle portfolios
- The Commission will work 'under the political guidance of its President'
- The President will receive a mandate from the Parliament.[18]

The 1999 Three Wise Men Report stressed that the authority of the President of the Commission had been increased at Amsterdam, but as the President's role is fundamental to the operation of the Commission and the coherence of the EU operation *per se*, further strengthening was desirable. Much also depends on the personality and personal clout of the incumbent. A strong President can have his own way. A weak President is perforce obliged to preside over dissent, occasional incoherence amongst his team and, in the case of Santer, over outright censurable practice or at the very least inappropriate behaviour. The list of improprieties in the Santer Commission, if not all to do with corruption and fraud, was long and it fed public anxiety in a way which fostered the view that Parliament's role should be increased. The commission seemed unable to run a recruitment system without some candidates receiving the exam questions in advance. A Commissioner (Bangemann) was accepting fees for speeches; another (Cresson) had emloyed friends with official money for private political purposes. There had been cover-ups in the 'mad cow' affair. One Commissioner (Flynn) had expressed the view that it was hard to live on his salary; another (Bjerregaard) had published a diary of life in the Commission without consulting Santer. A former Commission official (Buitenen) had 'blown the whistle' on corruption and been rewarded by suspension from office. In addition, journalists had turned from reporters to investigators and had become keen to expose malpractice.[19]

But the Amsterdam Treaty now legitimises the right of the President to select his own team. Whereas the Commission President was formerly 'consulted' on nominations for Commissioners, he will now have the right to agree or disagree and, unless practice proves the opposite, to settle alone the distribution of his team's portfolios.

The amended articles of the Treaty read:

Appointment of the Members of the Commission
Article 158(2):
The governments of the Member States shall nominate by common accord the person they intend to appoint as President of the Commission; the nomination shall be approved by the European Parliament.
The governments of the Member States shall, by common accord with the nominee for President, nominate the other persons whom they intend to appoint as Members of the Commission.

New first paragraph to Article 163 (composition and organization of the Commission):
The Commission shall work under the political guidance of its President.

At Cologne, Prodi stressed that it was likely that the EP might in future require quarantees from individual Commissioners that they would resign if an individual motion of censure by the Parliament required it. His view was that he, Prodi, and not the Parliament should decide. He would require their commitment in advance to compliance. The EP would then be free to censure the Commission as a whole, if it disagreed with the Commission President's decision. During the 1999 parliamentary hearings each Commissioner affirmed his or her readiness to resign at Prodi's request – a considerable *de facto* reform and one which the next IGC may have to include with a view to Treaty amendment.

Vice-Presidents and the need for coordination

Since the Maastricht Treaty, the Commission has had two Vice-Presidents, by tacit agreement the two longest-serving Commissioners, as opposed to the original six. Governments used to distribute Vice-Presidencies between the five larger member states with the remaining position given to a smaller country. The Italian government's inability to choose between the country's two Commissioners delayed Vice-Presidential appointments for seven months in Delors' third Commission until July 1993.[20] A Vice-President sometimes, but rarely, deputizes for the Commission President, as in July 1993 when Delors was too ill to travel to the Tokyo G7 Summit.

Member States view Vice-Presidents essentially as coordinators rather than policy leaders. With the exception of the field of external relations, the Amsterdam Treaty produced no change in the *status quo*. In the IGC, the Commission's starting point was the need for a Vice-President responsible for external affairs, providing the interface between the Commission and the foreign ministers of the Member States. The Commission also advocated a higher profile for itself in the CFSP as part of a new troika consisting of the Presidency, the High Representative of the CFSP and the Vice-President of the Commission. The Commission stressed the importance of bestowing actual policy roles on Vice-Presidents rather than a purely coordinating role, arguing that it could improve overall policy management by a better use of Vice-Presidents. Article 161 EC would then have to be amended.

The Commission's view did not quite echo Spierenburg's argument in 1979. Spierenburg had deplored the lack of complementarity, the diversity of backgrounds and the slight likelihood of Commissioners knowing each other well before taking office. His report noted the lack of cohesion between Commissioners, an imbalance between portfolios, insufficient coordination between senior officials, a maldistribution of staff between departments and shortcomings in the career structure. These factors led to a tendency for responsibilities to be personalized. The Commission lacked a sense of collective purpose and taste for joint action, 'with the consequence that the priorities and selectivity in the development of the Commission's programme of work are not as clearly established as they should be'.

Poor coordination amongst Commissioners and their lack of encouragement of senior officials had in turn led to a dearth of coordination amongst Directors-General and a growth in the power and role of the *cabinets*. Spierenburg argued that the lack of coordination at College level could be remedied by systematic and permanent working parties of Commissioners with participation of the services and a Presidency actively responsible for directing coordination – a principle actually implemented under Santer. Spierenburg proposed a new style of Vice-Presidency, a kind of chief executive responsible for management of work programmes, coordination and supervision, leaving representation and chairmanship to the President. Commissioners without a formal portfolio could assist those under particular pressure.

It was only in the area of external affairs that the Amsterdam Council was to make explicit mention of the Vice-Presidency being based on a policy portfolio as opposed to a managerial and leadership role. The Commission's proposal for two other Vice-Presidents for economic affairs and for overall integration disappeared without trace.

After the resignation of the Santer Commission, the British government insisted that one of the Commission's Vice–Presidents should have responsibility for reform of management, personnel and budgets.[21] Prodi intented to create two Vice–Presidencies based on policy responsibility. The first would cover management of the reform of the Commission, linked to a related portfolio such as internal audit, financial control, fighting fraud or the budget. The other would be responsible for relations with the EP, linked either to overall oversight of institutional reforms and/or a new service for Citizens' Europe. This sounded coherent. In fact his proposals were diluted as the two Vice–Presidents, Kinnock and Loyola de Palacio, had portfolios mixed in curious ways.[22]

The Vice–Presidency for relations with the Parliament provides a means of keeping close to parliamentary affairs, trouble–shooting and thus heading off potential embarrassment. Closeness to EP committees will enable compromises to be worked out at an earlier stage, to avoid Parliament blocking legislation. The spin–off will be an increase in the Commission's role as mediator between Parliament and Council, allowing it to regain some of the ground lost following the introduction of the co–decision procedure. But the overall effect of the change, while lending credence to the idea of policy coordinators as Vice–Presidents, still begs the question of whether precisely these tasks were worthy of Vice–Presidencies rather than others.

The widely supported idea of a Vice–President for external affairs was abandoned, perhaps due to the appointment of former NATO Secretary–General Javier Solana as 'Mr CFSP' and Secretary–General of the Council. A strong Commission Vice–President might be viewed as a clear institutional and personal rival. The fact that lack of coordination in external affairs had led to obvious managerial inefficiencies in the Commission did not prove reason enough to alter the position.

Numbers and the principle of collegiality

The Turin European Council of March 1996 set a general guideline of 'greater efficiency, coherence and legitimacy' and a particular guideline for the Commission pertaining to 'how the Commission can fulfil its functions with greater efficiency, having regard to its composition and representative capability'. The accepted wisdom was that the Commission was already too large, but the new fear was that enlargement to include even the first seven potential new member countries (Poland, Hungary, the Czech Republic, Slovenia, Estonia, Malta and Cyprus) would boost the Commission from the current 20 to 28 members.

A fundamental dilemma faces both the Commission and the Member States. On the one hand, all Member States must retain the right to appoint a Commissioner regardless of their size, budget contributions and political clout in the Union if legitimacy and public acceptance of the Commission is to be consolidated. Indeed, the smaller Member States have made it clear in the past that they did not join a Union to be dominated by the larger countries. On the other hand, the operational capacity of the Commission could be seriously hampered if, in an enlarged Union, all Member States retain a Commissioner. One solution would be a core of Commissioners in charge of key portfolios, supplemented by rotating assistant (or junior) Commissioners without portfolio. Overall policy coherence might not be a foregone conclusion under this system, but the advantages of an 'inner cabinet' system, as practised by Member States, would be undeniable.

Are there too many Commissioners? The prevailing view has been that Commissioners need to travel to represent the Commission and cultivate links with their countries of origin and parliaments. This, plus the inefficiency of having three institutional locations, Brussels, Strasbourg and Luxembourg, implies an operational requirement for a large Commission reflecting Member State size in numbers of Commissioners. The Treaty makes no provision for political or geographical weighting of Commissioners, as it does for the Council and the Parliament. Indeed, there is a clear contradiction between the required independence of Commissioners (Article 155 EC) and the desirability that Commissioners actually ensure national interests are considered in College discussions.

But there is a compelling case for a smaller, tighter operation at political level in the Commission. A small Commission would coordinate better, make agreement easier to reach, facilitate clear conclusions and have more chances to kindle team spirit, and thus project a better image. Spierenburg had recommended that Member States appoint only one Commissioner each, but to no avail. Commission President Roy Jenkins, who authorized the report, bitterly remarked, 'The position of too many Commissioners chasing too few jobs, with which I was confronted in 1977 was exacerbated by the Greek entry of 1981 and the Spanish and Portuguese entry of 1986.'[23] The 1985 Dooge Report also recommended only one Commissioner per Member State. But neither the Single European Act nor the Maastricht Treaty addressed the issue, though even Margaret Thatcher argued that 'a Commission of 17 is liable to be too large for efficiency or to provide all members with serious portfolios'.[24] The House of Lords Select Committee on the European Communities argued in 1985 that 'it must be doubted whether the members of such a large body can work efficiently and harmoniously together as a "college" '.[25]

A team of German academics has argued that Commissioners should not be appointed on a national quota basis.[26] Karl Lamers, foreign policy spokesman of the CDU/CSU in the Bundestag, identified ten to twelve policy areas, recommending that the total number of Commissioners be reduced to fit the portfolios. Since the national right to a Commissioner would vanish, there would have to be 'an unwritten rule whereby a Member State which does not have a Commissioner during one legislative period should be considered for one during the next'. Lamers also postulated the emergence of the concept of a Deputy Commissioner without voting rights, if the national quota principle proved too difficult to reform.[27] Though not the line followed by Germany in the IGC, there was food for general thought in the proposal.

In practice, there has been reticence on the part of large Member States actually to countenance relinquishing their second Commissioner. Former Commissioner Etienne Davignon has argued that there will always be countries which oppose the idea, because they cannot agree on one name. As for the apparent German, French and British agreement to reduce to one Commissioner, Davignon cynically notes that 'they may have managed to come to an agreement because they were certain that in the long run one country or another would oppose the idea'.[28]

So, should the treaty stipulation that there should be at least one Commissioner per Member State be changed? One Commissioner once commented that 'inefficiency could hardly be organized in a more costly way'.[29] The debates in the College on the subject in preparation of the IGC focused on the difficult reconciliation between

> Le concept managérial d'un collège restreint à une douzaine de membres, a priori plus efficace, et le maintien d'au moins un commissaire par Etat membre, a priori plus 'légitime' pour chacun d'eux.[30]

There is arguably no intrinsic need for each Member State to have a Commissioner. After all, the Commission supposedly represents the European interest and not that of the Member States. One could conceive, for example, of a small College of highly qualified, democratically appointed Commissioners with national proportions maintained, perhaps, at the next level down, that of Directors-General. This view, argued forcefully by Commissioner Dahrendorf in 1971,[31] would require rethinking the question of national balance and the concomitant removal of states' automatic right to a Commissioner. As the debate in the IGC showed, it is highly unlikely that there would ever be such agreement. Though the larger Member States agree to a reduction of their share to one rather than two Commissioners, the smaller Member States will not agree to a system with no guarantees of national representation at the most senior level. The removal of states' rights to a Commissioner each is thus perhaps thinking the unthinkable, though the French actually implicitly called for it during the IGC.

The French line in the IGC was similar to an idea floated by one Commissioner, Sir Leon Brittan, before the IGC, advocating a compromise between the demand of national legitimacy and managerial efficiency.[32] He proposed the following senior Commissioner portfolios: President, handling coordination of the entire Commission; external relations, including development; economic affairs, including EMU; environment; transport and regional policy; agriculture and fisheries; industry, the internal market and energy; competitiveness, including social policy, education and research; competition policy; budget, financial control, personnel and administration. The selection of portfolios could, of course, be adapted, 'depending on the changing needs of the Union'.

Brittan argued for greater hierarchy, replacing the horizontal structure beneath the President with a two-tier College of full and junior Commissioners. This would imply continued presence of nationals from all Member States in the College, though not always with a senior Commissioner. The larger countries would always have a senior Commissioner, with the remaining senior Commissioners and the junior Commissioners drawn, on a rotating basis, from the other states. Each full Commissioner would have two votes. Each junior Commissioner, disallowed from voting against his or her senior Commissioner, would have one vote. At least half the number of Commissioners and half the votes would be required for approval of a Commission decision. Brittan asserted that such a reform would induce a streamlining of administration, an acceleration of the reallocation of staff and funds between competing priorities, an improvement in laws and actions and a more coherent image.

In the IGC, Member States rejected UK and French proposals leaning in this direction. The UK suggested three options: the smaller Member States would give up their Commissioner; the Commission would have voting and non-voting members; some Commissioners would not have a portfolio. There would, in short, be a two-tier system based on senior and junior Commissioners.

There are good reasons for the Commission to envisage a system of junior and senior Commissioners. Not only has the competence and workload of the Commission increased exponentially to cover all ministerial responsibilities in Member States, the Commission has become increasingly answerable to the Parliament. All Commissioners are present on Wednesday in every Strasbourg week and expected at some point to appear in the plenary session, despite the fact that Wednesday has always been the day on which the College meets. Commissioners and senior officials are also frequent visitors in Brussels to the parliamentary groups, where they explain and defend Commission policies. Reform in the Commission may bring more power to officials, in particular to the Directors-General. Yet, traditionally, parliaments claim the right to hear representatives of governments holding political rather than administrative office. It is thus appropriate for the EP to be addressed by Commissioners.

Junior Commissioners could appear in minor debates and defend legislative proposals at committee stage as they work through the co-decision procedure. Appearance in plenary on major issues of policy could then be left to full Commissioners, with the appropriate cabinet member responsible for parliamentary affairs effectively working to both levels of Commissioner and providing an enhanced liaison function between the Directorates-General and the

Commissioners. A system of junior and senior Commissioners would ensure that all states remain represented, that small members incapable of permanently filling big posts would be appeased, the current workload would be reduced and external representation would be more frequent at political level.

The Commission argued in the IGC that the number of portfolios needed to be reduced to around ten to twelve, as indeed did France. This would make it easier to monitor attainment of objectives. Members without portfolio would be entrusted either with specific tasks or with support functions, on the understanding that from one Commission to the next there would be a degree of alternation. The chief aim of this distinction would be to enhance the Commission's efficiency and coherence. The allocation of portfolios and tasks to members and any changes made during the Commission's term of office would be made under the responsibility of the President, who would refer them to the full Commission for decision. Unlike the Brittan proposal, junior Commissioners would have the same voting rights as those with portfolios and would participate fully in College discussions.

The Commission was concerned to strike a balance between equality of treatment of Member States on the one hand and functional efficiency of the College on the other. It therefore advocated that the number of Commissioners should immediately be reduced to one per Member State. When the Union exceeded 20 Member States, the system would have to be reviewed. In the end the large Member States made it clear that they would be unwilling to relinquish one of the ten permanent portfolios in a reduced Commission and further, that they required compensation for the loss of a Commissioner by the re-weighting of votes in the Council. For the smaller members this was a 'no-win' situation, so the issue remained unsettled. For them, the right of every Member State to nominate a Commissioner was part of the legitimacy of the Commission, a principle to be respected even if enlargement meant an oversized Commission and an obligation to envisage its reduction.

On the whole, the small states argued for maintaining the *status quo*. This would mean a College of 33 Commissioners in an EU of 27 countries. The idea of regional Commissioners (e.g. a Dutch Commissioner representing Belgium and Luxembourg as well) was explicitly rejected. The Netherlands followed the Commission line of a core cabinet underpinned by junior Commissioners without portfolio.

Germany was prepared to go as far as to give up one of its Commissioners but not both, considering the French proposition of ten members unrealistic. Like the Italians, Germany favoured a Commission of 15–20 members, thus depriving some small Member States of a Commissioner in an enlarged Union. It argued that ways would have to be found to compensate them by increasing their presence in other institutions such as the EP and the Court of Justice. Italy argued that the number of Commissioners should be consistent with functions, and should be fixed at a maximum of 15. Once the number of Member States exceeded 20, a new ceiling would have to be fixed. Not all Member States would have a Commissioner – not, apparently, a problem for Italy.

The implication of the French and Commission option was that large Member States would not only lose the right to two Commissioners, but also have to accept not having a Commissioner at all during certain periods. One *quid pro quo* was a corresponding shift in the weighting of Council votes, since enlargement would otherwise introduce a situation where the smaller and medium-sized Member States could always outvote the large. But this idea did not run in the end. The French proposal for a reduced Commission was no longer a viable option. Yet the issue still needed to be resolved. The Commission continued to argue for a procedure for reviewing its membership above a certain number of Member States, entailing amendment of Article 157 EC. The procedure would be triggered when the number of Member States exceeded 20. If this were to become the final solution, the larger countries made their acceptance conditional on a re-weighting of votes in the Council. The UK argued that voting in the Council should anyway be re-weighted to take account of population and qualified majority voting should not be extended. These two factors would give the larger Member States more power *vis-à-vis* the Commission.

The smaller states would have accepted the double (votes and population) majority principle. But even the flexible Belgians hardened their position when it became clear that the larger Member States, led by the Germans, would never countenance an even-handed approach implying rotation within a reduced Commission and possible periods with no German Commissioner. At the Noordwijk special European Council, the Germans persuaded the others that the *status quo* was preferable to an endless quarrel linking the two institutions. As the largest Member State in terms of population, Germany would not give up the principle of a permanent German Commissioner. Kohl argued that any proposition to the contrary would be rejected by the German Parliament and, in the run-up to a general election, public opinion was a prime concern. The Germans had Spanish and British support. They were probably right. The quarrel was exposing an issue that was generally recognized but contrary to Article 155 EC. Membership of the College bound Commissioners not to take instructions from any source. Linking national interests in sizes, numbers and weightings in the Council and the Commission was tantamount to admitting that the treaty was a sham.

A joint declaration of the Belgian, Italian and French governments stated that enlargement could only be agreed if prior institutional adjustments were made, in particular the extension of qualified majority voting. Since agreement was not possible and fearing that the Amsterdam Treaty would embarrassingly fail to come to grips with the basic issue of the size of the Commission, Member States deferred final agreement on the number of Commissioners. A Protocol thus envisages resolving the issue of re-weighting so as to allow the implementation of the one-Commissioner-per-country solution and a new IGC before the Union exceeds 20 members. This might discuss the question of a College smaller than the number of Member States, raising the issue of rotation and equality once again.

The text of the Protocol on the institutions with the prospect of enlargement of the EU reads:

Article 1
At the entry into force of the first enlargement of the Union ... the Commission shall comprise one national of each of the Member States, provided that, by that date, the

weighting of the votes in the Council has been modified, whether by re-weighting of the votes or by dual majority, in a manner acceptable to all Member States, taking into account all relevant elements, notably compensating those Member States which give up the possibility of nominating a second member of the Commission.

Article 2

At least one year before the membership of the European Union exceeds twenty, a conference of representatives of the governments of Member States shall be convened in order to carry out a comprehensive review of the provisions of the Treaties on the composition and functioning of the institutions.

By 1999 the situation had changed. In his proposals at Cologne, Prodi argued that the motion that it is not possible to carve out substantial jobs for 19 Commissioners needed to be dispelled. Each portfolio would carry with it a significant area of work; the main challenge was 'squeezing all the work of the Commission into 19 portfolios'. Some portfolios will remain unchanged (regional policy, economic and monetary affairs, employment and competition), but others regrouped to remove overlap and duplication, grouping DGs together under the responsibility of single Commissioners. This implies a net reduction in DGs.

Decision-making: the Commission as initiator and broker

Germany's overall stance on the Commission was of great concern to the Commission itself. Germany was challenging the Commission's monopoly of initiative under Article 189a of the Treaty, and therefore the Community's delicate institutional balance, which is part of the nature of Community affairs, planned by the founding fathers and confirmed by the ECJ. The Germans floated the idea of the Council obtaining a right of initiative or at least be allowed to insist the Commission make a legislative proposal in a given area.

In the end the Commission's right of initiative was actually strengthened in two key third pillar areas. These were the free movement of persons where, after an initial 5 years of co-initiative with the Member States, the Commission will enjoy an exclusive right of initiative and a right of initiative in police cooperation and criminal matters. It is also arguably the case that the Commission's overall power has been strengthened by the virtual disappearance of the cooperation procedure and its replacement by a streamlined co-decision procedure. If it could be argued that the co-decision procedure had originally weakened the Commission by its creation of a new, special relationship between the EP and Council, it is also a fact that the Commission received a specific treaty-based role of brokerage. Amended Article 189b(4) provides that 'The Commission shall take part in the Conciliation Committee's proceedings and shall take all the necessary initiatives with a view to reconciling the positions of the European Parliament and the Council.'

An enhanced role in Common Foreign and Security Policy

In second pillar matters, a proposed 'new' troika[33] idea proved acceptable and the presence of the Commission in the new Council CFSP planning unit desirable in a tripartite structure comprising representatives of the WEU, the Commission and the Member States.

The CFSP is a special area in which the Commission will now have an enhanced role. Outside the EU the Commission delegates throughout the world have always been the only stable element in a shifting constellation of troikas and Presidencies of the Council. In addition, the Commission, rather than the Presidency represents much of EU business to the outside world as a matter of course. The new troika (Presidency, Council Secretariat General, and Commission) will formally improve the Commission's status, but there is more to the change than the formality. The irony is that most Member States are not represented in most countries of the world, that the ambassadors of other Member States are thus obliged to take on the Presidency role and the Council Secretariat maintains an office only in Geneva and New York.[34] Outside the EU, whereas the concept of the troika may change, practice will remain fluid and the Commission will remain the only permanent member.

In overall political terms, the Commission's role is arguably not enhanced by the creation of a specific CFSP role for the Council Secretariat and its Secretary-General. Yet, the creation of a potential counterweight in the shape of the new Vice-President for external relations in the Commission augurs, at the very least informally, for a redefinition of roles in terms of external representation. Much will depend on the individuals appointed and the operating rules within the Council. The Council Secretariat does not have the extensive information and political resources available to it, which the Commission's External Service, with its 128 delegations and offices outside the EU, provides for senior decision-makers in the Commission. True, the Council Secretariat can call on the resources of Member States, but the effectiveness of such mechanisms will depend on the willingness of traditionally secretive foreign ministries.

The external relations portfolios were reorganised in the opening months of the Prodi Commission, with four Commissioners dividing responsibility according to policy areas (external relations, trade, enlargement and development) rather than geography. However, the major issue dogging the external relations arrangements in the Commission has been rivalry at all levels. Prodi though did not appoint a Vice–President for external relations with the task of coordination and arbitration.

Managing change: the issue of internal reform

There is general agreement that the balance between the Commission's role as initiator of policy and manager of policy has changed and the management methods and structures of the Commission have proved unable to meet the resulting challenges.[35] That the Commission has proved more capable in the role of policy maker than in that of policy manager is witnessed by the growth in criticism from all sides. There is a clear 'management deficit' in the Commission, as more than one observer has pointed out.[36]

The Commission's structures and methods remained pretty much the same in the 1990s as they were in the 1950s. The Commission may be 'rigorous and supple in structure and function', but it has proved itself no more able to rise to the challenge of internal reform than it has been able to meet the countless criticisms and many attempts to propose the institutional reform outlined above. Yet, the arrival of two Nordic Commissioners in the Santer Commission has provided the political impetus for far-reaching managerial change. Under its second Secretary-General, Sir David Williamson, and its current Secretary-General, Carlo Trojan, 'designing tomorrow's Commission' has become a byword for root and branch reform.

Again, the need for reform is not new. Spierenburg noted in 1979 that the workload of the services had increased inexorably, but that the distribution of staff between Directorates-General (DGs) and services did not reflect the differential growth of the workload. He deplored the proliferation of services and DGs and suggested merging several DGs into a small number of large administrative units in order to facilitate coordination between related sectors, remove obstacles to career mobility and contribute to stability and efficiency. He argued that it was difficult to reallocate staff between DGs and even within DGs. There seemed to be a lack of staff mobility, which, coupled with poor promotion prospects because of the age structure of staff and a feeling of alienation, had led to a decline in morale. Alienation was partly caused by failure of the Council to act on the basis of Commission proposals, which had taken months of preparatory work, the limited scope of work, lack of information about Commission policy in general and a feeling of remoteness from the real decision-makers. The fact was that 'the Commission is being managed in a manner and with techniques which are inappropriate in present circumstances and can only be more so after enlargement'. Twenty years on, it might seem that some of Spierenburg's proposals might be met.

From SEM 2000 to the 'Commission of Tomorrow'

Two broad features of management change have begun, slowly, to introduce management change. Santer and Williamson had identified the reform agenda early on in the Santer Commission. They stressed that the way to achieve greater transparency and legitimacy was not by reducing the political powers of the Commission (notably its right of initiative, which was challenged by the Germans in the IGC). Rather they could be produced by underpinning those powers through greater operational efficiency and by concentrating on a limited range of policy areas where the Commission could genuinely act more effectively than the Member States. Areas where the Member States could be more effective than the Commission would be left to them. This not only implied a commitment to internal reform but also to subsidiarity. It was an opportune time since the political climate in some Member States was hostile to the Commission's 'centralizing' and self-aggrandizing tendencies, as they saw it, under Delors.[37] Indeed, slogans such as focusing on 'l'essentiel', 'less action, more efficiency' and 'doing less, but doing it better' were underlying themes throughout the Santer Commission.

For the IGC, the Commission argued that to increase the efficiency, visibility and coherence of Commission action, notably in the enlargement context, its internal organization would have to be reviewed. This was not a matter for the Treaty but for the Commission Rules of Procedure. With the Commission's right of initiative no longer in doubt and its institutional position strengthened by the IGC, the Santer Commission is set to achieve a major streamlining of the institution's executive and managerial functions. The starting point is the Amsterdam declaration on the organization and functioning of the Commission, which gave Council blessing to plans for reform. The declaration stated:

> The conference notes the Commission's intention to prepare a reorganisation of tasks within the College in good time for the Commission which will take up office in 2000, in order to ensure an optimum division between conventional portfolios and specific tasks.
>
> In this context, it considers that the president of the Commission must enjoy broad discretion in the allocation of tasks within the College, as well as any reshuffling of those tasks during a Commission's term of office.
>
> The conference also notes the Commission's intention to undertake in parallel a corresponding reorganisation of its own departments. It notes in particular the desirability of bringing external relations under the responsibility of a Vice-President.

The hope was that the Commission would prove able to end the various practices in the realm of personnel policy and management denounced both by Commission staff and by various outside observers.[38] The main thrust of reform in the field of human resources is the MAP 2000 programme, a far-reaching and ambitious attempt to modernize personnel policy and administration. It grew out of the Sound and Efficient Management (SEM) 2000 initiative launched at the beginning of the Santer Commission and formally approved in April 1997. MAP 2000 was structured in three phases: 1997–98 was to see a simplification of procedures and decentralization of powers from DGIX (personnel) to other DGs. Thereafter, in 1998–99 responsibilities were delegated vertically within each DG and increased in an effort to create greater autonomy in the allocation of managerial and administrative resources. The final phase was to be 1999–2000. This would involve further rationalization of the structure of Commission services in the light of a major screening of DGs in 1998. Implementation of the recommendations was suspended until the Prodi Commission took office.

MAP 2000 envisaged 25 measures including allowing administrative expenditure in each DG to increase to cover auxiliary and temporary staff, so as to decrease spending on technical assistants, studies and missions; allowing DGs greater responsibility for calculating expenses relating to equipment and estate management, and administrative posts gradually being transferred from DGIX to other DGs. In October 1997, Secretary-General Trojan launched five reflection groups of Directors-General on topics deemed most relevant to Commission reform, namely programming of work, training, mobility, information technology and simplification of procedures. The groups produced reports for January 1998 discussions between the five Heads of Unit responsible in DGIX, the Directors-General and the Secretary-General.

La Commission de demain[39]

In a paper entitled 'Designing Tomorrow's Commission' (April 1998), Trojan raised the question of shedding some of the Commission's purely managerial tasks for which it is ill-equipped and perhaps transferring these to outside agencies,[40] or at least streamlining them considerably. A screening exercise, 'dessiner la Commission de demain', was to provide a blueprint for the future Commission. Agenda 2000 had stipulated that contributions to the Community budget would be maintained at the current level of 1.27 per cent of GDP. Faced with enlargement and an increasing workload on the one hand and zero-growth of officials on the other, the Commission had no option but to streamline its management, though by the end of 1998 references were being made to the impossibility of the Commission continually taking on new tasks without concern for the human resources needed to manage the work implications.[41]

The screening foreseen by MAP 2000 began in January 1998. There were twelve screening teams, each headed by an official of Director level. They interviewed Heads of Unit, who gave a description of their Unit's activities and assessed the effectiveness with which priorities are met. A seven-page questionnaire was sent prior to the interviews. The Relex team was the largest, covering not only Relex DGs but also Commission delegations, the Task Force for the Accession Negotiations, the external relations units of other DGs and the new Service Commun Relex (SCR).

Implementing change and maintaining support

The implementation of MAP was not without problems. A controversy surrounding a proposed reform of the staff regulations (the 'statut') arose in April 1998. It was precipitated by the appearance of a paper drafted by a senior official of DGIX. The paper argued for far-reaching reforms on several 'taboo' subjects: a reduction in officials' salaries; the introduction of a performance-related pay scheme; dismissal of officials for incompetence or consistent underperformance; curtailing certain 'perks' such as the payment of an educational allowance in addition to a child allowance, and a reduction in the overall expatriate allowance; an increasing use of a national quota system to recruit officials from countries currently underrepresented, if necessary by means of publishing competitions limited to one country; the recruitment of translators with proven administrative and executive skills which would allow for mobility later on in their career; a greater use of teleworking to improve quality and efficiency in translation.

Both Commissioner Liikanen and the paper's author underlined that the report was not an official communication of the Commission but a personal view.[42] For the unions, the fact that reform proposals had been drafted without prior consultation was unacceptable, whatever the official status of the report. The Commission offered to set up a high-level Reflection Group composed of representatives from the Commission, the Parliament, the Council and the unions to discuss reform. It also proposed the creation of a joint body of the Commission administration and the unions with a view to evaluating the new method of assessing staff. No agreement was reached on these proposals and there followed a strike on the 30 April 1998. Subsequently, on 24 June 1998, former Secretary-General Williamson was appointed chairman of a 'Reflection Group on Staff Policy'. The Reflection Group on Personnel Policy was set up with a commitment by all parties to 'an independent, competent and permanent European civil service, and to a single set of staff regulations applying to all'.[43] Its final report was presented to the Commission on 31 October 1998. The report summed up many of the issues ripe for settlement in the Commission's personnel management, but there are as yet no concrete proposals to resolve many of the key issues underlined by Spierenburg and others[44] – such as the influence of the *cabinet* system in appointments (*piston*), national balance amongst officials, *parachutage* etc.

Promotions, national balance and parachutage

Staff mobility was one of MAP 2000's priorities. Promotion policy is still a cause for grievance among many officials. Indeed, people who joined through the *concours* and have worked in the Commission for many years can suddenly find themselves bypassed for promotion, with merit seeming to play little role. Team spirit among staff is not helped by the machinations involving '*piston*' and '*soumarins*'.[45] It is widely felt by officials that producing good work is less important than knowing the right people and networking, often by drumming up support from fellow countrymen or interest-based groups in other services. These tendencies are particularly common in the lower and middle ranks of the administration. In the higher ranks, *parachutage* from *cabinets* or national administrations is a common feature, leading to accusations of 'home-grown' ability being sacrificed to the interference of national politics. It is also true that newcomers in high posts can upset the sophisticated internal mechanisms and 'culture' of a DG.[46] *Parachutage* is not only a method of maintaining balance in national patronage. It is useful for the Commission to have senior officials within its ranks who have experience of *cabinets*, national administrations, politics and working methods at the highest levels. The links between detached national experts and their national administrations can be similarly beneficial.

The 1999 Herman Report[47] considered that 'the current need for geographical and political balance among senior office holders in the Commission may reduce the independence and efficiency of the European civil service', arguing that 'ability and relevant experience (should) play a greater role in the appointments process'.

The problems relating to national balance reflect an inherent dilemma which the Commission has always faced, that of maintaining a fair tally between nationalities while also not compromising the independence and high working standards of the organization. From a broader perspective, it highlights a split between intergovernmentalism and supranationalism in the administration. 'la Commission de demain' recognizes that there are 'des recrutements parfois trop politiques'[48] and that mobility and objectivity in promotion need to be enhanced. MAP 2000 set out to remedy this.

The cabinet *system and relations between the* cabinets *and the services*

The *cabinet* system is a product of strong French administrative influence on the Community in the early years. According to the Spierenburg Report, *cabinets* shield Commissioners from their services, *chefs de cabinet* usurp responsibilities of Directors-General and meetings of *cabinet* members and *chefs de cabinet* question proposals without consulting the responsible officials in the services. Henceforth, argued Spierenburg, no policy document should be edited without consultation of the appropriate Director-General and there should anyway be no radical departure from the theme of the basic proposal. Spierenburg also criticized the *cabinets'* widespread interference in appointment issues and the 'undue' attention to nationality factors, itself compounded by *parachutage* of *cabinet* members into services. While not offering a solution to the problem of *parachutage*, Spierenburg recommended reinstatement of officials only into their former posts on leaving the *cabinet*. While not dismissing the fact that *cabinet* members would have acquired considerable skills while working in *cabinets*, there should, it was argued, be fair competition for posts.

On balance, the *cabinet* system has probably been beneficial. There is however a widespread feeling that Spierenburg was right to argue that the *cabinets* had become too large and too powerful. Most Commissioners have a seven-member *cabinet*, including career officials and appointees who came to Brussels with the Commissioner.[49] A good *cabinet* can boost the standing of an otherwise poor Commissioner, and a poor *cabinet* can compromise an otherwise good Commissioner. It is no coincidence that the most effective Commissioners in the current Commission have the best-staffed and best-organized *cabinets*.

Questioning the *raison d'être* of the *cabinet* system raises the issue of the power of Directors-General, both in relation to *cabinets* and to the Commissioners themselves. Over time, it is argued, the *cabinet* system has led to a usurpation of power, frequently rendering the Directors-General powerless. Sometimes skilful *cabinets* become 'shadow *cabinets*' for their Commissioners' administrations, undercutting the autonomy of the appointed leaders of the Directorates-General. *Cabinet* members, including the most junior of them, often reworked and rewrote the work of the services – sometimes 'just for the fun of it' in the words of Carlo Trojan.[50] Santer's *chef de cabinet*, Jim Cloos, and Secretary-General Trojan set up a steering committee of *chefs de cabinet* and Directors-General. The aim was to analyse how to avoid the excesses of the present system by keeping the *cabinets* political and keeping them out of the day-to-day running of the services. Trojan's 'Commission de demain' paper recognized the problems and proposed limiting the *cabinets'* interventions, possibly by means of a code of conduct. It also raised the possibility of reducing the number of members, the idea being to improve relations between services and *cabinets* and act as a brake on *parachutage*. It also suggested the inclusion of the relevant Directors-General at the weekly meeting of heads of *cabinet*. This would be a logical and sensible development given that one of MAP 2000's aims is to devolve more responsibility to Directorates-General. The Herman Report argued that *cabinets* should have no more than six members with only one or two members of the same nationality as their Commissioner. Prodi took the message on board.

In an address to the 23 Directors-General in March 1991, Delors is said to have threatened to fire the most inefficient of them. But his inability to sanction poor performers and the power of national governments to influence senior positions underline the serious managerial deficit in the Commission's senior echelons. The Spierenburg Report also pointed to these problems. Neither the number nor the responsibilities of the DGs correspond to the number or the portfolios of the Commissioners. The responsibilities of a DG may also be spread over the portfolios of more than one Commissioner, as was formerly the case with DGI, with a north–south section and a general trade and OECD section, each reporting to a different Commissioner. The Directors-Generals' loss of power (and the consequent increased power of the *cabinets*) prompted Spierenburg to argue for them to regain importance. They should be solely responsible for management and coordination with other Directors-General, play a central role on key staff appointments, attend relevant Commission meetings and be entrusted with high-level missions, thus lightening the burden on Commissioners and simultaneously enhancing the profile of the Directors-General themselves. Criticized by staff for remoteness, the Directors-General were to hold frequent senior staff meetings, ensure flows of guidance texts and information, and take a personal interest in staff matters. There has been little evidence until the MAP 2000 programme and the Commission of Tomorrow initiative that they do.

'Unbundling' the Commission: the issue of agencies

In terms of the overall political direction of the Commission, a much canvassed issue is the idea of delegating the managerial functions of the Commission to a series of agencies.[51] The idea is that the tasks of the Commission would be 'unbundled' into three main areas corresponding to different managerial functions: a Commission for the Single Market, a Treasury Board responsible for all spending programmes, and an external trade Commission. The Commission's judicial functions would be hived off to special judicial bodies, for example a European Competition Authority. Under these proposals the Commission would become an even smaller, high-powered general staff, providing the European Council and its subordinate councils with proposals on strategy and policy. Politicians have been reluctant to tread this path. Seemingly, one part of the *acquis communautaire* is the continued existence of the Commission in the broad form in which it has operated since the outset. Thus, though the SEM 2000 and MAP 2000 initiatives have addressed the issues raised by the proponents of 'unbundling', the method of implementing the principles involved has taken a different form. Reforms have included the creation of units within each Directorate-General specialized in financial management and control and the introduction of enhanced systems of management, rather than the hiving off of the functions involved. This may be because internal reform has so far been proposed and managed by the very senior staff that management change might target. Unlike the more radical of Member States, there has been no attempt to appeal to outside management consultants unsullied by positions within the structures to be reformed. Yet there is nevertheless the outline of a move towards a Commission composed of a number of integrated ministry-like structures, in which the vertical lines between the political and civil service levels resemble those of Member State governments.

Conclusion

Reform of the Commission is thus under way but there remains a fundamental debate. National, intergovernmental and supranational tendencies often collide. This was not only demonstrated by the 1996–97 IGC but is also manifest in attempts at internal reform. Although the Commission possibly enjoys greater public legitimacy than it did at the beginning of the 1990s, the drive towards efficiency, embodied in the MAP 2000 programme, means the creation of a new management culture which is difficult to reconcile with the traditional ethos of the Commission as 'policy initiator'. Intellectual powers have always been valued highly whereas the practical skill of managing staff effectively has taken second place.

Creating a modern management culture is difficult enough in a national administration, but is even more problematic in an international institution, where the working methods and values of national administrations coexist, and where the linguistic and cultural diversity among staff does not automatically facilitate the exercise of authority. Some observers have noted a gradual change from the hierarchical structures of the early Commission, based on the French administrative model to a new 'management culture'.[52] The desire to create a managerial ethos within the administration does not, however, imply that the Commission will inevitably become a 'manager' of an intergovernmentally driven integration process in which the Council calls the shots. Rather, the 'doing less but doing it better outlook' could produce a Commission which has passed on many executive responsibilities to outside agencies and become an 'independent' authority like the European Central Bank with a high-powered general staff offering political and strategic advice to the Council. Some say that this would forestall charges of 'faceless bureaucrats' and thus improve public acceptance, while others contend that such a shedding of responsibilities would lead to a loss of legitimacy. The balance sheet of the period between the resignation of the last Commission and the beginning of the work of the Prodi Commission reveals that there is some way to go before the changes in the Amsterdam Treaty become second nature to the actors involved. Europe watchers will need to be vigilant in assessing whether fundamental reform is achieved or whether, as Tancredi in de Lampedusa's book 'The Leopard' reflected, 'it is necessary to change something in order that everything remains the same'.

The Commission has a fundamental problem as it approaches the next millennium: the lack of clarity about its role, emanating from the conflicting functions which it performs or to which it aspires; initiator, administrator, mediator, negotiator, on the one hand or, on the other, a proto-government within a federal Europe. The vital question is whether the 'La Commission de demain' initiative will produce a fundamentally different Commission in time for the next Commission in 2000 and whether the promise of reform in the Amsterdam Treaty will actually be realized. 'Come back Spierenburg, all is forgiven?' Or will it once again all be forgotten?

Endnotes

1. Committee of Independent Experts, *First Report on Allegations regarding Fraud, Mismanagement and Nepotism in the European Commission*, Brussels, 15 March 1999.
2. See G. Edwards and D. Spence, 'The Commission in Perspective' in G. Edwards and D. Spence (eds), *The European Commission*, 2nd edn, London: Cartermill, 1997.
3. 'The European Commission as Regulator', in G. Majone (ed.), *Regulating Europe*, London: Routledge, 1996, p. 61.
4. For a comprehensive review of the issues, see C. Docksey and K. Williams, 'The Commission and the Execution of Community Policy', in Edwards and Spence (eds), *The European Commission*. Recent practical examples are discussed in M. Van Schendelen, *EU Committees as Influential Policymakers*, Aldershot: Ashgate, 1998.
5. Case C-25/94, *Commission of the European Communities v Council of the European Union*, judgment of 19 March 1996, European Court Reports 1996 page 1–1469 and Case C-327/91, *French Republic v Commission of the European Communities*, judgment of the Court of 9 August 1994 [1994] ECR page 1–3641.
6. 'Dishing the pasta, not the dirt', *The Economist*, 21 November 1998.
7. In 1998, as in 1996 and 1997, the Budget Committee of the European Parliament approved an amendment by former Commission Director-General and Head of Delegation, Laurens-Jan Brinkhorst, creating a budgetary reserve to be lifted only on delivery by the Commission of management reforms in the External Service. For the 1999 budget the same applied. See Draft amendment 3451 (C4-0300/98) to budget line A-650 Global reserve for Delegations.
8. This is the title of the ambitious programme of decentralized financial management introduced by budget Commissioner Erki Liikanen. For a commentary see, B. Laffan, 'From Policy Entrepreneur to Policy Manager: The Challenge Facing the European Commission', *Journal of European Public Policy*, Vol. 4, 1997, pp. 422–38.
9. J. Newhouse, *Collision in Brussels. The Common Market Crisis of 30 June 1967*, New York: Norton, 1967.
10. F. Vibert, *The Future Role of the Commission*, London: European Policy Forum, 1994.
11. Inaugural Address to the European Parliament, 7 January 1995.
12. See W. Weidenfeld (ed.), *Europa '96: Reformprogramm für die Europäische Union*, Gütersloh: Bertelsmann,1994.
13. Reply by President Santer during question time, 2 December 1998.
14. D. Spierenburg, *Proposals for Reform of the Commission of the European Communities and its Services*, Brussels, 24 September 1979. The all-male Review Body was composed of the chairman, Ambassador D.P. Spierenburg, K. Buschmann, P. Delouvrier, G. Petrilli and D. Taverne.
15. L. Tindemans, 'Dreams come true, gradually', in M. Westlake (ed.) *The European Union beyond Amsterdam: New Concepts of European Integration*. London: Routledge, 1998, pp. 130–41.
16. See P. Ludlow, 'The European Commission', in R. Keohane and S. Hoffmann (eds), *The New European Community: Decision-making and Institutional Change*, Oxford: Westview, 1991, pp. 88–132, and Edwards and Spence, 'The Commission in Perspective'.

17. EP rule number 33, Chapter VI, 14th edn, June 1999.
18. For an account of the growth in Parliament's powers in this respect, see M. Westlake, 'The EP's Emerging Powers of Appointment', *Journal of Common Market Studies*, Vol. 36, 1998, pp. 431–44.
19. J. Nicolas, *L'Europe des Fraudes*, Brussels, Editions PNA, 1999.
20. *Agence Europe*, 2 July 1993.
21. The Next European Commission: *Efficiency through Management Reform*, London, 1999.
22. If the Commission were aiming at implementation of the principle of joined up government, this was hardly apparent in the appointments it made. Kinnock was given the reform portfolio, but the linked portfolio of the IGC went to Barnier, who also handles regional policy. Responsibility for relations with the EP, arguably also a dossier linked to reform, was given to Loyola de Palacio along with the energy and transport portfolios, both of which had warranted a sole Commissioner's responsibility hitherto.
23. Roy Jenkins, *A Life at the Centre*, London: Macmillan, 1991, p 376.
24. See 'Europe – the Future', paper tabled by Margaret Thatcher at the Stuttgart Summit, reproduced in *Select Committee on the European Communities European Union* (HL 226), 1985.
25. *Select Committee on the European Communities European Union* (HL 226), 1985, p. xxiv.
26. Weidenfeld (ed.) *Europa '96*, p. 38.
27. K. Lamers, 'Why the EU Needs to Strengthen its Institutions', in *What Future for the European Commission?*, Brussels: Philip Morris Institute, 1995, p. 43.
28. E. Davignon, 'The Challenges that the Commission must Confront', in *What Future for the European Commission?*, p. 16.
29. R. Dahrendorf, writing as 'Wieland Europa', 'A New Goal for Europe', *Die Zeit*, no. 28, 9 July 1971, translated and reproduced in M. Hodges (ed.), *European Integration*, London: Penguin, 1972, p. 85.
30. The formula is that of the Director of the Commission's IGC 1996 Task Force, Michel Petite. See 'L'avis de la Commission européenne: renforcer l'union politique et préparer l'élargissement', in A. Mattera (ed.), *La Conférence intergouvernementale sur l'Union européenne: répondre aux défis du XXIe siècle*, Paris: Clément Juglar, 1996.
31. Dahrendorf, 'A New Goal for Europe'.
32. Sir Leon Brittan, *Europe: the Europe We Need*, London: Hamish Hamilton, 1994, pp. 238–43. Similar views were voiced by Sir Christopher Tugendhat in evidence to the House of Lords' Select Committee in 1985, p. 201. There are parallels between Brittan's view and the UK government position in the IGC. See S. George, 'The Approach of the British Government to the 1996 IGC', *Journal of European Public Policy*, Vol. 3, 1996, p. 55.
33. Previously the former, current and future Presidency plus the Commission, the misnamed 'troika' would be composed of the Presidency, the Council Secretariat and the Commission.
34. See D. Spence, 'EU Foreign Ministries between Reform and Adaptation', in B. Hocking (ed), *Foreign Ministries: Change and Adaptation*, London: Macmillan, 1999.
35. See Laffan, 'From Policy Entrepreneur to Policy Manager'.
36. One such observer is L. Metcalfe. See his 'Building capacities for integration; the future role of the Commission', in EIPASCOPE, no. 2, 1996.
37. For an analysis see G. Ross, *Jacques Delors and European Integration*, Cambridge: Polity Press, 1995 and C. Grant, *Delors: Inside the House that Jacques Built*, London: Nicholas Brealey Publishing, 1994.
38. A good summary of the issues can be found in E. Page, *People who Run Europe*, Oxford: Clarendon Press, 1997.
39. *La Commission de demain*. SEC98 70.1, p. 7.
40. Peter Ludlow, by contrast, argues that at a time when 'the Commission's lack of accountability is widely regarded (not least by Commission representatives themselves) as problematical, it would be perverse to compound the problem by devolving executive responsibilities to apolitical agencies', Keohane and Hoffmann (eds), *The New European Community*, pp. 126–7.
41. Santer, EP question time, 2 December 1998.
42. The 'issues' paper on the reform of the staff regulations was made available on the Commission's Intranet. Its purpose, as the Director-General described it to all staff was 'to help identify issues and options ... not to draft specific proposals'. Message from the Director-General for Personnel and Administration, 5 April 1998.
43. Reflection Group on Personnel Policy: interim report, 28 July 1998, p. 6.
44. For a review of the issues, see D. Spence, 'Staff and Personnel Policy in the Commission', in Edwards and Spence (eds), *The European Commission*.

45. Spence, 'Staff and Personnel Policy in the Commission'.
46. I. Belier, 'La Commission européenne: hauts fonctionnaires et culture du management', *Revue Française d'Administration Publique*, Vol. 70, 1994, p. 253.
47. F. Herman, *Report on Improvements in the Functioning of the Institutions without Modification of the Treaties, Committee on Institutional Affairs*, PE 229.072/fin, 26 March 1999.
48. *La Commission de demain*, p. 9.
49. See M. Donnelley and E. Ritchie, 'The College of Commissioners and their *Cabinets*', in Edwards and Spence (eds), *The European Commission*.
50. Ross, *Jacques Delors and European Integration*, p. 161.
51. See, in particular, Vibert, *The Future Role of the Commission*.
52. Belier, 'La Commission européenne' p. 253.

Chapter 3

The European Parliament

Francis Jacobs

Introduction

The European Parliament's role in the European Union (EU) reform process is a paradoxical one. On the one hand it is the only directly elected parliamentary body at Union level, and is more continuously and deeply involved in the EU reform process than the individual national parliaments. On the other hand, it has no formal say on the outcome of that reform process and, unlike the national parliaments, cannot ratify or reject formal proposals for Treaty change. In spite of this handicap the European Parliament (EP) has itself been a major beneficiary of the Treaty reform process, both at Maastricht and Amsterdam.

This chapter first examines how the nature of the Parliament's involvement in this process of Treaty reform has changed over time and, in particular, between the two most recent Intergovernmental Conferences (IGCs). Secondly, it looks at the EP's attitudes to the reform process from Maastricht to Amsterdam and at the main policy positions adopted by the Parliament on EU reform issues in the period covered by this book, both as regards the development of the EP's own powers and those of the EU as a whole. It concludes by examining the evolution of the EP's own powers during this same period, including the new powers given by Maastricht, the main ways in which they have subsequently been developed and implemented, and finally the likely implications of the decisions taken at Amsterdam for the future role and powers of the European Parliament.

The European Parliament's involvement in the reform process

A characteristic of the EP's involvement in Treaty reform has been in the drawing up of draft Treaties designed to influence those with the power to negotiate them. This approach can be traced back to the Parliamentary Assembly of the European Coal and Steel Community which drew up a draft Treaty for a European Political Community, but it assumed particular prominence in the 1980s when the then directly elected EP played an important part in the Treaty reform process through its adoption, on 14 February 1984, of a draft Treaty on European Union. Prepared under the leadership of the veteran Italian federalist, Altiero Spinelli (and still familiarly known as the Spinelli draft Treaty), it won support from the parliaments and governments of a number of Member States and led to the creation of an *ad hoc* committee of personal representatives which was to examine changes to the Treaty. The committee, known as the Dooge Committee after its Irish chairman, Jim Dooge, did not entail formal Parliament involvement but did include several sitting and former MEPs, Fernand Herman of Belgium, Ioannis Papantoniou of Greece, and Enrico Ferri of Italy. The work of the Dooge Committee led in turn to an IGC in 1985 and to the signing of the Single European Act (SEA) in February 1986. The EP's direct involvement in that IGC was minimal (although President Pflimlin and Spinelli attended a couple of ministerial meetings) and at the end of the process, as at all subsequent IGCs, it could only give a non-binding opinion. However, the Italian parliament established a linkage between its own binding ratification and the opinion of the EP: if the latter rejected it, so would the Italian parliament. In the event the SEA was approved by the EP, with reservations.

The EP obtained a somewhat more important role during the negotiating process leading up to the Maastricht Treaty. The Parliament put forward draft Treaty amendments on the basis of two earlier interim reports prepared by its general rapporteur, the British Labour MEP, David Martin. It also participated in 'Assizes' between it and national parliaments in Rome in November 1990, which adopted a common declaration proposing certain Treaty amendments. For the first time the EP was also involved in a continuing dialogue with the ministerial negotiators with roughly monthly meetings between a delegation of 12 MEPs and an equivalent number of ministers or their representatives from the Member States. At these meetings, which began in the period of preparation for the IGC and continued throughout the negotiations, the EP's delegation was informed of the key issues being discussed, and was then able to express its own views. It was not, however, a very satisfactory form of participation and gave little scope for influencing the negotiations. Almost certainly of greater significance were the visits that were made by members from Parliament's delegation to individual national capitals, which included face-to-face meetings with Heads of State or Government. For example, participants at the meeting with President Mitterrand considered that it had influenced him in adopting a more favourable attitude towards the extension of the proposed new co-decision procedure.

After the EP had given its unenthusiastic support for the outcome of the Maastricht Treaty (on the basis of another report from David Martin), attempts were again made to revert to a more radical approach to Treaty reform through the adoption of a draft European constitution. The text that was drawn up by Mr Herman within the EP's Committee on Institutional Affairs, however, was merely noted[1] and not formally examined or adopted by the full Parliament as it was considered to be too far-reaching by the majority of members in the sensitive period of the run-up to the 1994 European Parliament elections.

The EP's involvement in the most recent IGC, which concluded in the Amsterdam Treaty, was of a quite different and more detailed nature than that in previous IGCs. The first major innovation was that the Parliament was fully represented in the Reflection Group of personal representatives that was chaired by Carlos Westendorp of Spain and whose report of 5 December 1995 helped to set the detailed agenda for the new IGC. The EP representatives, Elmar Brok (German CDU) and Elisabeth Guigou (French Socialist), not only took part in the discussions and adoption of the final conclusions on the same basis as the Member State representatives, but also established a rapport with certain members of the Group who went on to become their country's negotiators in the main IGC.

This positive experience of EP participation in the Reflection Group led to support from most of the Member States for the EP being given observer status in the main IGC negotiations. A small minority of countries, most vociferously France and the UK, opposed observer status for the Parliament, and the stalemate continued during the period immediately preceding the opening of the IGC in Turin in March 1996. The compromise that was finally agreed fell short of full observer status but went well beyond what Parliament had obtained in the past.

The EP's involvement had several components. The Parliament's two representatives (Brok and Guigou were confirmed in this role) met on a roughly monthly basis with the IGC negotiators to discuss the substance of those negotiations. These meetings were far more than 'pro forma' and lasted for up to two or three hours.[2] In addition, Brok and Guigou were invited to a number of the personal representatives' working dinners and also received almost weekly briefings from the successive Presidency IGC representatives, Silvio Fagiolo (Italy), Noel Dorr (Ireland), and Michiel Patijn (Netherlands), who briefed them on the latest developments at the negotiations and on problems that were arising. A further element of the Parliament's involvement was the presence of the EP President at monthly meetings of the foreign ministers. The President was usually accompanied by Brok and Guigou. These meetings were, however, of much shorter duration than those of Brok and Guigou with the IGC negotiators, with the President tending to make a 10–15 minute statement and then briefly responding to comments from only a few of the ministers. A final and very significant feature of the Parliament's involvement was that the EP representatives received the various IGC papers at the same time as the Member State negotiators: while the EP had received many of the relevant papers during earlier IGCs it had not done so on such a systematic basis, and in so timely a manner.

The EP's representatives based their comments at the various meetings they attended on the IGC resolutions adopted by the Parliament, in particular the resolution of 17 May 1995 prepared by Mr Martin and Mr Bourlanges (French EPP) (and that constituted the first detailed position paper on the IGC adopted by any of the EU institutions) and that of 13 March 1996 prepared by Ms Dury (Belgian Socialist) and Ms Maij-Weggen (Dutch Christian Democrat). While these resolutions gave guidance to the EP representatives on many of the issues that were discussed, Brok and Guigou also had to respond to a number of new developments in the negotiations, and also sometimes had to expand on the EP position. For example, the Parliament had called for co-decision on all legislation but Brok and Guigou had to clarify the scope of co-decision in a specific area such as agriculture (i.e. only applying to the major policy decisions of a legislative nature and not to all the details of agricultural policy). The EP had also called for the abolition of the budgetary distinction between compulsory and non-compulsory expenditure, but Brok and Guigou found themselves instead negotiating an interinstitutional agreement somewhat restricting the EP's full budgetary powers as regards CFSP expenditure, but permitting the latter then to be classified as non-compulsory rather than compulsory expenditure.

To make their point on certain key issues Brok and Guigou also addressed a number of written proposals and comments to the IGC negotiators (but did not make use of a team of external legal experts as Spinelli had done for the draft Treaty or David Martin when converting his political priorities into draft Treaty articles). They reported back regularly to the EP's Committee on Institutional Affairs, and national parliamentarians were also invited to be present at their debriefings, and to take part in their discussions.

A further feature of the Parliament's involvement in the Amsterdam IGC was to seek input from non-governmental organizations (NGOs). Two open hearings were held in 1995 and 1996, at which any NGO which wished to address the European Parliament's Committee on Institutional Affairs was able to do so, and over 200 took up this opportunity. At the end of the IGC NGOs were also invited to submit written or e-mailed comments on the outcome, and to take part in a subsequent discussion in October 1997 with members of the EP's Committee on Institutional Affairs.

The Committee on Institutional Affairs also sought to exchange views on IGC issues with members of national parliaments, in particular from their respective European Affairs Committees. These contacts took place on a bilateral committee-to-committee basis, within the framework of COSAC[3] (for example at a special COSAC meeting in Luxembourg in July 1997), and even in the context of a special round table meeting between members of the Committee on Institutional Affairs and representatives of national parliaments that took place in Brussels in October 1997 to discuss the outcome of the Amsterdam Treaty. So although the Rome Assizes experiment of November 1990 was not repeated before Amsterdam, there was considerable contact between the EP and national parliaments.

At the end of all this the EP finally gave its positive but cautious opinion on the IGC in a resolution adopted on 19 November 1997 (A4-0347/97) on the basis of a report from Mr Mendez de Vigo (Spanish EPP) and Mr Tsatsos (Greek Socialist). The resolution concentrated on a few central political points (notably overall evaluation and future strategy) and the accompanying explanatory statement contained the rapporteurs' detailed assessment on specific issues. As before, the EP's opinion was only a non-binding one, unlike the formal 'yes or no' power given to individual national parliaments.

The way in which the Parliament was involved at Amsterdam was not as satisfactory as if the EP representatives had had full observer status and had participated in all of the meetings. The EP representatives' monthly rather than weekly attendance meant that some discussions had to be repeated in their presence and Brok and Guigou were often faced with the difficult choice as to whether they wished to respond to debates which had taken place among the negotiators just before their arrival, and which were still fresh in everyone's mind, or else to raise issues which had been discussed a week or two before but which were important and on which they had not had a chance to comment.

The form of the EP's involvement also posed a number of problems within the Parliament. The EP's involvement in Maastricht had been less intense but it had been broader-based and there were some within the Parliament who felt that IGC responsibilities were being concentrated within too few hands. At the beginning of the IGC some even called for the creation of an inter–institutional conference on Maastricht lines to act in parallel with the EP representatives, but this idea was not followed up later. There were also some criticisms that the EP representatives' involvement with the negotiations meant that the Parliament would not be able to maintain the necessary distance from the final outcome, and would risk being associated with its shortcomings.

However, whatever its disadvantages, the EP's involvement in the Amsterdam IGC brought it closer to the action than it had ever been before, and ensured far greater continuity in presentation of the Parliament's position. The EP representatives became well known to all the negotiators, and the details of the European Parliament's position became more familiar. The EP came to be seen as less maximalist and more realistic than many had imagined.

In the future, however, the EP will be seeking further development of its role. Some of its members argue forcefully that Amsterdam should mark the end of the road for narrowly based intergovernmental negotiations and that new and bolder forms of Treaty reform should be used, such as constituent assemblies.

The Parliament's own resolution of 19 November 1997, while not referring to constituent assemblies, did consider 'that the Amsterdam Treaty marks the end of an historical era when the work of European unification could be undertaken, stage by stage using the method of classic diplomacy' (paragraph 18). Instead, there should be a new method providing for much greater involvement of the EP and of national parliaments.

At the very least, however, and if more traditional means are still used, the EP will almost certainly push for full observer status at the negotiations, which will be more satisfactory both for its own representatives who will be able to follow all the discussions, but also for the Member State negotiators themselves, who will not have to repeat their discussions or to spend valuable time on additional briefings.

Even more fundamental, however, will be the question of the involvement of the EP in final Treaty ratification. As outlined above, the Parliament's role has evolved considerably as regards its contacts with the IGC negotiators, but not at all as regards the weight of its opinion on the final outcome. The EP has argued strongly throughout the IGC that it should be given the right of assent to Treaty change to match that granted to national parliaments. The EP's resolution of November 1997, for example, stated that even before former Article N (new Article 48) TEU, is amended 'the European Parliament should be fully involved in the next Intergovernmental Conference' and that a binding agreement (e.g. modelled on inter–institutional agreements) 'should be achieved to the effect that the Treaty may enter into force only with the Parliament's approval' (paragraph 20). The EP will undoubtedly continue to push hard for this in the future.

The European Parliament's general and specific views on the reform process

The European Parliament's underlying approaches to reform

As regards its attitudes to EU reform, the EP has never been a monolithic institution. Attitudes have varied from those who have been proud to call themselves federalists to those who have supported further integration but without a clear blueprint in mind, to those who have been more cautious and to those who have been opposed to the whole EU integration process and/or who have advocated withdrawal of their country from the European Community. Ever since 1979, for example, a number of members have been elected in Denmark who have been opposed to European integration and who have stood on a list or lists not represented in national elections. More recently the main rationale of one of the current European Parliament political groups, the 'Europe of Nations', whose best-known leaders have been Philippe de Villiers and the late Sir James Goldsmith, has been to defend the nation states and intergovernmentalism. These views are shared by other members as well, such as certain Gaullist members and members from right-wing parties such as the French Front National who constantly rail against the 'Europe of Maastricht'. If anything, the number of MEPs holding such views increased as a result of the 1999 European elections.

Intergovernmentalism or outright anti-European views have thus been consistently represented within the EP. They have always, however, been in the minority, and those members who have advocated deeper integration, whether through federalist conviction or on a more pragmatic basis, have always won the votes that mattered.

This has not meant, however, that the EP majority has been able to pursue a consistent strategy since federalist idealism and integrationalist aspirations have had to confront a much less tidy reality characterized by uneven progress in different areas and by suboptimal solutions.

At the risk of oversimplification, there have been two main reflexes within the EP pro-European majority in response to this discrepancy between objectives and results. The first has been to attempt to set out new and more ambitious blueprints for the future, by advocating far-reaching changes to the Treaty reform process, such as use of 'constituent assemblies' rather than classic intergovernmental negotiations, and by suggesting new European constitutional structures. This was first done in the early 1950s in the then Assembly's draft Treaty for a European Political Community, but the epitome of this approach was the Spinelli draft Treaty of 1984, initially concocted by an all-party ginger group of MEPs, the 'Crocodile Club'. More recently, and as described below, the method was again used in the Herman draft constitution of February 1994 and there are signs that this approach is being revived as a result of the creation in July 1997 of SOS Europe, a new all-party group of MEPs completely dissatisfied with the outcome of Amsterdam.[4]

This group of MEPs also contains the main advocates of the need to deepen the EU before widening it, and a considerable number of these members had voted against the most recent enlargement in consequence.

The second main grouping within the EP pro-European majority has been that which can perhaps best be described as the 'realists'. They argue that it is best to start from what already exists and/or that it is risky to adopt a more radical approach which has little chance of broad acceptance. Under this view the European Union has already developed, albeit in an *ad hoc* manner, a rough and ready constitutional structure and step-by-step reform is the only practicable way forward. Most of them would prefer EU deepening to take place in conjunction with widening, but believe that it is unrealistic to block the latter in the name of the former. Moreover, while many have expressed disappointment at the overall outcome of recent IGCs or else at more specific shortcomings, their general reflex has been to say 'yes, but ...', and to accept the result subject to a number of reservations and with the intention of taking up the struggle on these points at a later date.

This second or 'realistic' tendency has always won the support of a majority of MEPs at critical moments when the EP has been forced to choose between approval or rejection of an IGC or of enlargement, but it has also generally become stronger within the Parliament in recent years, even at less critical moments. A turning point in this respect was when the EP decided not to formally adopt the Herman draft constitution and in the Parliament elected in 1994 there has been a marked tendency to avoid use of emotive words such as 'federalism'. (In the 1989–94 Parliament, in contrast, the Martin reports on political union in the run-up to the Maastricht Treaty had continued to talk of the aspiration of a European Union of federal type). Even certain maximalists have accepted the need for this strategy on the grounds that threats of rejection cannot credibly be sustained within the present Parliament.

A clear illustration of all the above was provided by the votes in committee and in plenary on the Mendez de Vigo and Tsatsos report on the outcome of the Amsterdam Treaty. It criticized a number of aspects of the Treaty (in particular the absence 'of the institutional reforms needed for effective and democratic functioning of an enlarged Union' (paragraph 3 of the final resolution) but, nevertheless, considered that 'the Amsterdam Treaty marks a further step on the unfinished path towards the construction of a European political union', and that 'it represents some not inconsiderable advances for certain institutions' (paragraph 2 of the resolution). It, therefore, recommended that the Member States ratify the Treaty. This was adopted in committee on a vote of 22 in favour to 11 against and 3 abstentions and in plenary on a vote of 349 in favour to 100 against with 34 abstentions. The pro-European 'realists' were thus in a clear majority, with those voting against or abstaining including those who were opposed to European integration, those who felt that the Treaty went too far on specific points, those from SOS Europe and other members who felt that the Amsterdam Treaty was too weak, and that the Parliament was settling for too little.[5]

The European Parliament's specific views on reform

While the general dividing lines on reform issues are fairly easy to indicate, this is less the case as regards the EP's views on specific policy areas, since different committees have had different priorities. Nevertheless, certain horizontal concerns and common themes can be identified.

First, the EP has inevitably put a strong emphasis on increasing the democratic quality of the European Union. This has mainly taken the form of calling for an increase in its own uneven powers, but there has also been increasing awareness of the need for cooperation with national parliaments.

Perhaps the EP's most insistent demand has been for the introduction of full legislative co-decision between the Parliament and the Council and the consequent reduction or elimination of other legislative variants, such as the cooperation and consultation procedures.

The EP was initially somewhat critical of the form of co-decision (technically the Article 189b procedure) that was introduced at Maastricht, but quickly recognized its significance. During the Amsterdam IGC the EP put a major emphasis on the need for co-decision to be extended to all legislation, and for the procedure to be simplified.

Until the Amsterdam IGC the EP had also asked to be given the right of legislative initiative, but it has now changed its mind on this issue, on the main grounds that Article 138b of the Maastricht Treaty gave it the right to request the Commission to submit a legislative proposal, and that any more far-reaching new request would lead to parallel requests from the Council, resulting in too great a weakening of the position of the Commission.

A final legislation-related issue which is worth citing is that of 'comitology', in other words the procedures by which implementing measures (the EU equivalent of statutory instruments) are adopted. While the EP recognizes that these are decisions of an executive nature (and on several occasions has called for a classification of acts or 'hierarchy of norms' in order to establish a more rational EU framework for these decisions), it also believes that they are often very important (e.g. decisions on BSE or on genetically modified maize) and has called for the whole comitology system to be simplified, for the EP to be given full information and to be given the opportunity to comment in significant cases, above all when it has been involved through co-decision in the original legislative act. Seemingly obscure, this issue of 'comitology' has thus proved to be a key institutional battlefield in recent years. (The implications of the recent Council agreement on this matter are not yet clear but still fall short of the full demands of the Parliament.)

The EP has also long emphasized the need for full budgetary co-decision as well, ending the artificial distinction between compulsory and non-compulsory expenditure, which has led to a lesser position for the Parliament in such key areas as agricultural expenditure.

The EP's persistent demand to be given the right of 'assent' to Treaty change (in other words for it to have a binding say on approval or rejection but not for it to be able to amend) has already been cited. The Parliament has also asked for its right of assent to be extended to certain other decisions, such as ones on own resources, as well as all international agreements entered into by the EU (at present the EP only has the right to give its assent to certain limited categories of international agreements and is not formally consulted at all on Article 113 commercial agreements).

A special case is that of the EP's involvement in nomination to top EU posts, where the Parliament has asked not just for a reinforced role as regards the nomination of the Commission and of its President, but also for assent on nominations to the European Court of Auditors and to the European Court of Justice (and in the Martin/Bourlanges resolution of May 1995 also to nominations to the European Court of First Instance and to the Executive Board of the European System of Central Banks).

Among the other issues raised by the Parliament in the context of its own powers and position have been the need for it to be given a say over its own seat, and to finally achieve a uniform electoral system as well as a uniform statute for its members. The EP has also called for the powers of its temporary committees of inquiry to be reinforced.

In addition to its concerns on its own powers, the EP has recognized the need for a reinforced role on EU matters for national parliaments and also for enhanced cooperation between them and the EP in order to overcome 'the democratic deficit'. The latter is a term that the EP has helped to popularize, and is clearly particularly acute in areas where neither the EP nor national parliaments have adequate powers of control. The European Parliament has argued that the national parliaments and the EP have distinctive but complementary roles in this key task of democratic control of EU matters, the national parliaments in controlling their own government and the EP in controlling other EU institutions. A corollary of this position is that the EP has consistently opposed (as have a majority of national parliaments) ideas that the national parliaments be given a formal collective role on EU legislative and other matters, such as through a Senate of National Parliaments, a High Council on Subsidiarity, return to a nominated EP, or other such ideas. It has considered that these ideas would prove difficult to implement, could slow down EU decision-making and certainly further complicate the EU institutional structure, as well as undermining the role of the Parliament itself.

As regards means of cooperation between the EP and national parliaments, the EP initially gave a strong emphasis to the idea of common parliamentary 'assizes'. The EP was pleased with the outcome of the only assizes which were held, in Rome in November 1990, but has had to recognize subsequently that many national parliaments were less satisfied with the experience and the emphasis has since shifted to the need for other forms of cooperation, such as committee-to-committee contact.

Besides this issue of democratic control, the EP has also had a number of other continuing priorities on horizontal institutional and decision-making questions. Perhaps the most important of these has been the need to extend qualified majority voting to all legislative decisions, as well as to certain other decisions as well. The Parliament has considered this to be essential to increase efficiency within the EU, especially in the perspective of further EU enlargement, since a continuing requirement for unanimity in an EU which might have up to 27 or more Member

States is clearly even less likely to work than unanimity amongst the original six Member States. The EP has refined its position, however, to recognize that unanimity should continue to apply for certain very sensitive decisions of a constitutional nature, such as Treaty change, enlargement, own resources, electoral reform and application of Article 235 (now renumbered as Article 308) EC.

The EP has also strongly emphasized the need for a more open and transparent European Union, in particular one where the principle of open access to documents becomes an established rule, and where the meetings of the Council are to be open to the public when it takes decisions in its legislative capacity.

The Parliament has also considered that the need for 'transparency' implies a simplified and more comprehensible Treaty. The EP was unhappy with the hybrid pillar structure introduced at Maastricht and has called for the merger of the three Community Treaties and the other provisions of the Treaty on European Union into a single unified Treaty and for a simplification and restructuring of the content of the Treaty. It has also called for the European Union to be given legal personality.

The EP has generally been more cautious in its comments on other EU institutions, notably as regards working methods and voting weights in the Council. In the Martin/Bourlanges resolution of 17 May 1995, the Parliament did call for the maintenance of six-month presidencies (rather than seeking longer presidencies or explicitly calling for 'team' presidencies), but did not subsequently return to the issue. As regards re-weighting of votes in the Council, the EP has acknowledged (in the same resolution of 17 May 1995) 'that the system of voting within the Council may need to be adjusted' (paragraph 22(iii)), but has given no explicit guidance as to how this might be achieved, considering that this was ultimately a matter for the Council itself. However, it has supported limited re-weighting in favour of the larger Member States and it has come out against introduction of a new system of double majorities since 'Council represents states' and 'it is in the Parliament that population is represented' (paragraph 22(iii)).

On another particularly sensitive institutional question, namely the composition of the Commission, the Parliament has supported the maintenance of at least one Commissioner per Member State (thus accepting the loss of the larger Member States' second Commissioner), but a minority of EP members have supported, in the name of efficiency, a more radical reduction in the size of the Commission so that there would be fewer Commissioners than Member States.

In its resolution on the Amsterdam Treaty of 19 November 1997, the Parliament considered that further institutional reform was a prerequisite of any enlargement and that adjustments should 'be made to the weighting of votes in the Council and to the number of Commission members, with the Member States retaining equal status with each other' (paragraph 16).

A further institutional issue has been that of whether 'flexibility' or 'reinforced cooperation' should be introduced on a broader and more explicit basis than at present. The European Parliament has been cautious on this issue, recognizing that some degree of 'flexibility' is inevitable but calling for its introduction to be subject to strict conditions, for instance that it should not undermine the single institutional framework or the *acquis communautaire*, and should not lead to Europe '*à la carte*'.

Besides these, the EP, both in its general institutional resolutions and in other resolutions, has made a large number of IGC-related proposals in specific policy fields. Among the most important of these have been the following:

- the need for the current weak concept of European citizenship to be developed in a more meaningful way
- incorporation within the Treaty of a list of human rights and fundamental freedoms (the European Parliament itself adopted a suggested such list on 17 April 1989) or else accession of the European Union to the European Convention on Human Rights
- attainment of proper freedom of movement within the EU accompanied by enhanced internal security, to be achieved, *inter alia*, by communitarization of as much as possible of the justice and home affairs pillar agreed at Maastricht and improvements to the residual third pillar (better decision-making structures and procedures, greater role for Community institutions, etc.)
- greater democratic accountability of Economic and Monetary Union, as well as the introduction of social and other counterpart measures to EMU (including the inclusion of a chapter on employment in the Treaty)
- enhanced commitment to high European standards for the environment, and for consumer protection and public health
- a more effective Common Foreign and Security Policy, including incorporation of the WEU within the EU (this last was strongly contested by a significant minority within the EP).

The evolution of the European Parliament's own powers from Maastricht to Amsterdam

The new powers given to the European Parliament at Maastricht

The most striking features of the evolution of the EP's powers have been first, the extent to which they have developed since direct elections were introduced (although some major advances, for instance in the budgetary field, had already taken place before 1979), and second, the *ad hoc* and uneven nature of these developments which have left the Parliament with highly variable powers, very considerable in some areas and very weak in others. Both of these features have been confirmed in the period between Maastricht and Amsterdam.

The most important of the new powers for the Parliament that were brought in by the Maastricht Treaty was the introduction of the co-decision procedure in certain legislative fields, notably Article 100A concerning the internal market. The key new element of co-decision was that, for the first time, it enabled the EP to reject definitively a legislative text without either the Commission or the Council being able to do anything about it. The real significance of this was less that it would be likely to lead to a large number of rejections (this has, in fact, only happened on two occasions since the Maastricht Treaty came into force), but that it gave the EP greater bargaining power than ever before. The second key feature of the new procedure was that it introduced a new framework for negotiations between the institutions by creating a 'conciliation' committee for use in case of continuing disagreement between the EP and Council after the EP's second reading on draft legislation. The implementation of the new procedure was subsequently facilitated by an inter–institutional agreement on the workings of the conciliation committee.

In the period since it has been implemented, the co-decision procedure has had a number of longer-term impacts, leading, for example, to the creation of new structures (a special conciliation service, etc.) and greater professionalism within the EP, and to a change in the balance between the Parliament, Commission and Council, with closer and more direct links between the Parliament and the Council and with the Commission in a still important but less central position than in the past. The co-decision procedure has thus been a major step forward for the EP.[6]

Besides introducing co-decision the Maastricht Treaty led to other increases in the EP's legislative power, first by extending the cooperation procedure that had been introduced by the Single European Act to 15 new policy areas (and maintaining it in three other areas: most of the other pre-existing areas were 'promoted' at Maastricht into co-decision), by extending the assent procedure to six new areas and finally by extending the consultation procedure to 24 new cases. Maastricht also provided a partial response to the EP's long-standing request (since modified, see above) that it be given a power of legislative initiative by providing (in its Article 138b) that 'the European Parliament may, acting by a majority of its Members, request the Commission to submit any appropriate proposal on matters on which it considers that a Community act is required for the purpose of implementing this Treaty'.

Another important innovation of Maastricht was to give the Parliament a new role as regards certain EU appointments. Before Maastricht the only appointments on which the EP had been formally consulted were those to the European Court of Auditors. As a result of Maastricht the EP was also to be consulted on the nominations to the Presidency of the European Monetary Institute, and later to the Presidency and Vice-Presidency of the European Central Bank. The Parliament was also to be consulted on the nominee for Presidency of the Commission and once the other members of the Commission had been nominated the Commission was to be 'subject as a body to a vote of approval by the European Parliament' (Article 158(2) EC). Finally, the EP was actually given the full right of appointment in one case, that to the newly elected post of Ombudsman (Article 138 EC).

These new powers have subsequently been used by the EP. The first interesting precedent was as regards the nomination of Mr Alexandre Lamfalussy to be the first President of the European Monetary Institute, when the nominee not only agreed to take part in a confirmation hearing at the Parliament's relevant committee (the Committee on Economic and Monetary Affairs and Industrial Policy), but also to respond .in writing before the hearing to a questionnaire sent to him by the Committee.

The better-publicized follow-up to this was when the EP then held confirmation hearings on the individual nominations to the new Commission. Jacques Delors, outgoing Commission President, had been unenthusiastic, to put it mildly, about such hearings, but Jacques Santer, who had only just scraped through his own vote of approval by the EP[7] (a tense vote that had already highlighted the Parliament's new position), not only agreed that they could take place, but also undertook to distribute the proposed portfolios in sufficient time before such hearings. The EP could not refuse individual nominations but its final vote of approval on the Commission as a whole was made subject to an overall assessment of how the prospective Commissioners had performed at their respective hearings.

These new procedures have certainly reinforced the position of the EP, but also strengthened its links with the Commission, strengthened by the fact that another reform of the Maastricht Treaty was to introduce a five-year term of office for the Commission as well as for the Parliament.

The EP's other scrutiny and control powers were also strengthened at Maastricht. The most important reform was the formal recognition in Article 138c EC of the Parliament's right to set up temporary committees of inquiry to investigate alleged contraventions or maladministration in the implementation of Community law.[8] After lengthy negotiations, conditions of implementation were then laid down in a new inter–institutional agreement. These new powers have now been used on two occasions, firstly to look into the problems of the Community transit system, and secondly to look at the Commission's handling of the BSE crisis. In the latter case there was also a follow-up committee to look into the implementation of the Parliament's initial recommendations. The BSE inquiry had a particularly high profile, but in both cases the Commission, and indeed the Member States in general, were made aware of the Parliament's new powers. Finally, the Maastricht Treaty also confirmed the EP's standing as a plaintiff and defendant in cases before the European Court of Justice.

All these were useful steps forward for the European Parliament. Nevertheless, the EP's powers remained very uneven. The co-decision procedure as agreed at Maastricht was itself not a fully balanced one. Much more significantly, however, it continued to co-exist for Community legislation with the consultation and cooperation procedures, and in some cases even with the assent procedure. There were cases of overlap in particular policy areas, with the guidelines for trans-European networks, for example, coming under co-decision, and other decisions under cooperation. Environmental policy came under the co-decision, cooperation and consultation procedures. The multi-annual framework programme for research and technology came under co-decision, whereas the specific programmes were to entail mere consultation rather than cooperation as before Maastricht. At the very least these varying forms of involvement of the EP have been a recipe for conflict over the appropriate legal base.

In other areas that were introduced by Maastricht the situation was much less satisfactory for the European Parliament, notably as regards its extremely weak role in the new intergovernmental pillars of Common Foreign and Security Policy and on justice and home affairs, and also as regards Economic and Monetary Union.

The situation after Amsterdam

The EP has been portrayed as one of the 'winners' as a result of the Amsterdam Treaty, and it is undoubtedly true that some of its powers have been extended and that its role has been usefully reinforced. On the other hand, it is important to put this into perspective: the Parliament's powers are still uneven after Amsterdam, and many of the weaknesses outlined above are still present.

This is well illustrated by what has happened as regards legislative procedures. As far as the EP is concerned, a number of positive steps have occurred. Legislative procedures have been simplified by the virtual abolition of the cooperation procedure. It will only survive as regards four mainly minor cases in the field of Economic and Monetary Union, where the IGC negotiators were reluctant even to change a comma of what had been agreed at Maastricht. In addition, the co-decision procedure has been successfully streamlined and made more balanced. There is now the possibility for agreement to be reached after the EP's first reading, and for the Parliament to proceed directly to reject a proposal rather than having to go through the cumbersome intention-to-reject stage. Moreover, the possibility for the Council to impose a common position in the absence of agreement with the EP in conciliation unless the Parliament could find the necessary absolute majority to override the Council text has now been deleted. A proposal will thus now fall if there is no agreement in conciliation. Some new time limits have also been introduced. The scope of the co-decision procedure will also be extended to 14 existing Treaty provisions, as well as to eight new ones, and by unanimous Council agreement could be further extended in five years' time to many measures taken pursuant to the new Treaty title on the free movement of persons, asylum and immigration.[9]

Besides these changes to, and extension of, co-decision, there will also be a considerable extension of the consultation procedure, including to such important measures as framework decisions, decisions and conventions taken pursuant to article K11 (new Article 39) TEU of the residual third pillar, and proposed flexibility arrangements in the Community domain.

While the above are all significant improvements they nevertheless fall well short of the European Parliament's proposal that co-decision become the normal legislative procedure. The consultation procedure will continue in a number of very significant policy areas, such as agriculture, fiscal harmonization (in spite of this being so important for the internal market) and, for five years at least, most measures taken pursuant to the communitarized third pillar. In an issue closely related to legislation, that of the EP's role in implementing or 'comitology' measures, the IGC made no progress whatsoever, and indeed hardly discussed the point at all.[10]

Nor was there any serious discussion on the Parliament's demands in the budgetary arena. Thus, the existing and arbitrary distinction between 'compulsory' and 'non-compulsory' expenditure has been maintained. A slight strengthening of EP powers can be observed in third and second pillar operational expenditure being charged to the Community budget unless the Council unanimously decides otherwise. However, as mentioned above, the *quid pro quo* for this in the second pillar was an inter–institutional agreement somewhat reducing the Parliament's freedom of manoeuvre.

New information will also be provided to the EP in the field of external trade policy,[11] but the Parliament is still not mentioned in the main Treaty base dealing with the common commercial policy,[12] and its role in the field of external economic relations remains generally rather weak.

As regards the EP's role in nominations, one potentially important change has been made, in that the Parliament must now formally give its approval rather than just being consulted on the nominee for President of the Commission.[13] On the other hand, the EP's role as regards other EU appointments will not be extended.

Besides the existing areas in which it has to give its assent (accession treaties, the structural and cohesion funds, the uniform electoral procedure and the conclusion of certain international agreements), the Parliament has been given a new power of assent as regards sanctions in the event of a serious and persistent breach of fundamental rights by a Member State.[14] The EP's requests, however, to be granted the right of assent on such issues as own resources, use of Article 235,[15] all international agreements and (as we have seen above) treaty change, were not granted at Amsterdam.

A few other changes were also made at Amsterdam that will affect the EP. There is to be a ceiling of 700 to its membership,[16] necessitating some difficult decisions on down-sizing existing national delegations before any significant new enlargement of the Union. Poland alone would have a right to 64 MEPs under present rules and the accession of the six countries suggested by the Commission for initial negotiations, Poland, the Czech Republic, Hungary, Estonia, Slovenia and Cyprus, would result in around 770 MEPs! Adoption of a 'uniform' procedure for European Parliament elections will be facilitated by a new procedure that such a system need not be identical in all Member States but merely be 'in accordance with principles common to all Member States'.[17] The EP will also be authorized to make proposals as regards the statute of its own members[18] and also itself to consult the Economic and Social Committee and the Committee of the Regions.[19] Much more controversial is the new Protocol which incorporates the Edinburgh agreement on the seat of the Parliament, obliging it to hold 12 plenary sessions in Strasbourg and to keep much of its secretariat in Luxembourg, thus limiting its ability to fix its own working conditions.

Finally, a particular problem may well be posed for the EP if the new Treaty provisions for flexibility are to be used, whereby some but not all the Member States may decide to establish closer cooperation amongst themselves in a particular area and then may make use of the institutions, procedures and mechanisms laid down by this Treaty. The implications of this for the EP are less clear. What will be the role of MEPs from non-participating countries, especially given the fact that the EP's voting majorities are laid down in the Treaty and naturally assume that the Parliament is indivisible?

The Amsterdam Treaty has thus had a number of positive and negative features for the EP. In addition, several of the reforms that it has been seeking have been put into abeyance, and will undoubtedly be reviewed in future IGCs.

In the meantime, however, the EP will be seeking to make the best use of the reforms that were achieved at Amsterdam. As mentioned above, it has already called for the Treaty to be ratified and will be closely following the ratification process and seeking the best possible rules of implementation. For example, it will be involved through co-decision in the development of the implementing rules on openness and there will probably be new inter–institutional agreements as there were after Maastricht: one such agreement is actually called for in the Treaty as regards the quality of legislation, and the EP has already reached agreement with the Council and Commission on a new joint declaration on the practical arrangements for the new co-decision procedure that replaces the existing agreement and seeks, in particular, to encourage more intensive contacts and cooperation between the EP and the Council. The EP has also extensively revised its own internal Rules of Procedure to make the most of its new post-Amsterdam powers.

The EP is also likely to push for a number of institutional and procedural changes not requiring formal Treaty change, such as ones promoting greater efficiency and openness, and enhanced democratic control in such fields as Economic and Monetary Union. Finally, the EP will, of course, also continue to test already existing procedures, such as those concerning temporary committees of inquiry, which were not changed at Amsterdam and whose strengths and weaknesses will become more apparent after further practical experience.

Both the EP's involvement in the reform process and its powers have thus evolved considerably in the period from Maastricht to Amsterdam but still fall short of what the EP has been requesting. While Eurosceptic views are also forcefully represented within the EP, the majority of members are likely to push for a stronger EP role and powers in the future, but in this process the 'realists', and those who do not wish to undercut their own national governments, still appear to have the driving hand over the 'idealists' and the more far-reaching federalists.

Endnotes

1. It was annexed to a resolution.
2. They were often felt by a number of the personal representatives to be helpful in opening up a more general debate.
3. Conférence des Organes Specialisés dans les Affaires Communautaires, bringing together members of the European Affairs Committees of the national parliaments and members from the European Parliament.
4. Its founders were three French MEPs (Jean-Louis Bourlanges, Dany Cohn-Bendit (of 1968 fame) and Olivier Duhamel), one Italian (Gianfranco Dell'Alba) and one Belgian (Antoinette Spaak, daughter of Paul-Henri Spaak).
5. From a British perspective, one can note that the vast majority of Labour MEPs voted in favour (50 in favour and 3 against with 1 abstention) and that the 2 Liberal Democrats, 2 SNP and 1 SDLP

member also voted in favour. With their party at home committed to opposition to the Treaty, and with the incorporation of the Social Chapter a negative factor even for many pro-European Conservatives, 11 of the Conservative MEPs voted against and 4 others abstained.

6. The reluctance of certain Member States to call a spade a spade has meant that the procedure is nowhere referred to as 'co-decision'. The British government even tried, unsuccessfully, to label it as the 'negative assent procedure'. In fact, it was known as the 'Article 189b procedure'; and now after Amsterdam its correct name will become the 'Article 251 procedure'.

7. On a vote of 260 in favour to 238 against with 23 abstentions.

8. The possibility of setting up such committees had previously existed in the European Parliament's Rules of Procedure, and had been used on nine occasions, but the EP's position was much weaker.

9. In two cases under this title such extension of co-decision would be automatic.

10. Although, as mentioned above, the situation has now been modified as a result of a recent Council agreement on Comitology.

11. Pursuant to amended Article 228 EC, to become new Article 300.

12. Currently Article 113 EC, to become new Article 137.

13. Revised Article 158 EC, to be new Article 214.

14. New Article F1, to be renumbered Article 7 TEU.

15. To be new Article 308 EC.

16. Amended Article 137, to be renumbered Article 189 EC.

17. Amended Article 138.2, to be renumbered Article 190 EC. The EP has since submitted a new proposal which is currently under consideration within the Council.

18. That is, the regulations and general conditions governing the performance of the duties of its members, Article 138(4), new Article 190 EC. The EP has also submitted a proposal to this effect on the basis of a report by Mr Rothley of the Legal Affairs Committee, but final agreement between the EP and the Council did not prove to be possible before the 1999 European elections.

19. Modified Articles 198 (new Article 262) and 198(c) (new Article 265).

Chapter 4

The European Court of Justice

Takis Tridimas

Introduction

The Treaty of Amsterdam, although less ambitious than the Treaty on European Union (TEU), introduces a number of important changes to the Community and the Union. Among others, it extends further the competence of the Community, it formalizes 'differentiated integration' by establishing procedures for closer co-operation,[1] and it blurs the distinction between the Community pillar and intergovernmental action.[2] The Treaty accepts that the Community and the Union have a role to play in areas traditionally reserved to the nation state and continues the trend towards social and political, as opposed to merely economic, integration heralded by the TEU.[3]

The most important changes made by the Treaty of Amsterdam concerning the Court of Justice are the introduction of new preliminary reference procedures under new Title IV of the EC Treaty and under the third pillar. The new provisions, although limited in their scope, mark a qualitative change of approach in that the Court acquires differentiated jurisdiction in two respects. First, the preliminary reference procedure ceases to be uniform throughout the EC Treaty. Secondly, although for the first time the Court acquires power in relation to the third pillar, submission to the Court's jurisdiction is optional for the Member States.

Article 46 TEU

Under Article 46 [ex Article L] TEU, as amended, the Court of Justice acquires jurisdiction in relation to three new areas:

- the provisions of the third pillar, under the conditions laid down in Article 35 TEU
- the provisions concerning closer cooperation (Title VII) but only as far as they concern the third pillar and the EC Treaty
- Article 6(2) TEU with regard to action of the institutions, in so far as the Court has jurisdiction under the EC Treaty and under the TEU.

The jurisdiction of the Court remains excluded from the second pillar concerning Common Foreign and Security Policy (CFSP). According to Article 46(c), the Court has jurisdiction in relation to the provisions on closer cooperation, but only 'under the conditions provided by' Article 11 EC and Article 40 TEU. In effect, the Court's jurisdiction is excluded only in relation to closer cooperation in the field of the CFSP where, in any event, the Court has no jurisdiction and in relation to which the Treaty of Amsterdam makes no specific provision for closer cooperation and uses instead the model of constructive abstention.[4] The Court has jurisdiction to review whether any closer cooperation entered into by the Member States respects the principles of the EC Treaty.[5] It does not, however, possess any such jurisdiction *ex ante* (i.e. to determine whether closer cooperation envisaged by the Member State may conflict with the *acquis communautaire*).[6]

It will be noted that acts of the institutions adopted under provisions of the TEU in relation to which the Court does not have jurisdiction do not escape judicial control altogether.[7] In *Commission* v. *Council* (transit visas case)[8] the Court held that it has jurisdiction to determine whether such acts encroach upon the powers conferred on the Community by the EC Treaty. Thus, an act adopted under a non-justiciable provision of the TEU may be annulled if its correct legal basis lies in the EC Treaty. The Court based its power to annul such an act on Article M (now Article 47) TEU which states that, save as otherwise provided, the provisions of the TEU are without prejudice to the provisions of the Community Treaties.

An interesting feature of the Treaty of Amsterdam is the position which it gives to the Court with regard to the protection of fundamental rights. Article 46 TEU states that the Court has jurisdiction in relation to Article 6(2) [ex Article F(2)] TEU with regard to action of the institutions, 'in so far as the Court has jurisdiction under the Treaties establishing the European Communities and under this Treaty'. This provision merely formalizes what has been the position under the existing law and does not extend the powers of the Court.

Article 7 TEU, as amended, provides for the first time for an enforcement mechanism in the event that a Member State is found guilty of a serious and persistent breach of the principles laid down in Article 6(1), namely liberty, democracy, respect for human rights and fundamental freedoms, and the rule of law. In such a case, the Council may suspend certain of the State's rights deriving from the application of the TEU, including its voting rights in the Council. It was envisaged by the Intergovernmental Conference (IGC) that such a draconian penalty would be used only in the most exceptional of cases. It appears striking, however, that the process of enforcement is purely a political one involving solely the political institutions of the Union to the exclusion of the Court. Article 46 suggests that Article 7 is not included among the articles in relation to which the Court has jurisdiction. If that were the case, it would mean that the concept of 'serious and persistent' breach is not amenable to judicial control, and that severe penalties could be imposed against a Member State without the latter having the means of challenging the Council's decision before the Court of Justice. The Court, however, does have jurisdiction in so far as the enforcement mechanism provided for in Article 7(2) TEU affects the rights of a Member State under the EC Treaty.

This is because Article 309 EC is justiciable. That provision states that, where a decision has been taken under Article 7(2) to suspend the voting rights of a Member State in Council, those rights must also be suspended with regard to the EC Treaty.[9] The Council may also decide, acting by a qualified majority, to suspend certain of the rights deriving from the application of the EC Treaty to the Member State.[10] Much as it seems unlikely that this provision would ever be used in practice, it would be unacceptable for the rights of a Member State to be suspended under the EC Treaty without that State having the right to judicial protection.

Article 7 was included in the Treaty of Amsterdam in response to calls by certain Member States who argued that the Union or the Community should accede to the European Convention of Human Rights (ECHR). It is, however, no substitute for such accession. Following the ruling of the Court in Opinion 2/94,[11] the accession of the Community to the ECHR may not be effected without amending the EC Treaty. The opportunity was present but not taken in the 1996 IGC. As has been pointed out, if the Union is so committed to the protection of fundamental rights, why is it reluctant to submit to external control?[12]

Title IV of the European Community Treaty

The Treaty of Amsterdam revises substantially the third pillar concerning cooperation on justice and home affairs. A significant part of it is now incorporated in Title IV of Part Three of the EC Treaty (Articles 61–69). Those provisions concern visas, asylum, immigration and other policies related to the free movement of persons. The remaining third pillar provisions (Articles 29–42 TEU) concern police and judicial cooperation on criminal matters. The jurisdiction of the Court of Justice is substantially affected. The Court has jurisdiction to give preliminary rulings in relation to matters falling within Articles 61 to 69 EC but its jurisdiction is more limited than under Article 234 [ex Article 177] EC. In particular, Article 68(1) provides that a preliminary reference may be made only by national courts against whose decisions there is no judicial remedy under national law.[13] Such a court is under an obligation to make a reference if it considers that a decision by the Court of Justice is necessary to enable it to give judgment.

The effect of Article 68(1) is that the preliminary reference procedure ceases to be uniform under the EC Treaty. In relation to Title IV, the jurisdiction of the Court may be activated only by national courts of last instance. This may not be easy to operate in practice as in some cases the same dispute, and indeed the same question referred, may give rise to issues pertaining both to the interpretation of Articles 61 to 69 and other articles of the EC Treaty. The restriction of the preliminary reference procedure to courts of last instance encounters both practical objections and those of principle. One of the main reasons why Community law has had such a major impact on the laws of the Member States is its ability to assist the citizen at the lowest level in the administration of justice.[14] Article 68(1) plainly limits access to justice. The Court of Justice itself has stated that limiting access,

would have the effect of jeopardising the uniform application and interpretation of

Community law throughout the Union, and could deprive individuals of effective judicial protection and undermine the unity of the case-law ... The possibility of referring a question to the Court of Justice must therefore remain open to all ... courts and tribunals.[15]

Also, there is much to be said about the enforcement value of the power of lower courts to make a preliminary reference. Such power mitigates the adverse effects that would ensue if a court of last instance failed to make a reference in circumstances where it was under an obligation to do so. In a subsequent case where the same legal issue arose, a lower court would be able to make a reference, thus provoking a ruling by the Court of Justice on that issue.

The jurisdiction of the Court under Title IV is limited not only in relation to the courts which may make a reference but also in relation to the issues which may be subject to judicial determination. Article 68(2) provides that the Court does not have jurisdiction to rule on any measure or decision taken pursuant to Article 62(1) relating to the maintenance of law and order and the safeguarding of internal security.[16] Article 68(2) is striking in that it denies the right to judicial protection, the most valued right guaranteed by the Court's case law.[17] At the very least, it must be interpreted restrictively. It should be noted that the interpretation of Article 68 itself is subject to the jurisdiction of the Court. Therefore, the meaning of 'maintenance of law and order' and 'internal security' in Article 68(2), and whether a measure can be said to relate to them, are justiciable issues. Nonetheless, the total exclusion of the Court's jurisdiction is undesirable. It poses serious problems of constitutionality, sets a bad precedent, and contradicts the principles of protection of fundamental rights, the rule of law, and democracy, commitment to which is affirmed in the Treaty of Amsterdam.

Article 68(3) provides that the Council, the Commission or a Member State may request the Court of Justice to give a ruling on a question of interpretation of Title IV or of acts of the institutions of the Community based on that Title. It adds that the ruling given by the Court of Justice in response to such a request does not apply to judgments of courts or tribunals of the Member States which have become *res judicata*. It is arguable that pursuant to that provision, the Court may decide on issues in relation to which its jurisdiction is excluded under Article 68(2), i.e. issues pertaining to law and order and internal security. Such interpretation is supported by the generality of Article 68(3), the economy of Article 68 as a whole, and the rationale for excluding the jurisdiction of the Court under Article 68(2). That rationale is that the Court of Justice should not have jurisdiction on reference from a national court to rule on issues which are perceived as highly sensitive and should be dealt with by interstate and institutional dialogue. But it does not prohibit a Member State or a Community institution from referring such issues to the Court of Justice.

Finally, it will be noted that Article 68 refers only to references for a preliminary ruling. It is not clear whether the provision affects at all, and if so how, direct actions pertaining to Title IV brought under Article 230 (formerly 173) of the EC Treaty.

Other amendments to the European Community Treaty

Following renumbering, the provisions pertaining to the Court of Justice are now contained in Articles 220–245 [ex Article 164–188] EC. The Court of Auditors is granted *locus standi* in actions for judicial review on the same footing as the European Parliament (EP) and the European Central Bank (ECB), namely, for the purposes of protecting its prerogatives.[18] This amendment reflects the growing importance that the Member States attribute to the supervision of Community finances. What is perhaps more interesting is that the position of the EP remains unchanged. It continues to enjoy limited standing and does not acquire the status of a privileged applicant. In some ways, the EP has been the victim of its own success. Since the seminal judgment in *Chernobyl*,[19] it has pursued jealously a tactical litigation policy challenging virtually every Council measure which it considers infringes its prerogatives, even if it agrees with the substance of the measure. In some cases, that policy has borne fruit.[20] It may have been feared that further extension of the EP's standing would lead to more actions and have the effect of moving to the judicial arena disputes that are better left to political negotiation. It remains to be seen whether the extension of the EP's powers in the legislative process through the elevation of co-decision to the main procedure for the adoption of Community acts will alleviate the need to rely on litigation as a means of influencing the political process.

It will also be remembered that, under Article 300(6) [ex Article 228(6)] EC, the EP does not have standing to request the Court to submit an opinion as to the compatibility with the Treaty of an international agreement that the Community envisages concluding. The EP, however, may submit observations once the procedure before the Court has been initiated.[21] This reflects the limited role given to the EP in relation to the external policies of the Community both in the sphere of trade and in the sphere of political relations.

The Treaty of Amsterdam does not liberalize the limited standing of non-privileged applicants in actions for judicial review under Article 230(4) EC. The requirements of direct and individual concern face three main objections: they impede access to justice;[22] they have led to an unruly body of case law which does not promote legal certainty; and they generate a significant amount of workload for the Court of First Instance, as litigants tend to submit extensive, and often ingenious, arguments in an attempt to establish standing. Whether those short-comings exceed the advantages which may flow from limiting standing for individuals is an open issue. It is notable that the Court of Justice itself has questioned whether the requirements of direct and individual concern are sufficient to guarantee for individuals effective judicial protection against possible infringements of their fundamental rights arising from legislative measures adopted by the Community.[23]

The third pillar

The third pillar (Articles 29–42 TEU), as amended by the Treaty of Amsterdam, provides for action in two diverse areas, namely police and judicial cooperation in criminal matters, and common action against racism and xenophobia.[24] In fact, the provisions of the pillar deal specifically only with the first of those areas. They single out certain particularly pernicious crimes against which common action should principally be directed[25] and provide for three means via which common action is to be pursued. These are the following:

- closer cooperation between police forces, customs authorities, and other competent national authorities
- closer cooperation between national judicial authorities
- the approximation of national criminal laws.

The provisions are innovative in that they provide for extensive cooperation in the criminal sphere, an area which traditionally falls within the exclusive province of the Member States. The pillar operates under an institutional structure the main feature of which is the enhanced role of the Council. The Court of Justice is granted jurisdiction to hear both direct actions and preliminary references. Under Article 35(1) TEU, the Court has jurisdiction to give preliminary rulings in relation to the following:

- the validity and interpretation of framework decisions and decisions
- the interpretation of conventions established under the third pillar
- the validity and interpretation of measures implementing such conventions.[26]

At first sight, it appears that the Court has no jurisdiction to rule on the interpretation of the provisions of the third pillar themselves. That would be incongruous and unworkable in practice, since the interpretation of acts of the institutions, such as decisions and framework decisions, may involve the interpretation of the provisions of the TEU themselves. Also, jurisdiction to rule on the validity of decisions and framework decisions necessarily implies jurisdiction to opine on the interpretation of the rules of primary law in the light of which the validity of such decisions is tested. It should therefore be accepted that Article 35(1) gives the Court of Justice implied jurisdiction to interpret the provisions of the third pillar. By contrast, it will be noted that the Court has no jurisdiction to rule on the validity of conventions since they are measures of primary Community law.

A distinct feature of Article 35 TEU is that the jurisdiction of the Court is optional. Article 35(2) enables a Member State to accept such jurisdiction by making a declaration to that effect any time after the Treaty of Amsterdam comes into force.[27] The provision seems to envisage that a Member State will make a universal declaration covering all conventions which may subsequently be adopted under the third pillar. That, however, does not foreclose the possibility that, upon signing a specific convention in the future, the Member States may agree that its provisions will not be subject to the Court's jurisdiction. An interesting problem which may arise as a result of Article 35(2) is whether the court of a Member State which has accepted the jurisdiction of the Court to deliver preliminary rulings may make a reference in relation to the law of another Member State which has not accepted that jurisdiction. It is submitted that in principle such a reference, which is admissible under the procedure of Article 234 [ex Article 177] EC, should not be precluded.

The jurisdiction of the Court is optional also in another respect. Under Article 35(3), a Member State has the option to extend the preliminary reference procedure to any domestic court or tribunal or restrict it to courts or tribunals of last instance, i.e. those against whose decisions there is no judicial remedy under national law. Under either option, a final instance court has the option and not the obligation to make a reference to the Court of Justice. This is an important difference between the preliminary reference procedure under the third pillar and its counterpart under Article 234 [ex Article 177] EC. Furthermore, Article 35(5) provides for a limitation on the Court's jurisdiction. It states that the Court has no power to review the validity or proportionality of operations carried out by the police or other law enforcement services of a Member State or the exercise of the responsibilities incumbent upon Member States with regard to the maintenance of law and order and the safeguarding of internal security. The interpretation of Article 35(5) itself is, however, subject to the jurisdiction of the Court.

Direct actions are governed by Articles 35(6) and 35(7) TEU. The first endows the Court with jurisdiction to review the legality of framework decisions and decisions in actions brought by a Member State or the Commission on grounds of lack of competence, infringement of an essential procedural requirement, infringement of the TEU or of any rule of law relating to its application, or misuse of powers. The proceedings must be instituted within two months of the publication of the measure. It is notable that neither the Parliament nor individuals enjoy *locus standi*. Also, no provision is made for the bringing of enforcement actions by the Commission. The exclusion of the EP from the list of potential plaintiffs may give rise to problems. The issue arises whether, on the basis of the *Chernobyl* judgment,[28] the EP may claim *locus standi* for the purpose of protecting its prerogatives, for example, in cases where the Council has failed to consult it although it is under an obligation to do so.[29]

Under Article 35(7), the Court has jurisdiction to rule on any dispute between Member States regarding the interpretation or the application of acts adopted under Article 34(2)[30] whenever such a dispute cannot be settled by the Council within six months of its being referred to the Council by one of its members. The Court is also given jurisdiction to rule on any dispute between Member States and the Commission regarding the interpretation or the application of conventions between Member States concluded under the third pillar. It seems that under those provisions the Court may be called upon to rule on the interpretation or the application of those measures *in abstracto* without reference to the facts of any specific dispute.

By way of conclusion, it may be said that the provisions of the third pillar leave a gap with regard to the protection of the rights of the individual. They extend the powers of the institutions to take measures which may affect individual freedoms without providing for a corresponding increase in the powers of the Court to safeguard individual rights. The system of optional jurisdiction means that individuals will not be able to challenge indirectly a Community measure or invoke it to their assistance in national proceedings unless the Member State in the court of which the dispute is pending has accepted the jurisdiction of the Court to deliver preliminary rulings. The Court's jurisdiction is further circumscribed by Article 35(5) and the foreclosure of direct effect.[31]

Court composition and organization

The agenda for the IGC, as established by the Turin European Council in March 1996, included the mandate to examine whether and how to improve the role and functioning of the Community judicature. In the end, the Treaty of Amsterdam did not address issues pertaining to institutional reform and, accordingly, it made no changes to the composition and organization of the Community courts. Indeed, the absence in the Treaty of any attempt to reform the institutional architecture with a view to preparing the Union for the next wave of accessions may be seen as the most important failure of the Intergovernmental Conference. Two thorny issues lie at the centre of the debate: a re-weighting of the votes in the Council and the size of the Commission. A Protocol annexed to the TEU and the Community Treaties provides that, at least one year before the membership of the European Union exceeds 20, a conference of representatives of the governments of the Member States shall be convened in order to carry out a comprehensive review of the provisions of the Treaties on the composition and functioning of the institutions.[32] Although the Protocol makes no reference to the Community judicature, it may be interesting to highlight at this juncture some issues pertaining to the composition and organization of the Community courts.

In its report on the application of the TEU, the Court of Justice drew the attention of the IGC to the problems that might ensue if the Union were enlarged further. The Court pointed out that a significant increase in the number of judges might lead to the plenary session of the court crossing 'the invisible boundary between a collegiate court and a deliberative assembly'.[33] Also, an increase in the number of judges and a concomitant increase in the number of chambers might pose a threat to the consistency of the case law. On the other hand, the Court conceded that the presence of a judge from each Member State enhances legitimacy and contributes to the harmonious development of the case law, providing due representation of the national legal systems.[34]

Clearly, a number of decisions will need to be made regarding the judicial architecture when the Union is further enlarged and the structure of the Community judicature as a whole may need to be rethought.[35]

As far as the appointment of members of the Court is concerned, the EP has suggested that they should be appointed for a longer, non-renewable period,[36] by a procedure involving the Council and the Parliament. The Court of Justice has expressed misgivings about the involvement of the EP in the process of selection but sees a longer, non-renewable, term of office as an added guarantee of independence.[37]

Finally, it may be noted that, in an effort to reduce the mounting workload of the

Court of First Instance, consideration is currently being given to the possibility of establishing single-member chambers to hear staff cases and other cases of limited importance. That will be an eminently sensible reform.[38] It will release valuable judicial time, thus enabling the Court of First Instance to concentrate on commercial disputes which form the main core of its jurisdiction namely, direct actions in the fields of competition law, state aid, and anti-dumping. Such disputes are by their nature more time-consuming and more important for the Community legal order.

Conclusions

The following conclusions may be drawn from this brief survey. The Treaty of Amsterdam abandons the principle that the jurisdiction of the Court must be uniform. The preliminary reference procedure ceases to be the same in relation to all provisions of the EC Treaty and, for the first time, aspects of the Court's jurisdiction become optional for the Member States. The limitations imposed on the Court's powers are the *quid pro quo* for bringing under the auspices of the Union politically sensitive areas traditionally reserved to the nation state. The end result is a curious mix and the boundaries between intergovernmental cooperation and Community action are not objectively ascertainable. The model of differentiated integration, now formally espoused by the Treaty of Amsterdam, will inevitably lead to variable jurisprudence applicable only to certain Member States. One of the key functions of the Court will be to preserve the integrity and coherence of the Community legal order in an era where diversity is the prevailing political model. Despite the avowed commitment of the Union to the rule of law and democratic values, the protection of fundamental rights remains problematic. The judicial protection of the citizen remains incomplete, particularly in areas which fall within the scope of the third pillar and Title IV of the EC Treaty. Also, the coexistence of three separate but interrelating structures for the protection of human rights, namely, the ECHR, Union law, and the laws of the Member States, is liable to lead to confusion.

Endnotes

1. See Articles 40, 43–45 TEU and Article 11 EC. The term 'differentiated integration' is used by P. Craig and G. De Búrca, *EU Law, Texts, Cases, and Materials*, 2nd edn, Oxford: Oxford University Press, 1998, p. 47.
2. Notably, Article 42 TEU provides that the Council, acting unanimously, may decide that action in areas falling under the third pillar shall fall under Title IV of the EC Treaty and determine the relevant voting conditions relating to it. This provision means that the boundaries between intergovernmental cooperation and Community action may change by act of the institutions and without amendment of the treaties.
3. See R. Dehousse, 'European Institutional Architecture after Amsterdam: Parliamentary System or Regulatory Structure?', *Common Market Law Review*, Vol. 35, 1998, p. 595.
4. See Article 23 TEU. It will be noted that the Treaty of Amsterdam has not made specific provision for closer cooperation in the fields of ECSC and Euratom.

5. This derives from Articles 43 TEU, 47 TEU, and Article 11 EC.
6. Compare with Article 300(6) [ex Article 228(6)] EC and the earlier proposals of P. Jacqué and J. H. Weiler, 'On the Road to European Union – A New Judicial Architecture: An Agenda for the Intergovernmental Conference', *Common Market Law Review*, Vol. 27, 1990, p. 185.
7. See also J. H. Weiler's discussion of the TEU before being amended by the Treaty of Amsterdam: 'Neither Unity nor Three Pillars – The Trinity Structure of the Treaty on European Union', in J. Monar, W. Ungerer and W. Wessels (eds), *The Maastricht Treaty on European Union*, Brussels: European Interuniversity Press, 1993, pp. 49–62.
8. Case C-170/96, judgment of 12 May 1998.
9. Article 309(1) EC first inserted by the Treaty of Amsterdam as Article 23b EC.
10. Article 309(2) EC. See also the equivalent provisions of Article 96 ECSC and 204 Euratom.
11. Opinion 2/94 on *The Accession of the Community to the ECHR* [1996] ECR I-1759.
12. See editorial, *European Law Review*, Vol. 22, 1997, p. 290.
13. See T. Hartley, *The Foundations of European Community Law*, 4th edn, Oxford: Oxford University Press, 1998, pp. 272 *et seq.*
14. See for example, 6/64 *Costa* v. *ENEL* [1964] ECR 585.
15. Report of the Court of Justice on certain aspects of the application of the Treaty on European Union, Luxembourg, May 1995, reproduced in Court of Justice *Annual Report* 1995, p. 25.
16. Article 62(1) mandates the Council to adopt, within a period of five years from the entry into force of the Amsterdam Treaty, measures with a view to ensuring, in compliance with Article 14, the absence of any controls on persons, be they citizens of the Union or nationals of third countries, when crossing internal frontiers.
17. See for example Case 294/83 *Les Verts* v. *Parliament* [1986] ECR 1339; Case C-70/88 *Parliament* v. *Council (Chernobyl)* [1990] ECR I-2041; Case 222/84 *Johnston* v. *Chief Constable of the Royal Ulster Constabulary* [1986] ECR 1651.
18. Article 230 [formerly Article 173] EC, third paragraph. The Court of Auditors also has *locus standi* to bring an action for failure to act under Article 232 [formerly 175] EC as one of the 'other institutions' referred to therein.
19. Case 294/83 *Les Verts* v. *Parliament* [1986] ECR 1339; Case C-70/88 *Parliament* v. *Council (Chernobyl)* [1990] ECR I-2041; Case 222/84 *Johnston* v. *Chief Constable of the Royal Ulster Constabulary* [1986] ECR 1651.
20. See for example, Case C-295/90 *Parliament* v. *Council (Students' Residence Directive)* [1992] ECR I-4193; Case C-329/95 *Parliament* v. *Council (Visas Regulation)* [1997] ECR I-3213; Case C-22/96 *Parliament* v. *Council (Telematic networks)*, judgement of 28 May 1998.
21. This occurred in Opinion 2/94 *on the Accession of the Community to the ECHR* [1996] ECR I-1759.
22. See for example, Case C-231/95 P *Stichting Greenpeace Council* v. *Commission*, judgment of 2 April 1998 confirming on appeal the judgment of the CFI in Case T-585/93 [1995] ECR II-2205.
23. Report of the Court of Justice on certain aspects of the application of the Treaty on European Union, p. 30.
24. Article 29 TEU.
25. These are terrorism, trafficking in persons, offences against children, illicit drug trafficking, illicit arms trafficking, corruption and fraud. See Article 29 TEU.
26. Under Article 34(2), measures implementing conventions are to be adopted within the Council by a majority of two-thirds of the Contracting Parties.
27. Note however that any Member State, whether or not it has made a declaration, is entitled to submit statements of case or written observations to the Court where litigation arises: See Article 35(4) TEU.
28. See for example Case 294/83 *Les Verts* v. *Parliament* [1986] ECR 1339; Case C-70/88 *Parliament* v. *Council (Chernobyl)* [1990] ECR I-2041; Case 222/84 *Johnston* v. *Chief Constable of the Royal Ulster Constabulary* [1986] ECR 1651.
29. Under Article 39 TEU, the Council must consult the Parliament before adopting decisions, framework decisions and conventions.
30. This provision enables the Council to adopt common positions, decisions, and framework decisions, and also to establish conventions, which it recommends to the Member States to adopt in accordance with their respective constitutional requirements.
31. Article 31(e) TEU provides that judicial cooperation shall include 'progressively adopting measures establishing minimum rules relating to the constituent elements of criminal acts and to penalties in the fields of organized crime, terrorism and illicit drug trafficking'. Such approximation is to be effected by framework decisions which under Article 34 are to be adopted

by the Council acting unanimously. Framework decisions resemble directives in that they are binding on Member States as to the result to be achieved but leave to the national authorities the choice of form and methods. However, they may not produce direct effect. See Article 34(2)(b).

32. Protocol 7 on the Institutions with the Prospect of Enlargement of the European Union, Article 2. The Protocol also states that, at the date of entry into force of the first enlargement of the Union, the Commission shall comprise one national of each of the Member States, provided that by that date the weighting of the votes in the Council has been modified in a manner acceptable to all Member States.

33. Report of the Court of Justice on certain aspects of the application of the Treaty on European Union, p. 28.

34. Report of the Court of Justice on certain aspects of the application of the Treaty on European Union, p. 28.

35. See further, W. Van Gerven, 'The Role and Structure of the European Judiciary Now and in the Future', *European Law Review*, Vol. 21, 1996, p. 211; G. Vandersanden (ed.), *La Réforme du Système Juridictionnel Communautaire*. Bruxelles, 1994.

36. The Draft Treaty prepared by the European Parliament in 1990 suggested a period of 12 years. In its report of 6 July 1993, the Parliament's Committee on Institutional Affairs suggested a period of 9 years.

37. See for example Case 294/83 *Les Verts* v. *Parliament* [1986] ECR 1339; Case C-70/88 *Parliament* v. *Council (Chernobyl)* [1990] ECR I-2041; Case 222/84 *Johnston* v. *Chief Constable of the Royal Ulster Constabulary* [1986] ECR 1651.

38. It will be noted that the introduction of such a reform will not necessitate Treaty amendment and can be effected by Council decision.

POLICY DEVELOPMENTS

Chapter 5

European Monetary Union: one money, one Europe?

Nigel M. Healey

The monetary unification of 11 of the European Union's 15 Member States took place on January 1, 1999. On January 1, 2002 a monetary conversion will begin, with a new single currency, the euro, replacing the national currencies of the participating Member States over a six-month period. This represents a monumental achievement and one which, for most of the period since Economic and Monetary Union (EMU) was enshrined in the Maastricht Treaty, looked beyond the EU's grasp. Recession and turmoil in the international currency markets in the mid-1990s, combined with popular hostility in northern Europe and fiscal imbalances in the southern states, threatened to derail the project. Only in late 1997 did it become clear that a combination of political determination, notably on the part of southern states and France, which raised taxes and cut government spending in a concerted effort at fiscal consolidation, and unexpectedly strong economic recovery would make EMU possible.

The creation of a workable monetary union from 11 heterogeneous nation states in the absence of a wider political union is unprecedented. This chapter reviews the economics of monetary integration, outlining the likely balance of benefits and costs. It then considers the institutional framework of EMU, exploring the constitution of the European Central Bank (ECB) and the debate over the convergence criteria. Finally, it assesses the implications of EMU for the three countries which chose to remain outside the first wave of entrants, Britain, Sweden and Denmark.

The background to the Treaty on European Union

The Treaty on European Union (TEU) set out the blueprint for the transition to EMU, establishing January 1, 1999 as the latest date for the start of monetary unification. The idea of a single currency for Europe has a long history. The mid-nineteenth-century Latin Monetary Union represented an early attempt to gain the benefits of a common currency in continental Europe. More recently, the EC's Werner Report proposed a three-stage programme culminating in the introduction of a single currency by 1980. The Werner Plan received a setback with the disintegration of the global Bretton Woods exchange rate regime in 1971 when President Nixon restricted the convertibility of the US dollar into gold. The EC's 'snake' arrangement, intended to be a regional fixed exchange rate system which would be gradually hardened into monetary union, was further rocked by the first oil price rise in 1973 and the ensuing recession, in which Member States adopted divergent policy responses, with some (like Germany) favouring restrictive monetary policies to limit the inflationary consequences of the oil price rise and others (Britain, Italy and France) adopting expansionary fiscal policies in an effort to stem rising unemployment.

The European Monetary System

A continued desire for currency stability in the EC led to the creation of the European Monetary System (EMS) in 1979. At the heart of the EMS lay the Exchange Rate Mechanism (ERM), a modified version of the earlier snake.[1] All nine Member States except Britain joined the ERM, with Spain and Portugal joining after accession. The EMS included novel innovations like the ECU, a basket currency for internal accounting purposes, and the divergence indicator. These represented a genuine attempt to manage cooperatively the policy conflicts which had undermined the snake and derailed the Werner Plan.

The problem the EMS sought to address was the inherent asymmetry in the disciplines imposed on participating states. If a country follows expansionary monetary policies, it will tend to suffer a balance of payments deficit. The deficit country can support its exchange rate by selling foreign exchange reserves, but at some point it must resort to a rise in interest rates to defend the exchange rate, reversing its earlier expansionary stance. A country pursuing restrictive monetary policies can, in contrast, hold down its exchange rate in the face of a persistent balance of payments surplus indefinitely, since it is selling its own currency in the open market and accumulating foreign exchange reserves.

This asymmetry in the capacity of deficit and surplus countries to make independent monetary policies means that fixed exchange rate systems tend to be dominated by surplus countries which pursue deflationary policies. States which favour expansionary policies will eventually have to abandon their preferred stance to defend their exchange rate or devalue. This bleak choice characterized British economic policy throughout the Bretton Woods years (the era of 'stop-go' policies) and plagued France and Italy in the 1970s as they repeatedly joined and left the snake. The design of the EMS was intended to make the system symmetrical, so that surplus and deficit countries alike would be required to align their monetary policies, rather than forcing the whole burden of adjustment on the latter.

In the event, the artificial devices created to impose symmetry had little impact. Germany pursued a restrictive monetary policy throughout the early 1980s, which was broadly shadowed by the Benelux countries and Denmark. France and Italy, with their national psyches moulded more by the fear of unemployment than abhorrence of inflation, reacted to the second oil price shock of 1979 and global 'stagflation' (recession and inflation) by adopting expansionary policies. There were eight realignments of exchange rate parities in the first four years of the EMS (1979–83) and the regime was widely dismissed as a failure.

The emergence of German policy leadership

In the early 1980s, however, political and economic forces reshaped the way governments approached policy-making. Politically, the New Right was in the ascendancy, most notably in Britain and Germany (and the United States). It echoed the traditional conservative attachment to 'sound money' (low inflation and fiscal rectitude), while stressing the importance of reducing the role of the state in the workings of the economy. At the same time, developments in economic theory, popularized by monetarists like Milton Friedman, suggested that expansionary monetary policies would always eventually lead to inflation. Monetarists argued that unemployment and economic growth could be influenced by monetary policy in the short run, but that in the long run 'real' economic variables were wholly determined by supply-side factors (that is, training and education, investment, technological change etc.). In the early 1980s, these factors proved mutually reinforcing, policy-makers incorporating the prescriptions of monetarists into policy design, while the marginalization of Keynesian economists from political debate hastened their decline within the economics profession.

In the 1970s, tensions within the snake stemmed from differences in countries' attitudes to inflation and unemployment, with the most inflation-averse governments running the tightest monetary policies, and *vice versa*. The new monetarist orthodoxy exposed this choice of inflation or unemployment as a fallacy, arguing that inflation was determined by monetary growth and unemployment by supply-side policy. For inflation-prone ERM countries, this implied that following Germany's tight money lead would, in the long run, bring them low inflation without any lasting increase in unemployment. Member States thus began to shadow German monetary policy, rather than running more expansionary monetary policies and periodically devaluing. Exchange rate realignments became much less frequent in the period 1983–92. By the mid-1980s, 'German policy leadership' was firmly established within the ERM and was seen as one of the system's greatest strengths. Membership appeared to deliver greater intra-ERM exchange rate stability, plus low and stable inflation.[2]

The Delors Report

There is a widely held view that renewed interest in monetary union in the late 1980s grew out of the success of the EMS, a single currency being seen as a logical development of a fixed exchange rate system. The truth is precisely the opposite. As a cooperative system of managed exchange rates, the EMS was a failure. The innovations of the ECU and the divergence indicator proved cosmetic. In comparison with the snake, the crucial difference was the shift in policy-making orthodoxy which made surrendering to German policy leadership more attractive in the 1980s than it had been in the 1970s. Like the snake, the ERM was a 'deutschmark bloc', rather than a cooperative project.

As finance minister, Jacques Delors had played a key role in persuading France to follow the German policy lead in 1983. In the late 1980s, as President of the European Commission, he played an even more crucial role in shaping the EU's monetary future. Delors recognized the political and economic weaknesses in the EMS. Politically, the Bundesbank's *de facto* role as the EU's central bank lacked legitimacy. Economically, German policy leadership hinged critically upon the business cycles of Germany and the rest of the ERM members remaining synchronized; should they ever become significantly decoupled, the short-term costs of shadowing German interest rates could be so high that the ERM would break up. The Delors Committee, formed to develop proposals for further monetary integration, concluded that the EMS could only be 'hardened' into a monetary union if, at the same time, monetary control were transferred from the Bundesbank to a European Central Bank.

The Delors Report advocated a three-stage plan for monetary union.[3] In stage one (to start in 1990), all EU Member States would join the ERM and adopt the 'narrow' exchange rate bands of 2.25 per cent. In stage two (to start in 1994), the European Central Bank would be established in provisional form to manage preparations for monetary union.[4] In stage three, exchange rates would be locked, the European Central Bank would take over monetary policy and, through a monetary conversion, a new single currency would replace the national currencies of participating Member States. This formed the basis of the negotiations over the TEU. For Chancellor Kohl, German reluctance to give up the deutschmark was outweighed by the political need to be seen to be locking Germany into the EU following reunification in 1990, when other Member States were wary of a larger, more assertive Germany.

The economics of monetary union

In technical terms, a monetary union consists of an arrangement between participating countries in which:

- bilateral exchange rates (i.e. the exchange rates between one member state and another) are permanently fixed, with no margins for permissible fluctuations; and
- there are no institutional barriers (e.g. legal controls) to the free movement of capital across national frontiers.

In addition, the form of monetary union agreed at Maastricht involves replacing national currencies with a common currency. Currency union is not a necessary condition for monetary union, but analytically the two are similar. If DM1 = FFr3, then the two currencies are perfect substitutes and it makes little economic difference whether they are replaced by a single currency.

The economic arguments for and against EMU are an extension of the 'fixed versus floating exchange rates' debate.[5] This debate turns on whether the economic benefits of stabilizing the exchange rate (reduced exchange rate uncertainty) outweigh the costs of giving up exchange rate flexibility (sacrificing 'monetary sovereignty'). These costs, in turn, depend critically upon the characteristics of the national economies (e.g. degree of wage flexibility) and the linkages between the economies whose exchange rates are pegged. The additional dimension of EMU is the transition to a single currency managed by an independent central bank, which promises extra benefits over and above reduced exchange rate uncertainty. A single currency makes prices more transparent and underscores the permanence of the monetary union, while the ECB is mandated to pursue price stability. The following sections examine the main benefits and costs of EMU in turn.[6]

The economic benefits of EMU

The benefits of EMU are reasonably uncontentious: an end to exchange rate uncertainty on intra-EU trade and investment; elimination of transactions costs on cross-border trade; greater price transparency; and a guarantee of future monetary stability through the commitment of the ECB to price stability.

Reduced exchange rate uncertainty. EMU will end the uncertainty that exchange rate fluctuations bring to intra-EU trade and investment. While financial futures markets provide a form of insurance against exchange rate uncertainty, such 'hedging' facilities are not costless. Moreover, for long time horizons, so-called 'forward' facilities are not universally available. Such considerations have a special importance for members of the EU, the *raison d'être* of which is to facilitate cross-border movements of goods, services, labour and capital. To the extent that uncertainty about the future course of intra-EU exchange rates inhibits the restructuring of production, EMU should accelerate economic integration and growth.[7]

While a single currency will eliminate exchange rate risk from intra-euro zone trade, the euro will still be prone to fluctuations against other major trading and investment currencies, notably the US dollar and the Japanese yen. The benefits to Member States will depend on the proportion of trade undertaken with the EU rather than third countries. Table 5.1 shows that for the smaller Member States, trade with other EU countries dominates their trade (measured by imports) with the rest of the world. The greater the ratio of intra-EU to extra-EU trade, the greater the potential gains from membership of EMU.

Transaction costs. The transaction costs involved in changing currencies reflect the use of banks' resources (e.g. personnel and equipment) as well as the costs of holding stocks of foreign currencies (e.g. the interest foregone). Small and medium-sized companies which lack sophisticated treasury departments and business and leisure travellers will benefit most from the euro. Likely savings will be between 0.25 per cent and 0.5 per cent of GDP.

Table 5.1 Intra-EU and extra-EU imports (1995)

	Intra-EU imports (% GDP)	Extra-EU imports (% GDP)
Austria	21.4	8.4
Belgium/Luxembourg	40.2	12.8
Denmark	16.4	7.6
Finland	14.0	9.7
France	11.3	6.4
Germany	10.5	8.3
Greece	14.5	6.9
Ireland	27.5	21.7
Italy	12.0	6.2
Netherlands	26.1	14.2
Portugal	24.3	8.5
Spain	13.1	7.1
Sweden	17.7	10.6
United Kingdom	12.9	10.6
EU 15	**14.1**	**8.5**

Source: European Commission Directorate General for Economic and Financial Affairs (1998), *Annual Economic Report for 1998*, European Economy.

Transparent prices. After 2002, when national currencies are replaced by the euro, there will be common currency prices throughout the euro zone. This means that consumers and corporate buyers will be able to compare prices across national markets, in the same currency, enabling them to identify unjustified price differences and switch to more competitive suppliers (see Table 5.2). The result should be greater competition across the euro zone.

Low and stable inflation. The ECB should be a guarantor of low, stable inflation across the euro zone. Table 5.3 shows the average inflation rates over the last four decades. Germany has successfully achieved low inflation since 1961; countries (Netherlands, Belgium, Luxembourg, Denmark, Austria and, more recently, France) which have pegged their currencies to the deutschmark have 'imported' a similar

Table 5.2 Average price differences (net of taxes) of same car (cheapest country = 100)

	1993	1995
Belgium	116	122
France	121	121
Germany	124	128
Ireland	115	112
Italy	100	102
Netherlands	115	121
Portugal	108	108
Spain	108	105
United Kingdom	120	120

Source: European Commission, reported in *The Economist*.

Table 5.3 Average inflation rates (private consumption price deflator)

	1961–70	1971–80	1981–90	1991–97
Austria	3.5	6.3	3.6	2.6
Belgium	3.1	7.2	4.6	2.4
Denmark	5.8	10.4	5.8	1.9
Finland	4.7	11.5	6.4	2.5
France	4.3	9.8	6.2	2.1
Germany*	2.8	5.2	2.6	3.0
Greece	2.5	13.2	18.3	11.9
Ireland	5.1	14.0	7.1	2.2
Italy	3.8	14.6	10.0	5.0
Luxembourg	2.5	6.5	5.0	2.4
Netherlands	4.1	7.6	2.3	2.3
Portugal	2.8	17.3	17.3	6.1
Spain	5.8	15.0	9.3	4.8
Sweden	4.1	9.6	8.2	3.8
United Kingdom	3.9	13.3	6.0	3.7
EU 15	**3.9**	**10.6**	**6.5**	**3.6**

* West Germany only 1961–91
Source: European Commission Directorate General for Economic and Financial Affairs (1998), *Annual Economic Report for 1998*, European Economy.

inflation performance. In contrast, Italy, Spain, Portugal and Greece have poor inflation records and EMU offers a way to break with their inflationary past.

The economic costs of EMU

The costs of monetary union are more controversial and stem from the 'pooling' of monetary sovereignty that EMU entails; that is, transferring the power to change interest rates and exchange rates from national governments (where it can be used with exclusive reference to national economic conditions) to the ECB (where it will be used to set policy for the euro zone as a whole). The monetary stance appropriate to any single Member State may not perfectly coincide with the stance appropriate to the euro zone group. The Stability and Growth Pact also limits the extent to which governments may use the other instrument of stabilization policy, fiscal policy, since budget deficits for participating Member States may not normally exceed 3 per cent of GDP. The clear risk is that by taking away one instrument (monetary policy) and restricting the use of the other (fiscal policy), EMU may prevent governments from adequately stabilizing their national economies in response to economic shocks.

A useful starting point is to identify the conditions under which EMU would *not* result in greater instability of national output and employment. Pooling monetary sovereignty will be costless if:

1. The business cycles of Member States are synchronized *and* the effects of the ECB's common monetary policy are the same on each state; or

2. Fiscal policy (at national or EU level) can be used to differentially adjust demand in Member States; or
3. Wages within Member States are perfectly flexible; or
4. Labour markets are perfectly integrated across the euro zone.

If Condition 1 is fulfilled, it makes no difference whether monetary policy is pursued centrally by the ECB or independently by national governments. If it is not, EMU may still be costless provided that at least one of the adjustment mechanisms set out in Conditions 2–4 is available; that is, either demand can be stabilized by fiscal policy or asymmetric shocks to Member States can be absorbed through changes in wages or movements of labour from areas of high to low unemployment. Consider each in turn.

'*One monetary policy fits all.*' Condition 1 is the 'one monetary policy fits all' requirement. If it is fulfilled, then the monetary policy stance taken by the ECB will be identical to, and as effective as, the policy response that each national government would choose in isolation. Economic theory suggests that with growing economic integration and a common monetary policy stance, business cycles should come into line. However, asymmetric economic shocks (that is, shocks which disproportionately affect one country more than the rest) may lead to sharp divergences in the future. The economic structures of Member States are not identical; a sharp rise in the price of oil, for example, will deliver a positive boost to Britain as a net oil-exporter, but a negative shock to the rest of the EU. Moreover, further economic integration may increase national specialization in production. The danger of asymmetric shocks causing business cycles to become desynchronized may actually increase in future.[8]

For EMU to be costless, national economies must also behave in broadly the same way in response to a change of monetary policy. There are historical and cultural differences between spending and borrowing patterns in different countries which will mean that the interest rate chosen by the ECB is not optimal for every state, even if each were at the same point in the business cycle. On the other hand, increasing integration in the financial sector is likely to lead to a convergence in borrowing and saving behaviour over time. It is also significant that the high levels of home ownership in Britain (see Table 5.4) are, partly at least, a rational response by individuals to monetary mismanagement by successive British governments in the 1970s and 1980s, when housing provided a tax-efficient hedge against high inflation.

As, on balance, Condition 1 is not satisfied, it is important that at least one of the alternative shock absorbers set out in conditions 2–4 can help to stabilize national output and employment.

Table 5.4 Homeowners as a percentage of total households, 1994

Britain	**France**	**Germany**
66%	54%	40%

Source: Council of Mortgage Lenders

Fiscal policy. In the short run, fiscal policy provides an alternative instrument to monetary policy for stabilizing demand. Governments can borrow against future tax revenue to stimulate demand during a recession and repay past borrowing to depress demand during a boom. National fiscal policy could, after EMU, provide a partial replacement for monetary policy. However, the architects of the TEU were fearful that the increased ease of borrowing to finance budget deficits might lead some governments to pursue unsustainable fiscal policies. The Stability and Growth Pact imposes a limit of 3 per cent of GDP on the size of the budget deficit. Although larger deficits are permitted to combat severe downturns, EMU will constrain governments in their use of fiscal policies for stabilization purposes.

An alternative way in which fiscal policy within the euro zone could replace the stabilizing role of monetary policy would be through transfers between different states. In a unified state, if one region suffers an asymmetric shock then demand is partially stabilized by a change in the net balance of fiscal transfers to other regions. MacDougall explored this issue in the context of the EC.[9] For inter–country transfers to play a significant stabilizing role after EMU, the EU's central budget would have to be much larger than the present 1.27 per cent of GDP. The design would also have to alter. Fiscal instruments like the European Social Fund and the European Regional Development Fund account for only 33 per cent of total spending and are directed towards equalizing structural differences in living standards rather than correcting short-term fluctuations in income and employment. The challenge is to build into the central budget transfer funds from countries with output above the trend to those with output below the trend, independent of *per capita* income. But there is little political appetite for such reforms, suggesting that the stabilizing effect of the EU budget is likely to remain negligible.

Wage flexibility. The above discussion suggests that EMU may mean that centrally made monetary policy is periodically inappropriate to the needs of individual economies, while at the same time restricting the ability of national governments to use fiscal policy for stabilization purposes. The need for active stabilization policy stems, in turn, from the inflexibility of labour markets. If wages were highly flexible, economic shocks could be absorbed by changes in wages, rather than changes in employment and output. While labour market institutions vary across the EU, in general they are much less flexible than in the United States.[10]

The responsiveness of wages to shocks is not, however, a linear function of the degree of trade union monopolization. When wage setting is very decentralized (at the limit, to company level), workers and employers can observe the effects of their wage bargains on their competitiveness, so that wages tend to adjust more quickly to external shocks.[11] The same is true for corporatist systems, in which national employers' federations negotiate directly with national unions. Here unions and employers can also take full account of the implications of their wage setting behaviour for competitiveness and employment. It is in countries where there is partial centralization that wages tend to be most unresponsive. Where trade unions represent only a proportion of workers in an industry and negotiate with a proportion of the employers, it is difficult for wage bargainers to gauge the impact

Table 5.5 Centralization of wage bargaining

Low centralization	Intermediate centralization	High centralization
United States, Canada, Switzerland, Japan	Germany, Netherlands, Belgium, France, Italy, United Kingdom, Australia	Norway, Austria, Denmark, Sweden, Finland

Adapted from L. Calmfors and J. Driffill, 'Bargaining Structures, Corporatism and Macroeconomic Performance', *Economic Policy*, Vol. 6, 1988.

of their settlements on the employment prospects of the workers affected. The tendency is for unions to fight for wage increases and resist cuts, knowing that their rivals are doing the same.

Table 5.5 suggests that countries in the intermediate centralization category are likely to suffer most from future asymmetric shocks after EMU, since they experience the greatest wage rigidities. This classification was based on labour market institutions before 1988 and places Britain in the intermediate group. It is likely that the reforms undertaken by the 1979–97 Conservative government pushed Britain towards the low centralization group, so that Britain may actually be better placed than Germany, France and Italy to deal with future economic shocks.

Labour mobility. In the absence of monetary or fiscal stabilization, labour mobility provides an alternative to wage flexibility as a way of absorbing asymmetric shocks.[12] If unemployed workers can move to take new jobs in prosperous Member States, then equilibrium could be restored by movements of people rather than wages. Labour migration thus provides a buffer in lieu of wage flexibility.[13] In contrast to the United States, where large-scale movements of labour have occurred in response to the changing economic fortunes of different regions, labour mobility in Europe is more limited.[14] Although the Single Market programme abolished many legislative obstacles to the free movement of labour, different social traditions restrict the ability of workers to move to jobs. Moreover, it is doubtful if the EU has the political will seriously to increase inter–country labour mobility. The prospect of large numbers of unskilled southern labour taking jobs in the richer northern states of the EU and placing demands on welfare systems, is not appealing to many politicians. The EU has preferred to use regional policy initiatives to 'take work to the (unemployed) workers', rather than the reverse. It does not seem likely that labour mobility will provide a significant alternative to greater wage flexibility in the foreseeable future.

Predictable benefits versus uncertain costs?

On balance, it is clear that, from an economic perspective, the benefits of EMU are reasonably predictable and fairly modest, although to the extent that the euro stimulates more rapid integration, they may be cumulative over time. Far more contentious are the economic costs of EMU which are uncertain and unquantifiable. It seems likely that, although there are pressures leading to greater convergence of business cycles, the EU may be plagued by asymmetric shocks. Pooling monetary sovereignty necessarily means that the less-integrated countries may be disadvantaged by a 'one monetary policy fits all' rule after EMU and fiscal policy will be unable to take over adequately a stabilizing role. Adjustment will be thrown more heavily on wage flexibility and, to a lesser extent, labour mobility. The leading EU states are characterized by rigid labour markets and major structural reform of labour market institutions may be necessary if EMU is not to lead to greater instability.

The Treaty on European Union

The TEU included provisions for the establishment of an independent ECB with a mandate to pursue price stability. Its design reflected a consensus that central banks should be independent of national governments and was closely modelled on the Bundesbank. The TEU also set out convergence criteria which Member States would be required to satisfy in order to join EMU. These have been criticized for appearing to ignore the economic literature on the need for alternative 'shock absorbers' (fiscal policy, wage flexibility, labour mobility) and including conditions related to public finances which have nothing to do with monetary integration. In reality, the criteria were motivated primarily by political, rather than economic, considerations, notably the need to assuage Germany's fear that the commitment to price stability in EMU would be undermined by the southern states' fiscal laxity. The public finance conditions were intended to exclude countries which could not demonstrate a sustained commitment to fiscal rectitude.

The European Central Bank

The design of the ECB was heavily influenced by modern economic theory, which suggests that if the ultimate power over monetary policy is vested with democratic governments (or a body representing their interests like the Council of Ministers), the outcome is likely to be higher inflation than if it is delegated to an independent central bank.[15] In contrast to the political pressures which bear upon elected governments, a constitutionally independent central bank has no incentive to depart from the socially optimal objective of price stability. Delegating control of monetary policy to an independent central bank may therefore insulate the policy-making process from electoral considerations. International evidence confirms a strong relationship between the degree of central bank independence and inflation.[16]

An independent central bank may also make monetary policy announcements more 'credible', reducing the unemployment costs of fighting inflation. 'Credibility' refers to the extent to which people believe the pronouncements of a policy-making body. Inflationary expectations will adjust favourably to the announcement of a tightening of monetary policy only if wage bargainers believe

Table 5.6 Measures of political independence

Central Bank	1	2	3	4	5	6	7	8	9
Germany		*		*	*	*	*	*	6
Netherlands		*		*	*	*	*	*	6
Italy	*	*	*		*				4
Denmark		*					*	*	3
Ireland		*				*		*	3
France		*		*					2
Greece			*					*	2
Spain				*	*				2
Belgium				*					1
Portugal					*				1
United Kingdom					*				1

Adapted from V. Grilli, D. Masciandaro and G. Tabellini, 'Political and Monetary Institutions and Public Financial Policies in the Industrial Countries', *Economic Policy*, October 1991, pp. 368–9.

Key to Table 5.6
1 Governor not appointed by government.
2 Governor appointed for 5+ years.
3 Executive not appointed by government.
4 Executive appointed for 5+ years.
5 No mandatory government representative on executive.
6 No government approval of policy decision required.
7 Statutory requirement for central bank to pursue price stability.
8 Explicit conflicts between central bank and government possible.
9 Index of political independence (sum of asterisks in each row).

the policy changes will be carried through. Given the incentives for a government to renege on promises of price stability as elections loom, the private sector is unlikely to pay much heed to politicians. A central bank which is constitutionally independent of the government and bound by a statutory obligation to fight inflation is liable to command much greater credibility, allowing it to achieve stable prices at a lower cost in terms of unemployment.

There are two dimensions to central bank independence. First, the central bank must be politically independent, in the sense that its decisions should be not subject to the approval or direction of the government. Ideally, the government should not be able to 'rig' the bank's policy-making executive by appointing its governor or senior staff. If the government makes such appointments, the interests of political independence are best served by having lengthy, secure terms of tenure for key executives, only a small proportion falling due for renewal within the lifetime of a single government. Table 5.6 sets out the main dimensions of political independence, ranking the EU's central banks as they stood in 1992.

Secondly, the central bank should be economically independent, in the sense that it can execute monetary policy without being undermined by government actions. For example, in many countries, the government has an account with its national central bank, which it can effectively overdraw at will, thereby increasing the

Table 5.7. Measures of economic independence

Central Bank	1	2	3	4	5	6	7	8	9
Germany	*	*	*	*	*	*	*	*	8
Belgium		*	*	*	*	*		*	6
United Kingdom	*	*	*	*		*	*		6
Denmark		*			*	*	*		4
France				*	*	*	*		4
Ireland		*	*	*		*			4
Netherlands				*	*	*	*		4
Spain				*	*			*	3
Greece				*		*			2
Portugal				*		*			2
Italy				*					1

Adapted from V. Grilli, D. Masciandaro and G. Tabellini, 'Political and Monetary Institutions and Public Financial Policies in the Industrial Countries', *Economic Policy*, October 1991, pp. 368-9.

Key to Table 5.7
1 Government credit from central bank not automatic.
2 Government credit from central bank at market interest rate.
3 Government credit from central bank for temporary period only.
4 Government credit from central bank limited in amount.
5 Central bank does not take up unsold government bond issues.
6 Discount rate set by central bank.
7 No government qualitative controls on commercial bank lending since 1980.
8 No government quantitative controls on bank lending since 1980.
9 Index of economic independence (sum of asterisks in each row).

money supply. Central banks may also be obliged to buy any issue of government bonds that is not taken up by the private sector, with the same effect on the money supply. Some instruments of monetary policy may also be under the control of the government. Historically, British governments have imposed both qualitative and quantitative controls on commercial bank lending. Table 5.7 shows how the national central banks of the EU Member States ranked on the main dimensions of economic independence at the time of signing the TEU.

The constitution of the European Central Bank

Under the terms of the TEU, the ECB comprises:

- the ECB itself, which has a president[17] and an executive of six members appointed by the European Council for eight-year terms, and a governing council (the executive plus governors of the national central banks from participating Member States); plus
- the European System of Central Banks (ESCB), consisting of participating national central banks, which act as regional agents in carrying out the policy instructions of the ECB.

Table 5.8 The independence of the European Central Bank

	1	2	3	4	5	6	7	8	9
Political independence:									
European Central Bank		*		*	*	*	*	*	6
German Bundesbank		*		*	*	*	*	*	6
Economic independence:									
European Central Bank	*	*	*	*	*	*	*	*	8
German Bundesbank	*	*	*	*	*	*	*	*	8

Adapted from V. Grilli, D. Masciandaro and G. Tabellini, 'Political and Monetary Institutions and Public Financial Policies in the Industrial Countries', *Economic Policy*, October 1991, pp. 368–9.

Key to Table 5.8
1 Governor not appointed by government.
  Government credit from central bank not automatic.
2 Governor appointed for 5+ years.
  Government credit from central bank at market interest rate.
3 Executive not appointed by government.
  Government credit from central bank for temporary period only.
4 Executive appointed for 5+ years.
  Government credit from central bank limited in amount.
5 No mandatory government representative on executive.
  Central bank does not take up unsold government bond issues.
6 No government approval of policy decision required.
  Discount rate set by central bank.
7 Statutory requirement for central bank to pursue price stability.
  No government qualitative controls on commercial bank lending since 1980.
8 Explicit conflicts between central bank and government possible.
  No government quantitative controls on bank lending since 1980.
9 Index of independence (sum of asterisks in each row).

Table 5.8 shows that on all indices of independence, the ECB is identical to the German Bundesbank. Because the ECB will operate through national central banks, the TEU requires that the latter end their links with their national governments, becoming fully politically and economically independent before they may be admitted to the ESCB. Article 7 TEU forbids any national central bank in the ESCB to seek or take instructions from any other EU institution or its national government. Since 1991, all Member States have passed legislation ceding greater autonomy to their central banks (increasing their political and economic independence). The Labour government has granted the Bank of England greater operational independence.

Political accountability and control

There has been widespread concern that an independent ECB will worsen the 'democratic deficit'.[18] Once appointed, the president, executive board members and national central bank governors will be outside the control of elected representatives. The French government has been particularly insistent that the ECB is subject to political scrutiny. Much of the debate, though, fails to distinguish between political accountability and control. There is no necessary conflict between *ex-post* accountability to elected representatives and operational independence. The ECB may be required to specify in advance its inflation targets for the year ahead, for example, and then at the end of the year defend its record at the European Parliament. In New Zealand, the central bank has a high degree of independence, but is accountable in this way to parliament and is subject to penalties, including the dismissal of the governor.

The convergence criteria

The TEU set out five convergence criteria which Member States must satisfy before acceding to EMU. The criteria fall into two categories: inflation criteria, which are designed to ensure that the transitional costs of joining are tolerable; and fiscal criteria, which are intended to guarantee that the ECB will not find its commitment to price stability undermined by profligate governments.

If countries enter EMU at different points in their business cycles, adherence to a common, low inflation monetary policy will cause recession in the higher inflation countries. The inflation criteria are intended to provide a guide to the extent to which such convergence has taken place; the logic of these conditions is that, if satisfied, the short-run costs of pooling monetary sovereignty will be modest and outweighed by the likely benefits. The three indicators of inflation convergence are:

1. Successful candidates must have inflation rates no more than 1.5 per cent above the average of the three EU countries with the lowest inflation rates.
2. Long-term interest rates should be no more than 2 per cent above the average interest rates in the three countries with the lowest rates.
3. The national currency must not have been devalued and must have remained within the normal bands of the EMS for the previous two years.[19]

The significance of the second condition lies in the fact that long-term interest rates provide a guide to the financial markets' expectations of inflation in the longer term. Put simply, today's long-term interest rate is a weighted average of expected future short-term interest rates. If investors expect inflation to be high in the future, they will expect short-term interest rates to be correspondingly high in the future as well. Critics of the inflation criteria point out that inflation is only one dimension of the business cycle. The level of cyclical unemployment, the size of the output gap or the scale of the cyclical budget deficit all provide information about the extent to which business cycles are harmonized. More seriously, by concentrating on nominal indicators, there is a danger that member governments seeking admission to EMU will focus their efforts on reducing inflation, risking the development of unsustainable real pressures (e.g. higher unemployment).

Two further convergence criteria impose limits on public finances, namely that:

1. National budget deficits must be less than 3 per cent of GDP.
2. The national debt must be less than 60 per cent of GDP.

The rationale of these fiscal criteria stems from the implications of creating an independent ECB with a statutory responsibility for maintaining price stability for national governments. An independent ECB would constrain national public finances in two ways.[20] First, the right to issue 'fiat' money (notes and coin) is transferred from national governments to the ECB, so that 'seigniorage' profits would be lost to member governments.[21] Seigniorage profits arise as governments 'sell' newly created currency to their national banking systems for its full face value, while the actual production costs of printing notes and minting coins are much lower.

Secondly, the requirement of economic independence for the ECB will deny governments the right of automatic, unlimited access to central bank credit. National governments will no longer be able to finance budget deficits or refinance maturing government debt by selling bonds to their central banks and increasing the money supply. The TEU requires that Member States should control their budget deficits (limiting them to not more than 3 per cent of GDP) and stabilize their public debt: GDP ratios (at or below 60 per cent) prior to joining EMU.

The fiscal criteria, and their incorporation in the Stability and Growth Pact, have been strongly criticized. As discussed above, the need to use fiscal policy more actively will increase after EMU, since governments will need a replacement for the stabilization role played by monetary and exchange rate policy. However, the architects of the TEU provided room for discretion in the interpretation of the fiscal criteria, which suggests that they may not prove excessively binding in practice. Article 104c TEU states that the Commission shall examine compliance with budgetary discipline on the basis of the following two criteria:

1. Whether the ratio of the planned or actual government deficit to gross domestic product exceeds a reference value (3 per cent), unless either the ratio has declined substantially and continuously and reached a level that comes close to the reference value; or, alternatively, the excess over the reference value is only exceptional and temporary and the ratio remains close to the reference value.
2. Whether the ratio of government debt to gross domestic product exceeds a reference value (60 per cent), unless the ratio is sufficiently diminishing and approaching the reference value at a satisfactory pace.

The first wave of EMU

In May 1998, the European Council decided which Member States met the convergence criteria. Britain and Denmark had opt-outs, and both exercised their option to 'wait and see'. Sweden does not have a formal opt-out, but also decided not to join in the first wave. Of the convergence criteria, the provisions for exchange rate stability had been overtaken by events. In August 1993, following a long period of speculative pressure on the foreign exchange markets, the EU

Table 5.9 Convergence criteria and outturns in 1998

	Inflation rate (%)	Long-term interest rate (%)	ERM membership	Budget balance (% GDP)	Debt ratio (% GDP)
1998 criteria	**2.8**	**7.5**	**Membership**	**–3.0**	**60.0**
Austria	1.5	5.6	Yes	–2.3	64.7
Belgium	1.3	5.7	Yes	–1.7	118.1
Denmark	2.1	6.2	Yes	1.1	59.5
Finland	2.0	5.9	Yes (1)	0.3	53.6
France	1.0	5.5	Yes	–2.9	58.1
Germany	1.7	5.6	Yes	–2.5	61.2
Greece	4.5	9.8	Yes (2)	–2.2	107.7
Ireland	3.3	6.2	Yes	1.1	59.5
Italy	2.1	6.7	Yes (3)	–2.5	118.1
Luxembourg	1.6	5.6	Yes	1.0	7.1
Netherlands	2.3	5.5	Yes	–1.6	70.0
Portugal	2.2	6.2	Yes	–2.2	60.0
Spain	2.2	6.3	Yes	–2.2	67.4
Sweden	1.5	6.5	No	0.5	74.1
United Kingdom	2.3	7.0	No	–0.6	53.0

Source: European Monetary Institute (1998), *Convergence Report.*
Notes: (1) since October 1996; (2) since March 1998; (3) since November 1996.

decided to widen the target bands from 2.25 per cent to 15 per cent, making depreciations of up to 30 per cent technically possible within the 'normal' bands of the ERM. In the run-up to the May 1998 summit, there was a great deal of discussion about whether the exchange rate criterion actually had any meaning, the Council deciding that membership *per se* was a sufficient condition.

Table 5.9 shows how Member States fared regarding the convergence criteria, based on the European Monetary Institute's 1998 Convergence Report. Only Denmark (which opted out), Finland, France, Luxembourg and Portugal unequivocally met all five conditions. The European Council agreed to admit a further seven countries, six of which violated a strict interpretation of the public debt limit (Austria, Belgium, Germany, Italy, the Netherlands and Spain) and one, Ireland, exceeded the inflation condition for what appear to be exceptional reasons (unexpectedly strong economic growth). Of the non-entrants, Denmark met all the requirements, while Britain and Sweden failed on the (contested) grounds of their non-membership of the EMS. All three are voluntarily choosing to remain outside EMU. Greece failed the requirements for inflation, long-term interest rates and public debt, but has made significant advances in recent years.

An EMU of 'ins' and 'outs'

Four Member States are outside the euro bloc. Of these, Greece has indicated its intention to join EMU by 1 January 2001 and Denmark will retain its EMS membership and peg its currency to the euro. Only Britain and Sweden, the only two present non-members of the EMS, will be free to pursue independent monetary and exchange rate policies. The problem for them is that the costs of continued monetary sovereignty seem likely to increase now that EMU is under way.

In Britain, much of the debate about EMU has involved a comparison of the estimated costs and benefits of membership, where the alternative is, implicitly, the *status quo*. The creation of an EMU of 11 states destroys the rationale of this approach. The alternative to membership for Britain is no longer the *status quo*, but a single currency bloc which excludes Britain. The resulting configuration of economic costs and benefits is transformed in a way which commentators are still trying to understand.

Two provisional conclusions are clear, however. The first is that the exercise of independent monetary policy by Britain and Sweden will be regarded by the euro states very differently after EMU. A monetary expansion which results in a depreciation of, say, sterling relative to the euro may be construed as an attempt to gain an unfair competitive advantage. Euro states may then retaliate by imposing non-tariff barriers against the outsiders. The second conclusion is that as EMU becomes the central issue in European integration, non-members may find themselves increasingly marginalized from policy-making. Already the Euro-11 group excludes non-EMU Member States from its discussions about monetary policy. This group may begin to coordinate other areas of economic policy (e.g. national fiscal policies) in ways that further damage the interests of the 'outs'. In all likelihood, the British government, which has declared its intention to join EMU when its economic cycle is more closely aligned with those in continental Europe, is almost certain to shadow the euro and avoid making policy decisions which could close off the option of joining in 2002.

The early months of EMU

Decades of theorizing about the likely economic costs and benefits of a single European currency came to end on 1 January 1999. The strides made in reducing inflation and budget deficits by the 11 participating states, the design of the European Central Bank – which is closely modelled on the Bundesbank – and the appointment of a hawkish Dutch president, Wim Duisenberg, all suggested that the euro would be a worthy successor to the deutschmark as Europe's hegemonic currency. Indeed, many comentators anticipated an early appreciation in the value of the euro *vis-à-vis* the US dollar, as central banks around the world reduced their official holdings of dollars in favour of the new European currency.

In fact, as Table 5.10 illustrates, the euro depreciated almost 15 per cent against the US dollar over the period between its launch in January and July 1999. Critics of monetary union have interpreted this decline as evidence of fundamental flaws in its institutional design, which have manifested themselves in the early weakness of the currency.

The counter-view is that, while the ECB is required under its statutes to give

Table 5.10 Selected euro cross-rates, January – July 1999

	January	February	March	April	May	June	July	% change Jan. – July
$/euro	1.17	1.13	1.10	1.08	1.07	1.04	1.02	−14.7
yen/euro	135.00	127.00	131.00	131.00	129.00	124.00	123.00	−9.8
£/euro	0.70	0.69	0.67	0.68	0.66	0.65	0.65	−7.7

Source: The Economist

Table 5.11 Short-term interest rates (three-month interbank rate), 1999

	January	February	March	April	May	June	July
Euro-11	3.24%	3.09%	3.08%	2.90%	2.58%	2.60%	2.66%
United States	5.07%	4.76%	4.82%	4.82%	4.79%	4.89%	5.13%
Britain	6.19%	5.66%	5.31%	5.19%	5.25%	5.19%	5.00%

Source: The Economist

overriding priority to maintaining price stability (in practice, keeping inflation below 2 per cent pa), the real problem facing the economies of the Euro-11 states in the first half of 1999 has been slow growth and high unemployment. Without compromising its inflation targets, the ECB has been able to reduce interest rates in order to stimulate growth. Table 5.11 shows that the ECB allowed short-term interest rates to fall between January and July 1999, with the result that the euro depreciated against the dollar and the pound. Together, the combination of lower interest rates and a 'cheap' euro should boost investment and exports, so accelerating economic growth in 2000.

The ECB's use of a 'cheap' euro to stimulate the Euroland economy highlights the dangers to the 'pre-ins' of being outside the currency bloc. For example, approximately 60 per cent of Britain's trade is with other members of the EU. Movements in the £/euro exchange rate have a profound effect on economic conditions in Britain. For the ECB, however, its interest rate decisions are driven wholly by economic circumstances within the euro bloc. If conditions dictate a depreciation of the euro against other currencies – notably, the dollar and the yen – the euro will also depreciate against sterling. Avoidance of this kind of 'beggar-thy-neighbour' policy, whereby the depreciating country (or bloc) effectively exports its unemployment to the outside world, remains one of the most powerful arguments for British participation in monetary union. The first half of 1999 has been a salutary lesson to British manufacturing of the consequences of non-membership.

Conclusions

The business cycles of the EU Member States are desynchronized and their responsiveness to the guiding hand of monetary policy variable. The TEU restricts the ability of governments to use fiscal policy to stabilize demand and a centralized budgetary system capable of making significant interstate transfers is many years away. Many EU states are characterized by labour market rigidities and labour mobility is limited in comparison with mature monetary unions like the United States. While the introduction of a single currency will benefit the EU by eliminating exchange rate risk and promoting international trade and investment between Member States, there is a significant threat of greater, rather than reduced, volatility in national economies. The key problem is that, while the convergence criteria have reduced the transitional costs of 'settling into' EMU (by forcing convergence before, rather than after, monetary unification), there is a strong likelihood that participating states will be buffeted by asymmetric shocks after the introduction of the euro.

The calculation of economic costs and benefits ignores the political dimension. For the EU, economic integration has always been a means to political unification, rather than an end in itself. The commitment of key Member States to political union means that EMU must be seen as part of a wider commitment to a unified Europe rather than a limited exercise in trading off economic costs for economic benefits. EMU will inevitably cause transitional problems for first wave states, but the extent of the political capital invested by Member States in the project means that its failure is unthinkable. The abandonment of EMU would threaten the continued existence of the EU and, for this reason alone, it is 'doomed to success'. For non-entrants, the creation of EMU fundamentally reshapes the benefits and costs of membership, increasing the former and reducing the latter. It seems certain that Greece and Britain will join by 2002, making it likely that Denmark and Sweden may follow suit.

Endnotes

1. M. Artis and N. Healey, 'The European Monetary System', in N. Healey (ed.), *The Economics of the New Europe*, London: Routledge, 1995, pp. 45–67.
2. See C. Mastropasqua, S. Micossi and R. Rinaldi, 'Interventions, Sterilization and Monetary Policy in European Monetary System Countries, 1979–87', in F. Giavazzi, S. Micossi and M. Miller (eds), *The European Monetary System*. Cambridge: Cambridge University Press, 1988, pp. 252–88; A. Haldane, 'The Exchange Rate Mechanism of the European Monetary System: A Review of the Literature', *Bank of England Quarterly Bulletin*, February 1991, pp. 73–82.
3. J. Delors, *Report on Economic and Monetary Union in the European Community*, Committee for the Study of Economic and Monetary Union, European Commission, 1989.
4. This became the European Monetary Institute in the TEU.
5. See, for example, J. R. Artus and J. H. Young, 'Fixed and Flexible Exchange Rates: A Renewal of the Debate', *IMF Staff Papers*, Vol. 26, 1979, pp. 654–98.
6. On the pros and cons of EMU, see B. Eichengreen, *Costs and Benefits of European Monetary Unification*, CEPR Discussion Paper, No. 435, London: Centre for Economic Policy Research, 1990; M. Emerson, *One Market, One Money*, Oxford: Oxford University Press, 1992; D. Currie, *The Pros and Cons of EMU*, London: HM Treasury, 1997.
7. Emerson, *One Market, One Money*.
8. P. Minford and A. Rastogi, 'The Price of EMU', in K. O. Pohl *et al*, *Britain and EMU*, London: Centre for Economic Performance, 1990, pp. 47–68; T. Bayoumi and B. Eichengreen, *Shocking Aspects of European Monetary Unification*, CEPR Discussion Paper No. 643, London, Centre for Economic Policy Research, 1992.

9. D. MacDougall, *Public Finance in European Integration*, European Commission, 1977.
10. F. Heylen and A. van Poeck, 'National Labour Market Institutions and the European Economic and Monetary Integration Process', *Journal of Common Market Studies*, Vol. 33, 1995, pp. 573–95.
11. L. Calmfors and J. Driffill, 'Bargaining Structure, Corporatism and Macroeconomic Performance', *Economic Policy*, Vol. 6, 1988, pp. 13–61.
12. R. A. Mundell, 'A Theory of Optimum Currency Areas', *American Economic Review*, Vol. 51, 1961, pp. 657–64; R. McKinnon, 'Optimum Currency Areas', *American Economic Review*, Vol. 53, 1963, pp. 717–25.
13. D. Gros, *A Reconsideration of the Optimum Currency Approach. The Role of External Shocks and Labour Mobility*, Brussels: Centre for European Policy Studies, 1996.
14. P. de Grauwe and W. Vanhaverbeke, *Is Europe an Optimum Currency Area? Evidence from Regional Data*, CEPR Discussion Paper No. 555, London: Centre for Economic Policy Research, 1991.
15. See K. Kydland and E. Prescott, 'Rules rather than Discretion: the Time Inconsistency of Optimal Plans', *Journal of Political Economy*, Vol. 85, 1997, pp. 473–92; A. Alesina and V. Grilli, *The European Central Bank: Reshaping Monetary Politics in Europe*, CEPR Discussion Paper No. 563, London: Centre for Economic Policy Research, 1991.
16. A. Alesina and L. Summers, 'Central Bank Independence and Macroeconomic Performance: Some Comparative Evidence', *Journal of Money, Credit and Banking*, Vol. 25, 1993, pp. 151–62.
17. Wim Duisenberg, who was head of the European Monetary Institute.
18. T. Teivainen, 'The Independence of the European Central Bank: Implications for Democratic Governance', in P. Minkkinen and H. Patomaki (eds), *The Politics of Economic and Monetary Union*, Helsinki: The Finnish Institute of International Affairs, 1997.
19. The ERM normal bands were 2.25 per cent, with a wider band of 6 per cent for new members. In August 1993, the normal band was widened to 15 per cent following a speculative crisis.
20. N. Healey and P. Levine, 'Unpleasant Monetarist Arithmetic Revisited: Central Bank Independence, Fiscal Policy and European Monetary Union', *National Westminster Bank Quarterly Review*, August 1992, pp. 23–35.
21. V. Grilli, 'Seigniorage in Europe', in M. de Cecco and A. Giovanini (eds), *A European Central Bank? Perspectives on Monetary Union after Ten Years of the EMS*, Cambridge: Cambridge University Press, 1989, pp. 53–79.

Chapter 6

The paradox of the social dimension

Jeff Kenner

At the June 1997 Amsterdam European Council, the EU's leaders moved with remarkable alacrity to reunite the disparate social provisions of the EC Treaty, thereby bringing to an end the twin-stream process for making social policy that had formally operated since the signing of the Maastricht Protocol on Social Policy in 1992. The United Kingdom's lengthy disengagement from mainstream Community social policy, beginning with Mrs Thatcher's refusal to accept the Community's 1989 Social Charter, will, however, have longer-term effects not just for the UK, which has to bring its laws into conformity with the *acquis* already adhered to by the 'Fourteen', but also for the Community as a whole, now that there is an apparent political consensus and no pariah state to blame for inactivity in the social policy field.

This chapter assesses these longer-term effects in the context of prevailing social and economic impulses by, firstly, evaluating the development of Community social policy from Maastricht to Amsterdam, and then assessing the extent to which the apparent restoration of a unified 'Social Chapter' masks a new, and more complex, bifurcation of Community social policy objectives into employment protection and employment creation streams that may prove incapable of reconciliation. Early indications suggest that despite the removal of the most obvious obstacle to progress, the 'Social Chapter' will be sparingly used while the new Employment Title will be the principal instrument and guide for policy development.

The road to Maastricht

For forty years social policy has operated in the Community's 'twilight zone'. While economic and sectoral integration has proceeded apace, social laws have emerged spasmodically after long gestation periods, either in the form of non-binding soft laws, for example on sexual harassment and equitable pay,[1] or as diluted directives with many substantive aspects subject to derogations within a framework of basic minimum standards, as in the case of measures concerning working time and young workers.[2] Full harmonization is not, and never has been, a social policy objective because of the need to 'respect the diversity of European societies'.[3] Rather, the approach has been to seek to establish a floor of rights for Community workers that can be built upon at national level while ensuring a broadly level playing field consistent with the requirements of market integration and competitiveness. This does not mean that the Community has always lacked ambition in the social field. On the contrary, bold efforts have been made, notably in 1974, when the first Social Action Programme was launched,[4] and in 1989 when the rights-oriented Social Charter was signed by 11 Member States.[5] But the promise of a strong social dimension has repeatedly foundered upon the rocks of economic recession and an exiguous legal base in the Treaties.

The Maastricht Treaty was negotiated at a time when the European economy was relatively buoyant and the Community's social policy activism was at its zenith. Eleven Member States were prepared to undermine the essential unity of the EC Treaty by adopting amongst themselves an Agreement on Social Policy (SPA) allowing them to have recourse to the 'institutions, procedures and mechanisms of the Treaty' in order to take 'acts and decisions' applicable *inter se* as an expression of their combined will to 'implement the 1989 Social Charter'.[6] The recalcitrant UK Government was prepared to consent to this arrangement on the questionable assumption that they could opt out from or block any future Commission proposals that ran counter to their own deregulatory approach to labour law. Furthermore, the SPA introduced important changes to the process of 'Social Dialogue' by granting the 'social partners', the representatives of 'management and labour', a direct say in the framing of Community social legislation. By using the ingenious device of the Protocol, and its annexed Agreement, the Eleven were able to establish, in a formal sense, a distinctive range of legal bases for the enactment of social policy legislation which went beyond the limited area of occupational health and safety permitted under the Single European Act (SEA),[7] albeit at the expense of 26 million workers based in the UK who were exempted from the Agreement's territorial effects.[8]

The SPA was originally intended as a direct substitute for Articles 117–122, the first Chapter of Title VIII of the revised EC Treaty, hence the misnomer of describing the Agreement as a 'Social Chapter'. The social policy provisions contained in Articles 117–122 were essentially programmatic in nature and placed primary responsibility for policy development at Member State level. Subsidiarity has always been axiomatic in this area of activity. Indeed, the only directly effective element in the Rome Treaty provisions, the Article 119 principle of equal pay between women and men for equal work, is a straightforward obligation on the Member States with no corresponding legislative base for Commission proposals.[9] This meant that any labour law measures not connected with Article 119 had to have a specific market approximation justification usually arising from the need to lessen the effects of economic transition by safeguarding the rights of the employees concerned, providing for consultation, or establishing a compensation fund.[10]

The SEA introduced an additional legislative route via Article 118a which allows for a diverse range of measures 'to encourage improvements, especially in the working environment, as regards the health and safety of workers'. The European Court of Justice (ECJ) has favoured a broad interpretation of 'health and safety' and the 'working environment' so as to encompass maximum working time and paid annual leave, pregnancy leave, and protection for young workers. Such measures are capable of falling within the remit of Article 118a so long as occupational health and safety is 'the principal aim of the measure in question'.[11] Thus, in the period between the SEA and the Treaty on European Union (TEU), social policy measures falling clearly outside Article 118a were caught by the double barrier of unanimity, under Articles 100 or 235, and exclusion from qualified majority voting (QMV) for internal market approximation measures, under Article 100a, of matters relating to the 'rights and interests of employed persons'.[12] After a decade of 'Thatcherism versus the social dimension',[13] the option presented at Maastricht of a twin-track approach to Community social policy appeared, despite its attendant risks, to offer a more attractive prospect than an indefinite period of stagnation.

The Agreement on Social Policy: scope and effect

Compromise at Maastricht led to the creation of two complementary but free-standing legal frames of reference for Community social policy.[14] All proposals must be introduced first as whole Community measures using the existing Treaty bases with a view to utilizing the SPA only as a fall-back device in the absence of consensus or where Article 118a is inapplicable. While such a process represents sensible politics it also serves to meet the requirement in the preamble of the Protocol for the operative elements of the SPA to be brought into effect 'without prejudice' to the provisions of the Treaty.[15] These requirements, coupled with the introduction of certain novel decision-making elements, render the SPA of interest as much for its procedural aspects as for its substantive provisions.

Article 1 of the SPA summarizes the objectives of Community social policy, in the context of the Community of Fourteen,[16] as encompassing:

> [T]he promotion of employment, improved living and working conditions, proper social protection, dialogue between management and labour, the development of human resources with a view to lasting high employment and the combating of exclusion.

Any substantive measures must take account of 'diverse forms of national practice, in particular in the field of contractual relations, and the need to maintain the competitiveness of the European economy' with Community action being supportive and complementary to the activities of Member States in the following fields enumerated in Article 2(1):

- improvement in particular of the working environment to protect workers' health and safety
- working conditions
- information and consultation of workers

- equality between men and women with regard to labour market opportunities and treatment at work
- integration of persons excluded from the labour market.

In each of these fields the Council can, without UK participation, adopt directives under QMV and the cooperation procedure with the European Parliament (EP).[17] These directives must be based on 'minimum requirements for gradual implementation, having regard to the conditions and technical rules' in each of the Member States. Such directives must avoid 'imposing administrative, financial and legal constraints in a way which would hold back the creation and development of small and medium-sized undertakings'.[18]

Article 2(3) requires unanimity among the Fourteen and permits only consultation with the EP in the following fields:

- social security and social protection of workers
- protection of workers where their employment contract is terminated
- representation and collective defence of the interests of workers and employers, including co-determination
- conditions of employment of third-country nationals legally residing in Community territory
- financial contributions for promotion of employment and job-creation.

The provisions in Articles 2(1) and 2(3) do not apply to 'pay, the right of association, the right to strike or the right to impose lock-outs'.[19] Notwithstanding the above, Member States retain the right to maintain or introduce 'more stringent protective measures' compatible with the Treaty.[20]

Article 6 contains the only other substantive provisions in the SPA, first repeating the principle in Article 119 of 'equal pay for equal work',[21] and then adding a paragraph drawn from the Equal Treatment Directives, allowing Member States to maintain or adopt measures providing for 'specific advantages in order to make it easier for women to pursue a vocational activity or to prevent or compensate for disadvantages in their professional careers'.[22] This derogation from the formal equality principle has been undermined in the equal treatment context following the ECJ's *Kalanke*[23] judgment and this has led to an amendment to the Amsterdam social policy provisions that will be discussed below.

Taken together these substantive provisions have offered the Fourteen, at the very least, scope to implement the outstanding legislative proposals under the 1989 Social Charter. At the time of the SPA's applicability, action was expected concerning outstanding proposals for the establishment of national and European works councils, rights to parental leave, and rights for atypical workers, such as temporary and fixed-term workers, homeworkers and teleworkers. In other areas, such as individual dismissals and harassment at work, progress was more likely first at national level with the prospect of Community intervention at a later date where necessary. Although Article 2(6) appears to rule out action in the areas of fair remuneration and freedom of association, aspects of two of the Community Charter's twelve fundamental social rights, these are not matters where the

Commission has ever proposed binding Community legislation.

Any assessment of the pace of social policy progress under the SPA has to take account of the procedural effects both of the need to act on a whole Community basis and, even where a decision is made to proceed under the SPA, the requirement both to consult management and labour and to allow for Community-level agreements to be reached between the social partners under Articles 3 and 4. Article 3 grants 'management and labour' a right to pre-empt all Commission proposals leading, under Article 4, to an option to conclude agreements that, if the substance relates to matters covered by Article 2, are to be adopted as Council 'decisions' on a proposal from the Commission. Article 3(4) provides for an extendible nine-month period allocated to allow the social partners to reach an agreement. The Commission may only proceed with its original proposal where the social partners decide not to exercise their right of pre-emption or if an agreement is not reached within the required time period. While this may not be a fully fledged form of European collective bargaining 'in the shadow of the law' as some have suggested,[24] it certainly represents a corporatist interface with the Community legislative process that undermines, and to an extent overtakes, the Commission's sole right of legislative initiative. Indeed it is for this very reason that the Commission has attempted to codify the process by seeking to determine the representativeness of the parties and to reserve a right to assess the extent to which the content of any agreement is consistent with Community law.[25]

In practice the 'big three' (UNICE, ETUC and CEEP)[26] have been able to take advantage of the fact that ultimately the Commission has decided that it is for the social partners to agree to negotiate with one another and determine the form of any agreement.[27] This approach has infuriated many smaller organizations, notably UEAPME, representing smaller businesses,[28] and precipitated a challenge to the legality of the Directive on Parental Leave,[29] the first measure to arise from a Framework Agreement. This Directive is no more than a legislative imprimatur of the full text of the Framework Agreement signed by the social partners. UEAPME's legal challenge pointed to the requirement in the SPA for proper consideration of the impact of any measure on small and medium-sized undertakings and this, they argued, can only be achieved through their full involvement in the process. These arguments were rejected by the Court of First Instance on the narrow grounds that no social partner has a general right to participate in these types of negotiations, whatever interest they claim to represent.[30]

There is no doubt that procedural and temporal complexities arising from the twin-stream legislative approach, coupled with the ability of the social partners to pre-empt the normal political process, have combined to decelerate the pace of progress in the arena of Community social policy. Indeed, at the time when the Amsterdam Treaty was negotiated the SPA legislative route had been successfully utilized on just two occasions.[31] In order to understand this process of deceleration it is first necessary to examine the economic and political considerations driving decision-making rather than these practical difficulties, for it has been the factors contributing to the former which have been the principal causes of legislative caution and inertia under the SPA.

Re-evaluating the European Social Model

At the Maastricht negotiations, there was an atmosphere of airy confidence about the immediate prospects for building on the 'European Social Model'. Average growth in the EC had dipped slightly from its late 1980s high of 3.3 per cent but employment was relatively buoyant and it seemed that the EC would bounce back from any looming downturn and cope fairly easily with factors such as German reunification. Five years later, the negotiations leading up to the Amsterdam Treaty were tempered by the harsh reality of growth levels down to an annual average of just 1.5 per cent and a net decline of 0.4 per cent per year in employment over the same period, a loss of 4.5 million jobs at a time when there was net employment growth in the United States and Japan.[32] Europe's slump in the world competitiveness league has been accentuated by technological and demographic changes affecting the labour market and the rising costs of social protection. Moreover, there was anxiety about the austerity measures required for compliance with the EMU convergence criteria and recognition that the Union's strategies for achieving economic and social cohesion will have to be updated to facilitate the next enlargement. Other policy dilemmas arise from uncertainties concerning the longer-term effects of globalization, the 'Millennium bug' and climate change. Against this backdrop it is hardly surprising that social policy priorities have been fundamentally reassessed, leading to a decisive shift away from the objectives of comprehensive social protection and security in employment and towards the creation of a more flexible modernized labour market intended to be globally competitive and capable of creating employment opportunities for all, including the socially excluded.

This change of direction was signposted in the Commission's 1993 White Paper on 'Growth, Competitiveness and Employment'.[33] The new approach is encapsulated in the Commission's call for '... a thoroughgoing reform of the labour market, with the introduction of greater flexibility in the organization of work and the distribution of working time, reduced labour costs, a higher level of skills and pro-active labour policies'.[34]

At first glance this appears to be a *volte-face* and, ironically, an acceptance of the very Thatcherite ideology that the SPA was designed to circumvent. But, upon reflection, is there compatibility between the agenda of 'labour market flexibility' and the notion of a 'European Social Model' based on shared values of 'negotiation, solidarity and a high level of social protection'?[35] Put more succinctly, is the Community's dual task of attaining a 'high level of employment *and* social protection' achievable?[36] Those who claim that higher labour standards bring about socio-economic benefits through improved productivity, and are therefore an integral part of the competitive economic model, are pitted against the advocates of a deregulated labour market who advocate reducing the costs of production on the basis that the Community's social costs have become unaffordable and are destroying jobs.[37]

For much of the post-Maastricht period the Community has been seeking to find a 'third way' involving intensive but consensual 'social partnership' and adherence to a set of common minimum standards, on the basis that competitiveness and social progress represent 'two sides of the same coin'.[38] This has allowed those engaged in Community social policy to make a case for a limited further extension of employment protection and employee participation initiatives alongside a measure of reorganization of work based on the need to improve employment and competitiveness. Running parallel with this debate has been a more radical agenda for establishing a collection of fundamental civic and social rights to replace the Social Charter with a more societal approach to work. This period of introspection has replaced legislative action with social reflection in the form of, *inter alia*, Green Papers on Social Policy[39] and Work Organization,[40] a White Paper on Social Policy[41] – all promulgated by DGV of the Commission – and a report by a *Comité des Sages* appointed by the Commission to advise it on future social rights.[42]

Published in 1993, the Green Paper on Social Policy, 'Options for the Union', sought 'to stimulate a wide-ranging and intensive debate within all Member States about social policy in the European Union'. The Commission identified three main factors for discussion. First, the 1989 Action Programme was virtually exhausted, with 47 proposals presented and the majority adopted. Second, the SPA opened up new opportunities for Community action in the social field by giving a stronger role to the social partners. Third, the changing socio-economic situation resulting from higher levels of unemployment required a new look at the link between economic and social policies at national and Community level.[43] The extent to which this third factor was to become the driving force of social policy was already apparent. The Commission added one caveat: 'the premise at the heart of this Green Paper is that the next phase in the development of European social policy cannot be based on the idea that social progress must go into retreat in order for economic competitiveness to recover'.[44]

Faced with economic adversity, a bold approach was needed, based on a notion of social inclusiveness which was to be pursued through a shift in the bias of social policy away from those in full-time paid employment and towards those who were marginalized from the workplace through social exclusion arising from such factors as low skills, poor education, disability, racism and xenophobia, homelessness and urban decay.[45] An embryonic Community employment policy was emerging, arising in part from the redesignation of the European Social Fund and vocational training policies in the amended EC Treaty,[46] and focusing in particular on the needs of young people and the long-term unemployed in the less-developed and declining regions of the Union. In this way an indivisible link was being forged between the strands of social and employment policies and the broader goals of economic and social cohesion.[47]

The Community's priorities oscillated further with the appearance in 1994 of a White Paper on Social Policy. This document, heavily influenced by the Growth White Paper, marked a decisive turn in policy and has served as a *leitmotif* for subsequent developments. In the Growth White Paper, the Commission had boldly begun with the clarion cry that the 'one and only reason' for publication 'is unemployment', before limply confiding that the 'difficult thing, as experience has taught us, is knowing how to tackle it'.[48] The Growth White Paper offered few positive answers. There was no miracle cure for unemployment and any attempt to drastically cut wages would not only depress demand but would also be 'socially unacceptable and politically untenable'. Instead, the themes of increasing competitiveness through skills and training, improved education, and investment in infrastructural improvements and research and technological development were identified as the main priorities. In this context 'social activism' no longer meant Community legislation to protect labour standards but instead involved a programmatic approach requiring action, primarily at Member State level, to integrate social policies with these wider competitiveness themes. Thus, while the Green Paper had recommended 'exploiting to the full'[49] the legislative opportunities offered by the SPA, the White Paper concluded that there was 'not a need for a wide-ranging programme of new legislative proposals in the coming period' because a 'solid base' of European social legislation had already been achieved.[50] Instead, there was to be a period of consolidation based on completing the existing social action programme, updating Community legislation and concentrating on enforcement, while directing all of the Community's spare energy towards active labour market policies capable of generating employment intensive growth.

Three of the potential areas for Community legislative intervention pinpointed in the White Paper – European works councils, parental leave and rights for part-time workers – have been followed up with Directives and Framework Agreements under the SPA.[51] A fourth priority, for a directive on the posting of workers temporarily in another Member State, has been followed up with a free movement of services measure under Article 57(2) EC.[52] Each of these legislative steps has met the requirements of labour market flexibility while providing a modicum of procedural rights or employment protection in specific circumstances. Thus, the Directive on European Works Councils is principally intended as a device to enable 'economic activities to develop in a harmonious fashion' in the internal market.[53] The Posted Workers Directive is as much about fair competition as respect for the rights of workers.[54] Although the two measures arising from Framework Agreements, on Parental Leave and Part-time Work, are derived from employment protection considerations in the Social Charter, they have, to an extent, been subverted by the 1990s labour market agenda. In the case of the Parental Leave Framework Agreement, the driving motivation is to allow for an easier return to working life, flexible organization of work and time, and for men and women to reconcile their occupational and family obligations.[55] The Framework Agreement on Part-time Workers is even more explicit, relying directly on the conclusions of the 1994 Essen European Council, which called for measures aimed at 'increasing the employment intensiveness of growth, in particular by more flexible organization of work'.[56]

Conversely, there were several other areas identified in the White Paper where legislation, although covered by the legal bases in the SPA, was not proposed and has not progressed despite the launch of a limited 'Medium Term Social Action Programme' in April 1995.[57] Instead, the Commission suggested debate and detailed studies in such areas as protection against individual dismissal, rights of privacy for workers, rights to payment of wages on public holidays and during illness, and prohibiting discrimination against 'whistle-blowers' who uphold their rights or refuse to perform unlawful tasks.[58] Significantly, in each of these areas, there has been no discernible sign of progress because neither the Commission nor the social partners have been able to construct a rationale for action based on flexible labour markets and competitiveness. The question has been left tantalizingly open by the White Paper, which notes that:

> With the completion of the existing social action programme, a substantial base of labour standards has been consolidated in European law. The question of where to go from there is complex and controversial because the issue of labour standards is at the heart of the debate about the relationship between competitiveness, growth and job creation ...
>
> It must be said that there is no clear consensus on this point and that Member States and others remain divided in their opinions about the need for further legislative action on labour standards at European Level.[59]

This statement crystallizes the dilemma facing the Community's social policy actors. The adoption of the Amsterdam Treaty and the election of a Labour government in the UK have created a veneer of consensus, but underneath the real debate about what is meant by 'flexibility' and 'employability' in the labour market and at the workplace is just beginning. Significantly, the areas where further Community legislation is likely in the short term, such as directives on other aspects of atypical employment and measures to extend the scope of equal treatment in employment, are precisely those that fit most easily within the flexible work organization and equal opportunities rubric. Proposals based primarily on 'labour standards' show little sign of consensual resolution.

In searching for a 'third way' and a coherent response to the flexibility debate, the Commission has developed its ideas in a Green Paper on partnership for a new organization of work published in April 1997.[60] By seeking to reaffirm the goal of higher labour standards whilst promoting the desirability of a more flexible organization of work the Commission hopes to switch the focus of debate. In the introduction to the Green Paper the Commission notes that:

> [W]hile much has been written about the need for flexibility of the labour market and its regulation, much less has been said about the need for flexibility *and* security in the organization of work at the workplace ...
>
> An improved organization of work will not, in itself, solve the unemployment problem, but it can make a valuable contribution, firstly, to the competitiveness of European firms, and secondly, to the improvement of the quality of working life and the employability of the workforce.[61]

Viewed from this perspective, a strong case can be made for increasing the job security of those in work, whether or not they are in permanent full-time work, and for adapting working hours and other aspects of the organization of work. Such arrangements, allied with improvements in training and greater employee participation, are a feature of many successful 'flexible firms' and meet the requirements of employers for a reliable workforce with interchangeable skills and adaptable work patterns capable of coping with fluctuations in demands for their goods and services. In return it is hoped that employees will have greater job satisfaction, higher skills and long-term employability.[62] Security is no longer possible without flexibility. Therefore the *quid pro quo* for greater security, the Commission implies, is a review of the basic foundations of systems of labour law, industrial relations, wage regulation and social security.[63] Whilst not making any concrete proposals, the Commission has at least pointed to some of the rigidities of the labour market that are a feature of the systems in many Member States and has paid regard to the importance to welfare provision of ongoing reforms that are provoking such disquiet throughout the Community. By raising these issues now, however difficult they may be to develop politically both at national and Community level, the Commission hoped that during the consultation process and beyond a measure of consensus can be reached and progress will be made.

This debate over flexibility in labour markets and work organization has been the dominant feature of post-Maastricht social policy discourse and there are few signs that it will abate. Throughout this period, however, an undercurrent of debate has been taking place concerning the importance of building fundamental social rights, or social citizenship, as an alternative rights-based model serving to constitutionalize social rights and duties within the EU. In essence it is argued that social citizenship rights should evolve as free-standing rights that are not dependent solely on the goals of economic integration but instead represent a direct link between the citizens of the Member States and the Union.[64] As long ago as 1987 the Economic and Social Committee had recognized the significance of such an approach in an Opinion on the Social Aspects of the Internal Market where it is stated that: 'adoption of Community legislation guaranteeing basic social rights immune to competitive pressures is therefore a key stage in the creation of the single market'.[65]

In the lead-up to the Amsterdam IGC there were many voices amongst academics and from within the Community institutions and lobby groups, notably in the EP and from the ETUC,[66] arguing the case for developing the citizenship concept introduced at Maastricht by incorporating fundamental social rights into any new Social Chapter of the revised EC Treaty or as a separate binding instrument in the form of a 'Bill of Rights'.

The starting point for any discussion about fundamental social rights is the 'Social Charter', the most influential social policy document throughout the 1990s. By 1995 it was widely recognized that the Charter needed revision to take account of the TEU and the emergence of the citizenship concept. The *Comité des Sages* appointed by the Commission issued a report in March 1996 entitled 'For a Europe of Civic and Social Rights' at a meeting of the European Social Policy Forum.[67] The *Comité* took the view that social rights and civic rights were indivisible and a set of core rights should be included in the EC Treaty as a first step. These should include the prohibition of all forms of discrimination, equality between men and women, equality before the law and free movement within the Union. An additional general series of rights should be included in a further revision of the Treaties after a period of consultation and debate. Within this enumerated list the *Comité* suggests, *inter alia*, the right to education, work, social security and protection of the family, housing and a minimum income. It proposes that fundamental civic and social rights should add to rather then replace Community social policy and concludes that:

> Europe must innovate in the social field, it will succeed in postulating an attractive social model only if it takes account of the new competitiveness constraints arising from globalization, demographic and social developments, and of fundamental human needs.[68]

In support of this approach, commentators have pointed to the importance of social rights in the constitutions of Member States, the core Conventions of the International Labour Organization, the commitments made in the European Social Charter of the Council of Europe of 1961, and in the Community's own 'Social Charter'.[69] While there are some differences of approach as to the extent to which any catalogue of rights or international instruments should be legally binding or directly effective under an amended EC Treaty, it is widely accepted that Article F.2 of the TEU, respecting fundamental rights at a Union level, falls outside the jurisdiction of the ECJ.[70] The challenge for the Union's political leaders at Amsterdam was how, if at all, to develop their collective adherence to fundamental rights, including social rights, beyond the stage of well-meaning but ultimately vacuous declarations.[71]

Amsterdam: re-unifying social policy?

At Amsterdam the EU's political leaders went further than many expected in both incorporating the SPA within the EC Treaty and developing the scope of the principle of non-discrimination. Furthermore, fundamental social rights are to be taken into account when developing Community social policy, although there will be no 'Bill of Rights' in the form suggested by the *Comité des Sages*. Perhaps the greatest import lies, however, with the new Employment Title and the wider labour market agenda developed at the Employment Summit held in Luxembourg in November 1997.

1. Articles 136–145 [ex Articles 117–122] – social policy

The immediate legal effects of the new 'Social Chapter', Articles 136–145 in the amended EC Treaty,[72] to abolish the Social Protocol allowing for the United Kingdom's 'opt-out' and to incorporate a revised form of the SPA as a direct substitution for the social provisions in Articles 117–122 EC. The Amsterdam Presidency Conclusions stated that the UK had agreed to implement the SPA directives before entry into force of the Amsterdam Treaty and that a means would have to be found to give legal effect to their wishes. In a remarkable throwback to the 1970s, the Council has used Article 100 as the legal base for adopting new Directives on European Works Councils, parental leave, part-time work and the burden of proof in sex discrimination cases.[73] With the return of consensus the choice of legal base is unproblematic on the whole, although once the Treaty is ratified Articles 136–145 must be used for measures where the principal aim is social policy within the scope of those provisions.[74] These Article 100 directives do not alter the substance of the existing directives but there will be some consequential transitional measures required in certain Member States and the UK has been allowed a two-year implementation period. In return, the UK was given permission to chair the Social Affairs Council during its Presidency in the first half of 1998 and to have its views taken into account during any discussions on SPA legislative proposals.

In substantive terms, Article 136 contains two important changes to the preamble of the SPA and Article 1 thereof. First, the express commitment to 'implement the 1989 Social Charter' is removed and replaced by a preface to the objectives of the new social provisions whereby the Community and Member States, 'having in mind fundamental social rights such as those set out in the European Social Charter and in the … Community Charter', shall implement measures which, as with the SPA, shall take account of the diversity of national practice and competitiveness. This nuanced adjustment frees the present-day leaders of the Community from any commitment to fulfil the remainder of an inherited agenda from the 1980s that would now be regarded as too regulatory. In the context of areas such as pay and freedom of association, Article 137(6), replacing Article 2(6) of the SPA, confirms that these matters are outside the scope of action under the social provisions. Although the European Social Charter and the constitutions of Member States are, in certain respects, even wider than the Community Charter, EC institutions will only have to take them into consideration in the context of broad objectives such as social protection and the promotion of employment. Reference in the social provisions to the term 'fundamental social rights' does, however, create the potential for development of this concept by the ECJ as part of the general principles of law enunciated in a succession of leading cases including *ERT* [75] where the Court declared that:

> Fundamental rights form an integral part of the general principles of law observance of
> which is ensured by the Court. For this purpose the Court proceeds from the
> constitutional principles common to the Member States and from pointers in international
> instruments concerning the protection of human rights in which the Member States have
> co-operated or to which they have adhered … Measures incompatible with the protection
> of fundamental rights thus recognized and safeguarded cannot be accepted in the
> Community.

The ECJ has accorded itself the role of constitutional guardian of the fundamental rights of Union citizens and the explicit reference to fundamental *social* rights in Article 136 will add force to this judge-made general principle of law by serving as a supplemental means of Treaty interpretation similar in effect to the foundation of the principles of non-discrimination and equality, drawn from Articles 6 and 119 EC. While this will not allow an individual to rely on 'fundamental social rights' in a directly effective sense, it will form a basis for the Court to strike down any measure or activity which amounts to an arbitrary violation of clearly understood and accepted social rights. This may be used to delimit or prohibit any future attempts to deregulate Community social laws.

The second important change in Article 136 removes the direct link between the objective of 'improving living and working conditions' and the possibility of 'harmonization while the improvement is being maintained'. Although the final paragraph states that the development of the common market will 'favour the harmonization of social systems', retaining the language of Article 117 EC, this amendment does more than merely tidy up the myriad social provisions.[76] It removes the very explicit link between improved labour standards and legislative harmonization which has previously guided attempts to build up and develop directives in these areas. In practice the approach of legislating as a last resort, derived from the White Papers, is being further underlined.

Article 137 appears to replicate Article 2 of the SPA by dividing the scope of supplementary and complementary Community directives into two spheres subject to either QMV or unanimity. However, there is a significant operative change. While the legal bases subject to the unanimity rule in Article 137(2) will continue to involve only consultation with the EP, proposals in those areas listed in Article 137(1) will be subject to the co-decision procedure. As the EP has been the strongest institutional advocate of Community social policy and the strengthening of equalities laws, this is likely to act as a spur for policy development and as a further brake on deregulation. A serious drafting problem also arises from this change and renders uncertain the Parliament's role in the legislative process where there is a Framework Agreement between the social partners. Articles 138 and 139 restate Articles 3 and 4 of the SPA *in toto*. Article 139(2) refers to implementation of any agreement concerning matters in Article 137 – including those areas covered by co-decision – as being subject to 'a Council decision on a proposal from the Commission'. This raises the prospect of the EP being unable to block or amend the substance of any directive arising from a Framework Agreement and, should such an interpretation be followed, may lead to an action for annulment to test the compatibility of these Treaty provisions. The simple restatement of the provisions concerning the social partners also leaves unresolved any problems arising from the uncertain and rather exclusive approach taken by the Commission to the question of who are 'management and labour' at Community level? Moreover, the Court of First Instance's 'hands off' approach in the *UEAPME* case indicates a disturbing tolerance of both a democratic and an accountability deficit in this area.[77]

Article 137(6), by merely restating the exclusion of such matters as pay, the right of association and the right to strike from legislation under the social provisions, appears to preclude the possibility of action in these areas as a Community of Fifteen. However, legislation may be permitted if its principal aim is the establishment and functioning of the common market under Article 94 [ex Article 100] EC.[78] For example, once EMU is fully operational, there would be a powerful economic case for harmonizing national laws on minimum wages.

Article 141 replaces both Article 119 EC and Article 6 of the SPA, considerably strengthening the sex equality provisions. Article 141(1), on the principle of equal pay, adds to these provisions by defining the principle as 'equal pay for equal work *or work of equal value*'.[79] This welcome addition of the equal value concept reinforces the existing position of the ECJ which regards the equivalent provisions in the Equal Pay Directive as implicitly part of Article 119 and therefore of direct effect both vertically and horizontally.[80] Article 141(3) adds a completely new legal base, independent of the listing in Article 137 and therefore explicitly outside the remit of the social partners, for:

> Measures to ensure the application of the principle of equal opportunities and equal treatment of men and women in matters of employment and occupation, including the principle of equal pay for equal work or work of equal value.

Article 141(3) provides for QMV and co-decision and it has the potential to encompass matters such as sexual harassment at the workplace, a subject of considerable disagreement when the current Equal Opportunities Action Programme was drawn up.[81] Article 141(4) replaces Article 6(3) of the SPA with the following:

> With a view to ensuring full equality in practice between men and women in working life, the principle of equal treatment shall not prevent any Member State from maintaining or adopting measures providing for specific advantages in order to make it easier for the under-represented sex to pursue a vocational activity or to prevent or compensate for disadvantages in professional careers.

This amendment is remarkable because by referring to the goal of 'full equality in practice' it extends the Community's area of concern beyond the notion of *formal equality*, comprising equal opportunity and equal access, and embraces the philosophy of *substantive equality* whereby a remedy is sought to redress the structural advantages which are perpetuated by unequal outcomes.[82] The immediate purpose of Article 141(4) is to mitigate the effects of the Court's judgment in *Kalanke*[83] where quota systems favouring women were outlawed in the German public service on the grounds that they violated the overriding principle of equal treatment. In the longer term this provision may have a wider impact upon the approach of the Community to the concept of equality. The first signs are already apparent with the clarification of *Kalanke* in the *Marschall*[84] case where the Court took account of substantive equality considerations, relying on a 1984 Council Recommendation on positive action for women,[85] and approved positive measures providing they contain a saving clause allowing individual circumstances to be considered. While Article 141(4) was not applicable in *Marschall* it may well have had a subliminal influence on the Court's decision not to follow the Advocate General's advice in his pre-Amsterdam Opinion.

2. Article 13 – non-discrimination

Developments in the equalities field, narrowly confined to sex equality in the social provisions, may be furthered by the insertion of a new Article 13 forming part of the general principles of the Community.[86] This clause, building on the well-established principle of non-discrimination on the grounds of nationality,[87] states that:

Without prejudice to the other provisions of this Treaty and within the limits of the powers conferred upon it by the Community, the Council, acting unanimously on a proposal from the Commission and after consulting the European Parliament, *may take appropriate action* to combat discrimination based on sex, racial or ethnic origin, religion or belief, disability, age or sexual orientation.[88]

Simultaneously, the Member States have widened considerably their legal competence to act against discrimination while accepting no obligation to legislate and conferring no direct rights upon individuals. Some additional assistance is offered by a separate declaration on disability stating that the institutions of the Community, when drawing up internal market measures, 'shall take account of the needs of persons with disability'. The absence of any duty to bring forward proposals in these areas and the unanimity requirement are disappointing but the significance of Article 13 should not be understated. In equalities terms it represents a quantum leap because it not only broadens and helps to define the scope of what the Community means by non-discrimination but also, as part of an established general principle of law, it will influence the ECJ's approach when interpreting all Community measures and actions. Furthermore, by including areas such as sexual orientation, age, disability and belief, as well as religion within its remit, Article 13 is wider than similar provisions in the constitutions of several Member States and, while the unanimity obstacle is formidable, the experience of the 1970s, when Article 235 was used for directives on equal treatment between women and men,[89] demonstrates that progress can be made where the political will exists. An early test will come if, and when, the Commission follows through its commitment in the 1998–2000 Social Action Programme to propose a directive to combat race discrimination.[90]

3. Articles 125–130 – employment

Title VIII on Employment, Articles 125–130,[91] will give legal effect and momentum to the ongoing political process stemming from the adoption at Essen in December 1994 of priorities for job creation and the launch at Florence in June 1996 of a 'Confidence Pact' for employment. Moreover, coordination of employment policies has been added to the Community's tasks in Article 3 alongside the objective of achieving and maintaining a 'high level of employment' in Article 2. The employment provisions must be viewed together with two European Council Resolutions, firstly, on stability and growth, the so-called Stability Pact, and, secondly, on growth and employment. A further statement in the Presidency Conclusions concerns 'Employment, Competitiveness and Growth'. Most significantly, the Employment Title has been given 'immediate effect' by the political decisions taken at the 'Jobs Summit' held in Luxembourg in November 1997.[92]

At the core of the Employment Title is a renewed commitment to the elusive objective of a coordinated employment strategy among the Member States who, by virtue of Article 126(2), 'shall regard promoting employment as a matter of common concern'. The Community's task, under Article 127(1), shall be to 'contribute to a high level of employment' by complementing action at national level. Article 127(2) provides that the objective of a high level of employment shall be taken into consideration in the formulation and implementation of all Community policies and activities.

Article 126(1) requires that employment and labour market policies shall be consistent with the broad economic guidelines adopted by the Community. In Articles 128(2)–(5) it is to be made clear that these economic guidelines will be supplemented by new employment guidelines to be implemented by Member States and monitored by the Council and Commission jointly. Article 130 provides that coordination and formulation of opinions shall be undertaken by a newly established Employment Committee with advisory status which must consult management and labour and have representation from the Member States and the Commission. Finally, the only specific legal base can be found in Article 129 whereby incentive measures, not involving harmonization, may be adopted by co-decision in order to support employment initiatives.

The Employment Title sends mixed messages. Most importantly, by making employment policy a 'matter of common concern' the Community is seeking to avoid, so far as is possible, unfair competition arising from subsidies and 'social dumping'. By linking high levels of employment and social protection with competitiveness, the Community is rejecting a simplistic deregulatory approach and adhering to the case for high skills, training, and above all, security and flexibility in work, as the key to a coordinated employment strategy. Governments and, if necessary, the Structural Funds and the European Investment Bank, will provide incentives for employers and the public sector will also have an important role. Such an interpretation has to be read into the Employment Title and it is noticeable that the most powerful declaratory commitments are made in the accompanying 'soft law' resolutions and Presidency Conclusions. This is made abundantly clear in the Presidency Conclusions where, expanding upon the Treaty coda of 'a high level of employment', it is stated that the ultimate goal remains 'full employment' and the Employment Title should be made immediately effective because:

> The European Council attaches paramount importance to creating conditions in the Member States that would promote a skilled and adaptable workforce and flexible labour markets responsive to economic change. This requires active intervention by the Member States in the labour market to help people develop their employability. *Such action is important if the European Union is to remain globally competitive, and in order to tackle the scourge of unemployment.*[93]

This surprisingly *dirigiste* statement represents the Community's most explicit rejection yet of the Thatcherite agenda of high unemployment 'as a price worth paying' for economic competitiveness. Moreover, the Resolution on 'Growth and Employment' seeks to utilize the 'possibilities offered to the social partners by the Social Chapter … to underpin the Council's work on unemployment'.[94] The Social Chapter and the Employment Title are regarded as mutually compatible tools for promoting employment goals. Notwithstanding these bold declarations, several vital questions remain to be answered. How effective in practice will be the

Community's attempts to monitor and enforce these commitments in the absence of any direct sanctions on a par with those operating in the framework of EMU? Is it possible to reconcile economic and employment guidelines issued separately? In the absence of any significant new Community resources, are any targets set achievable? Is there not a danger of increasing the degree of divergence in levels of labour market participation between Member States?

The answers to many of these questions remain open, but an indication of the way ahead can be found in the Presidency Conclusions and the accompanying 1998 Employment Guidelines issued at the Luxembourg 'Jobs Summit'. While broadly endorsing the Commission's draft proposals,[95] the European Council eschews the Commission's suggestion of a 70 per cent long-term target in line with Europe's global competitors. Nor is there any mention of the Commission's five-year target employment rate of 65 per cent, up from the current level of 60.4 per cent, involving the creation of at least twelve million new jobs. Instead, the European Council proposes only to 'arrive at a significant increase in the employment rate in Europe on a lasting basis'.[96] To achieve this objective, the 1998 Employment Guidelines will centre on four main lines of Member State action to promote entrepreneurship, employability, adaptability and equal opportunities.[97] The European Council urges Member States to make structural reforms, including restructuring of expenditure and reductions in the overall tax burden 'without jeopardizing the recovery of public finances',[98] while there is a 'window of opportunity' offered by improved growth. The essential elements of the Green Paper on work organization are also endorsed.[99] At Community level there will be an additional 450 million ECU over three years for a 'European employment initiative' to help small and medium-sized enterprises create sustainable jobs and an Action Plan for the European Investment Bank to 'find' up to an extra ten billion ECU in loans for 'small and medium-sized enterprises, new technology, new sectors and trans-European networks' aimed at expanding employment.[100] These initial guidelines, perhaps necessarily broad and non-specific, must respect the principle of subsidiarity and be compatible with the broad economic policy guidelines.[101] The European Council seeks to explain the relationship between the two sets of guidelines as follows:

> *The idea is*, while respecting the differences between the two areas and between the situations of individual Member States, *to create for employment, as for economic policy, the same resolve to converge* towards jointly set, verifiable, regularly updated targets.[102]

In fact there is a remarkable alignment between the two sets of guidelines. The 1997 Economic Guidelines point to, *inter alia*, higher employment growth fostered by the maintenance of appropriate wage trends, reductions in non-labour costs, reform of taxation and social protection systems, new patterns of work organization and adaptation of the whole educational system to increase employability. This level of congruity between the respective guidelines suggests that, despite the vagueness of the overall employment target, the existence of the Employment Title and the Employment Guidelines should serve to enhance the status of the Community's employment and social policies.

Social policy after Amsterdam: a paradoxical outcome?

In the Commission's Work Programme for 1998, just one social policy directive was proposed and this measure, to extend the Working Time Directive to sectors previously excluded from its provisions, was provided for in the Directive itself.[103] While this legislative vacuum might be attributed partly to the hiatus arising from the Treaty ratification process, the main reason lies with the absence of an institutional dynamic for a substantive action programme to drive forward social policy. Rather, policy will develop piecemeal, starting perhaps with measures concerning atypical workers not covered by the Directive on Part-time Workers. Paradoxically, just as the UK has returned to the fold and the potential exists for a wide-ranging programme, the process of social legislation has dried up and the only measures being considered are those connected with work organization and flexible labour markets. Social policy is being subsumed by the competitiveness agenda and the demands of globalization, with each proposed measure having to pass a competitiveness test. Moreover, there is little prospect of developing free-standing fundamental social rights at Community level along the lines advocated by the *Comité des Sages* and others. The statement in the Social Policy White Paper referring to the lack of consensus over the issue of labour standards is just as valid today.[104]

Consideration of the social policy provisions in isolation, however, paints a misleading picture. After Amsterdam the dynamic of social policy increasingly lies with the Employment Title and the enhanced status of employment policies in the Community's activities. An employment strategy based on high or full employment has the capacity to develop macro-economic policies to boost growth, employment, competitiveness and labour standards. As the Union enters a period of stronger growth, with inflation holding steady and unemployment declining,[105] a favourable climate now exists for policies to be developed, principally at Member State level, both to create employment and to boost labour standards. A balanced approach to employment security and labour market flexibility, coupled with a degree of consensus between the social partners, can facilitate progress through reductions in working time, improved leave arrangements, more effective health and safety measures and strengthened equal opportunities. Seen in this context, the absence of a programme of social policy legislation is not problematic so long as the Social Chapter can be activated as both a facilitator for change and as a back-up to Member States' own efforts. The 'third way' offered by the Commission in its Green Paper on work organization has the potential to succeed so long as there is social harmony and steady growth.

The real test will come when the Community faces another recession. In these circumstances the institutional power and monetary dictates of the European Central Bank, backed up by firm Treaty powers, will become far more significant than any platitudinous statements from the Employment Committee or other institutional actors concerned with employment policy. In the absence of 'verifiable' employment targets and significant extra Community resources will the 'same resolve to converge' the Community's macro-economic and employment objectives be sustainable? Moreover, if there is a shift in the bias of employment policy away from social protection, will the Social Chapter operate as a safety valve to protect labour standards? Therein will lie the ultimate explanation of the paradox of the Community's 'Social Dimension'.

Endnotes

1. See respectively, Commission Recommendation 92/131/EEC of 27 November 1991, OJ L49, 24 February 1992 and COM (93) 388 final of 1 September 1993. On soft law in the social policy context, see J. Kenner, 'EC Labour Law: The Softly, Softly Approach', *International Journal of Comparative Labour Law and Industrial Relations*, Vol. 11, 1995, pp. 307–26.
2. Council Directive 93/104/EC of 23 November 1993, OJ L307, 13 December 1993 and Council Directive 94/33/EC of 22 June 1994, OJ L 216, 20 August 1994.
3. Commission White Paper, *European Social Policy – A Way Forward for the Union*, COM (94) 333 of 27 July 1994, Introduction, para. 18. This is reinforced by Amsterdam Treaty Article 136 [ex Article 117] EC where it is stated that all measures must 'take account of the diverse form of national practices, in particular in the field of contractual relations'.
4. Bulletin of the EC Supplement 2/74.
5. The Community Charter of the Fundamental Social Rights of Workers adopted as a 'Solemn Declaration' by all Member States, except the UK, at the Strasbourg European Council, December 1989.
6. Article 1 of the Fourteenth Protocol on Social Policy and the preamble to the Agreement on Social Policy, both annexed to the EC Treaty, as amended by the TEU.
7. Article 118a EC.
8. European Commission, *Employment in Europe*, COM (94) 381 of 14 September 1994, p. 184.
9. Article 235 had to be relied upon as the basis for a series of directives on equal treatment for women and men. For example, equal treatment in employment, Directive 76/207/EEC of 9 February 1976, OJ L 39, 14 February 1976 and social security, Directive 79/7/EEC of 19 December 1978, OJ L6, 10 January 1979.
10. Under Article 100 EC. See respectively, Directive 77/187/EEC on transfers of undertakings of 14 February 1977, OJ L61, 5 March 1977, Directive 75/129/EEC on collective redundancies of 17 February 1975, OJ L48, 22 February 1975, and Directive 80/987/EEC on employer insolvency of 20 October 1980, OJ L283, 20 October 1980.
11. The importance of the 'principal aim' of any proposed measure was made clear by the Court in Case C–84/94, *United Kingdom* v. *Council* [1996] ECR I–5755, paras. 20 and 22. See the note by J. Kenner, *European Law Review*, Vol. 22, 1997, p. 580.
12. Article 100a(2)EC.
13. B. Hepple, 'Social Rights in the European Economic Community: A British Perspective', *Comparative Labour Law Journal*, Vol. 11, 1990, p. 425.
14. See the Commission's Communication concerning the application of the Agreement on Social Policy, COM (93) 600 final of 14 December 1995.
15. When the TEU was signed, there was some doubt as to the legality of the SPA. Although the ECJ has not been required to consider this question there is a broad consensus in favour of its legality derived from Article 239 EC which states that Protocols annexed to the Treaty by 'common accord of the Member States shall form an integral part thereof'. The SPA is an annex of the Protocol and is not excisable from it. The SPA is founded upon the *acquis* although it allows a temporary derogation. Ultimately it will assist the process of integration. See P. Watson, 'Social Policy After Maastricht', *Common Market Law Review*, Vol. 30, 1993, pp. 489–94; B. Bercusson, 'The Dynamic of European Labour Law After Maastricht', *Industrial Law Journal*, Vol. 23, 1994, pp. 6–7; P. Fitzpatrick, 'Community Social Law After Maastricht', *Industrial Law Journal*, Vol. 21, 1992, p. 203.
16. Austria, Finland and Sweden joined the 11 other signatories on accession to full EU membership on 1 January 1995. They had already been committed to its provisions by virtue of their membership of the European Economic Area established in 1993.
17. Article 189c EC. The QMV required has to be numerically adjusted to take account of the exclusion of the UK, but there is no impact on voting procedures in the EP where UK MEPs are

unaffected by the opt out. This creates a rather bizarre reverse form of 'democratic deficit' whereby these MEPs have a say over matters that will have no direct application in their constituencies.

18. Article 2(2).
19. Article 2(6).
20. Article 2(5).
21. Article 6(1) and (2).
22. Article 6(3). See Article 2(4) of Directive 76/207/EEC of 9 February 1976, OJ L39, 14 February 1976.
23. Case 450/93, *Kalanke* v. *Freie Hansestadt Bremen* [1995] IRLR 660.
24. Bercusson, 'The Dynamic of European Labour Law after Maastricht', pp. 13–18, 37–9 and 40–3.
25. Commission Communication concerning the application of the Agreement on Social Policy, COM(93) 600 final of 1 December 1993.
26. Respectively, the Union of Industrial and Employers' Confederations of Europe; the European Trades Union Confederation; and the European Centre of Enterprises and Public Participation.
27. COM(93) 600, para. 31.
28. European Association of Craft, Small and Medium–Sized Enterprises.
29. Directive 96/34/EC of 3 June 1996, OJ L145, 19 June 1996. The Framework Agreement was concluded between UNICE, ETUC and CEEP on 14 December 1995.
30. Case T–135/96, *UEAPME* v. *Council* [1998] ECR, judgment of 17 June 1998.
31. Directive 96/34/EC on Parental Leave, see n.29, and Directive 94/45/EC of 22 September 1994 on European Works Councils, OJ L254, 30 September 1994.
32. Annual Economic Report for 1997, *European Economy* No. 63, Luxembourg: OOPEC, 1997, p. 13.
33. *Growth, Competitiveness, Employment – The Challenges and Ways Forward into the 21st Century*, Bulletin of the EC Supplement 6/93.
34. *Growth, Competitiveness, Employment*, Ch. 8, p. 124.
35. See the Commission's White Paper, *European Social Policy – A Way Forward for the Union*, COM(94) 333 final of 27 July 1994, Annex, Ch.1, para.12.
36. Article 2 EC. My emphasis.
37. See S. Deakin and F. Wilkinson, 'Rights vs Efficiency? The Economic Case for Transnational Labour Standards', *Industrial Law Journal*, Vol. 23, 1994, pp. 289–310.
38. White Paper on Social Policy, COM(94) 333, Introduction, para. 17.
39. COM(93) 551 final of 17 December 1993.
40. *Partnership for a New Organization of Work*, Bulletin of the EU Supplement 4/97.
41. COM(94) 333 of 27 July 1994.
42. *Working on European Social Policy – A Report on the Forum*, Luxembourg: OOPEC, 1996.
43. J. Kenner, 'European Social Policy – New Directions', *International Journal of Comparative Labour Law and Industrial Relations*, Vol. 10, 1994, pp. 56–63.
44. Green Paper, p. 7.
45. Council Resolution on Social Exclusion, OJ C277, 31 October 1989; Commission's Communication 'Towards a Europe of Solidarity: Intensifying the fight against social exclusion fostering integration', COM(92) 542 final of 23 December 1992.
46. Articles 123–127 EC.
47. See Article 130a EC.
48. *Growth, Competitiveness, Employment*, p. 9.
49. Green Paper, p. 69.
50. White Paper on Social Policy, Introduction, para. 22.
51. Following the Commission's proposal for a Directive on Part–time Work, COM(97) 392 final of 23 July 1997, the Council unanimously adopted a Directive based on the text of a Framework Agreement between the social partners; Council Directive 97/81/EC of 15 December 1997, OJ L14 of 20 January 1998.
52. European Parliament and Council Directive 96/71/EC of 16 December 1996, OJ L18 of 21 January 1997. See also, P. Davies, 'Posted Workers: Single Market or Protection of National Labour Law Systems?', *Common Market Law Review*, Vol. 34, 1997, p. 571–602.
53. Directive 94/45/EC, see n. 31, ninth recital of the preamble.
54. N. 52, fifth recital of the preamble.
55. N. 31, paras 3–6 in the general considerations set out in the preamble of the Framework Agreement.
56. N. 51, para. 4 in the general considerations set out in the preamble of the Framework Agreement.
57. COM(95) 134 final of 12 April 1995.
58. White Paper, Ch. III, paras. 13–14.
59. White Paper, Ch. III, paras. 10–12.

60. Bulletin of the EU Supplement 4/97.
61. Bulletin of the EU Supplement 4/97, paras. 3–4. My emphasis.
62. Bulletin of the EU Supplement 4/97, para. 31.
63. Bulletin of the EU Supplement 4/97, paras. 41–61.
64. See J. Kenner, 'Citizenship and Fundamental Rights: Reshaping the European Social Model', in J. Kenner (ed.), *Trends in European Social Policy*. Aldershot: Dartmouth, 1995, pp. 1–84; C. Closa, 'A New Social Contract? EU Citizenship as the Institutional Basis of a New Social Contract: Some Sceptical Remarks', EUI Working Paper, RSC No. 96/48.
65. CES 1069/87, p. 2.
66. For example the call by the Civil Liberties Committee of the European Parliament for a right to work as an integral part of social citizenship. PE Doc. 174.605, 10 January 1994.
67. The meeting was held in Brussels on 27–30 March 1996. See, *Working on European Social Policy – A Report on the Forum*, Luxembourg: OOPEC, 1996. The committee, comprising academics and former politicians, was chaired by former Portuguese prime minister, Maria de Lourdes Pintasilgo.
68. *Working on European Social Policy*, p. 6.
69. See S. Deakin and C. Barnard, 'Social Policy in Search of a Role: Integration, Cohesion and Citizenship', in A. Caiger and D. Floudas (eds), *1996 Onwards: Lowering the Barriers Further*, London: Wiley, 1996, pp. 177–95; B. Hepple, 'Social Values and European Law', *Current Legal Problems*, Vol. 48, 1995, pp. 39–61; B. Bercusson *et al., A Manifesto for Social Europe*, Brussels: European Trade Union Institute, 1996; R. Blanpain *et al., Fundamental Social Rights: Proposals for the European Union*, Leuven: Peeters, 1996.
70. By virtue of Article L of the TEU.
71. For a critique see, A. Neal, 'Labour Law in the 1990s: An Unweeded Garden that Grows to Seed?', *International Journal of Comparative Labour Law and Industrial Relations*, Vol. 13, 1997, pp. 11–78.
72. The revised numbering of Articles of the EC Treaty used throughout this chapter, when referring to the Amsterdam amendments, is based on the text of the Amsterdam Treaty signed on 2 October 1997 (OOPEC, 1997).
73. Respectively, Council Directive 97/74/EC of 15 December 1997, OJ L10 of 16 January 1998; Council Directive 97/75/EC of 15 December 1997, OJ L10 of 16 January 1998; Council Directive 98/23/EC of 7 April 1998, OJ L131 of 5 May 1998; Council Directive 98/52/EC of 13 July 1998, OJ L205 of 22 July 1998. In each case the preamble of the Directive justifies the use of Article 100 on the basis that these measures will improve the functioning of the Common Market by removing a source of distortion of competition linked to the application of different standards, or, in other words, 'social dumping'.
74. Case C–84/94 [1996] ECR I–5755.
75. Case C–260/89 [1991] ECR I–2925 at paras. 41–2 of the judgment.
76. The social provisions also incorporate, *inter alia*, Article 140 [ex Article 118], concerning cooperation between the Member States and coordination by the Commission in a diverse range of social policy fields, and Article 142 [ex Article 120], concerning the Member States' endeavour to maintain equivalence between paid holiday schemes.
77. Case T–135/96, OJ C318, 28 October 1996. See also, L. Betten, 'The Democratic Deficit of Participatory Democracy in Community Social Policy', *European Law Review*, Vol. 23, 1998, pp. 20–36.
78. Case C–84/94 [1996] ECR I–5755.
79. My emphasis.
80. Council Directive 75/117/EEC of 10 December 1975, OJ L 45 of 19 February 1975; Case 43/75, *Defrenne v SABENA II* [1976] ECR 455.
81. The Fourth Action Programme on equal opportunities for women and men (1996–2000), Council Decision of 22 December 1995, OJ L335 of 30 December 1995.
82. See S. Fredman, 'European Community Discrimination Law: A Critique', *Industrial Law Journal*, Vol. 21, 1992, pp. 119–34; H. Fenwick and T. Hervey, 'Sex Equality in the Single Market: New Directions for the European Court of Justice', *Common Market Law Review*, Vol. 32, 1995, pp. 443–70.
83. Case 450/93 [1995] IRLR 660.
84. Case C–409/95, *Marschall* v. *Land Nordrhein–Westfalen* [1998] IRLR 39.
85. Council Recommendation 84/635/EEC of 13 December 1984, OJ L331, 19 December 1984.
86. Numbered as Article 6a in the unconsolidated text.
87. Article 12 [6] EC/Article 7 EEC.
88. My emphasis.

89. Most notably Council Directive 76/207/EEC of 9 February 1976, on equal treatment of women and men in employment and vocation training, OJ L39, 14 February 1976.
90. See, COM 98 (259) final of 29 April 1998.
91. Numbered as Articles 109n–109s in the unconsolidated text.
92. National action plans have been drawn up for each Member State in accordance with Articles 128(2)–(5). See, COM (98) 316 final of 13 May 1998.
93. Amsterdam Presidency Conclusions of 16 June 1997, doc. CONF 4001/97. My emphasis.
94. European Council Resolution on Growth and Employment, 16 June 1997, para. 12.
95. COM(97) 497 final of 1 October 1997.
96. Luxembourg Presidency Conclusions, para. 22.
97. Luxembourg Presidency Conclusions, para. 22.
98. Luxembourg Presidency Conclusions, para. 67.
99. Luxembourg Presidency Conclusions, paras. 69–73.
100. Luxembourg Presidency Conclusions, para. 8.
101. Council Recommendation of 7 July 1997, *European Economy*, No. 64, Luxembourg: OOPEC, 1997.
102. Luxembourg Presidency Conclusions, para. 3. My emphasis.
103. IP/97/202, 22 October 1997.
104. Bulletin of the EU Supplement 4/97.
105. Annual Economic Report for 1997, *European Economy* No. 63, Ch. 1, Luxembourg: OOPEC, 1997.

Chapter 7

The regions and Amsterdam: Whatever happened to the third level?

Charlie Jeffery

One of the most widely discussed features of the Maastricht Treaty was the success of a broadly based regional lobby in securing formal recognition in the EU's treaty arrangements and important rights of access for regions to European decision-making. This lobby could count three major achievements in the Treaty. First, the Committee of the Regions (CoR) was established as an advisory body to Council and Commission, formally adding the sub-national level to the existing forms of representation in the EU: Member States (in the Council), popular representation (the European Parliament) and socio-economic interests (in the Economic and Social Committee).[1] Second, a semantically anodyne but highly significant amendment to Article 146 of the EC Treaty opened up the possibility for regional-level ministers to lead their countries' delegations in the Council. And third, the principle of subsidiarity was incorporated formally in Article 3b of the Treaty, albeit in a form which did not explicitly extend the application of the principle to the sub-national level.

Given that the Maastricht Treaty foresaw the need for its own revision in a clause requiring a subsequent Intergovernmental Conference (IGC) to be convened by 1996, representatives of the regional lobby looked keenly forward to continuing their work in entrenching a 'third level' (i.e. below that of the EU and the Member States) in the Treaty foundations of the EU. Maastricht was seen not just as a 'decisive breakthrough'[2] for the third level, but also a first stepping stone on the way to a fully fledged, three-level Union.[3]

This combination of euphoria and anticipation did not last. The 1996–97 IGC which culminated in the Treaty of Amsterdam did not see a concerted mobilization of the third level, nor was an especially coherent or ambitious third level agenda presented at the IGC. Regional expectations of the IGC were muted and the advances in terms of enhanced possibilities for regional level participation in EU decision-making were at best incremental. Maastricht's decisive breakthrough was followed by a damp squib at Amsterdam. This chapter examines why. It starts with a discussion of the particular confluence of conditions in the Maastricht process which facilitated the third level breakthrough. The following three sections then examine how the contrasting conditions which existed prior to and at Amsterdam were not conducive to a significant furtherance of the third level agenda of the early 1990s. These focus in turn on: the wider political context surrounding the Treaty negotiations; the operation of the Committee of the Regions as a representative body of the third level during the IGC; and the nature and purpose of 'strong' region input into the IGC process.

The Maastricht context

The parallel IGCs on Economic and Monetary Union (EMU) and Political Union which culminated in the Maastricht European Council meeting in December 1991 produced the biggest widening of the scope of European integration since the Rome Treaties. This in part continued the impetus established by the Single European Act and the 1992 Single Market programme it spawned, with further steps in economic integration and in particular EMU being seen as necessary to consolidate the Single Market and maintain EU-Europe's competitiveness in an increasingly internationalized economic environment. In addition, the end of the Cold War, and German unification in particular, added a new slant to the integration process. The end of the Cold War unbound a German 'Gulliver' hitherto tied down by national division and the sclerotic nature of Cold War international relations.[4] This image of an unrestrained Germany, while provoking visceral historical resentments in some quarters, produced through the French President, François Mitterrand, and the European Commission under Jacques Delors the revival of one of the founding philosophies of the European integration: integrate in order to bind German power into multilateral structures. As David Spence put it:

> If an enlarged Germany posed challenges for the Community and for the balance of economic power between its members, here was an opportunity for the Commission to use Member States' worries to speed up progress on economic, monetary and political union. EMU and Political Union would bind Germany even more tightly into the Community system.[5]

The result was a French-sponsored acceleration of the EMU agenda, based on the premise of absorbing as quickly as possible the power of the Bundesbank into a European Central Bank. The German leadership under Helmut Kohl, keen to reiterate the now united Germany's pro-integrationist credentials, acquiesced in this agenda – but on condition that parallel steps be made towards Political Union. The two IGCs on EMU and Political Union were thus launched in an unprecedented atmosphere combining improvisation with urgency. As a result, the agenda for the IGCs became unusually fluid and open, extending far beyond the original economic agenda into new areas of policy integration and – of most importance for the regional issue – new questions of institutional design.

The shifting goalposts of the integration agenda in the early 1990s were one precondition for the third level breakthrough at Maastricht, opening up unexpected opportunities for new ideas and initiatives to be fed into the IGC process. The opening up of such opportunities coincided with the emergence of a third level 'movement' of regional mobilization focused on breaking the monopoly of the Member States in EU decision-making.[6] This 'movement' had a range of stimuli: the progress of federalization/regionalization processes in Belgium and Spain and, to a lesser extent, France and Italy; the growing proliferation of regional cooperation and lobbying associations, focused largely on European integration issues; and the intensifying discourses of the 'Europe of the Regions' and subsidiarity – all of which seemed to signify a potent, 'bottom-up' demand for the incorporation of regional governments as policy players in the European-level game. The final – and most important – ingredient in the mixture was the leadership provided by the German Länder.

Frustrated by the way in which transfers of competence to the European level had, especially since the Single European Act, eroded areas of their own constitutional competence domestically, the Länder were keen to 'strike back'.[7] This they did in part by seeking to boost their domestic rights of input into defining the German position on EU issues. However, they also struck back via the Maastricht process by riding and steering the emergent third level 'movement' as a means of generating multiple pressures directed at securing regional rights of input into European-level decision-making.[8] Their agenda, established in outline as early as 1987, and repeatedly refined and reiterated in the following years, conceived of a three-level European federation structured around the principle of subsidiarity:

- Federalism and subsidiarity, which have proved themselves as the characteristic structural features of German politics for decades, must be the architectural principles of the (European) Political Union.
- The Political Union is to be built up on three levels, which means, in consequence, that a state level beneath the level of the nation state must exist or be created in every Member State.[9]

By 1990 four tightly defined aims had been developed as the first steps in realizing this agenda:

1. Incorporating the subsidiarity principle in the Treaty
2. Regional-level access to the Council
3. The Committee of the Regions
4. A regional right of appeal to the Court of Justice.

In an intensive lobbying and coordination effort, this agenda was pushed simultaneously – and mostly more or less word for word – through a range of channels: together with other 'strong' regions, either bilaterally (especially with Flanders), or in the framework of the Bavarian-led initiative, the Conference 'Europe of the Regions'; by the Europe-wide Assembly of the European Regions, which comprised the whole range of sub-national government from 'strong' regions in federal states to weak local authorities in the more centralized Member States; and within Germany in the domestic coordination structures established with the federal government to feed in Länder concerns to the German negotiating position for the IGCs. Of these various channels, the latter was undoubtedly the most significant given that the Länder had a right of veto over the ratification of the

Treaty under renegotiation – a right they were certainly not shy in threatening to use. The Länder could therefore compel the federal government in most cases to pursue their agenda in the IGC discussions. The range of bodies speaking with a strong Länder accent in and around the IGC both helped to legitimize the Länder cause and offered alternative routes for pushing issues onto the IGC agenda on those few occasions when the federal government declined formally to adopt Länder positions.

The results of the Länder pressuring the federal government and skilfully harnessing the regional 'movement' to infiltrate the open agenda of the pre-Maastricht IGCs were impressive: a 75 per cent 'hit-rate' on their four key aims, with only that of securing regional access to the ECJ failing to be incorporated in some form in the Maastricht Treaty. Subsequent experience suggests, however, that the successes of the third level 'movement' at Maastricht were highly contingent. They depended first on a favourable political context which opened up the parameters of the IGC debates to an unprecedented – and perhaps unrepeatable – extent. They also depended on the coherence of the third level voice, repeatedly chanting a simple mantra of common aims, and the capacity and will of the Länder to lead the third level movement. None of these conditions were met in the IGC which culminated in 1997 at the Amsterdam European Council.

The political context of Amsterdam

The IGC on the revision of the Maastricht Treaty had an inherently narrower agenda than its predecessors on EMU and Political Union. No major step towards deepening the Union was foreseen; the IGC was intended only to review the provisions of Maastricht with a view to preparing the Union for the planned eastward enlargement to the first tranche of former communist states in central and eastern Europe. A major step towards deepening was also regarded as politically unfeasible given the protracted difficulties encountered in the Maastricht ratification process: the initial rejection of the Treaty in the first Danish referendum; the narrow majority in the French referendum; the slowness of a divided UK government in completing its parliamentary ratification process; and the delay in ratification in Germany caused by the need to wait for the Federal Constitutional Court to issue its (ultimately positive) judgment on the Treaty's validity in terms of German constitutional law. This stumbling ratification process, compounded by popular dissatisfaction in some Member States over the prospect of EMU and in others over the deflationary implications of meeting the EMU convergence criteria, amplified the perception that Maastricht was a 'treaty too far' for – and from – public opinion and that future initiatives in European integration would have to proceed on a less ambitious basis. This was a perception overtly reflected in the 1996–97 IGC in the overtly Euro-sceptical and occasionally obstructionist position taken by the Conservative government in the UK and the decidedly unenthusiastic stances on deeper integration struck by the Danish, Finnish and, to a lesser extent, Swedish governments.[10]

These background factors narrowed the parameters of the IGC agenda. This did not anticipate major change, focusing on technical issues of legislative procedure, the future operation of the two extra-Community pillars established at Maastricht, the structure of the Commission, voting weights in the Council, limited additions to the list of Union competences and the wider application of qualified majority voting (QMV) rules, and the question of flexible integration. The regional issue – apart from some expectation of minor tinkering with the structure and powers of the Committee of the Regions – certainly did not figure high on the agenda. Nor, indeed, did the agenda widen out notably in the course of the IGC negotiations. Rather, energies were deflected, especially in European Council meetings ostensibly dedicated primarily to pushing the IGC forward, by the parallel issue of preparations for EMU. The EMU issue held a far higher priority for most governments – including those unlikely to figure in the first stage – than the IGC. Indeed, towards the end of the IGC negotiations, EMU more or less overtly invaded the IGC agenda following the election of the Jospin government in France in June 1997. Jospin's election was due in part to EMU-related economic sluggishness in France, and Jospin used this as capital to force the IGC to accord a higher priority to discussing employment policy initiatives. This crowded out discussion of other issues[11] in the final – and typically most fluid – phase of the IGC negotiations and removed the possibility which had existed at Maastricht[12] for the Länder or other regional forces to extract last-minute concessions.

And finally, if the Member States had half an eye or more on EMU throughout the IGC, then the attention of the third level was also less than 100 per cent on the IGC. Again, rumbling in the background, was an issue of far more urgent, direct interest than the reshaping of the Treaty: Agenda 2000, and in particular the debate on the future of the Structural Funds after 1999. Jockeying for position to secure material best advantage – or least disadvantage – in future funding flows certainly consumed a large part of the limited administrative resources available to most EU regions during the IGC.

The 1996–97 IGC did not, then, present a favourable context for progressing the third level agenda of the early 1990s. The unhappy legacies of the Maastricht ratification process, compounded by the unwillingness of a number of Member States to countenance further integrationist steps, a constrained agenda, and the crowding-out effects of important issues in parallel policy debates limited the opportunities for third level forces to shape the outcomes of the IGC. What was also lacking was a coherent and purposeful third level voice capable of articulating such clear and consistently presented demands as those which impacted significantly on the Maastricht Treaty. This was somewhat ironic given that the Committee of the Regions (CoR) had been established to represent the sub-national level in EU decision-making. The establishment of the CoR has not, though, had the effect of coordinating and consolidating the third level 'movement' which mobilized around the Maastricht process. Moreover, none of the 'strong' regions of the EU proved capable of, or willing to, replicate the leadership role the German Länder had played at Maastricht. Whatever happened to the third level at Amsterdam? The next two sections offer some indications.

The Committee of the Regions and the IGC

The Committee of the Regions certainly attempted to establish itself as the voice of the sub-national level at the IGC. It established an *ad hoc* Special Commission for Institutional Affairs in May 1994 to prepare a CoR Opinion on the IGC. This was duly published in April 1995 to feed into the deliberations of the Reflection Group established to define the parameters of the IGC agenda. A steady flow of supplementary documents was then drawn up, culminating in the report 'Regions and Cities, Pillars of Europe' for the grandiosely entitled 'European Summit of the Regions and Cities' held a month prior to the Amsterdam European Council, also in Amsterdam. This three-year process of discussion and opinion-formation in the CoR produced, as Reilly notes,[13] some 11 core proposals on the CoR's 'wish-list' for the IGC:

1. The full administrative and budgetary separation of the CoR from the Economic and Social Committee (Ecosoc), with which it had hitherto shared a joint infrastructure.
2. The right of the CoR to adopt its own rules of procedure, without having first to secure Council approval.
3. The requirement that CoR members have an electoral mandate.
4. The enshrining of the principle of local self-government in the Treaty.
5. The extension of the institutional scope of CoR's consultation rights to include, alongside Commission and Council, the European Parliament.
6. The extension of the fields in which the CoR has to be consulted in the EU policy process.
7. The rewording of Article 3b on subsidiarity to clarify the application of the subsidiarity principle and to extend it explicitly to the sub-national level.
8. The award of institutional status to the CoR (alongside the Council, Commission, Parliament and Court of Auditors).
9. A right of appeal of the CoR to the European Court of Justice (ECJ) to defend its own rights.
10. A right of appeal of the CoR to the ECJ in cases where the principle of subsidiarity is infringed.
11. The right of those individual regions endowed with their own legislative powers to defend those competences before the ECJ.

Of these 11 agenda items, the first three were entirely uncontroversial, essentially technical points, and the separation from Ecosoc and the rules of procedure question were duly implemented in line with CoR wishes in treaty amendments. The self-evident notion that CoR members should hold an elected post at the sub-national level was not addressed formally in the Treaty. But, given the informal convention which is emerging on the issue, in particular that members who lose their mandate should resign their membership within six months, it did not really need to be. Likewise, while the fourth item on local self-government did not make it into the Treaty, the issue was not an especially urgent one given the growing scope of the signatories – including, after the 1997 election, the UK – to the European Charter of Local Self-Government. And on items 5 and 6, given the generally positive assessment of the Opinions the CoR issues in its advisory role, as reflected in the feedback reports the Commission now presents on those Opinions, the extension of the CoR's consultation rights to the European Parliament and the extension of the fields in which it has to be consulted were uncontentious and accepted in the Treaty. The new consultation fields comprise employment, social matters, the environment, the European Social Fund, vocational training and transport.[14]

The remaining items were more controversial, either foundering on the opposition of the Member States or failing to be incorporated into the Treaty in the form suggested by the CoR. This was hardly surprising given the widespread suspicion which still exists in at least some (especially the more centralized) Member States over according the sub-national level a fuller role in EU decision-making. What was more surprising was that, although these remaining items were put forward in collectively adopted CoR Opinions, there was still a large measure of disagreement among the constituent members of the Committee over their value. In particular, the old issue of the regional–local divide in the CoR was never far from the surface.[15]

It is worth recalling in this respect that although the CoR was hailed as a great breakthrough at Maastricht, representatives of the 'strong' regions in the EU (broadly defined as those with constitutionalized status and some range of exclusive legislative powers)[16] were disappointed both by the relatively weak, consultative powers the Committee was awarded, and by its 'dilution' through the incorporation of 'weak' local authorities in its membership.[17] The potential for these disappointments to be reflected in the emergence of a local–regional divide in the operation of the Committee was confirmed in the initial squabbles and consequent regional–local fudge over the CoR Presidency, and in persistent mutterings on the part of strong regions that the CoR might be divided into two chambers, one regional, one local, the former ideally with fuller rights in the EU legislative process. The question of dividing the Committee even appeared in an early draft of the CoR's IGC Opinion,[18] before the regional–local divide was reconciled in what the coordinator of the Special Commission charged with drafting the IGC Opinion termed 'a compromise without consensus'.[19]

The subsequent CoR discussions and supplementary documents on the IGC bore all of the hallmarks of this 'compromise without consensus'. As Adrian Reilly has shown in his invaluable survey of sub-national opinion on the IGC, there remained a subterranean, but nonetheless clear divide between the regional and the local camps throughout the IGC discussions.[20] This was evident in the items on the CoR wish-list dealing with subsidiarity, institutional status, and rights of appeal to the ECJ. On these issues, the views of local level representatives, as expressed outside of the formal, collective CoR framework – for example, in their national CoR caucuses or in the documents of their domestic local authority associations – demonstrated the superficiality of the CoR consensus. While there was general consensus in the Committee on tightening up the definition of the subsidiarity principle – as broadly accepted in the Protocol on subsidiarity attached to the

Amsterdam Treaty[21] – the local level was typically ambivalent or opposed to the explicit extension of any tightened-up subsidiarity principle to the sub-national level. This was no doubt a reflection of the fact that the CoR's formulation was one restricted to sub-national governments with guaranteed policy competences in their domestic political systems; this was a 'strong' region issue with little relevance to local level representatives. The question of institutional status also revealed the local–regional divide. This was a key issue in the CoR package of demands given that the items dealing with access to the ECJ – which is open only to fully fledged EU institutions – depended on it. Again, this was a strong region agenda which extended back to Maastricht;[22] recourse to the ECJ makes sense if one has legally guaranteed and substantial powers to defend. The local level naturally did not share this agenda, dismissing it as a distraction 'from concentrating on more urgent matters' which would 'further the cause of the CoR itself'.[23]

The coolness of the local level response to these more far-reaching items on the CoR wish-list for the IGC illustrates the 'latent conflict' between strong regions and their weaker sub-national counterparts throughout the discussions flanking the IGC.[24] This latent conflict points up a crucial difference in comparison with the pre-Maastricht IGCs. The broad-based third level 'movement' of the early 1990s which had been capable of articulating the aspirations of the strong and the weak together no longer existed. Paradoxically, the creation of the CoR at Maastricht as an institution representative of the third level has established a forum in which the inevitable differences of perspective and priority which exist among the vastly different units of sub-national government across the EU have come clearly to light. There is, in effect, no longer a single third level joined by common purpose but an array of highly differentiated sub-national bodies remarkable precisely for their lack of uniformity.[25] This was clearly manifested in the CoR's discussions on the IGC; it also, of course, limited the credibility of the CoR's demands of the IGC. 'Compromise without consensus' is not a strong basis from which to press for Treaty changes. The only possible outcome for the CoR in this context was incremental change: minor tweaks of institutional structure and limited extension of the scope of the CoR's existing powers. More radical advances – on subsidiarity, institutional status and the ECJ – were outside the realm of possibility. This was all the more so, of course, given that the CoR had no formal role in the IGC proceedings. Formal input was restricted to the Commission, to a limited extent the EP and, most importantly, to the Member States. As Reilly has noted, 'effective sub-national influence [in the IGC] depends therefore not just on generating a coherent sub-national voice across the Member States, but also on the generation of common sub-national/national positions *within* Member States'.[26] It is to this alternative route into the IGC negotiations that discussion now turns.

Regions and the IGC: the national route

This route was effectively open only to a select band of strong regions which, in the aftermath of Maastricht, had established codified domestic rights of input into the

European policy process: those in Austria, Belgium and Germany (though with the Spanish autonomous communities perpetually, if usually frustratedly, knocking at the door). These domestic rights provided a basis for the Austrian, Belgian and German regions to claim a right of input in shaping their respective national positions for the IGC. In each case this input was awarded without controversy and effected through consensual coordination processes linking the regions, acting collectively, to their central government.[27] In contrast to the pre-Maastricht IGCs, these domestic rights of input were not flanked by international cooperation on the IGC agenda among the strong regions. An initiative by North Rhine-Westphalia to establish a formal 'Dialogue of the Constitutional Regions' of Germany, Austria, Belgium, Italy and Spain on the IGC – an equivalent to the pre-Maastricht Bavarian-led 'Conference "Europe of the Regions"' – quickly ran into the ground, as did a Basque Country initiative to append a 'Protocol on the Role of Regions with Autonomous Legislative Responsibilities' to the new Treaty.[28] The strong regions were therefore restricted to a purely national route into the IGC debates.

Their capacity to use this route to press for the regional agenda delineated in the CoR and their own more specific concerns naturally varied. The Austrian Länder were able to persuade the Austrian federal government to include their concerns – essentially a reproduction of the CoR agenda – more or less wholesale in the Austrian position at the IGC.[29] It is not clear, however, given the relative weight of Austria as a Member State in EU negotiations, that this brought any notable tangible reward for the Länder cause. The same problem of limited political weight also applied in the Belgian case. The peculiarities of the internal coordination process in Belgium,[30] which brought the three communities and three regions into the Belgian delegation on a rotational basis, did not prove to be a potent vehicle for importing regional concerns into the IGC. Rotation limited the effectiveness of the regions/communities, not least by awarding an information advantage to the permanently present representatives of the federal government. This in turn led to a certain disillusionment at the sub-national level, manifested in a remarkable level of absenteeism in the relevant meetings. The only issue pressed with consistency and vigour was the specifically Flemish concern – rooted in the increasingly successful transformation of Belgium from a Francophone-dominated into a genuinely bi-communal state – to protect cultural/linguistic diversity. This found some recognition in the Treaty, but was not representative of any broader, specifically regional agenda. Indeed, this is a theme which Flanders has been pursuing in its 'Europe of the Cultures' project through a curious and rather incoherent collection of so-called 'cultural' regions (for example, Catalonia, Bavaria and Scotland) and small Member States (for example, Denmark and Ireland).

The German Länder had, of course, been the major force in pressing the third level agenda in the pre-Maastricht IGCs, using their interregional coalition-building capacities and their strong internal powers markedly to shape the Maastricht Treaty. In the 1996–97 IGC they offered no comparable leadership for EU-wide regional concerns, focusing instead on their own particular interests in the European integration process. This was a change of thrust quite clear in the first two Opinions – of May and December 1995 – the Länder issued, via their collective organ, the

Bundesrat, on the IGC. These followed part of the CoR agenda, but were pointed up much more strongly as 'strong' region issues.[31] The emphasis was on wider questions of the quality and structures of the relationship between the Union and Member States. This included: the application of the subsidiarity principle at the sub-national level in those Member States – such as, of course, their own – whose constitutional orders specifically empower sub-national authorities; a fuller definition of the respective competences of the Union and the Member States (the latter together, where appropriate, with their regions); and the right of constitutionally empowered regions to appeal to the ECJ on alleged infringements of their competences.

This focus on demarcating the competences of the Member States and their regions *vis-à-vis* those of the EU – in contrast to initial attempts in the pre-Maastricht debates to begin to delineate ideal-type competences of the third level more generally – reflects two things. First, the Länder were extremely successful in their quest, conducted during the German Maastricht ratification debates, to constitutionalize extensive internal rights of participation in co-determining German European policy with the federal government. Second, the Länder had invested more hopes than most in the prospects of a new era of third level politics in and around Maastricht, and were then disillusioned more than most with the highly limited reality of their creation – the Committee of the Regions – as a third level institution. In a consequent shift of priorities, the Länder bade 'farewell to the third level'[32] to focus increasingly on their intra-state rights of participation in EU decision-making.[33]

The Länder focus on EU–Member State relationships has to be seen in this light. They play a significant role in EU decision-making as part of the German Member State, and can achieve far more through that channel than by seeking to revive their now faded third level dreams. The transformation from third level leader to an introspective focus on the national context of European policy-making was confirmed in the later stages of the IGC. Two new issues came up on which the Länder sought – successfully – to have their views reflected: a defence of the operational peculiarities of the regional banking and regional broadcasting systems in Germany from Euro-regulation.[34] To point up the contrast to Maastricht, the Länder which had once demanded the creation of a 'Political Union ... on three levels' emerged from Amsterdam holding aloft the prize of protected regional broadcasting licence fees.

Conclusions

This is not to denigrate the significance of the broadcasting issue: the media are one of the core exclusive competences of the Länder, and their financing a matter of some considerable material interest for them. However, the broadcasting issue does neatly encapsulate the sea change in regional input into European treaty-making which occurred between Maastricht and Amsterdam. The earlier sense of collective purpose in establishing sub-national actors as Euro-level players, which skilfully exploited the favourable political context at Maastricht under the leadership of the German Länder, has been replaced by the pursuit of far narrower, but more tangible interests relevant to particular sub-national actors. The third level 'movement' has fragmented into a diverse mélange of sub-national interest politics. This was evident not just in the priorities of the German Länder at the IGC, but also the Flemish emphasis on cultural diversity, the difficulties in securing a common position in the CoR and the distractions of the funding issues in the Agenda 2000 debates. In this sense the wider political context surrounding Amsterdam, which was not conducive to far-reaching new integrationist initiatives, was irrelevant to the sub-national cause, because there is now no single sub-national cause to be pursued. Whatever happened to the third level? After the extraordinary circumstances and fleeting unity of Maastricht it has undergone a process of 'normalization' focused on the pursuit of real interests and far removed from the old chimera of a three-level political union.

Endnotes

1. J. Loughlin, 'Representing Regions in Europe: The Committee of the Regions', in C. Jeffery (ed.), *The Regional Dimension of the European Union*, London: Frank Cass, 1997, pp. 156–7.
2. U. Hoppe and G. Schulz, 'Der Ausschuß der Regionen', in F. Borkenhagen *et al* (eds), *Die deutschen Länder und Europa*, Baden-Baden: Nomos, 1992, p. 33.
3. G. Memminger, 'Die Forderungen der Länder im Gefüge des Grundgesetzes', in Borkenhagen *et al* (eds), *Die deutschen Länder und Europa*, p. 143.
4. See S. Bulmer and W. Paterson, 'West Germany's Role in Europe: Man-Mountain or Semi-Gulliver?', *Journal of Common Market Studies*, Vol. 28, 1989, pp. 95–117; W. Paterson, 'Gulliver Unbound: The Changing Context of Foreign Policy', in G. Smith *et al* (eds), *Developments in German Politics*, London: Macmillan, 1992, pp. 137–52.
5. D. Spence, 'The European Community and German Unification', in C. Jeffery and R. Sturm (eds), *Federalism, Unification and European Integration*, London: Frank Cass, 1993, pp. 140–1.
6. C. Engel, 'Das "Europa der Regionen" seit Maastricht', in F. Borkenhagen (ed.), *Europapolitik der deutschen Länder*, Opladen: Lesse and Budrich, 1988, p. 176.
7. The next section is based extensively on pp. 8–12 of C. Jeffery, 'The Länder Strike Back: Structures and Procedures of European Policy-Making in the German Federal System', *University of Leicester Discussion Papers in Federal Studies*, No. FS94/4, 1994.
8. C. Jeffery, 'Farewell the Third Level? The German Länder and the European Policy Process', in Jeffery (ed.), *The Regional Dimension of the European Union*, pp. 63–8.
9. H. Kilpert and R. Lhotta, *Föderalismus in der Bundesrepublik Deutschland*, Opladen: Lesse and Budrich, 1996, p. 226.
10. O. Schmuck, 'Die EU-Regierungskonferenz 1996: Zum Stand der Reformdebatte', *Integration*, Vol. 18, 1995, pp. 70–3.
11. Compare with S. Bulmer, C. Jeffery and W. Paterson, 'Deutschlands europäische Diplomatie: die Entwicklung des regionalen Milieus', in Bertlesmann-Wissenchaftsstiftung (ed.), *Effektivierung der deutscher Europapolitik*, Bonn: Europa Union Verlag, 1998.
12. Jeffery, 'The Länder Strike Back', pp. 10–11.
13. A. Reilly, 'The Committee of the Regions, Sub-National Governments and the IGC', *Regional and Federal Studies*, Vol. 7, 1997, pp. 134–64.
14. Reilly, 'The Committee of the Regions, Sub-National Governments and the IGC', pp. 139–40.
15. C. Jeffery, 'Whither the Committee of the Regions? Reflections on the Committee's "Opinion on the Revision of the Treaty on European Union" ', *Regional and Federal Studies*, Vol. 5, 1995, pp. 253–4.
16. Engel, 'Das "Europa der Regionen" seit Maastricht', p. 163.
17. Compare with Hoppe and Schulz, 'Der Ausschuß der Regionen'.
18. Jeffery, 'Whither the Committee of the Regions?', pp. 253–4.

19. U. Kalbfleisch-Kottsieper, 'Kompromiß ohne Konsens?', *EU-Magazin*, No. 6, 1995, p. 13.
20. Reilly, 'The Committee of the Regions, Sub-National Governments and the IGC'.
21. Reilly, 'The Committee of the Regions, Sub-National Governments and the IGC', pp. 144–6.
22. Jeffery, 'The Länder Strike Back', pp. 11–12.
23. Reilly, 'The Committee of the Regions, Sub-National Governments and the IGC', p. 142.
24. Compare with Engel, 'Das "Europa der Regionen" seit Maastricht', p. 165.
25. Compare with C. Jeffery, 'L'emergence d'une gouvernance multi-niveaux dans l'Union Européenne', *Politiques et Management Public*, Vol. 15, 1997.
26. Reilly, 'The Committee of the Regions, Sub-National Governments and the IGC', p. 135.
27. See M. Morass, 'Austria: the Case of a Federal Newcomer in European Union Politics', in Jeffery (ed.), *The Regional Dimension of the European Union*, pp. 89–92; B. Kerremans, ' "Bon Courage" to the Third Level? Multi-Level Governance and the Belgian Sub-National Involvement in the Council and the IGC from a Comparative Perspective', paper presented to the ECPR Joint Sessions, Berne, 1997; O. Schmuck, 'Der Amsterdamer Vertrag aus Sicht der Länder und Regionen', *Integration*, Vol. 20, 1997, pp. 230–1.
28. Engel, 'Das ' "Europa der Regionen" seit Maastricht', pp. 163–5.
29. Morass, 'Austria: The Case of a Federal Newcomer in European Union Politics', pp. 89–92.
30. Kerremans, ' "Bon Courage" to the Third Level?'
31. C. Jeffery, 'The German Länder and the 1996 Intergovernmental Conference', *Regional and Federal Studies*, Vol. 5, 1995, pp. 356–65.
32. Jeffery, 'Farewell the Third Level?'.
33. Indeed, their farewell to the third level as represented by the CoR was revealed in a phrase in the Bundesrat's resolution of May 1995: 'The structures of the Committee of the Regions are to be re-examined.' The subterranean meaning – reflecting exasperation over the local–regional divide in the CoR discussed above – was revealed in a policy paper of the European Ministers of the Länder as the 'reorganization of the Committee of the Regions in the long term into a representative organ solely of the regional level'.
34. Schmuck, 'Der Amsterdamer Vertrag aus Sicht der Länder und Regionen', p. 232; Engel, 'Das "Europa der Regionen" seit Maastricht', p. 178.

Chapter 8

An 'area of freedom, justice and security'? Progress and deficits in justice and home affairs

Jörg Monar

Introduction

The introduction of 'cooperation in the fields of justice and home affairs' was clearly one of the most innovative elements of the Treaty of Maastricht. It was also one of the most necessary, having regard to the new or increased transnational security challenges the Member States had to face after the end of the Cold War and the abolition of internal border controls in the framework of the Single European Market programme. Yet the Maastricht Treaty made of EU justice and home affairs the Cinderella of policy-making in the European Union: no other policy area of the Union had to content itself with weaker objectives, instruments and procedures.

The Treaty of Amsterdam now appears to come as the prince who redeems Cinderella from her poor circumstances. Not only have the basic provisions of Title VI TEU been substantially amended but major areas have been 'communitarized', partly in the form of an entirely new Title of the EC Treaty governed by a whole range of new specific provisions, and, last but not least, in both the 'old' intergovernmental and the newly communitarized parts of justice and home affairs the door to differentiated integration within the European Union has been pushed wide open. All this has been placed under the heading of maintaining and developing the Union as an 'area of freedom, justice and security' which has been made one of the central objectives of the Union Treaty.

The question is now what real possibilities for progress in the areas of justice and home affairs this overhaul of the former Treaty provisions offers to the Union and whether there are also new obstacles and problems to be expected. The following assessment will focus on a range of key issues such as objectives, instruments, decision-making and flexibility rather than provide an article-by-article analysis.

Objectives

The provisions on justice and home affairs introduced by the Maastricht Treaty did not provide for any policy objectives in the areas listed in Article K.1 TEU which were only described as 'matters of common interest'. The Treaty of Amsterdam brings considerable qualitative change in this respect. The first element is that amended Article 2 [ex Article B] TEU, fourth indent, now provides for the already mentioned new Treaty objective to maintain and to develop the Union 'as an area of freedom, justice and security'. This 'area' is further defined as one 'in which the free movement of persons is assured in conjunction with appropriate measures with respect to external border controls, immigration, asylum and the prevention and combating of crime'. This provision commits the Union to the adoption of measures in all of the core areas of the 'matters of common interest' of 'old' Title VI. Yet the 'appropriate measures' are explicitly linked to the 'old' Treaty objective of free movement of persons. This is a rather narrow basis which could make it more difficult for the Union to move beyond mere flanking measures of free movement.

The major part of the newly communitarized areas of the old third pillar has been transferred into the new Title IV [ex Title IIIa] EC on 'Visas, asylum, immigration and other policies related to free movement of persons'. According to Article 61(a) [ex Article 73i(a)] EC the Council shall adopt measures aiming at ensuring the free movement of persons in conjunction with a range of 'directly related flanking measures'. These are divided into two groups. Measures with respect to external border controls, to the conditions of travel of third country nationals to asylum and immigration are to be adopted on the basis of new Articles 62 and 63 [ex Articles 73j and 73k] EC, and measures to prevent and combat crime on the basis of new Article 31(e) [ex Article K.3(e)] EU within the third pillar. Each of these provisions governs selected issues of justice and home affairs such as standards for carrying out checks at external borders, minimum standards for giving temporary protection to displaced persons from third countries and the adoption of minimum rules relating to the constituent elements of criminal acts in specific fields.

What is of major importance here is that for the first time measures in the areas of justice and home affairs are not only linked to a specific aim but also to a clearly set deadline: the Council has to act within five years. This means that the successful Community method of combining integration objectives with deadlines for their achievement is for the first time applied to EU justice and home affairs.

Article 61(b) to (e) [ex Article 73i(b) to (e)] provides for the Council also to take measures in the following four groups of fields:

- asylum, immigration and safeguarding the rights of third country nationals
- judicial cooperation
- the strengthening of administrative cooperation and
- (under Title VI TEU) police and judicial cooperation in criminal matters.

Measures in these fields are not explicitly linked to the aim of free movement, yet they remain subject to the general aim of Article 61 (ex Article 73i] EC to establish an area of freedom, justice and security which, as already pointed out, focuses on the free movement of persons. This means that Member States favouring a restrictive approach to developing EU justice and home affairs could invoke this provision against any proposed measure which is not 'directly related' to the free movement of persons within the Union.

Article 63 [ex Article 73k] EC[1] dealing with measures on asylum, refugees and immigration, establishes as well a deadline of five years. Because of the importance of the subject matters covered this is clearly one of the most relevant new provisions. The types of measures listed in Article 63 [ex Article 73k] are described in great detail, ranging from criteria for determining the Member State responsible for considering an application for asylum, through minimum standards for giving temporary protection to refugees, to conditions of entry and residence for immigrants. Together they bear much resemblance to an extensive legislative action programme. Yet it needs to be emphasized that the list in Article 63 [ex Article 73k] EC is still far from being comprehensive enough to provide a basis for a 'common' policy worth the name: it covers, for instance, neither the development of common aims in the area of immigration policy nor the question of social integration of asylum seekers and immigrants. The central issue of burden-sharing between the Member States, an issue repeatedly brought up by Germany, is only vaguely and inadequately referred to in Article 63(2)(b) [ex Article 73k(2)(b)] as 'promoting a balance of effort' between Member States. This is hardly a strong basis for common policy-making on asylum and immigration.

This applies to an even greater extent to the policy areas mentioned in Article 61(c) [ex Article 73i(c)] EC: judicial cooperation in civil matters, and Article 61(d) [ex Article 73i(d)]: strengthening of administrative cooperation. Article 65 [ex Article 73m], which governs judicial cooperation in civil matters, limits the scope of measures in this area to those having 'cross-border implications' and identifies five areas ranging from improving the cross-border service of judicial documents, through the recognition and enforcement of decisions in civil and commercial cases, to the elimination of obstacles to the smooth functioning of civil proceedings. Important as these areas are, they do not provide a comprehensive basis for the creation of a common 'European judicial area'. It seems unlikely, for instance, that the wording of Article 65 [ex Article 73m] would allow for an incorporation of the 1968 Brussels Convention[2] into EC law and its extension to customs, revenue and administrative matters. As regards administrative cooperation, Article 66 [ex Article 73n] EC only refers in rather general terms to measures ensuring cooperation between relevant departments. There is also no deadline for the achievement of these objectives.

The measures in the field of police and judicial cooperation in criminal matters referred to in Article 61(e) [ex Article 73i(e)] EC are 'aimed at a high level of security'. This objective is repeated in almost identical terms in Article 29 [ex Article K.1] TEU which defines the general aims of cooperation under Title VI TEU. Articles 30 and 31 [ex 30 and 31] TEU specify in more detail the elements of 'common action' by the Member States in matters of police and judicial cooperation in criminal matters respectively. The former include, for instance, operational cooperation, data collection, training and common evaluation of investigative techniques. Yet no more precise objectives are set for cooperation in these areas and there is no time constraint.

Article 30(2) [ex Article K.2(2)] TEU deals mainly with cooperation through Europol providing, *inter alia*, for Europol to support specific investigative actions by Member States and to allow Europol to ask Member States' authorities to conduct investigations in specific cases. The wording here is rather precise and the Council has to take action within five years. Although the new provisions do not provide for the introduction of operational powers of Europol they nevertheless represent a step forward because a number of clear and deadline-linked objectives are set for developing Europol, especially as regards the support and the initiation of investigative action.

As regards judicial cooperation in criminal matters, Article 31 [ex Article K.3] TEU provides for 'common action' in a number of areas which include cooperation between ministries and judicial authorities, facilitating extradition, preventing conflicts of jurisdiction and the progressive establishment of minimum rules relating to the constituent elements of criminal acts. Yet, again, the areas listed here are far from comprehensive. There is no list of types of offences, such as fraud, money-laundering, corruption and disclosure of official secrets, on which Union action should focus. Issues of particular importance, such as the question of extraterritorial evidence, are not mentioned either. Lastly, there is no deadline by which 'common action' must be taken. It is also rather striking that there are no specific objectives set to combat drug-trafficking. After all, this is an area of common concern of the Member States which has consistently figured high on the Council's agenda during the last years.

The fight against fraud as far as it affects the financial interests of the Community, formerly under the third pillar, is now covered by Article 280 [ex Article 209a] EC. One new element has been added to the objectives of Community action: Article 280(1) now provides that measures taken 'shall act as a deterrent' and 'afford effective protection in the Member States'. According to Article 280(4) such measures shall be aimed at 'equivalent protection' in the Member States. This can provide a better basis for the sanctioning of financial fraud through national penal law. Yet the provision does not come near to establishing a basis for a European penal law on financial fraud which many experts believe to be the only efficient response to the increasing problems of fraud.[3]

Article 135 [ex Article 116] EC brings customs cooperation into the EC framework. Having regard to the EC's Customs Union competences this seems a highly sensible reform. Yet there are no precise objectives set.

What overall conclusions can be drawn from this bewildering range of new provisions? The total lack of objectives of former Title VI TEU has clearly been remedied, and some of the new objectives are strengthened by the five-year deadline set for the necessary Council measures. Yet the objectives cover a selection of issues rather than whole policy areas. This favours piecemeal problem-solving rather than a comprehensive policy approach. It is quite significant that the Amsterdam Treaty does not provide for the establishment of any 'common policy' according to the EC model in justice and home affairs, showing the limits of the communitarization introduced in these areas. In addition, the close formal link between most of the new objectives and the 'old' objective of free movement of persons could be used by some Member States as an argument for obstructing measures with a wider scope. All this means that the changes at the level of objectives are likely to bring about some progress, yet only in a fragmented form and with different speeds in the individual areas.

Instruments

Justice and home affairs cooperation under 'old' Title VI TEU has been affected by the weaknesses of its instruments and uncertainties as to their nature and scope. One basic problem was that the instruments introduced by the Maastricht Treaty had been largely taken over from the Common Foreign and Security Policy with its emphasis on political 'positions' rather than the legal acts normally needed within the areas of justice and home affairs. Conventions were the only instrument which did not cause controversies about its legal effects, but because of their need for ratification they were an unwieldy type of action. The Amsterdam Treaty again brings qualitative change in this respect. For the areas of the 'old' third pillar transferred to new Title IV [ex IIIa] EC, the third pillar instruments are now replaced by the EC legal acts. Yet the instruments under Title VI TEU have also been considerably modified.

With the 'framework decisions' of Article 34(2)(b) [ex Article K.6(2)(b)] TEU a new instrument has been created for the purpose of 'approximation of the laws' which shall be 'binding upon the Member States as to the results to be achieved but shall leave to the national authorities the choice of form and method'. This means that 'framework decisions' are very similar to EC directives, except in that they are legal acts outside of the Community framework and do not entail any direct effect. This instrument is clearly more appropriate to the legislative needs of police cooperation and judicial cooperation in criminal matters than 'common positions' or the former 'joint actions'. It should be appreciated by the Member States for the greater margin it leaves them as regards implementation.

The former 'joint actions' have disappeared from the range of instruments. Instead Article 34(2)(c) [ex Article K.6(2)(c)] TEU now provides for the new instrument of 'decisions' for any other purpose than approximation of laws consistent with the objectives of Title VI. 'Decisions' are to be binding on the Member States, but, again, any direct effect is excluded. As general-purpose instruments, 'decisions' could become the standard instrument for matters of limited scope requiring legal action.

'Conventions' have been maintained as an instrument, but some effort has been made to shorten the period between their adoption and their entry into force. Article 34(2)(d) [ex Article K.6(2)(d)] TEU now provides that Member States shall begin ratification procedures within a time limit set by the Council. Since the Council will have to decide on this limit by unanimity it is unlikely to be extremely tight, but it can certainly help to speed up ratification procedures. It is also stipulated that, unless otherwise provided, conventions shall enter into force as soon as they are adopted by at least half of the Member States. This can exercise additional pressure on

Member States to proceed with ratification. It may not always be practicable, however, to start applying a convention with only some of the Member States participating.

'Common positions' are still provided for in Article 34(2)(a) [ex Article K.6(2)(a)] TEU, with the addition that they 'defin[e] the approach of the Union to a particular matter'. Yet these terms are rather vague and the legal status of the act is not clarified. This and the fact that 'common positions' are the only acts listed in Article 34(2) [ex Article K.6(2)] TEU which neither fall under the jurisdiction of the ECJ[4] nor under the right of the European Parliament (EP) to be consulted,[5] suggest that a 'common position' has to be regarded as a decision on political strategy rather than a binding legal act. 'Common positions' could therefore become the preferred instrument of the Member States in cases in which they want to avoid a legally binding act or a consultation of the EP. It is obvious that frequent use of this instrument could seriously undermine prospects for substantial progress under Title VI.

Overall the Amsterdam Treaty clearly brings substantial progress in terms of the legal quality and potential effectiveness of instruments. The new provisions of Title VI offer for the first time the possibility to build up a clear-cut EU legal *acquis*. It seems very likely that the refined and extended legal instruments will lead to an increased legislative output in EU justice and home affairs. Yet it still remains to be seen to what extent the Member States will continue to use non-binding texts such as resolutions and what use they are going to make of the wild-card-like instrument of 'common positions'.

Division of competences between the EC framework and Title VI TEU

Justice and home affairs cooperation as established by the Maastricht Treaty was affected by uncertainties as regards the borderline between intergovernmental cooperation and EC competences. In a number of cases this led to controversies about the appropriate legal basis. By transferring major former third pillar areas into the EC framework, the Amsterdam Treaty removes a number of possible uncertainties and points of contention in respect to the scope of action taken in the two pillars. This applies not only to the areas closely related to free movement of persons, such as asylum, immigration and external border controls covered by new Title IIIa EC, but also to the communitarization of the fight against fraud affecting the financial interests of the Community and of customs cooperation. Yet the Amsterdam Treaty also offers scope for new controversies over the borderline between Community and intergovernmental action by creating an even more artificial split between communitarized and non-communitarized areas of justice and home affairs.

The fight against fraud affecting the financial interests of the EC is now an EC domain, but questions such as extradition and conflicts of jurisdiction between Member States, which can be of considerable importance in the fight against fraud affecting the EC, are governed by Article 31 [ex Article K.3] TEU. It also seems unfortunate that while measures against drugs-related health damage have to be based on Article 152(1) [ex Article 129(1)] EC, conversely, the fight against drug-trafficking is to remain fully within the scope of the third pillar.

While removing some of the existing problems of the division of competences the partial communitarization introduced by the Amsterdam Treaty therefore creates new potential for friction. This could complicate effective Union action on some issues of particular importance.

Cooperation with third countries

The 'old' third pillar provisions did not provide for cooperation with third countries. This has tended to reduce the effectiveness of cooperation under Title VI because in most areas of justice and home affairs effective action requires international cooperation.

The Amsterdam Treaty brings progress in this respect. The first element relates to the former third pillar areas now transferred to the EC framework. According to the case law of the Court of Justice (ECJ), the Community enjoys treaty-making power on all those matters of external relations which are inextricably linked to matters of internal competence covered by Community legislation. It can be argued, therefore, that on all those matters of justice and home affairs covered by EC legislation the Community will also be capable of entering into agreements with third countries. In the areas of asylum and immigration in particular this offers scope for effective external action building on and complementing internal measures.

The second element concerns the areas remaining under Title VI. New Article 38 [ex Article K.10] TEU provides that agreements referred to in Article 24 [ex Article J.14] TEU may cover matters falling under Title VI. This means that also on third pillar matters the Council can make use of the new CFSP provision enabling it to negotiate and conclude agreements with third countries. The curious aspect here is that a treaty-making authorization and procedure has been introduced, yet without granting legal personality to the Union. As a result the formal contracting partners on the Union's side of future international agreements concluded under Title VI will be the Member States only. They may still decide to attach a Union label to such agreement by signing as members of the EU or (in a political sense) on behalf of it, but the Union will not be a contracting party and there will be no transfer of competence to the Union.[6] Yet for the first time the Union will be capable of entering into conventional relations with third countries on justice and home affairs even in the intergovernmental sphere. Having regard to the increasing need for international cooperation, especially in the fight against international organized crime and drug-trafficking, this could significantly increase the Union's political capacity in these areas.

Decision-making

No other aspect of the 'old' third pillar has attracted as much criticism as its decision-making system: the problems of a particularly cumbersome multi-level structure of decision-making, of the predominance of the unanimity voting rule and the limited role of initiative of the European Commission were all seen as major reasons for a 'blockage' in the system. The question is therefore to what extent the new Amsterdam Treaty provisions remove the existing problems of decision-making.

As regards the structure of decision-making 'old' Title VI introduced a five-level decision-making system consisting of (a) the Working Parties, (b) the Steering Groups, (c) the K.4 Committee, (d) the Coreper and (e) the Justice and Home Affairs Council. This involved two levels more than the already cumbersome Community structure. In addition, occasional friction emerged between the K.4 Committee and the Coreper because the Treaty did not fully clarify the division of tasks between these two major Council bodies.

For the major part of the areas of justice and home affairs these structural problems are eliminated by communitarization. The role of the K.4 Committee (it should now be called 'Article 36 Committee') will henceforth be limited to the few areas still covered by Article 29 [ex Article K.1] TEU and is therefore likely to be much less influential. The Steering Groups are not mentioned in the new Treaty. It is very likely that they will be abolished, a measure which seems sensible enough after most of the areas of cooperation they had to coordinate have been moved to the EC pillar. This should help to simplify and to speed up procedures under Title VI.

As regards voting rules, one of the most difficult issues during the negotiations, one would assume that the communitarization of most areas of the 'old' Title VI into the EC framework would bring decisive change in this respect. In Amsterdam, however, Chancellor Kohl blocked the introduction of qualified majority voting in the areas of asylum and immigration because of German anxieties about the particular asylum and immigration pressures on Germany and the involvement of Länder interests in this area. Yet there were other advocates of unanimity in the newly communitarized areas, the British government, for instance, in the area of judicial cooperation in civil matters. As a result new Article 67(1)–(2) [ex Article 73o(1)–(2)] EC now provides that the Council shall act unanimously within a transitional period of five years. After this period the Council shall take a decision unanimously with a view to making all or parts of the Title on free movement governed by the Article 251 [ex Article 189b] EC procedure, which provides for qualified majority voting. This two-stage approach applies to all measures provided for by Title IV EC, with the exception of the already previously communitarized visa policy. On all of the newly communitarized matters of Title IV majority voting will therefore become possible after five years. Yet even then the passage to majority voting remains subject to a unanimous decision on which the Council can perfectly well fail to agree.[7] The major disagreements between the Member States over key questions such as burden-sharing do not augur well in this respect.

As regards the areas remaining within intergovernmental Title VI, all the different types of acts mentioned above must be adopted by unanimity. However,

Article 34(2)(c) [ex Article K.6(2)(c)] TEU provides that measures implementing a 'decision' can be taken by qualified majority. This majority voting on implementing measures represents a small step forward because so far it required a unanimous decision by the Council to proceed to qualified majority voting on measures implementing the 'decision's' predecessor, the 'joint action'.[8] Yet there is also a new hurdle because amended Article K.6(3) now provides for a 'double' qualified majority, requiring not only 62 votes but also that these are cast by at least ten Member States. With majority voting being limited to implementing measures and subject to the 'double' qualification it seems unlikely that the changes will greatly increase the Union's decision-making capacity under Title VI.

One would have expected that in the newly communitarized areas the Commission's weak position within the 'old' third pillar would be drastically improved by the exclusive right of initiative it normally enjoys within the EC framework. Yet according to new Article 67 [ex Article 73o(1) and (2)] EC the Commission will still have to share the right of initiative with the Member States in all the newly communitarized areas under Title IV EC during the transitional period of five years. Only after this period will its right of initiative become exclusive. This is clearly a serious restriction on the Commission's role which will be made worse by the maintenance of unanimity in the same areas during the transitional period. The question can be raised whether an integration of policy areas into the EC framework which departs, even only temporarily, from the principle of the Commission's exclusive right of initiative in conjunction with maintaining the unanimity principle in the Council should still be regarded as communitarization, or rather as an import of intergovernmental procedures into the EC framework.

However, some elements of progress can be found outside Title IV EC. The Commission will enjoy an exclusive right of initiative in respect to the measures countering fraud affecting the financial interests of the Community and to customs cooperation, the latter being an area in which the Commission did not previously have any right of initiative. In the third pillar, the Commission still has to share its right of initiative with the Member States, but by virtue of amended Article 34(2) [ex Article K.6(2)] TEU it now extends also to police and judicial cooperation in criminal matters.

Overall, the reformed decision-making system of EU justice and home affairs brings therefore a simplified structure and a slightly enhanced role of the European Commission, though with a very limited move towards more majority voting during the transitional period and uncertain prospects for the time after. If one looks at the long list of new objectives this result of the IGC, in terms of improving the Union's decision-making capacity in justice and home affairs, appears inadequate and the communitarization introduced hardly worth its name.

Democratic control

The communitarization of parts of Title VI TEU offered a chance to significantly strengthen the EP's so far rather ephemeral role in this area. Yet this has been largely missed. By virtue of Article 67 [ex Article 73o] EC the Parliament, during the transitional period of five years, needs only to be consulted on measures adopted in all areas transferred to Title IV EC. After the transitional period there could be a move towards the application of the Article 251 [ex Article 189b] co-decision procedure in part or all of the newly communitarized areas. This, however, remains subject to a unanimous decision of the Council, which cannot be taken for granted. There will be an immediate application of the Article 189b procedure only in the communitarized areas outside of Title IV, i.e. combating fraud affecting EC financial interests and customs cooperation.

As regards the areas remaining under Title VI TEU the Council, by virtue of new Article 39 [ex Article K.11] TEU, will now be obliged to consult the EP before adopting any measures with the exception of common positions. This means that on all legally binding instruments the EP will have a role similar to that under the EC 'consultation procedure'.

Its strengthened consultative role will give the EP enhanced possibilities to make a political input into the EU policy process in these areas. Yet since the reformed legal instruments are likely to lead to an increased legislative output in justice and home affairs it seems regrettable that, at least for the transitional period, the EP will only be able to influence legislation through the weak instrument of consultation. After all, this legislation can have a major impact on the life of EU citizens.

The Amsterdam Treaty 'Protocol on the role of National Parliaments in the European Union' provides for improved procedures of informing national parliaments on Commission consultation documents and legislative proposals. This may actually improve the scrutiny possibilities of those national parliaments which have not always been provided with adequate information by their governments. It is also of interest that Article 5 of the Protocol provides that the Conference of European Affairs Committees (COSAC) may examine any legislative proposal or initiative in relation to the establishment of an area of freedom, security and justice which might have a direct bearing on the rights of individuals. The terms 'direct bearing' may be open to different interpretations, and the contributions of the COSAC will have no binding legal effects for the EU institutions. Nevertheless, this provision could strengthen cooperation between the parliaments of the European Union and increase information on EU justice and home affairs in some national parliaments.

Role of the Court of Justice

The Maastricht Treaty had exempted all areas covered by the 'old' third pillar from the jurisdiction of the ECJ. The only exception was that the Member States could decide to give the Court jurisdiction in the framework of any third pillar conventions, a possibility which led to lengthy controversies between the Member States and delayed several major conventions. The ECJ itself emphasized in 1995 that the resulting deficit of judicial control was particularly serious as regards the judicial protection of individuals who might be affected by measures taken in the fields of justice and home affairs.[9]

The Amsterdam Treaty introduces major changes in this respect. The areas covered by 'old' Title VI, now transferred into the EC framework, come automatically under the jurisdiction of the ECJ. Yet as regards the areas communitarized under Title IV EC new Article 68 [ex Article 73p] EC imposes three limitations on the role of the Court.

The first one, provided for by Article 68(1) [ex Article 73p(1)] EC limits the use of the preliminary rulings procedure to national courts and tribunals against whose decisions there is no remedy under national law. This is an important limitation because Article 234 [ex Article177] EC provides that 'any court or tribunal' may request the ECJ for a preliminary ruling. On the one hand this could reduce the additional burden on the ECJ resulting from the extension of its jurisdiction to areas such as asylum and immigration which account for a considerable share of the workload of national courts. Yet this limitation will also reduce the ECJ's possibilities of consolidating the *acquis communautaire* in these areas. Some important questions of interpretation may reach the level of courts of last instance only after considerable delays or even not at all.

The second limitation results from Article 68(2) [ex Article 73p(2)] EC which provides that 'in any event' the ECJ shall not have jurisdiction over measures in view of ensuring the absence of any controls on persons at internal borders, if these relate to the maintenance of law and order and the safeguarding of internal security. This reflects primarily the preoccupations of the French government that the ECJ may interfere with national competence over controls on persons for national security reasons. The wording chosen here goes beyond the public order exemption in other parts of the EC Treaty, and some Member States may be tempted to give a very broad interpretation to 'maintenance of law and order' if it comes to limit the scope of the Court's jurisdiction.

The third limitation is contained in Article 68(3) [ex Article 73p(3)] which provides that the Council, the Commission or a Member State may request the ECJ to give a ruling on a question of interpretation of this Title or any Community act based thereon. However, the second sentence stipulates that in this case the ruling given by the Court shall not apply to judgments of national courts which have become *res judicata*. Individuals will therefore not be able to benefit retroactively from rulings of the ECJ under this provision. This is another questionable innovation in the framework of the Community Treaty.

As regards cooperation under Title VI TEU Article 35 [ex Article K.7] TEU introduces jurisdiction of the ECJ for three types of proceedings.

Article 35(1) provides that the ECJ shall have jurisdiction to give preliminary rulings on the validity and interpretation of 'framework decisions' and 'decisions', on the interpretation of conventions and on the validity and interpretation of measures implementing them. Yet this jurisdiction is not automatic but, by virtue of Article 35(2), dependent on a declaration made by the time of the signing of the Treaty or at any time after by those Member States willing to accept such jurisdiction by the Court. This formally introduces into the Union Treaty the possibility of differentiation between the Member States as to the acceptance of the ECJ's jurisdiction. A possibility for further differentiation is provided for by Article

35(3), which leaves the Member States the option of either accepting that requests for preliminary rulings may come from any court or tribunal or to limit such requests to courts or tribunals against whose decisions there is no judicial remedy under national law. The Member States are thereby left with a maximum of choice as regards their acceptance of preliminary rulings in the intergovernmental area, an *à la carte* approach which will do nothing to increase consistency and coherence in the EU legal *acquis* and could create differences between the Member States as regards the judicial protection of individuals in EU justice and home affairs.

Article 35(6) TEU introduces jurisdiction by the ECJ to review the legality of 'framework decisions' and 'decisions' in actions brought by a Member State or the Commission on the same grounds as provided for by Article 230 [ex Article 173] EC (action for annulment). Unlike in the case of the latter, however, there is no possibility for natural or legal persons to institute proceedings if a measure is of direct and individual concern to them.

Article 35(7) provides that the ECJ shall have jurisdiction to rule on any dispute between Member States regarding the interpretation or the application of acts adopted under the Title VI provisions whenever a dispute cannot be settled by the Council within six months. The ECJ is also vested with jurisdiction to rule on disputes between Member States and the Commission regarding the interpretation or application of conventions established under Title VI. The emphasis here is clearly on dispute settlement in the Council, with a very limited role for the Commission and no enforcement mechanism.

The jurisdiction of the ECJ under Title VI TEU is also subject to a limitation similar to the one in the newly communitarized areas. Pursuant to Article 35(5) the ECJ has no jurisdiction as regards the responsibilities of Member States with regard to the maintenance of law and order and the safeguarding of internal security. The scope of this exemption is further extended by the explicit exclusion of jurisdiction to review the validity or proportionality of operations carried out by the police or other law enforcement agencies of a Member State. Since nearly all common action in the fields of police cooperation and judicial cooperation in criminal matters is likely to have implications for 'law and order' and 'internal security', a broad interpretation of this clause could restrict effective jurisdiction by the Court under Title VI TEU even more than under Title IV EC.

Taken together these provisions will considerably increase the scope for judicial review by the ECJ on justice and home affairs in both the EC framework and under Title VI TEU. On the negative side, however, the ECJ's jurisdiction will be subject to a number of important limitations which mark another departure from the Community model and there are the risks of *à la carte* jurisdiction and wide-ranging exemptions in the third pillar.

Schengen and flexibility

Grown out of the increasing frustration of the Schengen members over the opposition of the United Kingdom to common policy development in justice and home affairs, the subject of 'flexibility'[10] became one of the key issues of the IGC. The question was whether Member States wanting to achieve progress within the EU system should be enabled to make use of the Union's existing institutional framework, its decision-making procedures and its legal instruments instead of having to resort to structures outside of the Union – like Schengen – which multiply decision-making structures and weaken the Union's political role. The IGC eventually agreed on the introduction of a wide range of cases of flexibility in the areas covered by 'old' Title VI TEU.

The first case is a long-expected one: the incorporation of Schengen into the Union *acquis*. Technically this takes the form of a Protocol to the Amsterdam Treaty which authorizes the at present 13 signatories of Schengen to establish closer cooperation among themselves within the scope of the Schengen agreements and provides that this cooperation shall be conducted within the institutional and legal framework of the European Union (Article 1).[11] With the entry into force of the Protocol the Schengen Executive Committee will be replaced by the Council which will take the necessary measures to incorporate the Schengen *acquis* (Article 2(1)). Proposals and initiatives to build upon the Schengen *acquis* will then be subject to the relevant provisions of the Treaties (Article 5(1)). All this sounds very straightforward.

Yet there are a number of provisions which make one expect that the Schengen *acquis* might not be so easily digested by the Union framework. One difficult issue is to determine an adequate legal base for each bit of the Schengen *acquis*. For some of these (e.g. visa requirements) an EC legal base may be most appropriate, for others (e.g. police cooperation) 'intergovernmental' Title VI TEU might be the obvious choice. To determine adequate legal bases for an *acquis* of around 3,000 pages – a process for which the elegant term 'ventilation' has been coined – is quite a task. It may well be that in the future former Schengen practitioners will be looking back with some nostalgia to the time when the Schengen *acquis* was not yet scattered over more than a dozen different legal bases across the Union Treaty and they did not yet have to struggle with the institutional and procedural requirements of the EU system.

Article 4 of the Protocol formally affirms that the United Kingdom and Ireland are not bound by the *acquis* but that they may 'at any time' accept some or all of the *acquis*. Yet the next paragraph says that the Council shall decide on such a request with the unanimity of the Schengen members and of the representative of the applicant country. This means that there is no right for non-participating Member States to join. The 'outs' will be dependent on the unanimous goodwill of the 'ins'.

So much for the incorporation of Schengen. Also of importance is the possibility of setting up new frameworks of 'closer cooperation'. As a result of the communitarization of most of the former third pillar areas, 'closer cooperation in justice and home affairs will need to be established on the basis of different legal provisions'[12] (Articles 11 [ex Article 5a] EC or 40 [ex Article K.12] TEU), depending on the subject matter covered. There are major differences between these two doors to flexibility.

The list of conditions to be fulfilled is much longer in Article 11 EC than it is in Article 40 TEU. One rather interesting difference in this respect is that the former Article provides that 'closer cooperation' should not concern the citizenship of the

Union or discriminate between nationals of Member States. Yet the same condition is not provided for by Article 40 TEU. This seems difficult to understand because 'closer cooperation' in police and judicial cooperation matters can certainly also concern EU citizenship and cause discrimination between nationals. The procedures for arriving at 'closer cooperation' are also different under these provisions. Under Article 11 EC the Commission plays a key role in the process due to its right of initiative; under Article 40 TEU it is the Council which is the sole decisive actor. Needless to say, the instruments and procedures after the establishment of 'closer cooperation' are those of the respective Treaty frameworks and therefore substantially different. This appears rather awkward if one thinks how closely interrelated are many of the areas covered by the two Titles.

There are other cases of flexibility provided for by the Amsterdam Treaty which may be described as the group of the opt-ins and opt-outs. The 'Protocol on the position of the United Kingdom and Ireland' guarantees the UK and Ireland a complete opt-out (the term is of course not used) from the new EC Title on free movement of persons, asylum and immigration. Yet Article 3 of the Protocol offers both Member States an opt-in possibility for the adoption and application of any measure proposed under this Title at the latest three months after the proposal has been made. Article 8 of the same Protocol gives Ireland a possibility to opt–out from this opt-out/opt-in Protocol if it no longer wishes to be covered by it. The 'Protocol on the application of certain aspects of Article 14 [ex Article A] EC' guarantees the United Kingdom the continuation of its right to exercise, at its frontiers with other Member States, controls on persons and gives a derogation to the United Kingdom and Ireland to continue to make between themselves the necessary arrangements for maintaining the 'Common Travel Area'. Denmark has been granted a similar opt-out to that of the United Kingdom and Ireland in the 'Protocol on the position of Denmark'. Yet the Danish case is obviously more complicated because Denmark is a Schengen member. Article 5 deals with this problem by providing that Denmark has six months in which to decide whether it will incorporate any Council decision building on the Schengen *acquis* into national law. In a Declaration attached to the Protocol on asylum for nationals of EU Member States, Belgium declares that in accordance with relevant international conventions it will carry out an individual examination of any asylum request made by a national of another Member State. This represents a partial Belgian opt-out from the agreement reached in this Protocol that Member States shall be regarded as safe countries of origin in asylum matters. Finally, Declaration 8 on Article 31 [ex Article K.3(e)] TEU exempts Member States whose legal system does not provide for minimum sentences from any obligation under Article 31(e) [ex Article K.3(e)] TEU to adopt them.

As a result of this amazing range of flexibility clauses, the Amsterdam Treaty allows the Schengen members to achieve their long-standing aim of incorporating the Schengen *acquis* into the Union framework while at the same time providing ample scope for satisfying particular national interests in form of opt-outs and opting-in possibilities. Yet the price to be paid for this 'flexibilization' of EU justice and home affairs is a plethora of new problems and risks.

Although legal acts adopted (or incorporated) under flexibility clauses will not become formally part of the *acquis communautaire* they will lead to the creation of different sets of legislation and case law of the ECJ with a corresponding fragmentation of the EC and EU legal order. Disputes over the scope of and conflicts between flexibility and non-flexibility legal acts are likely to arise. The need to distinguish, for instance, between EC Schengen and EC non-Schengen directives as well as between EU Schengen and EU non-Schengen 'framework decisions' in the third pillar is certainly not going to make the work of parliaments, courts and administrations easier.

There will be a risk of a widening political and legal gap between the 'ins' and 'outs' of Schengen and any other group establishing 'closer cooperation'. It is true that Article 43 [ex Article K.15(f)] TEU provides that closer cooperation shall not affect the interests of non-participating Member States. Yet with most areas of justice and home affairs being closely interrelated it is difficult to see how any substantial closer cooperation in one area can avoid affecting the interests of non-participating Member States in other areas.

An important factor in avoiding the perpetuation of different groupings is the possibility for non-participating Member States to join in 'closer cooperation' at a later stage. Article 43(1)(g) [ex Article K.15(1)(g)] TEU provides in this regard that all Member States shall be allowed to become parties to the cooperation 'at any time', provided that they comply with the basic decision and with the decisions taken within that framework. Yet, as shown above, the right of the 'outs' to join is not automatic but is dependent on the support of the Commission and/or the 'ins' in the Council, which in some way contradicts the 'at any time' promise. This contributes to the gap between 'ins' and 'outs' and can create political tensions. A foretaste of these was already given shortly after the Amsterdam European Council: the British and Irish delegations disputed the unanimity requirement for their possible adherence to the Schengen *acquis*, claiming that qualified majority had been agreed on at Amsterdam. It seems that Spain – engaged in the bitter Anglo–Spanish dispute over Gibraltar – insisted on unanimity because this would allow it to block the United Kingdom's adherence to Schengen.[13] The case shows how easily the politics of 'in' and 'out' can be abused for other political purposes.

Transparency

There can be little doubt that so far justice and home affairs have been one of the least transparent policy areas of the EU. This is partly due to the traditions of secrecy on internal security matters prevailing at the national level, but partly also to the unwillingness of Council and Commission to expose the nearly always complex and often sensitive negotiations on justice and home affairs issues to possible disruption by wider public debate.

Public access to documents is certainly a key issue in this respect, and so far the debate on 'transparency' in EU justice and home affairs has largely focused on this question. In spite of the long struggle of Tony Bunyan from Statewatch for access to Council documents, serious splits in Council over the issue and the Court's decision in the *Guardian* case[14] the Council has not departed from the basic rule of confidentiality of its proceedings codified in Article 5(1) of its Rules of Procedure. The number of documents made available to public access has certainly increased during the years, but documents of primary importance for understanding the decision-making process such as draft decisions, minutes of relevant Council bodies and even non-binding texts adopted by the Council are still only disclosed on a case-by-case basis.

The Amsterdam Treaty should bring some progress in this respect. First of all it seems likely that the communitarization of the major part of the 'old' third pillar areas (asylum, immigration, border controls, etc.) will lead to a spillover of the more generous public information practices of the EC framework into these areas, because of the stronger position of the EP within the Community system. Yet there are also two new treaty provisions which can make a difference: Article 255 [ex Article 191a] EC provides that any citizen of the Union shall have a right of access to European Parliament, Council and Commission documents subject to conditions determined by the Council in accordance with the procedure of Article 251 [ex Article 189b] EC within two years after the entry into force of the new Treaty. Since this procedure provides for co-decision by the EP, which has consistently advocated greater transparency, these conditions are likely to be less restrictive than the present ones. It should be noted, however, that this provision applies only to the EC Treaty and therefore does not cover the areas remaining under Title VI TEU. The other provision is new Article 41 [ex Article K.13] TEU which provides, *inter alia*, that Article 195 [ex Article 138e] EC shall apply to Title VI TEU. This means that the functions of the Ombudsman as regards inquiries into cases of mal-administration in the activities of the institutions will be extended to the inter-governmental areas of police cooperation and judicial cooperation in criminal matters. While the rather limited powers of the Ombudsman are unlikely to shed much light on the arcana of intergovernmental proceedings, the possibility for citizens to address formal complaints to the Ombudsman nevertheless makes what is left of the third pillar subject to some sort of public gaze and control and is in this sense a contribution to transparency.

The Treaty of Amsterdam therefore brings some elements of progress in respect to transparency. However, the extraordinary complexity of the new treaty provisions and the proliferation of 'flexibility' will also create new problems of transparency as regards public understanding of EU decision-making in justice and home affairs which may well obscure the limited progress achieved.

First steps towards the implementation of the new provisions

How difficult it may be for the Union to realize the potential of Amsterdam in justice and home affairs was shown during 1998 not only by the protracted struggle over the definition and incorporation of the Schengen *acquis* but also by the rather halfhearted character of the first major step taken towards the implementation of the new Treaty provisions. On the basis of a Commission Communication on the development of the new 'area of freedom, security and justice' of 14 July 1999[15] the Member States agreed on an 'Action Plan on how best to implement the provisions of the Treaty of Amsterdam on an Area of Freedom, Security and Justice' which was formally adopted by the Justice and Home Affairs Council on 3 December 1998.[16]

The 'Vienna Action Plan' has the merit of clarifying the rationale of the new 'area of freedom, security and justice'. As regards the concept of 'freedom' the Action Plan emphasizes that the new Treaty opens the way to giving freedom 'a meaning beyond free movement of persons across internal borders' which includes the 'freedom to live in a law-abiding environment' protected by public authorities at the national and European level. This marks a clear step beyond the old Schengen rationale with its focus on free movement and mere 'compensatory measures'.

On the meaning of 'security', however, the Action Plan takes a less forward looking view, reflecting the concerns of several Member States about retaining control over internal security instruments. It explicitly states that the new Treaty – although aimed at developing common action in the fields of police and criminal justice cooperation and offering enhanced security to Union citizens – does not pursue the intention to create a 'European security area' in the sense of uniform detection and investigation procedures. The Action Plan also provides that the Member States' responsibilities to maintain law and order should not be affected by the new provisions.

On the concept of 'justice' the Action Plan is again more ambitious, declaring that Amsterdam is aimed at giving citizens 'a common sense of justice throughout the Union' with an impact on day-to-day life which includes both access to justice and full judicial cooperation among Member States. The wording may fall short of the idea of a 'European judicial area', but it clearly goes beyond judicial cooperation as mere accompanying process of economic integration.

Part II of the Action Plan defines a number of 'priorities and measures'. These comprise both strategic objectives (such as developing an 'overall migration strategy') and a range of more concrete measures, most of which have to be taken either within two or within five years.

In the area of asylum and immigration policy the Action Plan focuses largely on restrictive measures such as the implementation of EURODAC, the limitation of secondary movements of asylum seekers between Member States, common assessment of countries of origin in order to design common prevention strategies and a coherent readmission and return policy, all this in combination with additional measures to combat illegal immigration. There are some elements, such as the definition of minimum standards on the reception of asylum seekers, which go slightly beyond the pre-Amsterdam *acquis*. Yet some major issues, such as the social integration of legally resident immigrants and asylum seekers or the potential use of external economic and CFSP measures to reduce immigration pressure, have not been addressed at all. Due to the opposition of France and Spain precise objectives regarding the difficult question of burden-sharing in the area of asylum policy had to be dropped from the Plan. The Action Plan uses the term 'European migration strategy'. Yet it is difficult to see such a term having any meaning without adequate policies on prevention, integration and burden-sharing.

In the area of police cooperation and judicial cooperation in criminal matters the Action Plan envisages a number of measures to improve the position of Europol such as the examination of Europol access to investigation data of the Schengen Information System and the Customs Information System as well as a stronger focus of its work on operational cooperation. Yet on some of the more sensitive issues, such as the nature and scope of the new power of Europol to ask competent authorities of the Member States to conduct and coordinate their investigations, the Action Plan remains vague and evasive. The same applies to the new possibility for Europol to participate in 'operational actions of joint teams' (Article 30(2) TEU). One cannot escape the impression that some Member States are concerned about any increase of Europol's role and therefore try to delay the implementation of the modest Amsterdam reforms in this area.

Positive elements in other areas of police cooperation are the renewed emphasis placed on the evaluation of investigative techniques in relation to the detection of serious forms of organized crime and on the expansion of operational cooperation between law enforcement services. Yet the Action Plan becomes again vague (and even tortuous in its wording) when it comes to the sensitive issue of cross-border law enforcement. The Plan speaks only about 'consideration' to be given to the 'determination of the conditions and limitations under which the competent law enforcement authorities of one Member State may operate in the territory of another Member State, in liaison and agreement with the latter'. This formulation reminds one of the very beginnings of the Schengen process in the mid-1980s.

The emphasis in judicial cooperation in criminal matters is largely on the implementation and the improvement of existing instruments and mechanisms such as strengthening the European judicial network and the effective implementation of the two extradition conventions. As regards the crucial issue of the mutual recognition of decisions and enforcement of judgments in criminal matters the Action Plan only provides cautiously for the 'initiation of a process with a view to facilitate' such recognition. The absence of concrete objectives on this point in the Action Plan will not help. The Action Plan is hardly more concrete on the question of the approximation of criminal law. It is true that the Plan provides, for instance, for the identification of behaviours in the field of organized crime for which it is urgent to establish minimum rules relating to the constituent elements of crime and to penalties. Yet no time limit is set for the adoption of such minimum rules, and as regards such important areas as rules on counterfeiting and fraud the possibility of approximation is only to be 'examined'. All this is not to say that the Action Plan is devoid of substance: there is a whole range of measures provided for which is likely to significantly improve data exchange, speed up and improve mutual assistance and to allow for better training and analysis of investigative techniques. Yet such limited measures are unlikely to realize the potential of the 'area of freedom, security and justice' and to fulfil the public expectations created by presenting this area as a major new benefit for the European citizen.

Conclusions

After the entry into force of the Treaty of Amsterdam there will be few other EU policy-areas which have a more wide-ranging set of objectives and offer more possibilities for Community and/or Union action than justice and home affairs. Because of the time limits set for action in the EC framework some of these possibilities will have to be used. There are also other elements of clear progress like the refined set of instruments under Title VI TEU, the new scope for cooperation with third countries and the strengthened role of the ECJ.

Yet at the same time the Amsterdam reforms in the areas of justice and home affairs are deeply flawed: the policy objectives focus on individual issues rather than comprehensive strategies, there is a highly artificial split between EC and intergovernmental areas of competence, the decision-making procedures retain much of the weakening features of the 'old' third pillar and, at least for the transitional period of five years, the areas communitarized in the new Title IV EC appear almost like an intergovernmental pillar within the EC framework. In addition, there are old as well as new constitutional problems: for the transitional period there will be hardly any improvement as regards the notorious democracy deficit of justice and home affairs, there are potentially serious limitations on the role of the ECJ and, perhaps most important of all, the enormous upsurge of flexibility means that there will be a major risk of legal fragmentation and political tensions between the 'ins' and 'outs' of Schengen and other frameworks of enhanced cooperation. The progress achieved in terms of new objectives, extended competences and the incorporation of Schengen has clearly been bought at a hefty price in terms of fragmentation, old and new structural weaknesses and an incomplete and intergovernmentalized communitarization in new Title IV EC.

Whatever legitimacy the Union system may be able to draw from the legal validity of its action and consent of its citizens, this legitimacy will in the longer term be eroded if it does not produce policies which effectively serve in a recognizable way the citizens' interest. With its emphasis on the Union as an 'area of freedom, security and justice' and the long range of new policy-making objectives under Titles IV [ex IIIa] EC and VI TEU, the Treaty of Amsterdam raises the stakes for the Union as regards securing legitimacy through performance. There has been no shortage of representatives of national governments and Union institutions who have hailed the Amsterdam reforms in the areas of justice and home affairs as a major breakthrough, making extensive use of these ringing terms of 'freedom, security and justice'. Yet all this means that the Union has placed additional programmatic demands on itself which are likely to raise citizens' expectations. The legitimacy of EU justice and home affairs will, therefore, much more than in the past depend on the Union's success or failure to meet these demands through actual performance. As Jürgen Habermas has pointed out in the context of his analysis of crises of legitimation, 'the penalty for this failure [to meet demands] is withdrawal of legitimation'.[17] The absence of a comprehensive basis for common policy-making and the persisting limitations as regards the decision-making capacity will not make it easy for the Union – at least during the transitional period of five years – to meet old and new demands for effective EU action in justice and home affairs. It will need considerable efforts by the Union institutions and the Member States to prevent the Union from falling into just another 'expectations-capability gap' which could seriously erode both its legitimacy and its capacity to respond to the increasing transnational security risks.

Endnotes

1. Referred to in Article 61(b) [ex Article 73i(b)] EC.
2. Brussels Convention on Jurisdiction and the Enforcement of Judgments in Civil and Commercial Matters.
3. See the report of Professor Mireille Delmas-Marty, 'Vers un espace judiciaire européen' presented to the European Parliament and the European Commission in 1996.
4. As provided for by Article 35(1) [ex Article K.7(1)] TEU.
5. As provided for by new Article 39 [ex Article K.11] TEU.
6. Declaration 4 annexed to the Amsterdam Treaty explicitly states that Article J.14 TEU shall not imply any transfer of competence from the Member States to the European Union.
7. The only newly communitarized areas to which majority voting according to the Article 189b procedure will be applied immediately are measures against fraud affecting the financial interests of the Community and customs cooperation, both being located outside of Title IV.
8. See 'old' Article K.3(2)(b) TEU.
9. Cour de Justice des Communautés européennes, *Rapport de la Cour de Justice sur certains aspects de l'application du Traité sur l'Union européenne*, Luxembourg, May 1995.
10. The term used in the relevant Treaty provisions is 'closer cooperation'. Yet during the IGC, 'flexibility' acquired a wider political meaning covering all possible forms of differentiated integration within the framework of the Treaties.
11. Protocol integrating the Schengen *acquis* into the framework of the European Union.
12. Both of which are linked to a new general clause on flexibility in Article 43 [ex Article K.15] TEU.
13. *Agence Europe*, No.7014, 11 July 1997, p. 2.
14. Case T-194/94.
15. COM (1998) 459.
16. OJ No. C19/1 of 23 January 1999.
17. J. Habermas, *Legitimation Crisis*, Boston: Beacon Press, 1976, p. 69.

Chapter 9

Common Foreign and Security Policy and defence: a lost opportunity?

G. Wyn Rees

Introduction

The Maastricht and Amsterdam Treaties witnessed an attempt to create in the European Union (EU) a fully capable foreign policy actor, with the capacity to draw upon military means to underpin its actions. From the time of the Treaty of Rome, the European Community had focused its efforts on economic integration and eschewed the pursuit of a foreign identity, whilst leaving defence issues in the hands of NATO. By the 1970s, however, a foreign policy mechanism entitled European Political Cooperation (EPC) had been established, in recognition of the fact that there was an external dimension to trade cooperation and that EC members needed to coordinate their voice in international affairs. Therefore, the forging of a Common Foreign and Security Policy (CFSP) in the 1990s was able to build upon the foundations that had been laid before in EPC.

However, whilst the CFSP was born amid ambitious hopes that reflected the end of the Cold War, it has proved to be an arduous process to realize these in practice. The spheres of foreign affairs and defence are notoriously areas in which nation states jealously guard their sovereign rights. Since 1990, this has been compounded by the turbulence of events in Europe and by the process of adaptation in international organizations other than the European Union. What has emerged is a foreign policy and infant defence identity within the EU that has surpassed its EPC-predecessor yet remains constrained and less capable than its proponents desired. Whether such an imperfect system is equal to the challenges that it faces is far from certain.

A moment of opportunity

The ending of the Cold War, by transforming the external political and strategic situation, provided a unique moment of opportunity to exceed the norms of EPC. The moment appeared to be propitious to advance the entire process of European integration that had started in the 1980s with the introduction of the Single Market.

A fully fledged political union, with its own dedicated foreign policy and defence resources, seemed to be within the grasp of Member States.

This was made possible by two fundamental changes to the environment in which the EC had historically developed. Firstly, with the demise of the Soviet threat, west European countries were no longer at risk of invasion from the east. This reduced their dependency on the United States for physical protection and enabled them to question America's right to demand its leadership position over its allies. The Europeans were now able to assert their independence from the United States, even if that risked antagonizing their erstwhile superpower patron. Secondly, the unification of Germany heralded the realignment of power relationships between the major west European countries. In so doing, it presented the need to tie the European states together for fear that old antagonisms, that had marred their histories, could be reignited. Closer integration within the EC offered the means to prevent the renationalization of policies in the western half of the continent, as well as offering a possible model of development to eastern Europe.

Nevertheless, although countries such as France, Germany Belgium, Spain and Luxembourg were eager to grasp the opportunities presented in 1990–91, there was considerable hesitation among the twelve members of the EC regarding the scope of the reform process. There were those, such as Britain, who were sceptical of the argument that unless the Community speeded up its integration process, then the whole post-war edifice of European cooperation was at risk of unravelling. Britain expressed doubts as to whether the Member States possessed a sufficiently broad range of shared interests to conduct a common foreign policy. The EC was also inexperienced in foreign affairs. The small EPC Secretariat represented the only institutional 'memory' in foreign policy because national Presidencies had always been responsible for the day-to-day conduct of EPC business. The past involvement of the European Commission in EPC had only occurred when economic instruments, such as sanctions, had been employed.

The prospect of developing a defence dimension within the EC posed numerous difficulties. West European states would have to develop a shared appreciation of their defence interests – in the absence of the traditional guidance by the United States – as well as plan and resource an operational military capability that could act independently of the Atlantic Alliance. A European defence identity already existed, albeit in nascent form, in the Western European Union (WEU). The WEU, which was grounded on the Modified Brussels Treaty of 1954, would have to be dismantled, or at best subsumed, if the EC was to become the defence expression of its members. It was inevitable that by undertaking such a course of action the Community would risk duplicating the pre-existing responsibilities of NATO, which itself was struggling to adapt to a post-Cold War role. Britain, the Netherlands and Portugal were deeply attached to the preservation of transatlantic defence structures and were acutely aware of the negative reaction that such efforts by the EC would cause in Washington. These Atlanticist countries advocated continuing reliance on the proven structure of NATO, rather than seeking to build up expensive military capabilities and command structures within a framework untested by the experience of the Cold War.

As a result, the EC decided to discuss these issues as part of an Inter-governmental Conference (IGC) on Political Union, which opened in Rome at the end of 1990. Foreign policy and defence formed a complex array of arguments at the heart of the conflicting visions of various Member States about the sort of European Union that should be created. Although foreign and defence policy were just two issues amongst many in the IGC, they encapsulated many of the contrasting ambitions amongst the Member States. At one end of the spectrum were countries that sought to create a genuinely integrated Union, with its own foreign and defence identity, separate from the United States. At the other end of the spectrum were states committed only to intergovernmental cooperation, in which foreign policy cooperation would remain limited, while defence would remain the prerogative of NATO. The goal of the IGC became to steer a path between these divergent outlooks. As Edwards and Nuttall commented of the IGC, the positions adopted by member states were 'determined more by the type of Europe they wanted than with the purpose and scope of a European foreign policy'.[1]

The Treaty on European Union

Title V of the Treaty on European Union (TEU) emerged as an elaborate compromise from among the negotiating positions of the Twelve. In the lead-up to the Maastricht European Council a variety of contrasting positions had been evident in relation to foreign policy and defence. France and Germany, with the support of countries such as Belgium and Spain, had pressed for a common foreign policy to be an integral part of the new European Union. Yet opposition to these ideas from countries such as Britain and Denmark led to a compromise being hammered out under the auspices of the Luxembourg Presidency in June 1991. This took the form of a pillared structure for the Union in which foreign policy was designated as an intergovernmental sphere of activity separate from the supranational Community pillar. This represented a significant dilution of the more ambitious designs for the EU. Preserving an intergovernmental approach increased the likelihood that EU foreign policy outputs would emerge as the lowest common denominators from among the national policies of the Member States.

As regards defence, Germany and France had called, in December 1990, for an organic relationship to be created between the WEU and the EC. This reflected the long-held vision of the French government for a capable defence identity to be embodied within a European organization. Both France and Germany envisaged the WEU becoming the defence expression of the Union until such a time as the Modified Brussels Treaty could be merged into the Treaty of Rome. Support for this position was forthcoming from the European Commission; its President, Jacques Delors, had argued that the poor showing of the EC in the 1990–91 Gulf War demonstrated the need for a Community competence over security and defence.[2] However, different lessons had been drawn from the Gulf experience by those nations with an Atlanticist predisposition and they argued the converse, that US–European cooperation needed to be reinforced. They vociferously opposed the subordination of the WEU to the proposed European Union and argued for the emphasis to be placed on the WEU's relationship with the Atlantic Alliance. There was a willingness to see the WEU made more operationally capable but the line was drawn at anything that resembled a duplication of NATO's command structures.[3]

The creation of the CFSP was a significant step forward in the history of European integration, comparable only, in the eyes of one commentator, to the Messina Conference of 1956–57.[4] But, because of the compromises that had to be negotiated between the Member States, the actual powers enshrined within the CFSP were limited and it represented little more than a codification of those practices that had grown up within EPC.[5] Its objectives were broadly drawn: to safeguard the common values and security of the Union (Article J1.2 TEU) and Member States were called upon to respect their obligation to inform and consult one another and to act collectively where possible. Member States who were United Nations Security Council members were expected to keep other states informed of relevant decisions so that, to the greatest extent possible, a broadly based foreign policy could be pursued.

The European Council was invested with the power to define guidelines for the CFSP, thereby ensuring an intergovernmental approach to foreign policy-making. This satisfied the demand of countries such as Britain and France who were determined to preserve national influence over foreign policy. The EC's external trade relations were confined to the first pillar and decisions relating to the exercise of relevant instruments, such as economic sanctions, stood outside of CFSP. Article M ruled that 'nothing in this Treaty shall affect the Treaties establishing the European Communities' (Article M TEU) whilst Article J.8.2 TEU made the Council responsible for maintaining consistency between the pillars. Nevertheless, the interface between the two pillars was recognized to be something that had to be monitored because of the risk of spillback from pillar two contaminating pillar one.

The question of the interaction between the intergovernmental CFSP and the Community's supranational institutions also exhibited potential for future tension. In the TEU the European Court of Justice was accorded no jurisdiction over the substance of the CFSP itself and its only point of contact would arise if there was overlap between the first and second pillars. For its part, the European Parliament's (EP) role in the CFSP was also deliberately restricted. The Parliament had been a strong advocate, throughout the period of the IGC, of incorporating foreign and defence policy within the Community's structures. It had hoped to play an influential role in such matters, increasing the Union's accountability in foreign affairs, once the Treaty was concluded. Yet Article J.7 TEU permitted the EP only to be informed and consulted on the CFSP and gave it no input into policy formation. Stipulated within the Treaty was the condition that an annual debate should take place in the EP on the progress of CFSP. Britain and France were instrumental in keeping the EP out of foreign and security policy on the grounds that not even national parliaments enjoyed a significant level of influence in this area. Indirectly, this has contributed to the overall criticism that the EU lacks democratic forms of accountability over its policies.

The negotiation of the TEU demonstrated that the Member States were reluctant to create a regular funding mechanism for the CFSP, due to the fact that it threatened to impose new demands on their national budgets. Two sources of funding were put forward: administrative expenditure in CFSP could be charged to the EC budget (Article J.11.2 TEU), while operational expenditures could either be drawn from the budget or charged directly to the Member States. In practice, this was likely to mean that initiatives would be funded from the Community budget, because in a crisis the EU would be unwilling to suffer the delay of requesting funds from its members. This process risked generating new frictions between the Council and the EP. The EP, while being denied the right of oversight over CFSP, was simultaneously being expected to relinquish its powers of accountability over the EC budget. This matter was not adequately addressed until the IGC of 1996–97 where it was agreed that operational expenditure could be drawn from the EC budget as a matter of course.

Similarly, the role of the European Commission in CFSP was tightly circumscribed. It was to be fully associated with the CFSP (Title V, Article J.9 TEU) and possessed a right of initiative, but in practical terms it was likely to play only a supportive role to that of the Presidency. The former EPC Secretariat was folded into the Council's Secretariat General and various working groups that provided an analytical focus on particular international issues were brought together. In addition, both the Permanent Ambassadors in Coreper and the Political Committee were accorded the right to assist in preparing the foreign policy agenda for the foreign ministers in the General Affairs Council.[6] This latter development contained the potential for dispute over spheres of responsibility as there were no clear lines of demarcation between the two bodies. Lastly, it was decided to inaugurate a dedicated division of the Commission to deal with foreign affairs; this became DG1A, which was placed under Commissioner Hans van den Broek. It was acknowledged that other Commissioners dealing with issues such as external economic relations would inevitably develop areas of overlap within the realm of foreign affairs. This was taken up in the early stages of the Santer Presidency when the foreign and external economic affairs portfolios were divided between four Commissioners resulting, in the eyes of some, in a dilution of the Commission's presence in international affairs.[7]

The instruments by which the CFSP could be carried out were divided into Joint Actions and Common Positions, to be defined in specific circumstances by the Council. Common Positions, a carry-over of the practice of EPC, made consultation amongst the Member States obligatory, although this was not legally enforceable. The Maastricht text represented a strengthening of the commitment of Member States to Common Positions as compared to what had hitherto been the case under EPC.[8] The more ambitious instruments, Joint Actions, were designed to develop the EU's ability to take decisive action. However, the breadth of issues that could be handled by Joint Actions was never specified and its precise distinction from a Common Position was left vague. Its viability depended on whether each Member State would be willing to act in concert with its partners and the choice of a Common Position was left to the circumstances of individual cases.

Decision-making in relation to Common Positions and Joint Actions confronted the fundamental question of whether Member States were willing to abrogate their national foreign policies in favour of a common policy. It was agreed that Joint Actions could only result from a unanimous decision amongst the Member States, on the basis of guidelines laid down by the Council (Title V, Article J.3.1 TEU). The British compromised to the extent that they accepted that once all states had agreed, the implementation of decisions could be taken by qualified majority voting (QMV). A qualified majority was defined as 54 votes in favour cast by eight states (Title V, Article J.3.2 TEU). This overcame a hurdle that had dogged the IGC negotiations but only at the expense of enshrining national vetoes over Joint Actions and the complexity of the QMV provisions made it likely that they would only rarely be used.

Defence and the Western European Union

Implicit within the negotiations on the IGC was a distinction between the issues of 'security' and 'defence': the latter was understood to relate to the planning and use of military power, whilst security was interpreted as covering a broader array of issues, such as arms procurement and disarmament. A subsequent report from a security working group recommended that four areas be considered as legitimate subjects for CFSP Joint Actions: namely, the Conference on Security and Cooperation in Europe (CSCE – renamed in 1994 the OSCE), arms exports, arms control negotiations and nuclear non-proliferation.[9] This recommendation was endorsed at the Edinburgh European Council meeting in December 1992. These subjects demonstrated the historical continuity of CFSP as they had all been topics of consideration within EPC.

As for defence, the TEU continued to exclude national defence industries from the provisions of the Single Market.[10] This was a source of frustration to those that believed that the inclusion of arms procurement could serve as a useful part of the integration process. More substantially, the Treaty fell short of investing the EU with the competence to take decisions over the use of military forces. This was because of the strident opposition of several Member States. However, a defence dimension was granted to the EU in terms of subcontracting military issues to the WEU, which was declared to be 'an integral part of the development of the Union' (Title V, Article J.4.2 TEU). For the first time an explicit linkage between the two organizations had been established. The WEU was given the task of 'elaborat[ing] and implement[ing]' actions on the Union's behalf (Title V, Article J.4.2 TEU) and while the European Council could not instruct the WEU to act, nevertheless it possessed the right to make 'requests' to the organization. This form of words ensured the institutional autonomy of the WEU, enabling it to act independently, while making it available for tasking by the EU.

This left considerable room for interpretation over how the relationship between the WEU and the EU was to develop in the future. Article J.4.1 TEU stated that the CFSP would include '...the eventual framing of a common defence policy, which might in time lead to a common defence'. Those states eager to develop the EU's defence identity envisaged a 'process involving successive phases' (Declaration on Western European Union, paragraph 1, TEU). Three stages were likely: first, the WEU would be merged into the European Union; second, a common defence policy would be negotiated and agreed and finally, a common defence would emerge over time.[11]

France and Germany interpreted the TEU as denoting a tight linkage between the European Union and the WEU, presaging the latter's rapid absorption into the EU. They were confident that once the taboo on including defence issues within the EU had been broken, it was reasonable to expect rapid progress in moving towards a common defence.

In contrast to the Franco-German interpretation, the British regarded the relationship between the EU and the WEU in much looser terms. They emphasized that the WEU had only a general responsibility to 'elaborate' defence issues on behalf of the Union and that no timetable had been agreed to realize an EU common defence policy. Those states with an Atlanticist disposition argued that there were considerable obstacles standing in the way of merging the two organizations. First, the territorial defence guarantees within the WEU had always been operationalized by NATO and it was unlikely that the United States would be willing to uphold these commitments if it foresaw the EU becoming a defence actor. Second, and linked to the issue of defence guarantees, was the fact that there were asymmetries between the memberships of the EU and the WEU. For example, Denmark was a full member of the EU but was not a member of the WEU. At Maastricht it was agreed that Denmark would be granted Observer status in the WEU in order to bring the memberships of the two organizations more closely together. Third, there were countries within the EU, such as Ireland (and later Austria, Finland and Sweden) who were committed to policies of neutralism. This would render it more complex for the EU to develop a genuine defence policy.

The Atlanticist states insisted that the Declaration on the WEU should give equal weight to the organization's continued linkage to NATO, as well as to the EU. Consequently, the WEU was endorsed as the 'European pillar of the Atlantic Alliance' (Declaration on Western European Union, paragraph 2, TEU) and closer consultation and working linkages were foreseen between the two organizations. This relationship between the WEU and NATO was consistent with the declared objectives of the Hague Platform of 1987, which had been drafted in order to assuage US fears concerning the reactivation of the WEU three years earlier.[12] The orientation of the WEU between the EU and NATO was therefore left open-ended and states with widely differing views over its future path of development were left to pursue their designs in the aftermath of the Treaty.

As a result of all these agreements relating to CFSP and defence, the overwhelming impression following the Maastricht summit was that a significant agreement had been negotiated, yet one that left a number of important questions unanswered. Perhaps more importantly, what was to follow the TEU was unclear. In the CFSP, much depended on the willingness of Member States to use the instruments that had been fashioned in the second pillar, to move beyond the coordination of national foreign policies that had characterized EPC. The goal of developing a single foreign policy, to which all states would be committed, remained a 'holy grail'. In defence, the WEU was left straddling the two larger organizations of NATO and the EU, uncertain of the roles it would fulfil in the future. Therefore, far from engineering a definitive treaty on the substance of a European foreign and defence identity, Maastricht signalled the widening of the debate on these subjects.

Between Maastricht and the 1996 IGC

The nature of the compromises agreed at Maastricht and the extent to which they contained ambiguities, guaranteed that the ensuing period was marked by heated debates and incessant institutional wrangles. Not only had the structures created at Maastricht to be given an operational capability, but the ambitions of the more integrationist states had still to be satisfied. However, in reality, it was difficult to bring into being even the limited goals of the TEU. Defining foreign policy interests that were held in common amongst the Twelve – and subsequently the Fifteen, when Austria, Sweden and Finland became members in 1995 – proved to be problematic. Parochial attitudes towards national foreign policy interests continued after the TEU. For example, at the end of 1991, Germany insisted upon the recognition of Croatia, despite the protestations of its allies that this could trigger off further instability in relation to Bosnia-Herzegovina, while Greece subsequently refused to accept a widely held EU position over Macedonia.

The CFSP failed, in the period following the signing of the TEU, to live up to the expectations of its proponents. It was commonly accepted that the Common Positions and Joint Actions that the EU undertook were distinctly modest in both scope and number. For instance, there were Joint Actions to monitor the Russian and South African elections; there was the provision of humanitarian assistance, under United Nations protection, to former Yugoslavia; the administration of the Muslim–Croat town of Mostar in Bosnia; the support for the peace process in the Middle East and the endorsement of the extension of the Non-Proliferation Treaty in 1995. All of the decisions in relation to these issues were taken on the basis of consensus and the only Joint Action that was ambitious in scope was the so-called 'Stability Pact', at the end of 1993, which was created between the EU and states of central, eastern and southern Europe. Meanwhile, the EU adopted Common Positions on a diverse range of topics as Sudan, Haiti, Rwanda and Ukraine.[13]

With the exception of the Stability Pact, there was little evidence from these initiatives that the EU was seeking to exercise the level of influence on the international stage commensurate with its economic muscle. Although officials in European foreign ministries argued that there were subtle benefits from the CFSP process, namely that a culture of foreign policy consultation and cooperation was being deepened, the actual policy outputs from the EU were unimpressive. It was evident that national priorities were still constraining any progress towards common policies and that the Union would remain an actor with limited influence. Even the Commission, fearful of upsetting the Member States, had demonstrated a marked reluctance to exercise its right of initiative in CFSP matters.

Similarly, in relation to defence, a sense of unfulfilled expectations pervaded the post-Maastricht period. The development of a working relationship between the WEU and the EC remained elusive, in spite of hopes that the two organizations would grow closer together. The WEU moved its headquarters from London to Brussels, created a Planning Cell that could prepare a range of options for likely types of crises and enhanced its operational capabilities, but its relationship with the EU continued to be strained. Information between the two organizations was not shared, meetings went unsynchronized and relations between the European Parliament and the WEU Assembly were frosty. Furthermore, progress in developing the operational tasks of the WEU was ponderous, while steps designed to take forward the innovations announced in the Maastricht Treaty were blocked. For example, attempts to define the sorts of tasks that the WEU might perform in fulfilment of the Petersberg Declaration, of June 1992,[14] were depressingly slow. France sought to elaborate the concept of a common defence policy, as outlined in Article J.4 of the TEU and move towards a European White Paper on defence, but was unsuccessful. This owed much to the fact that Britain was able to exercise its veto over any subject that it judged to be prejudicial to the primacy of NATO in European security.

As well as the inherent difficulties of the CFSP and defence, it must also be acknowledged that the external environment following the signing of the TEU in 1991 was a powerful constraint. This was evident in three important ways. First, the protracted and uncertain ratification process of the TEU, punctured by the Danish and French referendums, served to undermine confidence in the whole process of European integration and particularly cooperation in foreign affairs. It was evident that the doctrine of integration had outstripped its support amongst the ordinary voters and there was considerable disquiet over a perceived 'democratic deficit' within the European Union. This contributed to the fact that the TEU was delayed from entering into force until November 1993.

Second, external crises inflicted enormous stresses on the EU and subjected its infant foreign policy and security structures to demands for which they were woefully unprepared. In particular, the conflict in former Yugoslavia quickly proved to lie beyond the means of the Community to resolve. It was ironic that the crisis initially appeared to offer an opportunity for the EC to demonstrate its new-found unity, but it soon became apparent after Lord Carrington was unable to enforce a cease-fire that the economic mechanisms available to the Member States were insufficient incentives to halt the fighting. The ambitious rhetoric of the CFSP was shown to be hollow and it rapidly became clear that EC members had different interests in the region. By 1994, the focus of diplomatic effort was transferred from the EU–UN forum to a US-led 'Contact Group'. The Europeans had found that without the military support of the US, there was no stomach amongst them for large-scale intervention in Bosnia-Herzegovina. Troops were deployed nationally under a UN mandate to protect the distribution of humanitarian aid.

As far as the WEU was concerned, there had only been sufficient agreement amongst its members to deploy it for two limited missions. One was the maritime enforcement of the UN embargo on economic goods and arms (Security Council

Resolutions 713 and 757) in the Adriatic Sea, alongside NATO, and on the River Danube. The other mission consisted of assisting the EU in the administration of the Bosnian city of Mostar. The salutary lessons of the Bosnian experience led EU states to adopt a similarly passive policy during the subsequent crises in Rwanda in 1994 and in the Great Lakes region of Africa in 1996. Even in the case of Albania in 1997, on the doorstep of the west Europeans, a multinational *ad hoc* interventionary force, led by Italy, was the preferred option over the tasking of the WEU.

Finally, the EU was forced to come to terms with the fact that the NATO Alliance had demonstrated its ability to adapt to the security demands of post-Cold War Europe. Much of the early optimism surrounding the EU–WEU relationship was based on the assumption that it might come to rival or even supplant NATO as the continent's primary security forum. But the reassertion of American leadership in NATO and the Alliance's successful imposition of a peace in Bosnia-Herzegovina, resulted in a lessening of interest in alternatives to a transatlantic security framework. Although military forces with a specifically European vocation were established after Maastricht, namely the EuroCorps, EUROFOR and EUROMARFOR,[15] these were nevertheless reconciled and made compatible with NATO. This ensured that the central position of the Atlantic Alliance was maintained. NATO's Combined Joint Task Forces (CJTF) concept, launched at the Brussels Summit in January 1994, made it possible for Alliance assets, along with national forces, to be deployed for European-led military operations – thereby ending the implicit rivalry between NATO and the WEU–EU. By the time of the North Atlantic Council meeting in Berlin in June 1996 it was accepted that the Alliance will exercise first choice over whether it wants to lead in a military operation and will provide the structure in which European countries may conduct actions if the US is absent. NATO's dominance was further reinforced when it took the lead, after 1994, in the issue of organizational enlargement, culminating in its first invitations to Poland, Hungary and the Czech Republic to join the Alliance in 1999. Due to the greater economic and legal complexity of becoming a member of the EU, and the prior necessity of adapting its own structures, the prospect of the EU accepting new members was deferred to a later date.

Preparations for the 1996 IGC

It was stipulated at Maastricht that the TEU would be reviewed in its entirety in 1996, in order to resolve those issues that required further negotiation. In the light of the turbulence experienced by the EU in the period 1992–96, many of the states may have regretted this commitment to review the Treaty's provisions so soon. Nevertheless, a Reflection Group was tasked in 1995 to prepare a list of reforms to recommend to the European Council prior to the IGC being convened. Its subsequent presentation in December 1995, known as the Westendorp Report,[16] was viewed as disappointing, particularly in relation to CFSP. It was evident that fundamental disagreements remained between the Member States and all the Report could achieve was to present a range of options for consideration. A similar process of reflection had been undertaken within the WEU and a report was submitted in Madrid in November 1995,[17] with equally disappointing results. Although improving the Union's capacity for external action was declared to be one of the three main areas for reform when the IGC opened at Turin in March 1996, there was a good deal of scepticism about how much progress could be achieved.

France and Germany were once again in the driving seat of the reform movement. Germany remained eager to realize its strategic ambitions for the continent within an EU framework and was determined to achieve political recompense for its sacrifice of the deutschmark on the altar of monetary union. France continued to harbour a strong desire to partner Germany because of the importance it attached to being in the first wave of monetary union and this priority conditioned its attitude to the IGC process. At a summit meeting between the French and German leaders at Baden, it was agreed that the two governments would make a joint approach in the negotiations. Yet France could not hide its ambivalence about some of the German desires in the integration process: as of old, France still sought to realize a strong Europe but one with weak institutions that did not undermine the centrality of the nation state.

The ideological position of states in this IGC was broadly similar to the first: France and Germany continued to enjoy support for their efforts from countries such as Spain, Belgium and Luxembourg. Some changes in the positions of countries were evident since Maastricht: Italy, for example, was less willing to play the role of broker between Germany, France and Britain, whilst the Netherlands had shifted away from its earlier Atlanticist defence stance. Britain remained the country most opposed to the process of deeper integration and most committed to an intergovernmental approach. Despite finding itself isolated on some issues, the UK government was determined to adhere to its negotiating positions. Only when the Conservative government was replaced by a Labour administration in May 1997, just before the Amsterdam Summit, was a slightly more flexible negotiating stance in evidence.

Because it was impossible to force states to generate the required political will to enhance the potential of CFSP, the IGC attempted to increase the coherence and efficiency of foreign and security policy by focusing on institutional reform. Several areas were the subject of discussion: one was the question of the external representation of the Union and the setting up of a planning organization in Brussels to provide a conceptual underpinning to the CFSP. Another subject of protracted discussion was majority voting – while it was agreed that policy orientations should remain the preserve of the European Council, states of an integrationist disposition advocated that Joint Actions and Common Positions should be decided by majority voting. This would be likely to encourage states to seek compromise with their partners, rather than to fall back on the use of national vetoes. But the UK,[18] supported by Greece and Portugal, made clear its opposition to such a development on the grounds that forcing states to adhere to a foreign policy position, against their interests and better judgement, made a mockery of the concept of a common foreign policy.

In the face of British opposition to majority voting, two sorts of possibilities presented themselves. One was the concept of 'constructive abstention', which was designed to circumvent the problem of a Member State having to adhere to a policy with which it disagreed. France was initially sceptical of constructive abstention but after the meeting of foreign ministers from France and Germany, in Freiburg in February 1996,[19] France agreed to endorse Germany's view. According to this idea, a Member State would not have the power to veto a decision if there was a qualified majority in favour, but it could abstain and allow the decision to proceed.[20] The other possibility lay in 'flexibility', by which those states eager to cooperate more closely might be empowered to proceed independently of dissenting countries. In a joint submission to the IGC in October 1996,[21] France and Germany argued for flexibility or 'differentiation' to be made possible in all areas of activity, including the CFSP. The Irish Presidency considered this idea carefully but in the event the Amsterdam negotiations excluded foreign policy and defence from the proposed remit of flexibility.

In the sphere of defence, the thrust of the initiatives within the IGC was designed to orchestrate the eventual subordination of the WEU to the European Council. The WEU's Reflection Group had laid out three options for the IGC. Two of these options envisaged enhancing the powers of the European Council over the WEU; either allowing it to set guidelines, or to offer directives to the WEU. Both of these options, albeit according to different timetables, foresaw the eventual merging of the WEU into the EU, to create a 'single institutional framework for European security and defence'.[22] Prior to the Amsterdam Summit, in March 1997, Germany, France, Italy, Belgium, Spain and Luxembourg called upon the Dutch Presidency to seek the rapid absorption of the WEU into the EU structure. Britain was alone amongst the ten WEU states in opposing both of these two options and insisted upon a third alternative, namely preserving the institutional autonomy of the WEU.

The end game and the Treaty of Amsterdam

Disagreements over the substance of the reform agenda in the CFSP continued right up until the Amsterdam European Council in June 1997. By this time it had become apparent that the ambitious goals of some Member States would not be realized and a variety of other issues, such as Economic and Monetary Union, were dominating the attention of the Heads of State. Moreover, the key decisions in relation to continental defence had already been taken a year earlier at the NATO meeting in Berlin. Here the concept of Combined Joint Task Forces had been operationalized and it had been agreed that the European defence identity would be constructed within the confines of the Atlantic Alliance. Hence, the expectations for this Summit were much lower than those that had preceded Maastricht.

The Treaty of Amsterdam (ToA) accorded the European Council the right to establish 'common strategies' (Article 13.2 [ex Article J.3] TEU) in relation to Joint Actions under the CFSP. This ensured that decisions on the objectives, duration and instruments of Joint Actions would be decided by unanimity by the Member States, before being handed down to be implemented by qualified majority voting. Yet the Treaty also enables Member States to request a vote in the European Council. The potential result will be that, over issues where disputes arise, states will refuse to compromise their positions and will seek recourse to the European Council. This may have the effect of turning the European Council into a quasi-arbitration body preoccupied with resolving disagreements. This may carry the attendant risk of further slowing down the decision-making in the CFSP area.

As well as the power to lay down common strategies, the Treaty of Amsterdam affirmed that the European Council could conclude legally binding agreements on behalf of the Union (Article 24 [ex Article J.14] TEU). This helped to resolve the long-term debate in favour of the argument that the EU does not enjoy a legal identity as an international actor, whereas the EC does.[23] Although the EU was not granted the right explicitly to conclude international treaties, nevertheless a mechanism had been found by which such legally binding agreements could be initiated.

Regarding the thorny issue of voting procedures, Article 23 [ex Article J.13] TEU determined that a state could abstain from a foreign policy decision whilst not preventing the measure from proceeding. Even though this was not an innovation, further safeguards were introduced in order to prevent the impression of Member States being herded towards majority voting. The state choosing to abstain over an issue was given the opportunity to clarify its reasons for standing aside and was no longer expected to be bound by the outcome (whilst acknowledging the binding of its partners). This made abstention a highly visible rejection of EU policy and rendered the Union vulnerable to outside exploitation. There was now the danger that enemies of the EU could sow dissension by pointing to the existence of divisions within the body politic. Furthermore, if one third of the states abstained in this manner then no decision could be adopted. As well as risking the solidarity of the Member States it could be argued that the measures increased the complexity of decision-making, which was contrary to the stated aims of the IGC process.

Over the issue of appointing a 'High Representative for the CFSP', there was disagreement amongst the leading European states that reflected differing conceptions of the nature of the post. France lobbied hard for the candidate to be a political figure of prestige and significance whilst Germany and Britain preferred a more bureaucratic appointment. In Article 18 [ex Article J.8] TEU, the role of High Representative was given to the Secretary-General of the Council of Ministers, which appeared to reflect the preferences of Germany and Britain. Nevertheless, debate continued after the signing of the Treaty and eventually a consensus emerged around the appointment of a high profile figure that could speak with a sense of authority on the international stage. It was eventually agreed in June 1999 that Javier Solana, a former Spanish Foreign Minister and Secretary-General of NATO, would be the first High Representative.

As for the actual extent of the power to be invested in the High Representative, there was a lack of clarity on this point as well. It is not unreasonable to expect that the influence of the office will grow once the incumbent has stamped his personality on the post. One of the chief sources of strength attached to the position will be its long duration, particularly when compared to the position of the six-month EU Presidency.[24] Small states in particular are likely to find the office useful due to the limited resources they can bring to bear when they hold the Presidency. On the other hand, foreign ministers will be wary of the High Representative usurping any of their roles and will be eager to ensure that the incumbent acts as their servant and not their replacement.[25] The power of the foreign ministers to undercut the position will continue to exist either through refusing to grant their support to initiatives by the High Representative or through the mechanism of appointing *ad hoc* envoys to various parts of the world.

The Amsterdam Treaty announced the creation of a 'Policy Planning and Early Warning Unit' (PPEWU) at the disposal of the High Representative.[26] This represented an attempt to enable the EU to become more proactive in foreign policy terms, to consider the types of options that would be available in various scenarios and to avoid damaging differences of opinion emerging during crises. While Germany had earlier supported a more ambitious proposal for a planning body to be located within the Commission – which would have reduced dependency on national capitals and helped to define common European interests – it was eventually agreed that the PPEWU would reside within the Secretariat General of the Council.[27] This ensured that it would remain closely attached to the work of the Presidency. Its main focus remained unspecified: whether long-term planning and theoretical papers, which would be likely to limit its impact, or short-term planning and serving as a 'situation centre', which could substantially elevate its importance. Its effectiveness will depend to a large extent on the attitude and cooperation of the Member States; the lesson to be drawn from the experience of national planning staffs is unfavourable as they tend to be viewed as adjuncts to the policy-making process.[28] Member States may choose to limit the information that they submit to the PPEWU and disregard its outputs, thereby ensuring that its activities will be marginalized.

If the provisions of the Treaty relating to foreign and security policy represented cautious reforms, then those pertaining to defence were even more limited. There was never any question that decisions involving the use of military forces would retain the need for unanimity but even where there had been discussion of innovations, such as the inclusion of a statement that committed the EU to the defence of its own territorial integrity, this never survived the draft Irish treaty. On the central question of the WEU's future, British obduracy ensured that it continued to be autonomous.[29] Article 17 [ex Article J.7] TEU changed the right of the European Council from 'request' to 'avail' the WEU, thereby perpetuating the weak linkage between the EU and its defence arm. The word 'progressive' was used to replace 'eventual' in relation to the 'framing of a common defence policy'. The language at Amsterdam was more direct in referring to the 'possibility of integration' of the WEU into the EU, but the British were guaranteed the power of veto because only the European Council was to be capable of sanctioning such a development (Article 17 [ex Article J.7] TEU).

The only substantive defence provision in the Amsterdam Treaty was the inclusion of the Petersberg tasks into Article 17 [ex Article J.7] TEU. Through this mechanism military tasks at the lower end of the conflict spectrum were being declared to be within the purview of the CFSP and any tasking that might be undertaken by the European Council could now be prepared in advance. All EU Member States, including the neutrals (Ireland, Finland, Austria and Sweden), were to be fully associated with the planning and execution of these potential Petersberg tasks but only those states taking part in an operation would be expected to contribute to the costs. States such as Britain had argued throughout the IGC that the position of neutral states in relation to the CFSP provided a strong justification for perpetuating the separation of the WEU from the EU. They feared that the WEU could be prevented from acting in an emergency by the particular sensitivities of such neutral members.

It was only after the ToA had been signed, but prior to its ratification, that there were significant developments in relation to the WEU. The British government announced in the autumn of 1998 that it was reviewing its position on European defence and this served as the foundation for an informal meeting of EU defence ministers under the aegis of the Austrian Presidency. At an Anglo-French Summit at Saint Malo in December, it was announced that the two countries would seek a '...capacity for autonomous action, backed up by credible military forces...' for the European Union.[30] Furthermore, Britain has signalled its willingness to consider merging the WEU into the European Union, although a timetable has still to be worked out. This effectively reverses its long cherished position over the autonomy of the WEU. This change of stance has been made possible both by the reconciliation of the ESDI to NATO and by the recognition that European military paralysis during recent crises was contrary to the interests of all.

In all therefore, the Amsterdam Treaty effected only marginal improvements in relation to second pillar activities and contrasted with the substantive changes that were effected in the third pillar. Changes were made in the areas of decision-making and the visible representation of the CFSP, but majority voting and the subordination of the WEU were avoided. No significant communitarization of CFSP matters had been achieved and therefore the status quo position of the intergovernmentalists had prevailed. The overwhelming feeling was that the whole of the IGC process had served largely to expose underlying differences of objective amongst the Member States. Furthermore, after Amsterdam there was a consensus that the EU was inadequately prepared for the process of enlargement, which had been formalized at the Copenhagen European Council meeting in June 1993. The difficult decisions relating to enlargement had been avoided and deferred at the summit.

Conclusion

In seeking to assess the merits of the EU's CFSP in the 1990s, one should not understate the significance of the innovation: after all, it accorded the Union a salience in foreign affairs that the EC had not previously enjoyed. By adding foreign and security policy to the realm of European integration, CFSP gave the EU a full range of competencies. What can never be measured accurately is the contribution made by the relationship between the WEU and the EU to stabilizing the continent after the end of the Cold War, counteracting uncertainty and preventing the possibility of defence becoming renationalized amongst west European states. Also, very importantly, CFSP has provided the EU with the necessary framework to address the challenges of the future; across the spectrum of security problems from, at the lowest end, issues such as illegal immigration and terrorism, through to major issues such as overseas interventions and peacekeeping. The tools now lie at the disposal of the Member States to be developed at the speed that they deem to be appropriate.

But such an upbeat assessment needs to be tempered by honest criticism. There can be no doubt that the CFSP has fallen far short of the expectations of its founders and that the early exercise of its powers, after the signing of the TEU, has proved to be unimpressive. Whilst a period of opportunity to forge an ambitious foreign and defence identity existed prior to Maastricht, this window rapidly closed after the compromises in the Treaty had been hammered out. The subsequent period served to undermine, rather than reinforce, the political will of the Member States to make the system work. By the time of the preparations for the 1996 IGC, the momentum in foreign and defence cooperation had evaporated and hence the Treaty of Amsterdam became an exercise in institutional fine tuning, rather than substantive reform.[31]

The upshot of the situation has been that the EU has found itself weak and divided in the face of testing security issues, such as the crises in former Yugoslavia, Algeria and most recently Kosovo. When these problems arose, EU Member States have struggled to speak with one voice and have vacillated over how best to respond. The limitations of the CFSP have been all too apparent; namely the need to make foreign policy decisions by consensus and the inadequate role of the EU Presidency which accords only a short period of attention to a problem. As always, the issue of leadership remains at the heart of the CFSP conundrum.

Nevertheless, the experiences of the inadequacies of CFSP have created a broadly based constituency supportive of its enhancement. The crisis in Kosovo, for example, has further stimulated the desire to have military capabilities at the command of the European Union. Although these military means will not be designed to fight major wars and NATO will continue to be the organisation with the choice over whether to lead in a crisis; nevertheless, the taboo regarding the EU and defence has been overcome. In due course the EU will have military advice and capabilities at its disposal for the conduct of Petersberg tasks and it will be able to draw upon NATO assets for demanding types of operations. Whilst progress has been made on the institutional issues, it remains to be seen whether EU states will be successful in overcoming some of their military weaknesses such as in long range transport aircraft and satellite intelligence systems. Much depends upon what role the various Member States want for the EU in foreign affairs, whether they desire a robust and forceful actor that can pursue its interests on the world stage, or whether they will be satisfied to see the EU's external influence restricted to issues of trade. What is clear is that other international actors, such as the United States, are looking to the EU to shoulder a greater share of the responsibilities in global affairs and are eager for the EU to be able to wield political influence and military power more commensurate with its economic strength. To quote from a former British foreign secretary, Geoffrey Howe, 'In an era of superpower shrinkage ... Europe is going to have to bear more of the burden ... for defending the values we hold dear ...'.[32]

Endnotes

1. G. Edwards and S. Nuttall, 'Common Foreign and Security Policy', in A. Duff, J. Pinder and R. Pryce (eds) *Maastricht and Beyond: Building the European Union*, London: Routledge, 1994, p. 87.
2. J. Delors, 'European Integration and Security', *Survival*, Vol. 22, 1992, pp. 99–109.
3. The British position was summarized in a joint Anglo-Italian letter to the Dutch Presidency of the Council in October 1991.
4. M. Jopp, *The Strategic Implications of European Integration*, Adelphi Paper 290, London: Brassey's for the International Institute for Strategic Studies, July 1994, p. 12.
5. See M. Holland, 'Introduction', in M. Holland (ed.), *Common Foreign and Security Policy: The Record and Reforms*, London: Pinter, 1997, p. 5.
6. G. Edwards and S. Nuttall, 'Common Foreign and Security Policy', in Duff *et al., Maastricht and Beyond*, p. 93.
7. F. Cameron, 'Where the European Commission Comes In: From the Single European Act to Maastricht', in E. Regelsberger, P. de Schoutheete de Tervarent and W. Wessels (eds) *Foreign Policy of the European Union: From EPC to CFSP and Beyond*, London: Lynne Reiner, 1997, p. 102.
8. M. Eaton, 'Common Foreign and Security Policy', in D. O'Keefe and P. Twomey (eds), *Legal Issues of the Maastricht Treaty*. London: Wiley Chancery Law, 1994, p. 5.
9. Jopp, *The Strategic Implications of European Integration*, p. 22.
10. It was suggested that Article 223, which excludes defence industries from Single Market strictures, might have been abolished or at least amended in the subsequent revision of the Treaty in 1996, but in the event the Treaty of Amsterdam talks of nothing more than fostering 'cooperation in the sphere of armaments'.
11. For a more detailed discussion of the issue of a common defence, see L. Martin and J. Roper (eds), *Towards a Common Defence Policy*, Paris: Institute for Security Studies of the Western European Union, 1995.
12. WEU Ministerial Council Meeting, 'Platform on European Security Interests', The Hague, 27 October 1987.
13. H-G. Krenzler and H. Schneider, 'The Question of Consistency', in Regelsberger *et al., Foreign Policy of the European Union: From EPC to CFSP and Beyond*, pp. 143–5.
14. These were humanitarian operations, peacekeeping and the employment of combat forces in crisis management, including peacemaking.
15. In May 1992 the French and German governments announced the establishment of a 50,000 strong Corps to be based in Strasbourg. The 'EuroCorps' was subsequently joined by Belgium, Spain and Luxembourg. In May 1995, France, Spain, Portugal and Italy agreed to establish a land and naval force for the Mediterranean: these became the EUROFOR and the EUROMARFOR, respectively.
16. Report of the Reflection Group, Brussels, 5 December 1995.
17. WEU Council of Ministers, 'WEU Contribution to the EU Intergovernmental Conference of 1996', Madrid, 14 November 1995.
18. *A Partnership of Nations: The British Approach to the European Union Intergovernmental Conference 1996*, CM 3181, London: Foreign and Commonwealth Office, March 1996.
19. *Agence Europe*, No. 6677, 29 February 1996, p. 2.
20. France and Germany also argued for new weightings in qualified majority voting to safeguard the interests of larger states and to prevent the risk of being outvoted by coalitions of smaller countries. This was duly opposed by the smaller countries at the Amsterdam summit.

21. *Agence Europe*, No. 6836, 19 October 1996, pp. 2–3.

22. WEU Council of Ministers, 'WEU Contribution to the EU Intergovernmental Conference of 1996'.

23. For a more detailed discussion of this issue, see N. Neuwahl, 'A Partner with a Troubled Personality: EU Treaty-Making in Matters of CFSP and JHA after Amsterdam', *European Foreign Affairs Review*, Vol. 3, 1998, pp. 177–95.

24. Jürgen Trumpf, Secretary-General of the European Union Council, described the High Representative as having the potential to act as the 'memory of the CFSP', *Agence Europe*, No. 7154, 6 February 1998, p. 3.

25. A decision on the appointment was taken at the European Council Summit in Cologne in June 1999.

26. Amsterdam European Council, 'Declaration to the Final Act on the Establishment of a Policy Planning and Early Warning Unit', 16–17 June 1997.

27. It was later decided that the PPEWU will at the minimum consist of representatives of the 15 Member States, the European Commission and the WEU, *Agence Europe*, No. 7257, 6–7 July 1998, p. 4.

28. J. Monar, 'The European Union's Foreign Affairs System after the Treaty of Amsterdam: A "Strengthened Capacity for External Action?" ', *European Foreign Affairs Review*, Vol. 2, 1997, p. 416.

29. Martin Westlake has noted the fear of some critics that states may use the mechanism of Constructive Abstention to avoid having to contribute to the costs of Petersberg tasks.

30. 'Declaration on European Defence', Anglo-French Summit, Saint Malo, 3–4 December 1998, http://www.fco.gov.uk

31. Duff argues that the absence of an external stimulus, like the Gulf War, helps to account for the limited progress in the CFSP at Amsterdam. Yet this view can be questioned in the light of the pressure that was being exerted by the prospect of eastward enlargement. A. Duff (ed.), *The Treaty of Amsterdam: Text and Commentary*, London: Sweet and Maxwell for the Federal Trust, 1997, p. 124.

32. G. Howe, 'Bearing More of the Burden: In Search of a European Foreign and Security Policy', *The World Today*, Vol. 52, 1996, p. 24.

PART THREE

THE UNION AND ITS CITIZENS

Chapter 10

The place of the citizen in the European construction

Nanette A. Neuwahl

The notion of citizenship is most commonly associated with the existence of nation states, whose nationals are deemed to have rights of social protection and political participation, as well as duties towards the society (in this case the state) to which they belong. The use of the same notion in the context of the European Union (EU) goes some way towards challenging this well-entrenched conception. Yet, like the state of integration itself, the state of European citizenship is in flux and consequently, difficult to pin down.

In themselves, the provisions of the Treaty on European Union (TEU) on citizenship remain largely unaffected by the Treaty of Amsterdam. To assess any progress made, this chapter describes the evolution of the relation between nationals of Member States and the EU institutions from the inception of the Common Market to the present. As will become clear, Amsterdam has not maintained the momentum which previously existed. Renewed reflection on the significance of citizenship may be needed.

The 'market citizen'

The European Economic Community was founded in 1957 to help bring lasting peace, stability and increased prosperity to the peoples of continental Europe. But the EEC Treaty foresaw little for 'people'. It certainly did not provide for European citizenship. As is well known, political union was proved too elusive to be put on the agenda and the day-to-day business was geared towards the creation of a common market; the rest, if at all, would spill over from there. The EEC Treaty provided for certain economic benefits to individuals, notably relating to free movement and circulation (of persons, goods, services and capital). The fact that, in addition, provision was made for a few social rights, notably relating to equal pay for men and women, had to do with the wish to prevent 'social dumping' and to ensure that within the common market competition was not distorted. And initially it was uncertain whether any of such rights would be protected at court.

Arguably, it was the European Court of Justice (ECJ) which enabled the foundation of a supranational civil society (*société civile*), by conceding in the famous *Van Gend en Loos* case and subsequent jurisprudence that nationals of Member States could derive rights protected by national courts directly from the Treaty of Rome. This creative case law is based on a teleological interpretation of the Treaty, whereby the ECJ draws inspiration from the aims of the Treaty and the useful effect of its provisions. Meanwhile, it can be argued that the fact that some form of citizenship and indeed the very concept has eventually made its way into the EC Treaty was the necessary consequence of the internal market[1] and the earnest resolve to bring it about.

Undoubtedly, the direct effect of Community law has contributed to the emergence of an ever-increasing body of rights and their effective enforcement. It has facilitated the steady expansion of the rights of individuals through the intricate interaction between the judiciary and the legislature. The ECJ could induce legislation when laying down broad principles needing implementation (e.g. in *Cassis de Dijon*) or might interpret on a case-by-case basis principles laid down in primary or secondary Community law.

Therefore, the fact that private individuals have been allowed to invoke, directly before the national courts, the provisions of the Treaty and acts taken for its implementation can be said to mark the inception of a 'supranational civil society'. But it remained a rudimentary society, because the political institutions lacked legitimacy,[2] and because its subjects could not aspire to be more than privileged aliens. They were 'market citizens' at most.

Pressure for change came about partly at the instigation of the judiciary in several Member States, particularly Germany and Italy, who with their criticism of the lack of a fundamental rights catalogue and the lack of democracy were starting to question the observance of the rule of law and with it, the doctrine of supremacy of Community law.

This has undoubtedly contributed to the enactment by the Community institutions of several declarations of principle, including the 1977 Joint Declaration on Human Rights and the 1989 Social Charter. It is also believed to have precipitated the case law of the ECJ regarding fundamental rights protection in the Community. The Court made it clear that fundamental rights were protected in the Community legal order as general principles of law, and that the content of these rights was inspired by principles common to the constitutional traditions of the Member States and by treaties for the protection of human rights.[3] Moreover, the ECJ gave rulings on the right to a fair hearing, the right to privacy, the principle of non-retroactivity, and so forth.

The European Parliament (EP) for its part had improved its status since the introduction of direct elections in the late 1970s, and was constantly pushing for a greater role in the legislative process. By this time, the effects of economic integration were reaching the periphery of political integration.[4]

The issue of European citizenship would, however, not be confronted by governments until after the establishment of a truly 'common' market. Because the integration process had passed into a phase of relative stagnation in which the need to reach consensus blocked most prospects of advance, Member States resolved in the mid-1980s to amend the EEC Treaty: in 1987, the Single European Act brought about a speeding up of the decision-making process and the facilitation by the end of 1992 of a single market in which persons, goods, services, and capital could move freely.

In this context the Belgian government issued a Memorandum on Political Union[5] which presented a 'people's' Europe as being directly linked with the free movement of persons in the context of the Single European Market. Human rights should be written into the Treaty and the Community should accede to the European Convention on Human Rights (ECHR) and certain other agreements relating to social rights. A uniform election procedure for the European Parliament was needed, enabling all citizens in the Community to take part in such elections whatever their nationality or residence. Subject to conditions of residence, there should also be a right to participate in local elections in other Member States.

Nothing much came of these plans at first, but the nexus with the 'people' resurfaced in the Intergovernmental Conference (IGC) on Political Union which led up to the Maastricht Treaty. Intended to build upon previous achievements and to expand Community competencies, the twin IGCs of 1990–91 paved the way for the introduction of a single currency as a further step in a frontier-free market and the setting up of new political structures designed to enable the Community to act as a leading power in a rapidly changing world.

The making of the European citizen

In some respects the climate in the period leading up to Maastricht was particularly propitious for the citizen. For one thing, the expansion of the competencies and activities of the Union into ever wider fields prompted the concern with greater democratic control of the decision-making process.

At the same time, there was a growing concern with the social acceptability of the integration project as a whole, and the furtherance of European identity through the creation of a European Union citizenship was seen as a means to reinforce it. For instance, the right of Union citizens to participate in European and local elections on the basis of residence was seen as a possible way for individuals to be more involved in a process which increasingly affected their daily lives and to ensure that they would be determining factors in the Community.

The 1990–91 IGC, or at least the EMU IGC, centred on the establishment of Economic and Monetary Union and if one took the view, like Germany, that this could not be attained without establishing political union at the same time, the introduction of the European citizen was a matter of course.

In addition, there was an increasing concern that the nation state could no longer meet essential needs of present-day society. For some, the alternative solution of establishing a supranational political system was thus becoming expedient, and the granting of citizenship rights could be as instrumental in this respect as the creation of enforceable individual rights had proved to be in the propulsion of economic integration.[6]

It was in this type of climate that the Spanish prime minister, Felipe Gonzalez, proposed that a separate chapter on citizenship was required,[7] providing for an integrated space for the specific benefit of the citizens and giving them unlimited rights of free movement, establishment and access to employment, as well as the right to vote in local elections if resident in countries other than their own.

This idea was then taken up by the Greek government in a Memorandum on a People's Europe,[8] which stressed the need to strengthen people's feelings of belonging to one legal Community aimed at the harmonious development of their potential. This rendered it essential that the concepts of citizenship and human rights were given recognition in the Treaty and that the right to vote in local and European Parliament elections if resident in a Member State other than one's own, and simplified access to the ECJ be granted. The idea that the word 'economic' be eliminated from the EEC also originated from Greece.

In the same period the EP adopted a resolution[9] calling for voting rights in municipal and European elections in the country of residence and for the inclusion in the Treaty of provisions on human rights and fundamental freedoms, as well as provisions against racism and xenophobia. In its view, moreover, the ECJ should have jurisdiction for the protection of fundamental rights, and citizens of the Union should be able to access it directly after exhaustion of local remedies. The Community should accede to the ECHR to ensure the external review of Community actions and procedures, at least in the areas covered by the Convention.

The subsequent Spanish Memorandum on Citizenship[10] was a major contribution in that it provided a definition and categorization of citizenship which, although not literally reflected in the later Treaty on European Union, did inspire the solutions it adopted. Citizenship of the Union was defined as

> the personal and indivisible status of nationals of the Member States whose membership of the Union meant that they had special rights and duties that were specific to the nature of the Union and were exercised and safeguarded specifically within its boundaries, without dismissing the possibility that such a status of European Citizenship might also be extended beyond those boundaries.

The Memorandum stressed as special basic rights of European citizens the full right to freedom of movement and the right to participate in elections in one's country of residence. In addition there would be new rights in the field of social policy, health, education, culture, environment and consumer protection, which would grow with the exercise of the Community's new spheres of activity. Finally, there should be diplomatic and consular protection of citizens in third countries.

There were further contributions by other delegations, including a Danish Memorandum stressing, among other things, the need for strengthening the democratic process by greater openness. Certain Council meetings should be public and citizens should have access to general administrative acts or acts concerning them.

This propitious atmosphere then led the European Council to recommend that the IGC give substance to European citizenship. Both the Spanish government and the Commission submitted draft texts (of respectively, 10 and 11 articles). As they turned out to be largely compatible, they could be used as a basis on which Part Two of the Treaty was modelled.[11]

Of course, as often occurs with European integration, in the end the chosen solutions were the result of compromises. To expect a commonality of views of what European citizenship was or was meant to be would be wrong. Rather than a clear strategy for the future, Maastricht is a collection of provisions pointing in the direction of change. After all, the citizenship provisions of Maastricht have to be seen as part of a 'package' aimed at reviving and boosting further integration. A citizen-oriented outlook and the deepening of the political integration process were required as a consequence of the completion of the Single European Market and the broader aspirations existing in some quarters.

It is interesting to note the place of the citizenship provisions in the TEU and their relationship to other provisions of the Treaties. The Maastricht Treaty by which the Community became part of a wider European Union, is most of all notable for the introduction in stages of EMU and for its 'pillar' structure. The second and third pillars, governing respectively Common Foreign and Security Policy (CFSP) and justice and home affairs (JHA), are subject to intergovernmental cooperation. They are fields of common concern but remain outside the supranational context of the Community. By contrast, the fact that European citizenship is placed inside that context can be taken as a clear sign that citizens' rights and concerns are to be taken seriously indeed.

To take away anxieties that the EU was starting to change into a new 'super-state', replacing national identities and cultures, the TEU states in Article F that

> the Union shall respect the identities of its Member States and shall contribute to the flowering of the cultures of the Member States, while respecting their national and regional diversity and at the same time bringing the common cultural heritage to the fore.

On the insistence of Denmark, moreover, a declaration was annexed to the Treaty according to which citizenship of the Union did not replace Member State nationality. European citizenship was merely in addition to being a national of one's own Member State, and the Treaty on European Union would not encroach upon the latter.

Citizenship of the Union brought specific advantages. Whereas the Community had already brought about higher living standards through increased consumer choice, environmental improvements and new employment opportunities, the Maastricht Treaty takes this further by offering ordinary men, women and children new rights as 'citizens of the European Union', in particular the rights laid down in Articles 8a–e to, respectively:

- live and work in any Member State of the European Union
- vote and stand as a candidate in local elections in any European Union country
- vote and stand as a candidate in EP elections in any European Union country
- receive diplomatic or consular protection in non-European Union countries from any Member State in case the State of which one is a national has no embassy or consulate there

- petition the EP or complain to the Ombudsman in cases of maladministration by Community institutions.

In addition to the part specifically concerned with citizenship, the TEU brought improvements in several matters believed to be of concern to the citizen. For instance, it introduced in Article 3b EC the principle of subsidiarity, according to which decisions should be taken as near to the people as possible and only on an EC-wide basis where necessary. Henceforth, the Union would only take action where the desired policy objective could not be achieved by national governments. The subsidiarity principle prevents unnecessary bureaucratic interference in people's lives. Regions and local authorities were also given a bigger part to play by involving them in Community decision-making through the (consultative) Committee of the Regions.

Furthermore, the TEU constituted a move towards greater transparency and accountability. The Commission was to suggest measures to improve public access to information and the transparency of the Community's decision-making process, including the wider distribution of proposed policy initiatives[12] and the opening up of Council's decisions to the public (e.g. the Council's policy debates were to be retransmitted by audiovisual means).

The EP was given the power to appoint an independent Ombudsman to investigate cases of maladministration by EU institutions (except the Court of Justice). Individuals, companies and legal persons would be enabled to address complaints to the Ombudsman, especially through a Member of the European Parliament.

Maastricht considerably expanded the powers of the EP. The Parliament was to be more involved in decisions made by the Council, in particular through joint decision-making and greater scrutiny of the Commission, as well as through the right to set up a committee of enquiry to investigate breaches of Community law, bad management or maladministration by Community institutions.

In response to a perceived concern of the general public, there was to be tighter control of EC finances, and several measures were agreed to combat fraud. The Court of Auditors, the Community's financial watchdog, attained full institutional status. National governments were required to take steps to deal as effectively with EC fraud as they would do with national fraud. New penalties for failing to respect EC law were also introduced. The ECJ was enabled to fine Member States for failing to respect a judgment made against them for breach of EC law.

Finally, there were improvements in the social field, though they were disappointing in some respects. A Social Protocol, implementing the aims of the 1989 Social Charter, was designed to form part of the Maastricht Treaty. However, as the United Kingdom was unable to accept its provisions, it was laid down as a separate agreement between the other Member States, annexed to the EC Treaty. This meant that if the UK were unable to subscribe to a measure, the (then 11) countries could move ahead without it.

The Treaty of Amsterdam

The fact that the European citizen had not lost appeal or topicality at the start of the 1996 IGC is apparent from a reading of the Report of the Reflection Group on the revision of the TEU which was adopted in Brussels on 5 December 1995. The Group considered that

> a key element, not only for an understanding of the reasons for reform of the Treaty but also in order to guarantee the success of the Conference, is to place the citizen at the centre of the European venture by endeavouring to meet his [*sic*] expectations and concerns ...[13]

Indeed, developments so far might have led one to have high expectations. Yet, as in the past, seemingly straightforward slogans covered up an absence of commonality of views. Placing the citizen at the centre of the European venture did not necessarily mean the development of a fully fledged charter of citizenship rights. If Maastricht could be seen as the start of such a development – as it introduced a specific part on citizenship, Part Two of the EC Treaty – its advocates would be disappointed. A broader conception of the IGC's aims would involve, more simply, being seen to strive to meet concerns of the populace. This any political society would do in order to gather public support. As will be seen, it is especially in the latter sense that the negotiators, intent on avoiding a repetition of the negative outcome of the Danish and French referendums and keen on getting the people more interested in European affairs, must have interpreted the exhortation of the Reflection Group.

This approach is already apparent from the Conclusions of the Turin European Council, which defined in March 1996 the goals of the IGC. There is less emphasis on the essential elements of citizenship and more on what are to be considered to be the citizen's concerns.[14]

First of all, the European Council asked the IGC to 'base its work on the fact that the citizens are at the core of the European construction: the Union has the imperative duty to respond concretely to their needs and concerns'. This implied investigating avenues of progress with respect to fundamental rights:

> As Member States are committed to respecting human rights, democratic values, equality and non-discrimination, and as the Union is a community of shared values, the IGC should consider whether and how far it will be possible to strengthen these fundamental rights and improve the safeguarding of them.

It also implied a concern with justice and home affairs:

> European citizens pay growing attention to justice and home affairs. In an area of free movement for people, goods, capital and services such as the Union, the exercise of these rights according to the Treaties must be accompanied by adequate protection. A strengthened control of the Union's external frontiers shall contribute to it. In this context, the Conference is called upon to produce adequate results mainly on the following issues:
>
> > within the framework of defined objectives, better methods and instruments;

ensuring better protection of the Union's citizens against international crime, in particular, terrorism and drug trafficking;

developing coherent and effective asylum, immigration and visa policies;

clearing divergent views on jurisdictional and parliamentary control of EU decisions in the field of justice and home affairs.

Unemployment and environmental policy were also on the list of the European Council:

For the Union and the Member States the fight against unemployment is the priority task. Obtaining better employment opportunities requires a stability oriented economic policy, greater competitiveness and sound growth, i.e. through the completion of the single market and the implementation of the convergence criteria for the achievement of economic and monetary union. However, supplementary coordinated action is necessary. Therefore, in order to fulfil the objective of a high level of employment while ensuring social protection, the IGC should examine how the Union could provide the basis for better cooperation and coordination in order to strengthen national policies. The IGC should moreover examine whether and how the efforts of our governments as well as of the social partners could be made more effective and better coordinated by the Treaty. ... A healthy and sustainable environment is also of great concern to our citizens. Ensuring a better environment is a fundamental challenge for the Union. The IGC will have to consider how to make environmental protection more effective at the level of the Union, with a view to sustainable development.

Finally, closeness to the citizen through reinforcement of the principle of subsidiarity, transparency, and openness are briefly mentioned, as is the need to simplify and consolidate the Treaties. The general aim to work out institutional improvements for the benefit of a more democratic and efficient Union closed the list of tasks the IGC was charged to consider.

During the 1996–97 IGC there was considerable opposition by some Member States, notably the UK, France and Sweden, to extending the citizenship part of the EC Treaty. This attitude prevailed despite the more favourable views of Austria, Italy, Greece, Spain and the Netherlands. As a result, Part Two of the EC Treaty has remained virtually unchanged.

The only new right, included in Article 21 [ex Article 8d] EC, is the right to write to the Community institutions in one of the languages of the Treaties and to have an answer in that same language. This improvement comes along with the insertion of the reassurance in the text of Article 17 [ex Article 8] EC that European citizenship is additional to and not replacing national citizenship, an amendment which seems superfluous in the sense that none of the aspects of European citizenship currently provided for actually replaces national citizenship rights or duties. It may serve the purpose of appeasing sensitivities existing within Member States such as the UK and Denmark, as well as to give more political clout to those opposing future developments. On a side issue, it could also raise the legal issue whether, given the fact that European citizenship is complementary to national citizenship, national authorities will ever be able to prevent the Treaty provisions from being invoked against them by their own nationals, or whether European citizens in the sense of the Treaty are merely people claiming rights from Member States other than their own. Only time will tell how this works out.

The Commission in its Report to the Reflection Group,[15] noting that in some cases the Maastricht provisions were not being implemented, had stressed the importance of realizing the potential inherent in the citizenship rights introduced by the previous IGC: 'the Citizen enjoys only fragmented, incomplete rights which are themselves subject to restrictive conditions. In that sense the concept of Citizenship is not yet put into practice in a way that lives up to the individual's expectations.'[16]

The cumbersome procedure laid down in Article 22 [ex Article 8e] EC for new citizen-oriented Community legislation – beyond that intended to facilitate the exercise of the rights already granted in Articles 18–21 [ex Articles 8a–d] EC – has basically remained unchanged. The only procedural improvement is the substitution of the co-decision procedure for the assent procedure in connection with the implementation of the right to free movement in Article 18 [ex Article 8a]. Article 22 empowers the Council to add new citizenship rights in accordance with the respective constitutional requirements of the Member States. A proposal by the EP to simplify the procedure and to provide for majority voting failed due to opposition by several Member States. Rightly or wrongly, it was considered essential that the reinforcement of citizenship rights emanated from the will of all Member States, and even the Commission was against abolishing the unanimity requirement. Under Maastricht, Article 8e has never been used.

Exhortations by the European Commission and the EP to expand existing citizenship rights, notably through the completion of diplomatic protection in third countries and the realization of complete freedom of movement, have never been followed. The extension of voting rights in other than local elections was considered at the IGC but not sustained because of the lack of compatibility of the systems of several Member States.[17]

The most comprehensive set of (mostly unsuccessful) proposals tabled for the introduction of new citizenship rights came in the form of a joint Italian/Austrian Memorandum of 1 October 1996. It advanced the following new rights:

- (Proposed Article 8b EC): the right to enter the territory of all Member States including one's own, as well as to move and reside there. This was going against another proposal, by the Spanish, who insisted that European citizens should not be allowed to apply for asylum in another Member State. In the end, the proposal was abandoned, and the question of asylum dealt with in a separate protocol to the Treaty.[18]
- (Proposed Article 8c EC): the right, in principle, of access to documents held or issued by Community institutions. This right was later included in a new Article 255 [ex Article 191a] EC, for the benefit of all citizens and any national or legal person residing or having its registered office in a Member State. As there is no reference to this right in the citizenship part of the Treaty, it is well hidden in Part Five relating to the EC Institutions, and the second and third pillar are not covered by it.
- (Proposed Article 8e EC): the right of citizens to demand the adoption of

legislation if at least one-tenth of the electorate in each of at least three Member States underwrites the request. Most Member States were opposed to this embryonic form of direct democracy. For some, the will of 370 million people could only be formed coherently through the EP.

- (Proposed Article 8g EC, replacing Article 138a EC): the right to associate freely with political parties acting at European level and to participate in trade unions and other associations at European level. This right must have been shattered against the fear of governments of losing control over constitutionally delicate issues such as this, and the proposal was abandoned. The Treaty of Amsterdam does contain clauses dealing with European aspects of charities and with negotiations between the social partners, but they are not a substitute for what should be a basic citizens' right.

- (Proposed Article 8i EC): the right to receive an education taking account of the common heritage of European civilization, and to learn in school a language other than one's own. This must have conflicted, if not with subsidiarity, then with what most Member States consider a matter of national sovereignty or regional competence, and it would also have raised concerns about the financial implications of the amendment. The proposal was not adopted. Instead it was suggested that the preamble to the EC Treaty should include a clause to the effect that the Member States are 'determined to promote the development of the highest possible knowledge of their peoples through a wide access to education and its continuous updating'. This would effectively become the ninth recital.

The joint Memorandum of Italy and Austria further contained constructive proposals on human rights and non-discrimination. However, these were to be kept outside the part on citizenship because they were rights which were not specific to nationals of Member States, benefiting as they do all individuals throughout the Community. Also the Spanish delegation had argued strongly for keeping human rights in a separate part of the TEU. The outcome will be discussed below.

Assessment

The qualities of European citizenship can be measured against criteria traditionally developed in relation to citizenship of modern nation states. This is in line with the common European heritage deriving from the Enlightenment and the French Revolution, as well as the (real or perceived) success of the nation state model of society, the cohesion of which depended on a triad of rights, duties and political participation.

One may wish to argue that there is no need to apply a nation state model to the European Union, among other things because the nation state as an institution is no longer capable of catering for essential needs of present-day societies. The environment, asylum and immigration are examples of problems which the nation state has not been able to solve in a satisfactory manner, and are of increasing significance. The creation of a new European state is therefore not the answer. What is needed is a relationship not exclusively between the state and the individual, to the exclusion of the alien, but multiple allegiances between individuals and different circles of society.

Be this as it may, the triad of rights, duties and participation is still the basic pattern upon which societal relations are built, and in constitution-building there is no practical or more useful alternative. The following assessment therefore broadly follows that model.

Citizens' duties

Shortcomings in Union citizenship as compared to Member State citizenship are perhaps most clearly visible in relation to citizens' duties. Although the Maastricht Treaty does mention duties as a corollary of citizenship of the Union, there are no such duties explicitly laid down. For example, there is no military service and the Union is not endowed with an independent power to tax. The absence of such aspects can be seen as a missed opportunity to encourage a sense of solidarity or allegiance to the Union, and the lack of an EU power of taxation in particular reduces its possibilities of pursuing policies which have a considerable impact for the citizen, for instance in the social field. Nevertheless, it is not surprising in the light of the lack of democratic character of the European institutions or in the face of a lack of perceived usefulness of the Union in the eyes of the citizen who would be asked to make a contribution. Proposals by the EP to introduce voluntary Community services or to show taxpayers, on their national tax forms, how much they currently contribute indirectly to the Community budget have not been taken on board.[19]

Political participation

The powers of the EP have continuously been expanded since the inception of the Treaties, and Maastricht in particular constituted an important improvement, as the introduction of the co-decision procedure brought about a degree of parity between the Parliament and the Council, even though it applies to certain areas only and the Parliament does not have a right of legislative initiative. Amsterdam builds somewhat further on the *acquis*, notably by expanding and simplifying the co-decision procedure and by transferring certain subjects from the third to the first pillar.[20]

Of course, any improvement in this area has to be seen in perspective. To some, the broadening of the powers of the EP means nothing if that body is not representative of European public opinion. As long as seats in the EP are still distributed to Member States and there are no transnational political parties, no transnational political programmes or elections, this is unlikely to change. The EP in that sense does not really represent the European citizens.

In those areas in which the co-decision procedure does not apply, the democracy deficit at the European level is blatant and where it is not made up for by adequate control at the national level it is outright unacceptable. The Treaty of Amsterdam brings in its Chapter 19 a new Protocol on the role of national parliaments in the Union which is a necessary though insufficient improvement, as any such control is indirect.

The right, granted by Maastricht, to vote in and stand for municipal elections in one's country of residence, important though it may be, cannot make up for this. First of all, this is not a level of decision-making which influences European affairs to any significant degree. Second, it is a right which benefits only a very tiny proportion of the populace, namely those who live in a Member State other than their own and who comply with the requirements of the legislation concerned. It is therefore difficult to see how this right makes Member States' citizens feel more European.

The right to vote and stand as a candidate for European elections in one's country of residence has to be seen in the same light. As pointed out above, the EP is presently an institution of some consequence. It might have been possible to establish a right for all European citizens to vote in a constituency of their choice in the EU. However, so far this has not been attained. The extent of participation in the EP elections, the most recent of which, in 1999, was characterized by a very low turnout (barely 50 per cent) is indicative of the extent to which the citizen feels concerned.

Rights

The third element of the citizenship triad is constituted by individual rights, including free movement, social protection, a minimum standard of human rights, access to justice, and non-discrimination.

The right to free movement had been, since Maastricht, at the heart of the citizenship provisions, having previously largely been realized by two regulations, nine directives and a series of judgments by the ECJ. This did not include, however, the freedom from border controls on persons.

One of the central innovations of Amsterdam is the creation over time of an 'area of freedom, security and justice', which entails the transfer of certain policy areas from the third to the first pillar, and the 'communitarization' of much of the Schengen *acquis*. The UK, Ireland and Denmark do not, however, have to participate in this venture.

Commenting on this state of affairs, Commissioner Monti was positive about the inclusion of the Schengen *acquis* in the Treaty since this would make Community rules and procedures applicable – which is somewhat of an improvement especially in terms of the expansion of democratic control by EP and of the powers of the Court of Justice.[21] Yet from another perspective the solutions adopted are disappointing, even if the EP were capable of giving detailed attention to all of the *acquis*. The fact that free movement applies to some countries and not to others strikes at the heart of the citizenship provisions. For so long as there is no uniformity, the right to free movement granted in Article 8a EC is really destined to remain an empty phrase.

In addition, there is some unclear drafting in this area, particularly in relation to the use of the words 'freedom', 'security' and 'justice' in the title of the section. These are very strong words indeed, but they do not seem to be guaranteed by the Treaty. Seen in that light, the Amsterdam amendments would appear at best confusing and at worst misleading. Moreover, it is not immediately clear whether the variable geometry with regard to the Schengen *acquis* is compatible with the principle laid down in the new Article 11 [ex Article 5a] paragraph 1 sub c EC, according to which 'closer collaboration between [some] Member States may not concern the citizenship of the Union or discriminate between nationals of the Union'. Free movement is clearly a citizen's right and flexibility sits uneasily with this provision, even if one takes the view that Article 11 would appear to refer to new flexibility arrangements only, not those already agreed to at the IGC. The fact remains that it contains a principle, the universality of citizenship, which is not consistently applied throughout the Treaty.

Amsterdam clearly represents an advance in terms of the notorious Social Protocol, which has reverted wholesale to the Treaty. The British general election in May 1997, in which the Major government was defeated, made possible the reversal of the British opt-out in this field. However, this will not necessarily result in an improvement of social protection within the Union. On the contrary, one can expect an increase in disputes about the legal basis of proposed legal measures in this field and about their compliance with the principle of subsidiarity. As one commentator remarks:

> While the British now accept that there has to be a common base of social rights for all citizens, and are prepared to allow an enhanced role for the social partners, they will resist over-regulation and will deploy the principle of subsidiarity to kill draft directives that threaten labour market flexibility.[22]

Similar considerations hold good for the non-discrimination provisions in the Treaty. New Article 13 [ex Article 6a] EC, a general non-discrimination provision, allows the Council 'within the limits of the powers conferred' by the Treaty to take appropriate action to combat discrimination based on sex, racial or ethnic origin, religion or belief, disability, age or sexual orientation. In so far as this provision will not have direct effect, it will require further implementation by the institutions, and it is not always clear on what basis. A new indent to Article 141 [ex Article 119] asks the institutions to make progress in the equal treatment of men and women; but proposals to include references to measures for the elderly and disabled, for instance, did not make their way into amendments of the old Article 118(2). Progress may further be limited by the failure to further extend qualified majority voting in the field of social policy.

Limited improvements have also been made in the field of human rights, although the absence of a catalogue of human rights and of external judicial control is much regretted. Traditionally, the Treaty had not contained human rights provisions or competencies of the Community institutions in this field, and Maastricht changed little. Article F(2) TEU merely confirmed the situation arising under the case law of the ECJ, namely that the Union would respect human rights as general principles of Community law. The open hostility of certain Member States, notably the UK, to Community action in the field of human rights explains, at least in part, why the ECJ in its Opinion 2/94 took a minimalist attitude on Community powers, denying that it could become a party to the ECHR. Although the matter of treaty-making power in human rights questions appears to have been discussed at the IGC, the challenge was not taken up, depriving the European citizen of a valuable guarantee of compliance by the Community institutions with the required standards.

The newly proposed procedure in Article 7 [ex Article F.1] TEU for ensuring compliance with human rights by Member States, threatening suspension of their rights in case of serious and persistent disregard of human rights, the rule of law, or the principles of liberty and democracy, does not make up for this. Instead, the procedure is doomed to be both politicized and exceptional, and it excludes activities by the EC institutions.

The fact that the Amsterdam Treaty, given its Protocol on asylum rights, does not provide for asylum in another Member State may prove to be a setback for the protection of human rights against which the above procedure may be of no avail.

The confirmation and extension of the jurisdiction of the ECJ in matters of human rights is, of course, to be applauded. Article 46 [ex Article L] TEU does not merely codify the case law of the ECJ regarding human rights protection in the Community. It appears also to extend the jurisdiction of the Court, where acts of the institutions are concerned, beyond the framework of the EC Treaty. Notably, according to Article 35 [ex Article K.7] TEU, the ECJ has jurisdiction in various types of proceedings regarding framework and other decisions, JHA conventions and measures implementing them, and Article 40 TEU provide for closer cooperation in the field of JHA making use of Community institutions. The expansion of the Court's jurisdiction in this field and the control of the observance of human rights are much-needed improvements, even though activities of the Member States, for instance those in the implementation of acts of the institutions do not seem to be covered by Article 46. This impression is reinforced by the new clause in Article 7 [ex Article F.1] TEU according to which human rights and fundamental freedoms 'are upheld by the Member States'. The situation may, however, be different with regard to certain actions by Member States under the notorious Protocol on asylum for nationals of Member States of the Union, because this is a protocol to the EC Treaty for which the ECJ obviously has jurisdiction.

One must again regret the less than clear drafting and the compartmentalization of the Treaty which makes it difficult to read and understand. For instance, the citizen would have been better served by a reference to fundamental rights in the part on citizenship of the Union, even if fundamental rights are not the preserve of citizenship. Similarly, the lack of a catalogue of human rights is to be regretted as it would help awareness of fundamental rights.

The enlargement of protection is not accompanied by procedural changes, like the increased access to the courts (*locus standi*) for individuals, or the creation of a fast-track procedure in case of alleged infringements of fundamental rights.

'Bread and games' instead?

Whereas there was no breakthrough as regards the three traditional elements of citizenship, Amsterdam did bring progress on a variety of issues of concern to the general public, notably employment, environment protection and justice and home affairs.

As is well known, a high level of employment was already a well-established principle of the EC long before Amsterdam (Article 2 EC). Many of the changes made to the Treaty in this field seem to be fairly cosmetic, the EU not being able to do anything that it was not able to do beforehand. The provisions on employment appear to be the result, not so much of the view that individuals ought to be entitled to a job, or of a consensus that full employment is worth striving for, but rather of the idea that failing to be seen to be dealing with high levels of unemployment would be a public relations mistake.

Yet the thought that something can realistically be done about unemployment without spending any money at all would seem to be completely unrealistic. The refusal to commit such funding can therefore only mean there are as yet no serious intentions to take action on the Community level. According to Duff,[23] the belief that the EU holds the answer to structural unemployment implies a centralization of fiscal policy that is not consistent with the EMU programme, which insists that measures are taken at a national level to curb excessive government deficits.

In relation to environmental protection, much has been done to improve the existing provisions and to clarify the relationship between Community policy and action by the Member States. The link with citizenship is, of course, only indirect. But it is another area included in the Treaty because it is a major concern of the electorate. For much the same reasons, the sections in the Treaty dealing with public health and consumer protection as well as countering fraud and other illegal activities affecting the financial interests of the Community have been amplified and rendered more precise. Justice and home affairs are examined in more detail in Chapter 8. More generally, provisions on subsidiarity intended to ensure that Community measures are taken as closely as possible to the citizen are laid down in a Protocol to the Treaty of Amsterdam.[24]

Finally, there is an attempt to simplify the Treaties which, however, does not go far enough. Among the declarations appended to the Treaty of Amsterdam there is one on the quality of drafting of Community legislation.

Conclusions

After Amsterdam the individual is not much more a fully fledged citizen than before, and not much less a subject. Rather than strengthening essential elements of citizenship, the IGC mostly focused on citizens' concerns by way of a set of public relations actions. These are certainly areas of concern to the electorate, though they bring no direct improvement of the quality of European citizenship as such.

Previously, the citizenship provisions may have seemed to have an enormous or, depending on the perspective adopted, an altogether dangerously broad potential. The phrase in Article 8 EC, according to which 'Citizenship of the Union is hereby established' is reminiscent of a 'Social Contract' and creates expectations in the minds of people who share ideas of freedom, equality and social justice. The Union was going to take over, to protect and care, through actions of the political institutions and through the administration of justice. The Article even evoked a scenario in which the EU would sooner or later replace national allegiances and citizenship, just as the proliferation in the Treaties of the word 'Union' was indicative of an advanced degree of familiarization with the idea of complete (economic, monetary and political) integration.

By the time of the adoption of the Treaty of Amsterdam, opponents of further political integration succeeded in taking most of the steam out of the development of Part Two of the EC Treaty. In terms of citizens' rights, the Amsterdam Treaty changes are hardly substantial, and from the perspective of an integrated political system would definitely not go far enough.

It is regrettable that Amsterdam has not led to the elaboration of a fully fledged European Citizenship Charter. This would clearly have represented a recognition of achievements so far, if not a step forward in European integration. The awareness that belonging to the Union gives citizens added value undoubtedly contributes towards their greater involvement with the European idea. The interest in motivating European citizens for the integration process would have justified giving increased importance to citizenship of the Union, especially but not only with regard to social and economic rights.

Endnotes

1. E. Marias, 'From Market Citizen to European Union Citizen', in E. Marias (ed.), *European Citizenship*, Maastricht: European Institute for Public Administration, 1994, p. 1.
2. Marias, 'From Market Citizen to European Union Citizen', p. 3.
3. See for example, N. Neuwahl, 'The Treaty on European Union: A Step Forward in the Protection of Human Rights?', in N. Neuwahl and A. Rosas (eds), *The European Union and Human Rights*, The Hague: Martinus Nijhoff Publishers, 1995, pp. 1–22.
4. Marias, 'From Market Citizen to European Union Citizen', p. 4.
5. F. Laurssen and S. Vanhoonacker (eds), *The Intergovernmental Conference on Political Union*, Maastricht: European Institute for Public Administration, 1992, pp. 269–75.
6. See for example, G. Ferrari, 'Citizenship: Problems, Concepts and Policies?', in M. de la Torre (ed.), *European Citizenship: An Institutional Challenge*, The Hague: Kluwer International, 1997, pp. 51–64.
7. *Agence Europe*, No. 5252, 11 May 1990. See also, Spanish Delegation, 'Intergovernmental Conference on Political Union – European Citizenship', in Laurssen and Vanhoonacker, *The Intergovernmental Conference on Political Union*, p. 325.
8. Laurssen and Vanhoonacker, *The Intergovernmental Conference on Political Union*, pp. 277–81.
9. Official Journal of the European Communities 1990, C 231/97.
10. Laurssen and Vanhoonacker, *The Intergovernmental Conference on Political Union*, pp. 328–33.
11. Marias, 'From Market Citizen to European Union Citizen', p. 9.
12. Compare with the so-called 'green papers'.
13. Report of the Reflection Group, SN 520/95 (REFLEX)21, 11.
14. *Agence Europe*, No. 6699, 30 March 1996, p. 2.
15. *Intergovernmental Conference 1996, Commission Report for the Reflection Group*, Luxembourg, 1996.

16. *Commission Report for the Reflection Group*, pp. 21–22.
17. European Parliament, *Positions résumées des États Membres et du Parlement européen sur la Conférence intergouvernementale de 1996*. Task force 'Conférence intergouvernementale', Luxembourg, 4 December 1996, passim.
18. See below, the section on fundamental rights protection.
19. European Parliament, *Fiche thématique sur la citoyenneté européene*, no. 10. Secretariat working party, Task force 'Conférence intergouvernementale', Luxembourg, 20 February 1997, p. 13.
20. See Chapter 1.
21. Second Report on Citizenship, June 1997. http://europa.eu.int/comm/dg15/en/update/report/citen.htm
22. See A. Duff (ed.), *The Treaty of Amsterdam: Text and Commentary*, London: The Federal Trust, 1997.
23. See Duff, *The Treaty of Amsterdam*, note 22.
24. See also the Declaration by Germany, Austria and Belgium on subsidiarity. CONF 4002/97, p. 93.

Chapter 11

Flexibility and closer cooperation: evolution or entropy?

Philip Lynch

In the mid-1990s flexibility seemed a panacea for the ills of the European Union (EU), allowing some Member States to forge ahead with further integration without requiring the participation of states unwilling or unable to proceed. Flexibility was lauded by European zealots in Bonn and recalcitrants in London as a way of managing integration among states with diverse attitudes and attributes, and of preparing the Union for eastward enlargement. But there was no consensus on the character or mechanics of flexibility, evidenced in the variety of terms mentioned: multi-speed Europe, variable geometry, *à la carte* Europe, hard core and closer cooperation acquired their own political resonance.

The further development of intra-EU flexibility had a number of attractions. It would allow those states seeking further integration to proceed, subject to certain conditions, by-passing the vetoes of states unwilling to become involved in these areas. This vanguard could also move ahead more quickly than those states which supported further integration in principle, but who were unable to meet the conditions to join at that juncture. The Conservative government in Britain wanted flexibility arrangements which guaranteed that they would not be forced into further integration against their will. However, rules of good conduct for participants and non-participants would be necessary to ensure that all benefited from such arrangements, to protect the interests of 'outs' and minimize opportunities for 'free-riders'.[1] Flexibility also promised a more manageable route to eastward enlargement which allowed both a widening of the Union and a deepening of the integration process. But flexibility also carried with it risks for the EU, sitting uneasily with its goals of solidarity and cohesion while not guaranteeing enhanced efficiency, democracy or political progress.[2] The EU's smaller states and its Mediterranean members feared that they might be excluded from a developing hard core and involuntarily consigned to a second tier.

A number of flexibility arrangements have been included in the Treaty of Amsterdam: a general clause permitting a majority of states to proceed with closer co-operation, subject to certain conditions; specific clauses allowing closer cooperation in certain policy areas; and a range of special arrangements for individual states. Given this heterogeneity and the complexity of the authorization process, it is debatable whether flexibility marks a progressive stage in the evolution of an EU adapting to a changing environment (and if so, towards what kind of Union is this evolution leading?), or whether it is a sign of entropy, the tendency of things to fall apart over time as stability and order give way to disorder and inefficiency.

A typology of flexibility

This chapter utilizes a threefold typology of flexibility – identifying a multi-speed Europe, variable geometry and *à la carte* Europe as the most significant ideal types – and uses 'flexibility' as a generic term. Any classification is problematic, however, given the number of terms employed, their different usage in political debate, the blurred boundaries between the key variants, and the *ad hoc* arrangements found in the Treaties. Stubb's typology locates differentiation along three variables, time (multi-speed), space (variable geometry) and matter (*à la carte*).[3] Wallace and Wallace, though, note that a core might be organized around policies (for example, EMU, defence or immigration policy), countries (the Franco-German partnership) or institutions (as in the Western European Union [WEU] and EuroCorps), while differences between states might be based on taste or ability.[4]

1. Multi-speed Europe

In a multi-speed Europe, the pursuit of common objectives is driven by a vanguard or core group of states who are permitted (even obliged) to proceed with further integration in new areas at a faster pace than other states. Pro-integration states would not be bound to travel at a speed dictated by the slowest Member States, but could forge ahead. A key assumption of the multi-speed model is that all Member States will eventually adopt the agreed policies, the states in the slow lane of the integration process eventually arriving at the point of common destiny. Differences are, in theory, temporary and removed over time. Those states not joining the 'first wave' of states moving into new areas of integration are 'pre-ins' rather than 'outs'. To prevent a multi-speed Europe degenerating into a multi-tier EU with permanent divisions, the conditions of membership of the vanguard are predetermined and agreed by all states rather than just those joining at the outset. The *acquis communautaire* is preserved and differentiation occurs within the institutional framework of the EU, using EU methods and procedures.

The multi-speed ideal type embraces the goal of solidarity while recognizing the diversity of ability and capacity which exists in the Union. States agree on the same broad goals but move towards achieving them at different speeds. Core states may be expected to provide aid (financial and administrative) to help the 'pre-ins' join in a later wave, and should refrain from revising the conditions of membership upwards. The time scale for transition may be open rather than set at a fixed date in advance, but this risks semi-permanent derogations if an open-ended transition period disguises a lack of political will among non-participants.

The multi-speed model has a number of variants. A 'two-speed Europe' suggests two rather than multiple waves of states moving into new policy areas. 'Differentiated integration' also refers to differences in the time scale in which states move into new areas of integration which are agreed by all. Here the term is not used, as is sometimes the case, as a generic term but as a specific form of flexibility, namely the EC's traditional model in which states are granted temporary derogations or transition periods.[5] Wallace and Wallace have used the metaphor of 'flying geese' to suggest a Europe in which different states take turns in leading further integration according to the policy area in question and their relative capacity.[6] Stronger states move first into new, but agreed, territory, assisting weaker states on their journey towards a common destination.

The boundary between the multi-speed and intra-EU variable geometry models is blurred, as illustrated by Stubb's inclusion of a 'hard core' within his multi-speed family of terms.[7] The concept of a hard core errs towards rigidity in its outlook and mechanics, suggesting a predetermined core and/or a division within the EU which is unlikely to be eradicated in the short term given the gulf between the capacities or preferences of 'in' and 'pre-in' states. The ideal type multi-speed model may, through a deliberate or unintended corruption of the initial goal of eventual full participation by all, result in a rigid division along multi-tier rather than multi-speed lines. 'Pre-ins' may in effect become 'outs' if, formally or informally, the hurdles which a state has to overcome to gain entry in a later wave are raised. An economic core may become self-perpetuating if further integration produces winners and losers, propelling the 'ins' still further ahead of the 'pre-ins' in terms of capacity, or if the core states adopt new flanking policies which become additional hurdles to entry.

The concept of a multi-speed Europe is not new, being suggested in the 1975 Tindemans Report[8] and Spinelli's 1984 Draft Treaty of European Union. Examples of multi-speed integration in the EU include temporary derogations on Single Market legislation, transition periods for new Member States and the Maastricht Treaty's provisions for the multi-speed development of Economic and Monetary Union (EMU).

2. *Variable geometry*

The ideal type of the variable geometry model allows some EU Member States to develop further cooperation in new policy areas, recognizing that this produces a (semi-)permanent division between a core of states and those states unwilling or unable to take part. It thus admits to rigid differences in the objectives and/or capacity of current Member States.[9] Flexibility is presented as the optimal means of by-passing obstructions (deliberate or otherwise) on the road to 'ever-closer union'. Non-participants may in future opt in to the new areas of cooperation, but would have to accept those rules and arrangements already developed. Variable geometry arrangements have often developed outside of the EU framework, as in the case of the Schengen Group.

Variable geometry is conceptually less precise than the multi-speed idea, reflected in its family of concepts (including multi-tier, opt-in and concentric circles). Variable geometry may produce circles of further integration defined either by their membership ('space' in Stubb's formulation) or the policy areas covered.[10] These circles may have limited overlap in terms of membership. In a Europe of interlocking circles, those states pursuing integration in, say, internal security may not be identical with the group of states pursuing EMU or extra-EU defence cooperation. The 'concentric circles' scheme envisages a Europe in which states are grouped in a series of different circles of cooperation; in the 'Olympic rings' model, the lack of congruence between the different circles of cooperation is more pronounced and there is a proliferation of regimes.[11]

3. À la carte *Europe*

The *à la carte* Europe model envisages a looser form of flexibility in which EU Member States are able to pick and choose which policy areas they wish to participate in, opting out of further integration which they have no taste for. States are bound by a minimum number of common objectives such as Single Market legislation and the core *acquis*. However the *à la carte* model carries with it the danger that the *acquis* is undermined by opt-outs and demands for a repatriation of EC competences. Like the variable geometry model, it recognizes that irrevocable differences exist between states, but rather than having progressive virtues, it further erodes solidarity and the EU's single institutional framework, opening up large areas of EU activity to opt-outs.

The ideal type *à la carte* model has had limited impact on the EU's development, but the opt-outs incorporated in the Maastricht Treaty and Treaty of Amsterdam indicate an incremental drift towards *à la carte* solutions. Examples include the British opt-out from Stage III of EMU; British non-participation in the Maastricht Social Agreement; the provisions in the Edinburgh summit Conclusions on derogations for Denmark relating to defence, EMU Stage III and citizenship of the Union[12]; and the special arrangements relating to the UK, Ireland, Denmark and Belgium laid down in Protocols appended to the Amsterdam Treaty.

In terms of the likely implications of the three ideal types of flexibility for the future development of the EU, the multi-speed model has the clearest evolutionary ethos. It maintains the goals of solidarity and cohesion, seeks agreement on common objectives and safeguards the *acquis*. It looks to the evolution rather than dissolution of the Union's institutional framework and charges a vanguard of states with driving the integration process forward while aiding other states to join at a later date. Although the vanguard theoretically exerts centripetal pressure on the 'pre-ins', in practice the multi-speed model may produce semi-permanent divisions among states and across policy sectors, particularly if the vanguard develops into a hard core. The variable geometry and *à la carte* models both have a tendency towards entropy as differences in the capacity and political will of states are formalized in separate institutional arrangements. The *ad hoc* arrangements associated with a variable geometry outcome (intra-EU but particularly extra-EU) may result in greater complexity, inefficiency and lack of transparency. An *à la carte* outcome produces centrifugal pressures, added risks of contamination and further complexity as special arrangements for certain states threaten the *acquis* and work against a sense of common purpose.

Flexibility in the European Community

The classic Community method of integration implies full, uniform participation by all Member States, with EC legislation binding on all states from the same starting date. But Community secondary legislation has frequently allowed for differentiation, recognizing the special economic problems faced by some Member States, who are then granted partial exemptions (derogations) or temporary delays in the implementation of legislation. The Single European Act introduced traditional differentiation into primary Community law.[13] Article 8c SEA stated that in establishing the Single Market, the Commission 'shall take into account the extent of the effort that certain economies showing differences in development shall have to sustain', proposing appropriate derogations, though these would have to 'be of a temporary nature and must cause the least possible disturbance to the functioning of the common market'. Rather than just reflecting differences in the ability of Member States to implement EC legislation, the provision of derogations has often reflected a lack of political will on the part of some states, or has resulted from difficult negotiations with new members.

Variable geometry is evident in Article 233 EC which foresees the completion of the Benelux regional union, allowing Belgium, Luxembourg and the Netherlands to pursue integration in policy areas not covered by the Treaty. Article 130k SEA envisaged supplementary research and development programmes 'involving the participation of certain Member States only'. Article 100a (4) SEA stated that, subject to confirmation by the Commission that discrimination or trade restriction would not result, Member States might be permitted to maintain higher national environmental standards than those adopted by the Community. These provisions were partially amended in the Treaty of Amsterdam.

When it was created in 1979, all Member States agreed on the basic principles of the European Monetary System (EMS), but not all were obliged to participate fully. Thus, the UK joined the EMS in 1979, but did not join its most important part, the Exchange Rate Mechanism (ERM), until 1990 before unilaterally withdrawing from the mechanism in 1992. Greece did not join the ERM until 1998, whereas Sweden and Finland linked their currencies to the ERM before achieving EU membership. The bands within which currencies operated also varied, the majority having 2.25 per cent bands against their central parity, weaker currencies having 6 per cent bands. The bands for all but the deutschmark and guilder were increased to 15 per cent in 1993 following currency turbulence.

EU states have pursued flexible integration in a number of research ventures, including the European Space Agency and the Joint European Torus (JET) project on research into nuclear fusion. Variable geometry in defence cooperation is evident in the differential membership and role of NATO, the WEU and EuroCorps. In 1985, six EC states formed the Schengen Group with the aim of removing internal frontiers and developing further cooperation in areas concerning the free movement of persons. As this was a goal of the EC Treaties, Schengen was presented as a laboratory in which complex integration measures were given a trial run before being adopted more widely. An alternative perspective noted the dangers of this experiment: states chose to cooperate within the Schengen framework rather than the EC, while progress within Schengen was dogged by political and practical problems.[14] By 1997, Schengen membership stood at 13 (some non-EU states have associate status), the UK and Ireland remaining non-members. Another 'Byzantine structure' was created in 1994 when the European Economic Area (EEA), in which five European Free Trade Association (EFTA) states participate in the Single Market, introduced asymmetrical institutional arrangements.[15]

Flexibility and the Maastricht Treaty

In the 1990s flexibility has taken on a qualitatively and quantitatively different character. The Treaty on European Union (TEU) or Maastricht Treaty extended flexibility, employing its multi-speed, variable geometry and *à la carte* variants in a number of areas. Whereas earlier derogations had been granted to states with special economic problems, many of the TEU Protocols and Declarations (for example, on Irish abortion law) afforded exemptions to states facing political difficulties.[16]

Economic and Monetary Union

The TEU explicitly paved the way for flexibility in the development of Economic and Monetary Union. EMU would be a multi-speed process, a majority of Member States moving to Stage III (the irrevocable locking of exchange rates and adoption of a single currency) in 1997 or 1998 if they met the convergence criteria. If a critical mass of states did not meet the criteria by then, Stage III would begin on 1 January 1999 for those states adjudged to have met the criteria. The assumption was that states not joining in 1999 (the 'pre-ins') would strive to meet the criteria and join shortly after. This reflected a multi-speed ethos, although Denmark can be viewed politically as an 'out' with little intention of joining Stage III. States not participating in Stage III are treated as 'Member States with a derogation' and have some of the rights and privileges afforded to first wave 'ins' suspended, such as making appointments to the European Central Bank (ECB). The national central banks of 'pre-in' states are part of the European System of Central Banks (ESCB), but their Governors are members of the ECB General Council rather than its Governing Council.

EMU also has an *à la carte* element in that the UK and Denmark were granted opt-outs from Stage III. But EMU and the British opt-out were discussed and accepted by all Member States during the IGC and at Maastricht; all states, including the UK, accepted EMU as the 'irreversible' goal of the EC. In a Protocol, the Treaty signatories accepted that the UK 'shall not be obliged or committed to move to the third stage of EMU without a separate decision to do so by the United Kingdom Government and Parliament'. The UK was also granted exemptions on aspects of EMU legislation. It was obliged to inform the Council in advance if it did not intend to join Stage III at its launch. The UK can at any time thereafter revoke its opt-out and apply to join. Membership would not be automatic: the UK would have to meet the convergence criteria and be accepted by a QMV vote, although the requirement of two years' membership of the ERM might be waived. The Protocol on Denmark stated that it would notify the Council in advance regarding its position on participation in Stage III of EMU. Following the Danish referendum's 'No' to the Maastricht Treaty, Denmark indicated at the 1992 Edinburgh European Council that it would not participate in Stage III. Sweden decided that it would not sign up to the euro in 1999, though it had not explicitly been granted an opt-out.

More details on the management of an EMU of 'ins' and 'pre-ins' were fleshed out after Maastricht. Discussions covered codes of conduct on economic policy for 'ins' and 'pre-ins' and the arrangements by which first wave states would discuss EMU issues. A new Exchange Rate Mechanism (ERM2) replaced the existing system in 1999. It provides exchange rate stability between the euro-zone states and the 'pre-ins', preventing competitive devaluations and aiding the transition to membership of 'pre-in' states. Membership is voluntary, Sweden and the UK indicating that they have no plans to join. The Stability and Growth Pact ensures that EMU states continue to strive for long-term, sustainable convergence and avoid excessive deficits. Each EMU state aims for a 3 per cent public deficit target, presenting a stability programme to the Commission specifying its medium-term budget objectives and adjustment paths for surplus or deficit ratios. The Council can impose sanctions on states which breach the excessive deficit rule, but a deficit will be considered 'exceptional and temporary' if it is deemed to result from severe economic downturn or an unusual event outside the control of that state. The 'pre-ins' submit convergence programmes to the Commission and will be subject to EU surveillance and non-binding recommendations on the avoidance of excessive deficits, but will not face sanctions.

In 1997, agreement was reached on a new 'Euro-X' Council (now Euro-11) consisting of the finance ministers of EMU states. In this group, the 'ins' will discuss matters of mutual interest – for example, the euro's exchange rate and the operation of the Stability and Growth Pact – separately from Ecofin meetings of all 15 EU finance ministers. The Blair government claimed to have won assurances that Ecofin will remain the decision-making forum and that 'pre-ins' should not be excluded from discussions on wider economic issues, though the Euro-11 group may reach informal agreements prior to Ecofin meetings.[17] First wave states may try to establish inclusive or bilateral cooperation in EMU 'flanking policies' such as tax harmonization, creating intersecting circles of additional economic integration within the euro-zone. At the first formal Euro-11 meeting, held under the British

Presidency in June 1998, Chancellor Gordon Brown opened the session but was required to leave when the meeting proper began.[18]

The second and third pillars

The TEU introduced elements of flexibility into the new Common Foreign and Security Policy (CFSP) second pillar, and the justice and home affairs (JHA) third pillar. Article J.4 TEU allowed for closer cooperation on defence matters on a bilateral basis between two or more Member States in the framework of the WEU and NATO, provided that such cooperation did not impede CFSP cooperation. The WEU was designated an 'integral part of the development of the Union' and its defence component even though only nine EU states were full members of the WEU. Greece subsequently became a full member; the remaining EU states, namely Austria, Denmark, Finland and Ireland have observer status. EuroCorps was set up by France and Germany, then joined by contingents from Belgium, Luxembourg and Spain. In the third pillar, Article K.7 TEU allowed for closer cooperation between two or more Member States in JHA matters.

Social policy

Following John Major's refusal to agree to any extension of Community competence in social policy within the TEU proper, the other 11 (14 after the 1995 enlargement) Member States signed the Social Protocol and Agreement.[19] Britain's action was condemned as anti-*communautaire*, creating separate social policy regimes in the EU and free-rider benefits for the UK. The Protocol on Social Policy allowed the other 11 states to pursue additional social policy cooperation in areas outlined in the Social Agreement, using EU institutions and procedures. The UK would not take part in the deliberation and adoption of these measures, but was still involved in and bound by social policy legislation agreed under existing Treaty articles, including Article 118a EC on health and safety.

The Blair government accepted the incorporation of the Social Agreement into the Treaty proper at Amsterdam. Only two directives had been agreed and implemented under the Social Protocol route during the period of British non-involvement, the European Works Council Directive and the Paternity Leave Directive. The former nonetheless had repercussions in Britain as a number of transnational companies whose headquarters were in the UK set up works councils in their British branches.

Post-Maastricht debates

Flexibility was given additional impetus by the elucidation of German, French and British perspectives in 1994. The 'Reflections on European Policy' paper produced by senior CDU/CSU politicians Karl Lamers and Wolfgang Schäuble reflected Chancellor Kohl's belief that the pace of European integration should not be dictated by 'the slowest ship in the convoy'. It argued that a pre-determined hard core of states (driven by France and Germany, and including the Benelux states) 'oriented to the model of a federal state', should forge ahead with further cooperation in monetary, fiscal, economic, social and foreign policy. 'The countries of the hard core must not only participate as a matter of course in all policy fields, but should also be recognisably more Community-spirited in their joint action than others, and launch common initiatives aimed at promoting the development of the Union.'[20] The hard core would not be closed, but would act as a vanguard and persuader for 'ever closer union' of all Member States, however, other states seeking to join it would have to accept the common objectives and any new measures. Lamers and Schäuble characterized this as a 'variable geometry or multi-speed approach', recommending that arrangements for flexibility be 'sanctioned and institutionalized in the Union Treaty'.[21] Subsequent German submissions departed from these proposals in both tone and substance, dropping the idea of a pre-determined hard core.

In response, Major developed his idea of a 'multi-track, multi-speed, multi-layered' Europe in a speech in Leiden.[22] He ruled out the development of a hard core of either countries or policies; any arrangement which allowed a small group of states to use EU institutions must be agreed by all states, open to all who want to and are able to participate, and must not force reluctant states into further integration. All Member States would be bound by existing Single Market rules, but would be free to opt out of other policy areas such as further social policy cooperation or EMU. Major claimed his vision was one of variable geometry, but critics depicted it as an *à la carte* model, particularly when the UK sought a limited renegotiation of existing commitments at the IGC. Some Conservative Euro-sceptics went further, proposing a special status for Britain in a Single Market-only tier of the EU.[23]

French premier Balladur proposed a 'Europe of concentric circles', organized around three circles.[24] The first 'ordinary law' circle would be an enlarged EU; the widest circle would link EU applicants and non-members through political, military and economic agreements. A series of 'tighter circles' would permit closer cooperation in different policy areas, but unlike the German hard core proposal, the membership of, say, monetary and military circles need not overlap.

States clarified their positions in the IGC as the debate expanded to cover the mechanics as well as the principles of flexibility. Most rejected the *à la carte* and pre-determined hard core models, the original Six viewing 'enhanced cooperation' as a means of pursuing deeper integration ahead of eastern enlargement.[25] The newer and poorer Member States adopted a more cautious tone, concerned about the implications of flexibility and stressing the importance of safeguards. Greece and Portugal in particular had serious reservations. The 1995 Reflection Group Report noted that 'a large majority' accepted there was a case for 'flexibility' providing it met a number of criteria. Flexibility might be allowed on a case-by-case basis (especially in CFSP and JHA) when other solutions had been exhausted.

The *acquis* and single institutional framework must be preserved, while flexibility would be temporary and open to all Member States meeting relevant criteria. The Reflection Group rejected the *à la carte* perspective, its proposals echoing a multi-speed ethos of temporary differentiation utilizing EU institutions and procedures.[26]

The Reflection Group Report marked the beginning of a gradual convergence of the positions of most states, though much work on the mechanics of flexibility (for example, the triggering mechanism) lay ahead. An October 1996 Franco-German joint letter proposed a general Treaty clause authorizing 'closer cooperation' within the EU.[27] EC policy areas covered by unanimity, plus the CFSP and JHA pillars were identified as suitable for a form of flexibility in which no state would have a veto right, but no state willing and able to take part would be excluded. The Dublin II draft revision of the Treaty outlined three forms of flexibility: 'case-by-case flexibility'; 'flexibility in a specific area' with conditions outlined in a Protocol; and 'enhanced cooperation flexibility' through a general clause.[28] The Dutch Addendum to Dublin II proposed a general clause on flexibility supported by specific clauses for each pillar, setting out conditions for its use rather than providing a detailed positive list of policy areas in which flexibility would be possible or a negative list of areas in which it would be precluded.[29]

Flexibility and the Amsterdam Treaty

Flexibility was only briefly discussed at the Amsterdam European Council, where a proposed specific clause on closer cooperation in CFSP was dropped. Only at this final stage of the negotiations was it decided that closer cooperation be triggered by QMV but with a veto right reminiscent of the Luxembourg Compromise included. In the Treaty of Amsterdam, the term 'closer cooperation' is used to refer to differentiation authorized by the general and specific clauses, although no clear definition or philosophy of 'closer cooperation' is spelled out. The phrases 'opt in' and 'opt out' are not used in the special formulae Protocols and Declarations. Included in the Treaty are a general clause in the common provisions of the TEU confirming the right of some Member States to engage in closer cooperation within the EU, provided that certain conditions have been met; specific clauses outlining the conditions for, and mechanics of, closer cooperation in both the European Community and what remains of the TEU third pillar; plus a number of special arrangements.[30]

Although the Treaty marks a significant institutionalization and legitimization of intra-EU flexibility, it neither provides a definitive normative statement on the Union's preferred mode of flexible integration, nor a clear insight into its likely future use.[31] Rather, it contains a heterogeneous mix of provisions for, and types of, differentiation which variously mirror elements of the multi-speed, variable geometry and *à la carte* ideal types. The origins of the general and specific clauses lie in the desire of pro-integration states to circumvent the vetoes of sceptical states and move into new policy areas, but the cumbersome triggering mechanisms appear likely to frustrate their ambitions. There is little in the Treaty to suggest that the use of flexibility to manage eastward enlargement was a primary motivation.

The TEU general clause

The TEU general clause is an enabling clause[32] outlining the conditions under which some Member States might be permitted to establish closer cooperation (which itself is not fully defined), using the 'institutions, procedures and mechanisms laid down by the Treaties'. Article 43(1) [ex Article K.15(1)] TEU lists the conditions which must be met if this is to be authorized. Closer cooperation must be 'aimed at furthering the objectives of the Union and at protecting and serving its interests'; must 'respect the principles of the Treaties' and the EU's 'single institutional framework'; can be used only as a 'last resort'; must involve 'at least a majority of Member States' and must not affect the *acquis communautaire*. Safeguards for non-participants are included: closer cooperation must not 'affect the competences, rights, obligations and interests' of non-participating states; it must be open to all Member States who wish to join at any time, provided they 'comply with the basic decision and with decisions taken within the framework'. However, non-participants 'shall not impede' the implementation of closer cooperation once authorized. States seeking closer cooperation must also meet conditions set out in the appropriate specific clause.

Article 43(2) [ex Article K.16] TEU states that, when implementing decisions reached under closer cooperation, the 'relevant institutional provisions of the Treaty apply'. However, while all EU Member States take part in deliberations under closer cooperation, only participating states take part in the adoption of decisions taken under closer cooperation. Voting calculations will be adjusted to reflect this. Expenditure arising from closer cooperation will be borne by participating states only (except for administrative costs for EU institutions), unless the Council decides otherwise by unanimity. The EP is merely regularly informed of the development of closer cooperation. Although the general clause states that the EU's single institutional framework must be protected, flexibility by its nature suggests institutional complexity and fragmentation. Questions are likely to arise regarding the functioning of the Presidency when the Member State holding the office is not involved in all areas of closer cooperation. Issues may also arise concerning the role of the Court of Justice; the different legal instruments which exist in the broad spectrum of justice and home affairs and voting procedures in the EP.

The general clause is close to a multi-speed perspective in that closer cooperation occurs within the EU framework, the rights of non-participants are safeguarded and areas of closer cooperation are open to all states seeking to join, provided they meet certain conditions. Closer cooperation must be of a progressive nature, undertaken by a majority of states, must not undermine the EU's objectives, *acquis* or institutional order, and will be authorized only when normal procedures have been exhausted. However, it appears closer to intra-EU variable geometry in some respects: there is no suggestion of positive measures (such as side-payments) to prepare states who want to join but are unable to do so for future participation.[33] The vagaries of the conditions indicate that authorization will be a political rather than technical process. Determining whether closer cooperation is genuinely a last resort and does not affect the interests of non-participants will prove particularly sensitive, though such states can invoke the revised Luxembourg Compromise included in the specific clauses. Ultimately, the Court of Justice may be called upon to determine the fate of proposals for closer cooperation.

The specific clauses

The EC specific clause Article 11 [ex Article 5a] EC sets out further preconditions for closer cooperation in the first pillar, expressed in the form of a negative list of areas in which closer cooperation will not be permitted. Closer cooperation may be authorized provided that it 'does not concern areas which fall within the exclusive competence of the Union' and, crucially, must 'remain within the limits of the powers conferred upon the Community by the Treaty'. That is, it requires an existing legal basis in the Treaty and must observe existing legislative arrangements.[34] Additionally, authorization is possible only if closer cooperation 'does not concern the citizenship of the Union or discriminate between nationals of Member States', and does not lead to trade discrimination, trade restriction or a distortion of competition.

Article 11(2) [ex Article 5a(2)] EC sets out the triggering procedure for closer cooperation in the EC. States seeking closer cooperation must address a request to the Commission which may then submit a proposal to the Council. The Commission is not compelled to submit a proposal; it may refuse to do so, giving reasons for its negative view. Authorization is granted by the Council acting by QMV, having consulted the European Parliament (EP). Significantly, the provisions include a revised Luxembourg Compromise: any Member State may wield its veto, preventing a vote being taken if it states that it intends to oppose the authorization on the grounds of 'important and stated reasons of national policy'. If this happens, the Council may request by QMV that the matter is referred to 'the Council, meeting in the composition of the Heads of State or Government, for decision by unanimity'. States wishing to become a party to closer cooperation at a later stage must notify both Council and Commission, the latter playing the key role in deciding on the request. The rights of non-participating states are not further clarified in the specific clauses. The Commission decides whether to submit (or block) proposals for closer cooperation and formally decides whether to accept late entrants, though these are a rather poor reflection of its EC right of initiative and role as guardian of the Treaties. The authorization process strengthens intergovernmentalism in that the Council takes the final decision and, though it does so by QMV, individual Member States ultimately have veto rights. The EP has only a minor role.

Article 40 [ex Article K.12] TEU outlines the specific provisions for closer cooperation under Title VI TEU, covering those areas of the JHA third pillar which have not been communitarized, notably police and judicial cooperation in criminal matters. It replaces the more limited Maastricht Article K.7 provisions on closer cooperation. The TEU specific clause appears more dynamic than its EC counterpart as it does not contain a list forbidding closer cooperation in specified areas. Despite (or, more likely, because of) the link between internal security matters and citizenship rights, the TEU specific clause does not include the proviso that closer cooperation should not affect citizenship of the Union or discriminate between nationals of Member States. There are also differences in relation to the mechanics of closer cooperation, reflecting the intergovernmental basis of Title VI. Thus, the Commission has a lesser role, presenting an opinion rather than submitting or blocking an initial proposal, and offering only a non-binding opinion on late entrants. States can again block a decision on closer cooperation for 'important and stated reasons of national policy', but authorization by QMV requires a majority of at least 62 votes cast by at least 10 Member States.

A proposed specific clause on closer cooperation in CFSP was dropped during the final Treaty negotiations, but variable geometry action will continue outside the EU framework. The Amsterdam Treaty provides case-by-case flexibility provisions in CFSP through 'constructive abstention'. Here, a Member State which abstains can formally declare that it accepts that the EU is bound by a decision, though that state will not have to apply the measure. If at least one third of the weighted votes are from states utilizing this 'constructive abstention' mechanism, the decision will not be adopted.

Special arrangements

As Jörg Monar notes in Chapter 8, the Treaty includes a number of provisions for differentiation in the broad justice and home affairs spectrum. The Schengen Protocol incorporates existing Schengen provisions into the EU *acquis*, authorizing the 13 Schengen members to establish closer cooperation among themselves within the scope of the Schengen agreements. This cooperation will be conducted within the EU's institutional and legal framework. The Protocol also permits those states to 'build upon the Schengen *acquis*'. It affirms that the UK and the Republic of Ireland are not bound by the Schengen *acquis*, although they may request to take part in some or all of these measures at any time. However, such requests would be dealt with by the Schengen states on the basis of unanimity, prompting suggestions that Spain might unilaterally block a British request given the dispute between the two states over Gibraltar.[35] Iceland and Norway maintain Schengen associate status as part of the Nordic Council, in which three distinct regimes now exist.

A Protocol guarantees the UK's right to exercise controls on persons at its frontiers with other Member States and permits the UK and Ireland to maintain the Common Travel Area. The Protocol on the Position of the UK and Ireland guarantees their non-involvement in the Title IIIa EC arrangements on the free movement of persons, asylum and immigration, but both can opt in to any measure proposed under the new Title. Ireland can opt out of the Protocol altogether if it no longer wishes to be covered by it. Indeed, in a Declaration attached to the Treaty, Ireland declares that it intends to adopt Title IIIa measures 'to the maximum extent' compatible with the Common Travel Area. The arrangements reflect the dilemmas facing a reluctant 'out', an Irish government constrained as a member of the Common Travel Area by British refusal to remove border controls, but concerned at its exclusion from further integration.

The Protocol on Denmark allows it to opt out of the Title IIIa provisions, though the Danish government can decide to implement decisions which build on Schengen (of which Denmark is a member), thus creating an obligation under international law rather than EC law, or waive the Protocol altogether. In a Declaration attached to the Protocol on Asylum, Belgium declares that, contrary to an agreement reached in the EU, it will carry out individual examinations of any asylum request made by a national of another Member State.

Conclusions

The Treaty of Amsterdam further legitimizes and extends intra-EU flexibility but produces complex and asymmetric arrangements. Flexibility is enshrined as an operating code of the Union, but a definitive constitutional statement or philosophy of flexibility is not yet in place. Closer cooperation is not defined and a number of opt-outs are included in the Treaty despite the rejection of the *à la carte* model. The flexibility provisions are primarily managerial and technocratic in character, evidence (albeit unwelcome to purists) of the EU's capacity for adaptation. The closer cooperation clauses were born of compromise, being designed to pacify pro-integration states seeking to by-pass obstructionism, allay the worst fears of potential 'outs' and satisfy states determined to secure special exemptions.

It remains unclear to what extent the closer cooperation provisions will be used, though their extensive use is unlikely, particularly in the first pillar. Sizeable obstacles are placed in the path of states looking to pursue closer cooperation, notably the requirement of majority support, last resort status and the revised Luxembourg Compromise. The EC specific clause imposes additional limitations, prompting suggestions that closer cooperation in the first pillar will be rare and confined to uncontentious policy areas.[36] Cooperation in EMU 'flanking policies' such as employment, social protection and taxation appeals to some first wave states. The Lamers-Schäuble paper envisaged further economic and fiscal cooperation, though concerns about the impact on the Single Market and Franco–German tensions over EMU governance threaten its development. Given the procedural obstacles to intra-EU closer cooperation, flexible integration may instead occur via *ad hoc* arrangements outside the institutional structures of the EU.

The existence of closer cooperation provisions will affect the dynamics of EU negotiations, though contrasting scenarios can be envisaged. The possibility of some states seeking to resort to closer cooperation might encourage a more constructive approach from potential recalcitrants at an earlier negotiating stage should they fear being excluded from further integration.[37] Yet supporters of fast-track integration may view flexibility as a means of circumventing difficult negotiations in areas subject to unanimity in which lowest common denominator outcomes are the norm, or of excluding states deemed unfit for further integration. Some safeguards for non-participants are provided, yet states willing but temporarily unable to participate in closer cooperation are likely to balk at being consigned to the slow lane given that lengthy periods of exclusion are likely to prove damaging. However, die-hard states may use the threat of a veto to extract concessions, or invoke the revised Luxembourg Compromise 'emergency brake' if they feel strongly that closer cooperation will create a hard core or exercise an unwelcome centripetal pull.[38] This could foster political ill-will and drive pro-integration states towards extra-EU cooperation.

Flexibility was lauded as a means of easing eastern enlargement, but the new Treaty provides few signs that the EU is preparing for enlargement with great conviction or that the scale of the preparatory task facing applicant states has been sufficiently addressed. With regard to eastern enlargement, the EU's pre-accession strategy largely follows the traditional Community model of differentiated integration in which new Member States accept the existing *acquis* as a whole but are granted transition periods where necessitated by special economic problems.[39] Opt-outs will not (at least immediately) be on offer. Following EMU and the incorporation of the Schengen *acquis*, adapting to and implementing the EU *acquis* will prove more difficult than in previous enlargements. Eastern enlargement is conditional on the EU's ability to absorb new Member States. Agenda 2000 envisages reform of the Common Agricultural Policy and Structural Funds, while a Protocol states that institutional reform should be readdressed one year before EU membership reaches 20. Suggestions that eastern enlargement should follow a variable geometry route explicitly setting up a multi-tier EU in which new members are not fully involved in, for example, free movement provisions have so far been officially resisted. Even if multi-tier scenarios are rejected, flexibility will be a defining feature of a post-enlargement EU; diversity will increase and new members will have lengthy transition periods.

The extended use of flexibility would reshape EU institutions and policies, changing the character of European integration. But with EMU Stage III in its infancy, tough decisions on eastern enlargement still to be taken and the Amsterdam closer cooperation clauses as yet untested, the dynamics of flexibility and the relative influence of its centripetal and centrifugal forces remain uncertain. In some respects, acceptance of greater flexibility is a sign of the continuing evolution of the EU as it adapts to the challenges of a changing environment (including global-ization, enlargement and the greater diversity of capacity and political will among its present members). Through its qualified legitimization of flexibility, the EU has sought to prevent diverse capacities and interests from producing stalemate or disintegration, reconciling diversity and unity. Yet the evolutionary path the EU is taking as the new millennium approaches is not one anticipated by federalist or neo-functionalist accounts: the linear development of a federal Europe is unlikely, while policy spillover may only be evident in a hard core.

Intergovernmentalist assumptions about lowest common denominator outcomes and the limits of integration may also need to be reassessed given the impact of flexibility on interstate bargaining and the possibility of a core of states ceding sovereignty in areas of high politics. If flexibility is firmly established as a central adaptive feature of the EU's evolutionary process, the next stages and goals of European integration will need to be reassessed.

One possibility mooted in the mid-1990s was the emergence of a hard core of states, all of whom pursue further integration across a range of policy sectors (such as EMU, tax harmonization, foreign and defence policy, and internal security). However, the IGC rejected a predetermined hard core, the Treaty places limits on closer cooperation and many states remain wary of the possibility of a privileged inner circle. More likely is the development of a series of interlocking circles lacking a fixed centripetal hard core or an agreed road map to 'ever closer union'. Here, membership of the circles and their institutional arrangements would differ across as well as within policy areas. Further integration would be incremental rather than inevitably dynamic. Flexibility will offer further confirmation of the EU's status as a multi-level polity in which there is a range of policy actors and regimes, and differences are evident across policy sectors.

Despite the rejection of the *à la carte* ideal type, and the likelihood of only limited use of the closer cooperation clauses, flexibility carries with it a number of risks for the Union. Flexibility can validly be viewed as a sign of EU entropy, a loss of energy and effectiveness as established patterns disintegrate. The emergence of heterogeneous flexibility arrangements, particularly opt-outs, creates institutional complexity and policy inefficiency while eroding solidarity and political goodwill. The hurdles faced by states seeking intra-EU closer cooperation may result in continued reliance on extra-EU variable geometry, while the problems posed by eastern enlargement have yet to be effectively addressed in relation to future flexibility. Overall, the provisions for flexibility do not sit easily alongside the Turin European Council goals of democracy, efficiency, solidarity, cohesion, transparency and subsidiarity. Indeed, these goals appear more likely to be undermined than enhanced by incremental moves towards a multi-tier Europe.

Endnotes

1. Centre for Economic Policy Research, *Flexible Integration: Towards a More Effective and Democratic Europe*, London: CEPR, 1995, pp. 59–76.
2. The Turin European Council Presidency Conclusions stated that 'democracy, efficiency, solidarity, cohesion, transparency and subsidiarity' must be preserved in the European construction.
3. A. Stubb, 'A Categorization of Differentiated Integration', *Journal of Common Market Studies*, Vol. 34, 1996, pp. 283–95.
4. H. Wallace and W. Wallace, *Flying Together in a Larger and More Diverse European Union*, The Hague: Working Documents, Netherlands Scientific Council for Government Policy, 1995.
5. See C-D. Ehlermann, 'How Flexible is Community Law? An Unusual Approach to the Concept of "Two Speeds" ', *Michigan Law Review*, Vol. 82, 1984, pp. 1274–93; G. Edwards and E. Philippart, *Flexibility and the Treaty of Amsterdam: Europe's New Byzantium*, Centre for European Legal Studies, University of Cambridge, Occasional Paper No. 3, 1997, pp. 3–4.
6. Wallace and Wallace, *Flying Together in a More Diverse Europe*.
7. Stubb, 'A Categorization of Differentiated Integration', p. 285 and p. 289.
8. See W. Wessels, 'Flexibility, Differentiation and Closer Cooperation. The Amsterdam Provisions in the Light of the Tindemans Report', in M. Westlake (ed.), *The European Union Beyond Amsterdam: New Concepts of European Integration*, London: Routledge, 1998, pp. 76–98.
9. Stubb, 'A Categorization of Differentiated Integration', p. 287.
10. Stubb, 'A Categorization of Differentiated Integration', p. 287; C-D. Ehlermann, *Increased Differentiation or Stronger Uniformity?* Florence: European University Institute Working Paper No. 95/21, 1995, pp. 5–6.
11. F. de la Serre and H. Wallace, *Flexibility and Enhanced Cooperation in the European Union: Placebo rather than Panacea?* Paris: Groupement d'Études et de Recherches "Notre Europe", 1997, p. 21.
12. See D. Curtin and R. Van Ooik, 'Denmark and the Edinburgh Summit: Maastricht without Tears',

in D. O'Keeffe and P. Twomey (eds), *Legal Issues of the Maastricht Treaty*, London: Wiley Chancery, 1994, pp. 349–65.

13. Ehlermann, *Increased Differentiation or Stronger Uniformity?* p. 8.
14. J. Monar, 'Schengen and Flexibility in the Treaty of Amsterdam: Opportunities and Risks of Differentiated Integration in EU Justice and Home Affairs', in M. den Boer (ed.), *Schengen, Judicial Cooperation and Policy Coordination*, Maastricht: European Institute of Public Administration, 1997, pp. 14–15.
15. M. Cremona, 'The "Dynamic and Heterogeneous" EEA: Byzantine Structures and Variable Geometry', *European Law Review*, Vol. 19, 1994, pp. 508–26.
16. D. Curtin, 'The Constitutional Structure of the Union: A Europe of Bits and Pieces', *Common Market Law Review*, Vol. 30, 1993, pp. 17–69.
17. T. Blair, 'Neither a Surrender, Nor Isolation', *The Times*, 15 December 1997.
18. 'UK Tastes Life Outside the Euro Club', *The Financial Times*, 5 June 1998.
19. Curtin, 'The Constitutional Structure of the Union', pp. 52–61.
20. K. Lamers and W. Schäuble, *Reflections on European Policy*, Bonn: CDU/CSU Fraktion des Deutschen Bundestages, 1994, p. 7.
21. Lamers and Schäuble, *Reflections on European Policy*, p. 6.
22. J. Major, 'Europe: A Future that Works', William and Mary Lecture, Leiden, 7 September 1994. Major had talked of 'a multi-track, multi-speed, multi-tier' Europe in a speech at Ellesmere Port, 31 May 1994.
23. See, M. Thatcher, *The Path to Power*, London: Harper Collins, 1995, pp. 501–6.
24. E. Balladur, 'My Vision of A More Flexible Europe', *European Brief*, December 1994, pp. 20–2. Translated and reprinted from *Le Monde*, 30 November 1994.
25. European Parliament, *Intergovernmental Conference, Briefing Number 4. Differentiated Integration*, 1996; A. Stubb, 'The 1996 Intergovernmental Conference and the Management of Flexible Integration', *Journal of European Public Policy*, Vol. 4, 1997, pp. 37–55.
26. The Reflection Group Report. SN 520/95 (REFLEX 21), Brussels, December 1995, pp. 6–7.
27. *Agence Europe*, Europe Documents, 29 October 1996.
28. Conference of the Representatives of the Governments of the Member States, *The European Union Today and Tomorrow. A General Outline for a Draft Revision of the Treaties – Dublin II*, Brussels, 5 December 1996. CONF 2500/96.
29. Conference of the Representatives of the Governments of the Member States, *Addendum to Dublin II – General Outline for a Draft Revision of the Treaties*, Brussels, 20 March 1997. CONF 2500/96.
30. Early assessments include Edwards and Philippart, *Flexibility and the Treaty of Amsterdam*; C-D. Ehlermann, *Differentiation, Flexibility, Closer Cooperation: The New Provisions of the Amsterdam Treaty*, Florence: European University Institute, 1997.
31. J. Shaw, 'The Treaty of Amsterdam: Challenges of Flexibility and Legitimacy', *European Law Journal*, Vol. 4, 1998, pp. 63–86, depicts the flexibility provisions as 'generally non-ideological', reflecting a concern with technocratic management.
32. Editorial, 'The Treaty of Amsterdam: Neither a Bang Nor a Whimper', *Common Market Law Review*, Vol. 34, 1997, pp. 767–72, describes it as 'secondary flexibility'.
33. Wessels, 'Flexibility, Differentiation and Closer Cooperation', p. 91, notes that EU leaders wished to avoid a situation in which states able but politically unwilling to proceed with closer cooperation were eligible for side-payments.
34. Shaw, 'The Treaty of Amsterdam', pp. 72–3.
35. See the *House of Commons Foreign Affairs Committee, First Report. The Treaty of Amsterdam*. HCP 305, 1997, especially the evidence of Robin Cook (pp. 16–17) and chief minister of Gibraltar, Peter Carvana (pp. 37–45).
36. Shaw, 'The Treaty of Amsterdam', pp. 74–5, notes that culture, education and research have been suggested as potential fields in which closer cooperation might occur.
37. Wessels, 'Flexibility, Differentiation and Closer Cooperation', p. 95, suggests a 'best case' scenario in which 'the provisions might work as a negative incentive', increasing the incentives to reach consensus as potential 'outs' fear exclusion and 'ins' prefer normal EU procedures to the complex closer cooperation route.
38. Tony Blair declared that Britain had 'secured a veto over flexibility arrangements which could otherwise have allowed the development of a hard core, excluding us against our will', *Hansard*, Vol. 296, col. 314, 18 June 1997.
39. F. de la Serre and C. Lequesne, 'Enlargement to the CEECs: Which Differentiation?', in M. Moresceau (ed.), *Enlarging the European Union: Relations between the EU and Central and Eastern Europe*, London, Longman, 1997, pp. 349–57.

Chapter 12

Defining a constitution for the European Union

Robin C. A. White

Background

It is possible for lawyers to say that the question of whether there is a constitution of the European Community has been answered by pronouncements of the European Court of Justice. In *Les Verts*[1] the Court described the EEC Treaty as a 'constitutional charter'.[2] In its Opinion on the EEA Agreement[3] the Court said,

> The EEC Treaty, albeit concluded in the form of an international agreement, none the less constitutes the constitutional charter of a Community based on the rule of law. As the Court of Justice has consistently held, the Community treaties established a new legal order for the benefit of which the States have limited their sovereign rights, in ever wider fields, and the subjects of which comprise not only Member States but also their nationals.[4]

Much has been written on a 'European constitution'[5] indicating the importance of the topic, and simply to cite the Court's statements as a complete answer to the question is to duck the issue. All writers agree that the Community has no written constitution, but no legal writer denies the existence of constitutional principles which govern the legality of action at the Community level. The thrust of much of the writing is to draw attention to the constitutionalizing role of the Court of Justice. The absence of a written constitution has been noted by the European Parliament (EP). In 1994 it adopted a Resolution on the Constitution of the European Union,[6] which contained a Draft Constitution of the European Union. Among the principles which motivated the Parliament was the need for a constitution which is 'readily accessible and comprehensible to the citizens of the Union'.[7]

The Treaty on European Union has been criticized[8] as tinkering with the constitutional charter 'in an arbitrary and *ad hoc* manner which defied ... its underlying *constitutional* character'.[9] The Bundesverfassungsgericht (German Federal Constitutional Court) raised a number of fundamental questions about the constitutional legitimacy of the Union, and its planned development.[10] Those who hoped that the Treaty of Amsterdam would remedy the widely acknowledged[11] deficiencies and complexities will be disappointed. Some aspects of the 'bits and pieces' criticized by Curtin have been tidied up, but the overall structure remains just as complex, perhaps even more complex with a plethora of opt-ins and opt-outs.

The following sections trace the need for and recognition of constitutional principles from the early days and argue that the flexible unwritten constitution is more appropriate for the novel supranational arrangement that is the European Union.

The national paradigm

Understanding the nature of constitutions at the national level is far from straightforward. There is no agreed definition of a constitution.[12] Very broadly a constitution is the set of rules governing the composition, powers and methods of operation of the main institutions of government, and the general principles applicable to their relations with citizens.[13] The constitution may be written or unwritten, though on closer analysis this distinction is not clear cut. Those countries, like the United Kingdom, which do not have a written constitution have some written documents of a constitutional nature, while those countries with written constitutions also have some unwritten constitutional material.[14] Where there is a written constitution, it may be flexible or rigid, depending on the procedure required for its amendment. Constitutions may be descriptive or prescriptive, with the former formally enjoying no special pre-eminence in the hierarchy of norms.

It is generally agreed that, in a democracy, whatever the nature of the constitution, its authority flows from the people or polity. Thomas Paine said,

> A constitution is not the act of a Government, but of a people constituting a Government, and a Government without a constitution is power without right. ... A constitution is a thing antecedent to a Government; and a Government is only the creation of a constitution.[15]

A government is generally regarded as a requirement for statehood.[16] So, in summary, the national paradigm of a constitution would seem to require the ability to identify a set of rules dealing with the institutions of government and their relations with those governed. Those rules gain their legitimacy from the polity. Beyond that there is considerable flexibility. Content and style will be determined by whether the state is a unitary or federal one; whether the constitution is descriptive or prescriptive; whether it is flexible or rigid; and whether it is written or unwritten. How does the Union measure up against the national paradigm?

The constitution of the Community

In its broadest sense, a constitution is simply a set of rules for determining what may or may not be done in an organization. Clubs, societies and companies have constitutions, and generally the authority for their constitutions also flows from their members. But clubs, societies and companies are not governments. It is, of course, the political dimension which makes the question of whether the Community or Union can be said to have a constitution.

The Court of Justice has not only determined that the EEC Treaty (as it then was) is a constitutional document, but has also fashioned out of the objectives of the Treaty certain constitutional rules. The early case law drew on federal traditions in establishing certain fundamental constitutional rules on the application of Community law. As Bogdanor has noted, the founding Member States 'all have enacted constitutions prescribing what their legislatures can and cannot do and so power-sharing appears natural to them'.[17] So the notion of the supremacy of Community law embodied in the Court's ruling in *Costa* v. *ENEL* came to be accepted by the Member States,

> ... by creating a Community of unlimited duration, having its own institutions, its own personality ... and more particularly, real powers stemming from a limitation of sovereignty or a transfer of powers from the States to the Community, the Member States have limited their sovereign rights ... and have thus created a body of law which binds both their nationals and themselves.[18]

The Court went on to make a number of rulings establishing the direct effect of Community law, including directives, which have led to recognition of a constitutional right to effective legal protection.[19] The twin notions of the supremacy of Community law, and its direct effect have been joined by further constitutional notions which have also been elaborated by the Court. Pre-emption by Community law, which refers to the allocation of powers between the Community and the Member States, arises when a field is 'occupied' by the Community, with the result that Member States lose their powers to legislate in this area.[20] The Court has also wrestled with an issue flowing from the doctrine of supremacy which arose when certain Member States, concerned that Community law contained no catalogue of fundamental rights, sought to test the legality of Community law against the provisions of a national constitution. The Court responded by making it clear that fundamental rights are protected by Community law by reason of their status as 'general principles of law'.[21] In its Opinion on accession of the Community to the European Convention on Human Rights, the Court said,

> ... it is well settled that fundamental rights form an integral part of the general principles of law whose observance the Court ensures. For that purpose, the Court draws inspiration from the constitutional traditions common to the Member States and from the guidelines supplied by international treaties for the protection of human rights on which the Member States have collaborated or of which they are signatories. In that regard, the Court has stated that the Convention has special significance. (See, in particular, Case 206/89, ERT.)[22]

All this has led the Court to state that,

> ... the European Economic Community is a Community based on the rule of law, inasmuch as neither its Member States nor its institutions can avoid a review of the question whether the measures adopted by them are in conformity with the basic constitutional charter, the Treaty.[23]

This formulation has been repeated by Advocates General[24] and by the Court of Justice[25] on a number of occasions.

The Single European Act of 1987 did not change the constitutional structure of the Community, though it did introduce the so-called '1992 programme' designed to breathe new life into the creation of the Single Market. Weiler has divided the process of European integration into three phases.[26] The period from 1958 to the mid-1970s is characterized as one in which legal scholars celebrated constitution-building by the Court of Justice, while political scientists regarded the era as one of crumbling supranationalism. The next phase from 1973 to the mid-1980s is characterized as one of 'political stagnation and decisional malaise' but also as one in which the scope of the reserve power in Article 235 of the EEC Treaty was widely used to extend the competence of the Community. The implementation of the 1992 programme saw the erosion of unanimity and the development of majority voting in a less homogeneous Community.[27] The constitutional significance of this is the possibility of Member States facing binding rules adopted against their will.

The Treaty on European Union and the Community constitution

The creation of three pillars in the Treaty on European Union (TEU) has complicated the unwritten constitution of the Community. The Community is the supranational pillar of the Union, while justice and home affairs and Common Foreign and Security Policy are intergovernmental pillars. While the Community has legal personality,[28] the Union is not given legal personality. Even the Community pillar becomes much more complex with its introduction of 'variable geometry' in the form of opt-outs and opt-ins for individual Member States.

Perhaps more than anything else the tortuous process of ratification of the TEU with close calls in some of the Member States highlighted the very real risk of losing the support of citizens in the Member States.[29] The voice of the commentators on the TEU was uniformly critical because the new structure undermined the unity and coherence of the European Communities.[30]

The Treaty on European Union undermined the constitutional order of the three communities – European Economic Community, European Coal and Steel Community and the European Atomic Energy Community – by adding intergovernmental heads to the supranational structure of the communities. In particular, there was scope for a conflict concerning matters coming under the Community rules on free movement of persons and certain matters dealt with by the intergovernmental pillar on justice and home affairs.[31] The Maastricht Treaty failed to merge the three Communities, and the language of pillars and branches failed to convince. The Union is 'founded on the European Communities', yet its constitutional structure is very different. The result is a constitutional emulsion of supranational and intergovernmental ingredients which can never combine; they can be shaken and stirred, but left alone will separate out into the two disparate constituent parts.

Yet the Maastricht Treaty codified a most significant constitutional principle:

that of subsidiarity. Those with diametrically opposed ambitions for the development of the Community paraded new Article 3b of the EC Treaty as a triumph of, on the one hand, federal ambition, and, on the other, of recognition of the limits of supranationalism. Legal scholars had a field day seeking to unravel its true significance.[32]

The ramifications of the TEU were considered in a constitutional challenge to ratification by Germany, and the decision of the Bundesverfassungsgericht reverberated ominously around the Community.[33] Those reverberations flowed from the apparent conclusion of the German Court that as the scope of activity of the Communities and Union extended, there would need to be a parallel development in democratic legitimation of that progress, and, most significantly, it would be open to national courts to determine whether that development met the requirements of national constitutional standards such that it would be appropriate to agree to the transfer of sovereignty entailed in the developments. The decision is recognized as a warning to European ambition, but the reasoning has not gone unchallenged.[34]

Article N of the TEU had recognized that further work was required; it embodied a commitment for an Intergovernmental Conference (IGC) in 1996 in order to revise the Treaties on which the Union is founded. By the time of the entry into force of the Maastricht Treaty in November 1993,[35] it was clear that three items would need to be addressed by the IGC. Firstly, it was obviously necessary to undertake the task required by Article N . Secondly, it was necessary to revitalize the vision of European integration by a process of simplification and better presentation of the vision of Europe to its people. Thirdly, it was necessary to address those issues where a structure largely developed for a Community of six Member States would need to work for a Community of as many as 30 Member States.

In the period between the signing of the Maastricht Treaty and the signing of the Treaty of Amsterdam, one interesting development occurred in the European Parliament. A resolution was passed on 10 February 1994 proposing the establishment of a written constitution for the European Union.[36] The preamble to the resolution recognized the need 'to provide the European Union with a democratic constitution to enable the process of European integration to continue in accordance with the needs of European citizens'. It was stated that the constitution must be 'readily accessible and comprehensible' to European citizens. A Draft Constitution is appended as an annex to the resolution. There is a call in the resolution for the task of adopting a constitution to be added to the agenda of the IGC; that, unsurprisingly, did not happen.

The Treaty of Amsterdam

Stated aims

How does the Treaty of Amsterdam tackle some of the constitutional issues posed by the existing structures? The IGC was never about writing a constitution for Europe; political negotiating processes are prone to being side-tracked by political issues. The saga of British beef was fresh in everyone's mind in March 1996 when the IGC was launched in Turin, and a newly elected British government succeeded in making employment measures a key feature of the outcome of the IGC in the period leading up to the Amsterdam Summit in June 1997. The outcome of the IGC does not match up to the rhetoric. The Presidency Conclusions from the Madrid Council in December 1995 had committed the Member States to making institutional reforms 'a central issue of the Conference in order to improve the efficiency, democracy and transparency of the Union'. Results were to be achieved in three main areas:

- making Europe more relevant to its citizens
- enabling the Union to work better and preparing it for enlargement and
- giving the Union greater capacity for external action.

All three heads raise issues of constitutional significance. The word 'simplification' appears frequently in position papers, but the results of the IGC hardly represent a triumph of rationalization. A Declaration attached to the Treaty on European Union committed the IGC to examining 'to what extent it might be possible to review the classification of Community acts with a view to establishing an appropriate hierarchy between the different categories of act'.

The Treaty of Amsterdam is entirely silent on this issue, which reflects a lack of political willingness by the Member States to tackle such fundamental issues. Though the United Kingdom has come on board in signing up to the Social Policy Agreement, there remain a series of opt-outs and opt-ins which do not leave the overall position better than in 1993 on the entry into force of the Maastricht Treaty. Differentiation and variable geometry do not lend themselves to constitution-building when there is little common agreement on the shape of the edifice.

Reinforcing constitutional principles

What then has changed? Among the most significant changes from a constitutional perspective is the re-enforcement of principles of democracy. It will be recalled that Article F(1) TEU stated that the 'Union shall respect the national identities of its Member States, whose systems of government are founded on principles of democracy'. New Article 7 (ex Article F.1) TEU gives the Council power to determine the existence of a 'serious and persistent breach of the principles mentioned in Article F(1)' so long as:

- a proposal has been made by one-third of the Member States or by the Commission
- the European Parliament has assented, acting by a two-thirds majority of the votes cast representing a majority of its members
- the Council is unanimous
- the Council is composed of Heads of State or Government and
- the Member State in question has been invited to submit its observations.

The Council, having made such a determination, may by qualified majority decide to suspend 'certain of the rights deriving from the application of this Treaty'. It is expressly provided that this does not absolve the Member State of its obligations. Corresponding amendments to the three Community Treaties provide for suspension under those Treaties.[37] No recourse is available to the Court in respect of such decisions, which are in the political arena. Such provisions are, of course, not novel; they appear in the treaties establishing many international organizations.[38]

The principles of subsidiarity and proportionality are given a Protocol of their own,[39] but this adds little, essentially confirming the position adopted by the institutions. That is not to say that it is unimportant. The codification of these guidelines in a Treaty text is helpful. So, there is confirmation that subsidiarity does not apply where the Community has exclusive competence, though it provides a guide to the exercise by the Community of its own powers. It is not a principle designed to unravel the *acquis communautaire*. Paragraph (4) of the Protocol commits the institutions to giving reasons for concluding that an objective can better be achieved by Community action; the relevant indicators may be qualitative or quantitative. The Directive is stated to be the favoured legislative measure: 'Other things being equal, directives should be preferred to regulations, and framework directives to detailed measures.'[40]

The Commission must file an annual report on the application of Article 5 [ex Article 3b] EC for consideration by the European Council, the EP and the Council. The report is to be copied to the Committee of the Regions and the Economic and Social Committee. The vexed question of justiciability remains open since the final paragraph of the Protocol simply states the obvious: 'compliance with the principle of subsidiarity shall be reviewed in accordance with the rules laid down by the Treaty'.

Shifting competences

A completely revised Title VI has been added to the Treaty on European Union which is no longer the justice and home affairs pillar but is concerned with provisions on police and judicial cooperation in criminal matters. Visa, asylum, immigration and other policies related to the free movement of persons have been incorporated in new Title IV [ex Title IIIa] EC. This is a significant and welcome extension of the formal competence of the Community in this sphere and addresses many of the criticisms of the relationship under the Maastricht Treaty between the Community and JHA pillars. The jurisdiction of the Court of Justice is extended, *inter alia*, under Article 46 (revised Article L) TEU to the provisions of Title VI TEU on the conditions provided for in Article 35 [ex Article K.7] TEU.[41] More significantly, the Court is given jurisdiction in respect of Article 6(2) [ex Article F(2)] TEU[42] 'with regard to action of the institutions, in so far as the Court has jurisdiction under the Treaties establishing the European Communities and under this Treaty'.[43] This welcome change underlines the judicial supervision of the protection of fundamental rights both under Community and Union provisions.

Though care will be needed to avoid conflicting interpretations of protection afforded under Community and Union law and the Convention,[44] the effect of this amendment ensures that no adverse consequences will flow from the Court's proper conclusion that there is no power for the Community to accede to the European Convention on Human Rights.[45] The amendment does not, of course, subject the Community and Union to external supervision of its respect for fundamental rights.

Institutional change

Institutional change thought to be so necessary for impending enlargement has not been achieved. An apologetic Protocol[46] indicates the inability to grapple with this vital issue. Article 1 provides that on the date of entry into force of the next enlargement, the Commission is to comprise one national of each Member State. But even this sensible provision is conditional. By that date, the Member States must have agreed by unanimity the weighting of votes in the Council, such amendment to take 'into account all relevant elements, notably compensating those Member States which give up the possibility of nominating a second member of the Commission'. Article 2 of the Protocol provides that at least one year before the membership reaches 20, 'a conference of representatives of the governments of the Member States shall be convened in order to carry out a comprehensive review of the provisions of the Treaties on the composition and functioning of the institutions'.

In the meantime we know that the membership of the European Parliament is not to exceed 700.[47] The Parliament's existing obligation under Article 190(3) [ex Article 138(3)] EC 'to draw up proposals for elections by direct universal suffrage in accordance with a uniform procedure in all Member States' is modified by the addition of the words 'or in accordance with principles common to all Member States'.

Provision is made for Parliament to approve the person nominated as President of the Commission in place of the right to be consulted.[48] An amendment to Article 173 EC (now renumbered Article 230) codifies the right of the European Parliament, along with the Court of Auditors and the European Central Bank, to challenge Community acts for the purpose of protecting their prerogatives.

The provisions on access to documents are of greater moment in constitutional terms. Article 255 [ex Article191a] EC, newly introduced by the Treaty of Amsterdam, is worthy of reproduction:

1. Any citizen of the Union, and any natural or legal person residing in or having its registered office in a Member State, shall have a right of access to European Parliament, Council and Commission documents, subject to the principles and the conditions to be defined in accordance with paragraphs 2 and 3.
2. General principles and limits on grounds of public or private interest governing the right of access to documents shall be determined by the Council, acting in accordance with the procedure referred to in Article 251 [ex Article 189b] within two years of the entry into force of the Treaty of Amsterdam.
3. Each institution referred to above shall elaborate in its own Rules of Procedure specific provisions regarding access to its documents.

This enhanced entitlement to information is not matched by the grant of easier standing to challenge Community acts under Article 230 [ex Article 173] EC, where the barriers to action by natural and legal persons remain unchanged.

Article 255 may be read with the Protocol on the Role of National Parliaments in the European Union.[49] This Protocol provides that all Commission consultation documents shall be 'promptly' forwarded to national parliaments, and that Commission legislative proposals shall be 'made available in good time' so that Member States can ensure that national parliaments can receive them. Some bite is given to this second provision in that a six-week period must elapse between the date on which proposals are made available in all languages by the Commission to the Council and EP and the date when the proposal is placed on the agenda of the Council for decision. Failure to do so will constitute a breach of an essential procedural requirement which would open the measure to challenge under Article 230 [ex Article173] EC. An increased role for the Conference of European Affairs Committees (COSAC) is set out in Part II of the Protocol.[50]

Decision-making procedures

There was general agreement that the plethora of decision-making procedures was unhelpful and confusing.[51] The reasons for this complexity are rooted in difficult negotiations at each Treaty revision where sophisticated procedural devices have cloaked differences in the positions of Member States. It also reveals a reluctance by the Member States to entrust the EP with the same role in every legislative procedure. The co-decision procedure in Article 251 [ex Article189b] EC has been simplified and the position of the European Parliament marginally enhanced, but there has been no root and branch simplification of the decision-making procedure. In future, where Article 251 [ex Article 189b] EC applies, the EP will not be obliged to indicate its intention to reject the Council's common position in advance of its doing so, and the Council will no longer be able to override a failure by the Conciliation Committee to approve a joint text by reverting to its rejected common position. In an ideal world, there would only be two procedures: a single simplified co-decision procedure for legislative acts, and an assent procedure for international agreements. That position has not yet been reached. The cooperation procedure remains unchanged in Article 252 [ex Article 189c] EC. Consultation procedures are also retained, and the role of the European Parliament in Common Foreign and Security Policy and the rump of justice and home affairs remains minimal.[52]

The objective of simplifying the decision-making procedure has not been met.

Variable geometry

The EC Treaty will contain a new Article 11 [ex Article 5a] which will enable some of the Member States to establish closer cooperation among themselves using the institutions, procedures and mechanisms of the Community. This is the enabling provision for the incorporation into Community law by a limited number of Member States of the Schengen *acquis*. It is, however, drafted in such a way that it could encompass any future developments for closer cooperation among a smaller number of Member States than the 15. Authorization by the Council for such action is required. The cooperation proposed:

- must not concern areas falling within the exclusive competence of the Community[53]
- must not affect Community policies, actions or programmes[54]
- must not concern citizenship of the Union or discriminate between nationals of Member States[55]
- must remain within the limits of the powers conferred on the Communities by the EC Treaty[56]
- must not constitute a discrimination or a restriction of trade between Member States and not distort the conditions of competition between the Member States.[57]

The Council is to act on a proposal from the Commission[58] and is required to consult the EP, but if a Member State declares that, for important and stated reasons of national policy, it intends to oppose the grant of authorization by qualified majority, no vote can be taken. In such circumstances, the Council may, acting by qualified majority, refer the matter to the Council in the composition of Heads of State or Government, which may grant the necessary authorization if it is unanimous.

Variable geometry is a reality with the incorporation of the Schengen *acquis* into the EC Treaty and TEU.[59] There are further Protocols involving opt-outs: special provisions are made for the United Kingdom and Ireland in relation to Article 14 [ex Article 7a] EC and to new Title IV of the EC Treaty.[60] There are also special provisions for Denmark.[61]

Consolidated texts of the EC Treaty and Treaty on European Union

Article 12 of the Treaty of Amsterdam paves the way for the production of consolidated and simplified texts of the Treaty on European Union and the Treaty establishing the European Community. A scheme of renumbering Treaty articles is introduced, which helpfully gets away from the lettering system originally adopted for the TEU. Though this made it easy to remember which treaty was in issue, it made for great complexity when amendments were introduced. Consolidated texts of the two treaties were appended to the Treaty of Amsterdam on its signature on 2 October 1997. Amendment by reference is always potentially hazardous, and the early production of consolidated texts is to be welcomed.

This exercise also makes clear that the function of the Treaty of Amsterdam has solely been to amend the TEU and the three Community Treaties. It has happily not resulted in yet another Treaty base for Union and Community action.

Conclusions

Earlier it was stated that the national paradigm of a constitution would seem to require the ability to identify a set of rules dealing with the institutions of government and their relations with those governed, whose legitimacy flows from the assent of the polity. If this paradigm is followed, the constitution of the Union or Community soon comes up against what has been described as the 'no Demos thesis'.[62] Under this thesis, there can never be a European constitution since there is no European people. The concept of a people or nation is regarded as requiring a group which shares a collective identity and loyalty, and a homogeneity of 'organic national-cultural conditions on which peoplehood depends'.[63] Weiler challenges this thesis, while accepting the difficulties of identifying a European people. He says,

> I am arguing that to insist on the emergence of a pre-existing European Demos defined in organic national-cultural terms as a precondition for constitutional unification or, more minimally, a redrawing of political boundaries, is to ensure that this will never happen. The No Demos thesis which is presented by its advocates as rooted in empirical and objective observation barely conceals a predetermined outcome.[64]

That predetermined outcome is that the Union and Community is no more than an international organization created by treaty. Weiler also accepts the problems of defining a European citizenship and of addressing the democratic deficit that arises from European law-making. He concedes that European mechanisms do reduce individual empowerment and that this cannot be cured by simply seeking to replicate domestic democratic arrangements in Union decision-making. The development of the United States is sometimes put forward as an example of the creation of a citizenship, but, as Weiler notes, that was part of an explicit programme to create 'One Nation', which is not the current aspiration of the Union. Weiler's response is to argue for 'multiple demoi' whereby nationality and citizenship might be decoupled.[65] He says,

> The view of multiple *demoi* which I am suggesting, one of truly variable geometry, invites individuals to see themselves as belonging simultaneously to two *demoi*, based, critically on different subjective factors of identification. I may be a German national in the in-reaching strong sense of organic-cultural identification and sense of belongingness. I am simultaneously a European citizen in terms of my European transnational affinities to shared values which transcend the ethno-national diversity.[66]

This model is helpful because it is not limited by the traditional notions of constitutional authority for a novel organization; in Weiler's terms it has a 'special European specificity'.[67] There was a coherence and (as it now seems) simplicity to the Community model of integration, but the Member States wanted something more flexible in which to take forward progress in other areas. This has been provided by the twin pillars of the Common Foreign and Security Policy, and justice and home affairs in the Treaty on European Union. Significantly, the latter pillar has been considerably slimmed by the Treaty of Amsterdam.

As Dashwood has pointed out,[68] the genius of the Union structures is that each of the Member States continues to exist as a State 'in the fullest legal and political sense, and are so perceived by their own governments and peoples and by the outside world'.[69] He describes such an arrangements as 'a constitutional order of States'.[70]

In this model, there is no surprise at the centrality of the Council in the institutional structure of the Union, nor at the relationship between national parliaments and the EP, and the latter's role in the Union. The 'no Demos thesis' becomes a fallacious thesis. The Weiler response offers a better way forward in considering the development of European citizenship. It is also consistent with the objectives of securing 'an ever closer union among the peoples of Europe',[71] while respecting the 'national identities of its Member States',[72] and with a Union 'founded on the principles of liberty, democracy, respect for human rights and fundamental freedoms, and the rule of law, principles which are common to the Member States'.[73]

The Union is not yet at its final destination, and so it is too soon to write in constitutional language the ultimate form of integration which the Member States[74] will adopt. The Maastricht Treaty caused alarm because it seemed to some too definite about the ultimate destination. Messy though the language and practice of variable geometry and differentiation are, they are reassuring to particular Member States which are at different points on the journey to the unknown destination. What is emerging from the debate is greater recognition that the ever-closer union of the peoples of Europe does not necessarily mean the abolition of the Member States as full nation states.

If such reassurances could be regarded as inherent in the current construction of the Union, it would be easier for some Member States to recognize the transfer of sovereignty, in particular to the Community, inherent in membership.

Uncertainty about the ultimate destination and size of the Union requires a flexible approach to the building of a constitution. The unwritten constitution is the ideal vehicle for such a task. The *Oxford English Dictionary* definition of a constitution is instructive in this context,

> The system or body of fundamental principles according to which a national State, or body politic is constituted and governed. This may be embodied in successive concessions on the part of the sovereign power, implied from long accepted statutes or established gradually by precedent ... [In the case of an unwritten or written constitution] it is assumed or specifically provided that the constitution is more fundamental than any particular law, and contains the principles with which all legislation must be in harmony.

It is not difficult to recast that definition in a way which fits the current state of development of the Union. The unwritten constitution of the Union consists of the constitutional principles now to be found in the treaties, the statements of the Court of Justice, and the traditions common to the Member States. There are, of course, two sub-systems: the Union system and the Community system which sit uneasily together. But the fact of the matter is that they do coexist, and they more or less function well. Clearly States can exist with unwritten constitutions; the Community has always been regarded as *sui generis* and the Union includes the Community. Once we avoid falling into the 'no Demos' fallacy for what is a *sui generis* development, we can address issues of democratic legitimacy more imaginatively (as Weiler has done – and not uncritically) and satisfy ourselves that there is an effective and powerful unwritten constitution for the Union. It is too soon to crystallize the evolution of that constitution by seeking to reduce it to a written constitutional document.

NB. This chapter was submitted for publication at the beginning of 1998.

Endnotes

1. Case 294/83, *Les Verts* v. *European Parliament*,.[1986] ECR 1339; [1987] 2 CMLR 343.
2. Case 294/83, *Les Verts* v. *European Parliament*, [1986] ECR 1339; [1987] 2 CMLR 343, para. 22.
3. Opinion 1/91, *Re the Draft Treaty on a European Economic Area*, [1991] ECR I-6079; [1992] 1 CMLR 245.
4. Opinion 1/91, *Re the Draft Treaty on a European Economic Area*, [1991] ECR I-6079; [1992] 1 CMLR 245, para. 21.
5. See for example, F. Dowrick, 'A Model of the European Communities' Legal System', *Yearbook of European Law*, Vol. 3, 1983, p. 169; G. Mancini, 'The Making of a Constitution for Europe', *Common Market Law Review*, Vol. 26, 1989, p. 595; K. Lenaerts, 'Constitutionalism and Federalism', *American Journal of Comparative Law*, Vol. 38, 1990, p. 205; J. H. Weiler, 'The Transformation of Europe', *Yale Law Journal*, Vol. 100, 1991, p. 2403; F. Jacobs, 'Is the Court of Justice of the European Communities a Constitutional Court?' in D. Curtin and D. O'Keeffe (eds), *Constitutional Adjudication in European Community and National Law*, Dublin: Butterworth, 1992, p. 25; D. Edward, 'The Community's Constitution – Rigid or Flexible? The Contemporary Relevance of the Constitution Thinking of James Bryce', in D. Curtin and T. Heukels (eds), *Institution Dynamics of European Integration. Essays in Honour of Henry G. Schermers, Volume II*, Dordrecht: Martinus Nijhoff, 1994, p. 57; S. Weatherill, 'Beyond Preemption? Shared Competence and Constitutional Change in the European Community', in D. O'Keeffe and P. Twomey (eds), *Legal Issues of the Maastricht Treaty*, London: Chancery Law Publishing, 1994; P. Eleftheriadis, 'Aspects of European Constitutionalism', *European Law Review*, Vol. 21, 1996, p. 32; B. de Witte, 'International Agreement or European Constitution?' in J. Winter *et al.* (eds), *Reforming the Treaty on European Union – The Legal Debate*, The Hague: Kluwer Law International, 1996, p. 3; A. Dashwood, 'EC Powers and Member States' Powers. Position Paper', in A. Dashwood (ed.), *Reviewing Maastricht Issues for the 1996 IGC*, London: Sweet & Maxwell, 1996, p. 6.
6. [1994] OJ C61/155.
7. Recital C of the Resolution.
8. See, notably, D. Curtin, 'The Constitutional Structure of the Union: a Europe of bits and pieces', *Common Market Law Review*, Vol. 30, 1993, p. 17.
9. Curtin, 'The Constitutional Structure of the Union', p. 18.
10. *Application of Manfred Brunner*, judgment of 12 October 1993, 89 BVer GE 155; (1994) 1 CMLR 57.
11. Even officially, see Report of the Reflection Group.
12. P. Norton, *The Constitution in Flux*, Oxford: Basil Blackwell, 1984, p. 3.
13. W. Jennings, *The Law and the Constitution*, 5th edn., London: University of London Press, 1960, p. 33.
14. See generally, D. Pollard, N. Parpworth and D. Hughes, *Constitutional and Administrative Law, Text with Materials*, 2nd edn., London: Butterworths, 1997, ch.1.
15. T. Paine, *The Rights of Man 1791–1792* (edited by H. Collins), Harmondsworth: Penguin Classics, 1969, p. 93.
16. Along with a territory, a people and independence. See I. Brownlie, *Principles of International Law*, 4th edn., Oxford University Press, 1990, pp. 72–9.
17. V. Bogdanor, 'Britain and the European Community', in J. Jowell and D. Oliver, *The Changing Constitution*, 3rd edn., Oxford: Clarendon Press, 1994, p. 4.

18. Case 6/64, *Costa* v. *ENEL*, [1964] ECR 585, 593.
19. Chronicled in D. Curtin, 'Directive: The Effectiveness of Judicial Protection of Individual Rights', *Common Market Law Review*, Vol. 27, 1990, p. 709, and M. Ross, 'Beyond *Francovich'*, *Modern Law Review*, Vol. 56, 1993, p. 55.
20. See, for example, Case 83/78, *Pigs Marketing Board* v. *Redmond*, [1978] ECR 2347; [1979] 1 CMLR 177.
21. See, especially, Case 29/69, *Stauder* v. *Ulm*, [19699] ECR 419; [1970] CMLR 112; and Case 11/70, *Internationale Handelsgesellschaft*, [1970] ECR 1125; [1972] CMLR 255.
22. Opinion 2/94, *Re the Accession of the Community to the European Human Rights Convention*, [1996] ECR I-1759; [1996] 2 CMLR 265, para. 33 of Opinion. See also Case 206/89, ERT v. *Pliroforissis and Kouvelas*, [1991] ECR I-2925; [1994] 4 CMLR 540.
23. Case 294/83, *Partie Ecologiste 'Les Verts'* v. *European Parliament*, [1986] ECR 1339; [1987] 2 CMLR 343, para. 23 of Decision.
24. In Joined Cases 31/86 and 35/86, *LAISA*, [1988] ECR 2285; [1988] 2 CMLR 420, para. 38 of Opinion; Case 302/87, *European Parliament* v. *EC Council*, [1988] ECR 5615, para. 20 of Opinion; Joined Cases 193 and 194/87, *Maurissen*, [1989] ECR 1045, para. 52 of Opinion; Case C-70/88, *Re Radioactive Food: European Parliament* v. *EC Council*, [1990] ECR I-2041; [1992] 1 CMLR 91, para. 6 of Opinion; Joined Cases C-181/91 and C-248/91, *Re Aid to Bangladesh: European Parliament* v. *EC Council and EC Commission*, [1993] ECR I-3685; [1994] 3 CMLR 317, para. 21 of Opinion; Case C-65/93, *Re Generalised Tariff Preferences: European Parliament* v. *EU Council*, [1995] ECR I-643; [1996] 1 CMLR 4, para. 20 of Opinion.
25. Case C-2/88, *Re JJ Zwartveld and others*, [1990] ECR I-3365; [1990] 3 CMLR 457, para. 16.
26. See Weiler, 'The Transformation of Europe', p. 2403.
27. With the accession of the United Kingdom, Denmark and Ireland, followed by the southern European countries of Greece, Spain and Portugal.
28. Art. 281 [ex Art. 210] EC.
29. See generally, F. Laurssen and S. Vanhoonacker, *The Ratification of the Maastricht Treaty. Issues, Debates and Future Implications*, Dordrecht: Martinus Nijhoff, 1994. The import of the message was acknowledged in the Report of the Reflection Group received at the Madrid European Council on 15–16 December 1995.
30. See, for example, U. Everling, 'Reflections on the Structure of the European Union', *Common Market Law Review*, Vol. 29, 1992, p. 17; Curtin, 'The Constitutional Structure of the Union', p. 17; A. Dashwood, 'Community Legislative Procedures in the Era of the Treaty on European Union', *European Law Review*, Vol. 19, 1994, p. 343; and J. Lipsius, 'The 1996 Intergovernmental Conference', *European Law Review*, Vol. 20, 1995, p. 235.
31. See D. O'Keeffe, 'The Emergence of a European Immigration Policy', *European Law Review*, Vol. 20, 1996, p. 20; and R. Bieber and J. Monar (eds), *Justice and Home Affairs in the European Union. The Development of the Third Pillar*, Brussels: European Interuniversity Press, 1995, part 4.
32. See for example, J. Mackenzie Stuart, 'Subsidiarity – A Busted Flush?', in Curtin and O'Keeffe (eds), *Constitutional Adjudication in European Community and National Law*, p. 19; D. Cass, 'The Word that Saves Maastricht? The Principle of Subsidiarity and the Division of Powers within the European Community', *Common Market Law Review*, Vol. 29, 1992, p. 1107; N. Emiliou, 'Subsidiarity: an Effective Barrier against the "Enterprises of Ambition" ', *European Law Review*, Vol. 17, 1992, p. 383; A. Toth, 'A Legal Analysis of Subsidiarity', in O'Keeffe and Twomey (eds), *Legal Issues of the Maastricht Treaty*; A. Toth, 'Is Subsidiarity Justiciable?', *European Law Review*, Vol. 19, 1994, p. 268.
33. *Application of Manfred Brunner*, judgment of 12 October 1993, 89 BVer GE 155; [1994] 1 CMLR 57. See notes by H. Crossland, 'Three Major Decisions given by the Bundesverfassungsgericht (Federal Constitutional Court)', *European Law Review*, Vol. 19, 1994, p. 202; J. H. Weiler, 'Do we Need a Constitution? Reflections on Demos, Telos and the German Maastricht Decision', *European Law Journal*, Vol. 1, 1995, p. 219; and M. Zuleeg, 'The European Constitution under Constitutional Constraints: The German Scenario', *European Law Review*, Vol. 22, 1997, p. 19.
34. See, especially, Weiler, 'Do we Need a Constitution? Reflections on Demos, Telos and the German Maastricht Decision', and Zuleeg, 'The European Constitution under Constitutional Constraints: The German Scenario'.
35. Nearly a year later than had been hoped.
36. [1994] OJ C61/155.
37. Article 236 EC; Article 96 ECSC; and Article 204 Euratom.
38. Good examples are Article 8 of the Statute of the Council of Europe and Article 5 of the Charter of the United Nations Organization.

39. Protocol on the Application of the Principles of Subsidiarity and Proportionality; this protocol is attached to the EC Treaty.
40. Protocol on the Application of the Principles of Subsidiarity and Proportionality, para. 6.
41. There is a preliminary reference procedure but it is much more circumscribed than hitherto and is optional, requiring a separate acceptance of this jurisdiction of the Court of Justice.
42. Which reads, 'The Union shall respect fundamental rights, as guaranteed by the European Convention for the Protection of Human Rights and Fundamental Freedoms signed in Rome on 4 November 1950 and as they result from constitutional traditions common to the Member States, as general principles of law.'
43. Art. 1(13), Treaty of Amsterdam, amending Article L TEU (later Art. 46 TEU).
44. See F. Jacobs and R. White, *The European Convention on Human Rights*, Oxford: Clarendon Press, 1996, p. 413.
45. Opinion 2/94, *Re the Accession of the Community to the European Human Rights Convention*, [1996] ECR I–1759; [1996] 2 CMLR 265, noted by N. Burrows, *European Law Review*, Vol. 22, 1997, p. 58.
46. Protocol on the Institutions with the Prospect of Enlargement of the European Union.
47. Article 189 (2) [ex Article 137(2)] EC.
48. Artcle 214 [ex Article 158(2)] EC.
49. Developing a similar Protocol to the Treaty on European Union.
50. See K. Lenaerts and E. de Smijter, 'The Question of Democratic Representation: On the Democratic Representation through the European Parliament, the Council, the Committee of the Regions, the Economic and Social Committee and the National Parliaments', in Winter *et al.* (eds), *Reforming the Treaty on European Union – The Legal Debate*, pp. 182–9.
51. See Dashwood, 'Community Legislative Procedures in the Era of the Treaty on European Union', pp. 265–6; and Lipsius, 'The 1996 Intergovernmental Conference', p. 262.
52. New Article 21 [ex Article J.11] and new Article 39 [ex Article K.11] TEU.
53. Para. 1(a).
54. Para. 1(b).
55. Para. 1(c).
56. Para. 1(d).
57. Para. 1(e).
58. Which may be prompted by a request from Member States: Para. 2, sub-para. 3.
59. Protocol annexed to the Treaty on European Union and to the Treaty establishing the European Community integrating the Schengen Acquis into the framework of the European Union.
60. Protocol annexed to the Treaty on European Union and to the Treaty establishing the European Community on the application of certain aspects of Article 7a of the Treaty establishing the European Community to the United Kingdom and Ireland, and Protocol annexed to the Treaty on European Union and to the Treaty establishing the European Community on the position of the United Kingdom and Ireland.
61. Protocol annexed to the Treaty on European Union and to the Treaty establishing the European Community on the position of Denmark.
62. See Weiler, 'Do we Need a Constitution? Reflections on Demos, Telos and the German Maastricht Decision', p. 219.
63. Weiler, 'Do we Need a Constitution?', p. 229.
64. Weiler, 'Do we Need a Constitution?', p. 240.
65. See, *contra*, D. Grimm, 'Does Europe Need a Constitution?', *European Law Journal*, Vol. 1, 1995, p. 282.
66. Weiler, 'Do we Need a Constitution?', p. 253.
67. Weiler, 'Do we Need a Constitution?', p. 253.
68. A. Dashwood, 'EC Powers and Member States' Powers. Position Paper', in A. Dashwood, (ed.) *Reviewing Maastricht Issues for the 1996 IGC*, London: Sweet & Maxwell, 1996, p. 6.
69. Dashwood, 'EC Powers and Member States' Powers', p. 6.
70. Dashwood, 'EC Powers and Member States' Powers', p. 7.
71. Article 1 [ex Article A] TEU.
72. Article 6(3) [ex Article F (3)] TEU.
73. Article 6(1) [ex Article F(1)] TEU.
74. Including a significant number of potential new Member States.

CONCLUSIONS

Conclusions: Maastricht, Amsterdam and beyond

Philip Lynch, Nanette A. Neuwahl and G. Wyn Rees

The European Union in the 1990s

This book has examined the development of the European Community (EC) and European Union (EU) in the 1990s, focusing on the changes introduced by the 1992 Treaty on European Union (the 'Maastricht Treaty') and, in particular, the 1997 Treaty of Amsterdam. Successive chapters have assessed institutional reform, policy developments and the changing nature of the EU. Characterizing this period is a difficult task given the uneven development of the Union. The reform process which began with the 1986 Single European Act continued into the 1990s, the most notable achievements being the virtual completion of the Single European Market and Economic and Monetary Union (EMU). The two Treaty revisions have also brought about significant institutional and policy change. Alongside this deepening, a widening occurred in 1995 when Austria, Finland and Sweden joined the Union. However, the 1990s have also been a period of policy setbacks and frustrated reform, the Amsterdam Treaty being viewed as a disappointment by proponents of reform.

A division of the decade into pre-Maastricht and post-Maastricht periods points out the different political environments faced by the 1990–91 and 1996–97 Intergovernmenal Conferences (IGCs) respectively. Here, the early part of the decade is viewed as one of continued (though partially frustrated) dynamism, while the post-Maastricht period is one of eroded confidence and incrementalism. The Maastricht Treaty lies at the juncture of the two periods, marking the high-water mark of the elite-driven reform agenda of the 1980s relaunch yet, from a reformist perspective, proffering limited change and provoking a popular backlash which subsequently strained the reform process. But this neat division is problematic. In viewing Maastricht as the conclusion of the dynamism of the late 1980s, one must also recognize the fundamental changes which occurred during 1989–90 – changes which EU Member States did not fully come to terms with at Maastricht. The collapse of communism in eastern Europe, German unification and the end of the Cold War significantly altered the political dynamics of European integration. Equally, despite the problems facing the Union in the post-Maastricht period, EU leaders have embraced (albeit falteringly and with varying degrees of enthusiasm) two major 'leaps of faith' – the creation of a single currency and the eastward enlargement of the Union.

This uneven progress of reform in the 1990s fits the 'stop-go' pattern evident in the development of the EC/EU since the 1950s.[1] The 1970s are usually depicted as a period of 'Euro-sclerosis' in which momentum was halted by economic downturn and a reassertion of national interests. But important developments, such as the creation of the European Monetary System (EMS) and the first direct elections to the European Parliament also took place in this period. The mid-1980s brought renewed dynamism with the Single European Market programme as the centrepiece of a relaunch of the Community. This uneven development also reflects disagreements about the ultimate destination of the EU's 'road to reform', and indeed over whether an end goal is necessary or desirable. The various organizing frameworks employed in the study of European integration and the EU offer contrasting perspectives on the development of the EU and the destination of the integration process. Although integration theory has not been a primary concern of this volume, four broad approaches are briefly outlined.

1. Neo-functionalism. Central to neo-functionalist theories of integration is the concept of 'spillover', whereby the transfer of functions from the nation state to supranational bodies accelerates across policy sectors. Integration is a technocratic and dynamic process driven by interest groups and the Commission, ultimately resulting in the transfer of competences and loyalties to a supranational political community. With the advent of 'Euro-sclerosis' in the 1970s, neo-functionalism lost much of its intellectual lustre. However, the Single European Market programme prompted a reworking of elements of the neo-functionalist model, including spillover and pressure from transnational business in the light of changing economic imperatives.[2]

2. Intergovernmentalism. Drawing upon neo-realist theories of international relations, intergovernmentalists treat the nation state as the dominant actor in EU decision-making. The pace, direction and major features of European integration are determined by interstate bargaining. Moravcsik's 'liberal intergovernmentalism' is the most influential recent variant of this approach. He outlines a 'two-level game' of domestic policy-making – in which a range of domestic actors seek to influence the state's European policy – and interstate bargaining in the EU in which governments aim to increase their executive autonomy.[3] If there is a convergence of national interests, states may cede sovereignty to achieve shared collective interests (e.g. free trade) but ensure that sovereignty is retained in matters of 'high politics' and that supranational bodies have limited autonomy.

3. Constitutionalization. A number of political scientists and lawyers view the EU as an emerging polity, likening European integration to a state-building or constitution-making process. Comparative studies of the supranational elements of the EC focus on federal ideas and federal systems. Rather than envisaging a federal Europe being created through agreement on a European constitution, Pinder talks of a neo-federalism in which the strengthening of supranational institutions and Community competence is gradually transforming the Union into a federal polity.[4] Legal scholars have examined the leading role of the European Court of Justice

(ECJ) in the constitutionalization of the Treaties. The ECJ has described the EEC Treaty as a 'constitutional charter',[5] clarified the relationship between Member States, the EC and citizens (through the principles of direct effect and the supremacy of Community law) and established principles governing the division of competences.[6] This gradual constitutionalization was evident during the 'Eurosclerosis' of the 1970s as well as the relaunch of the 1980s.

4. *EC governance.* Drawing upon public policy and/or 'institutionalist' methodology, a number of studies have highlighted the complex nature of EU governance in which policy-making occurs at a number of levels and differs in character from sector to sector.[7] National governments remain significant actors, especially on 'history-making decisions' such as Treaty reform, but Community institutions,[8] sub-national governments[9] and interest groups may all have important inputs into lower-level policy-making in the EC. Majone has emphasized the regulatory character of EC governance, the Commission developing a regulatory (rather than redistributive) role in the Single Market.[10] Although not producing an overarching theory of European integration or the EU's road to reform, such studies add to our understanding of EU governance and the day-to-day activity of the Union.

As the new millennium approaches, the destination of the reform process is uncertain. Debates about 'deepening' versus 'widening' have been complicated by the extension of differentiated integration, differences across policy sectors and the need to marry more effectively efficiency and democracy in the EU. The following sections assess the achievements and limitations of the reform process in the 1990s, focusing in particular on the Treaty of Amsterdam.

From Maastricht to Amsterdam

The contrasting political environments forming the backdrop to the 1990–91 twin IGCs and the 1996–97 IGC shaped their respective outcomes. In comparing the negotiations, four factors are especially significant. Firstly, the extent of convergence and divergence in the negotiating positions of key Member States crucially affected interstate bargaining and the outcome of the IGC process. Secondly, a national government's stance in the IGC was itself shaped by domestic factors which produced either opportunities or constraints.[11] The liberal intergovernmentalist thesis recognizes the leading role of national governments in Treaty negotiations, but they are not the only relevant actors. A third significant factor was thus the role played by supranational institutions, particularly the European Commission, and non-state actors. Finally, wider factors such as globalization and the state of the European economy were also relevant.

The 1990–91 IGCs

Member States agreed to establish the 1990–91 IGCs on EMU and political union at a significant historical juncture. A range of factors propelled the integration process forward but raised difficult questions about its purpose and destination, questions which the Maastricht Treaty did not resolve. The Single European Market programme, a convergence of national economic policy outlooks and Commission activism hastened further economic integration. German unification altered the dynamics of Community politics. Chancellor Kohl saw the future of Germany in a Community moving more rapidly towards political union; President Mitterrand saw EMU as a means of containing Germany and enhancing French economic influence.

The IGC on EMU benefited from the sense of purpose provided by the Franco–German partnership. Germany had particular influence over the EMU negotiations, favouring a multi-speed EMU, tough convergence criteria and an independent European Central Bank (ECB), although no single actor had overall control of the process.[12] By contrast, the parallel IGC on political union was less well focused and prone to divisions between maximalist states seeking an extension of Community competence and supranational authority, and minimalist states favouring an enlarged intergovernmental EU. The late 1980s and early 1990s were a period of Commission activism.[13] Jacques Delors chaired the influential Committee of Central Bank Governors (which produced the Delors Report on EMU) but was disappointed by the Maastricht Treaty – particularly its limited provisions on political union.

The Maastricht Treaty extended the scope of differentiated integration, granting special arrangements to a number of states. The UK and Denmark gained opt-outs from Stage III of EMU, while Britain's refusal to accept an extension of EC social policy competence forced the other 11 Member States to settle for a Social Protocol authorizing its signatories to use EC institutions and procedures to make and apply legislation in areas specified in the Social Agreement. The inclusion of Article 3b on subsidiarity, the principle that decisions should be taken as close as possible to the citizen, was championed by Britain and Germany. But, as Jeffery has noted, the mobilization of sub-national governments was also significant, the German Länder successfully lobbying for subsidiarity and the creation of the Committee of the Regions.

As Rees has argued, the early 1990s represented a window of opportunity in foreign and defence matters. However, although the TEU established a framework for action in the CFSP, it left a number of issues unresolved and fell short of creating a viable EU defence capability. Reconciling the different positions of Europeanists, Atlanticists and neutrals proved difficult. The CFSP arrangements ultimately reflected an uneasy truce between states advocating and opposing a leading role for the EU in security and defence. The differences between Member States were further confirmed during the Gulf War and civil war in former Yugoslavia. The unwillingness of some states to accept a communitarization of sovereignty-sensitive issues such as immigration and internal security policy also determined the primarily intergovernmental character of the justice and home affairs (JHA) third pillar.

In terms of institutional change, the introduction of the co-decision procedure gave the European Parliament (EP) a greater voice in the legislative process in some policy areas, although this did not satisfy those hoping the EP would have a more positive input. As Neuwahl has noted, the provisions on citizenship of the Union were innovative and had potential although they did not provide sufficient 'hard' rights for citizens.

The 1996–97 IGC

The road to reform proved harder to navigate during the 1996–97 IGC, given the difficult post-Maastricht terrain, the lack of a sense of direction and the misfiring of the traditional engines of European integration, namely the Franco–German partnership and the Commission. Unlike 1985 and 1990, no underlying rationale existed for the launch of an IGC in 1996. Many Member States would have preferred to concentrate on preparations for the 1999 launch of the single currency and allow more time for the TEU arrangements to be bedded in. However, Article N of the Maastricht Treaty stated that an IGC would be held in 1996 to revise a number of areas. These included the extension of co-decision; a revision of the CFSP; new titles on energy, tourism and civil protection, and the introduction of a hierarchy of Community acts. The weighting of votes in the Council was added to the agenda following the 1994 'Ioannina Compromise'. Flexibility, employment and a 'Europe closer to its citizens' also emerged as key issues. The 1995 Reflection Report identified three broad themes for the IGC: the citizen and the Union, an efficient and democratic Union, and effective external Union action.[14] It also illustrated the difficulties facing the IGC: many states wanted to make the EU work better without radical change and Britain opposed much of the reform agenda.

The EU endured a crisis of legitimacy for much of the post-Maastricht period. The elite-driven integration process encountered a popular backlash as the Maastricht Treaty endured a tortuous ratification process. The Treaty was rejected in a 1992 Danish referendum which altered the Community's political landscape; narrowly approved in the French referendum; met fierce opposition in the British parliament and was cautiously approved by the German constitutional court.[15] This backlash produced a crisis of confidence in the EU, the Commission under Jacques Santer reverting to a more pragmatic and consolidatory outlook ('not more but better'). The smooth functioning of the EU was also hindered by a series of Council Presidencies in which the governments of states holding that office were distracted by national elections. High-profile policy failings such as the 1992–93 crisis in the Exchange Rate Mechanism (ERM) and the EU's impotence in former Yugoslavia, plus teething troubles in the third pillar, added to the gloom.

Economic downturn and rising unemployment also took their toll, recession raising doubts about a successful transition to Stage III of EMU. High interest rates resulting from German unification and pressure from the foreign exchange markets provoked a crisis in the ERM. Britain and Italy left the mechanism in 1992 and others were forced to devalue their currencies before, in 1993, the bands of permitted currency fluctuation within the ERM were widened to 15 per cent for all but Germany and the Netherlands. Predictions that EMU would be blown off course were confounded, although political will wavered for a time as senior politicians in

Italy, Spain and France speculated about a delay in the EMU timetable or a softening of the convergence criteria. Governments instead recommitted themselves to meet the convergence criteria, taking unpopular decisions to cut public spending and raise taxes.[16] The harsh economic climate contributed to a change of emphasis in EU social policy as Member States and the Commission sought to marry social protection with labour market flexibility and competitiveness.

National governments faced additional domestic constraints on their European policies in the post-Maastricht period. Opinion polls showed declining support for European integration, especially as EMU acquired a negative symbolism given the enforced cuts in public spending. Euro-scepticism manifested itself in anti-European fringe parties and dissent in mainstream parties such as the British Conservatives and French RPR, though a heightened concern with identity politics was evident across the political spectrum.[17] A number of governing parties were embroiled in political scandals or suffered election defeats. To placate discontented electorates, governments curtailed their pro-integration aspirations, looking towards a 'Europe closer to the citizen' and to a coordination of national policies rather than deeper integration.

Tensions in the Franco–German relationship contributed to the inauspicious political environment.[18] Chirac's pragmatic attitude towards European integration and concern with sovereignty were evident in the decision to reapply border controls shortly after the Schengen Accord came into effect. The most significant disputes arose over the governance of EMU. The French government wanted the ECB's authority to be countered by the involvment of national ministers in EMU policy decisions. At Amsterdam, Jospin's newly elected Socialist government urged intervention to reduce unemployment and sought to reopen discussions on the Stability and Growth Pact.[19] Kohl and Chirac's refusal to take part in a bicycle ride organized for EU leaders at the Amsterdam summit seemed to symbolize the relative inertia of the Franco–German relationship.

The EU's mechanisms for achieving Treaty change have been the subject of criticism, the 1996–97 IGC in particular proving ineffective in furthering long-term reform or strategic rethinking. The likelihood of a successful IGC is increased if there is a shared sense of strategic direction, broad consensus among leading Member States on the favoured road to reform and effective leadership. These were not in evidence in 1996–97. Treaty outcomes tend to be complex deals, characterized by uneasy compromises, side-payments to states who are not obvious 'winners' and opt-outs for recalcitrant states. Intractable problems are left until a frantic 'end game' of brokering by Heads of State or Government, but this still failed to produce agreement on institutional reform at the Amsterdam summit.

The Treaty of Amsterdam

Though regarded as a disappointment by many advocates of reform, the Amsterdam Treaty brings about a number of significant developments. Foremost among these are the changes to the justice and home affairs pillar. The EC Treaty provides for the progressive establishment of an 'area of freedom, security and justice'. Title IIIa on 'visas, asylum, immigration and other policies related to the free movement of persons' brings controls at external borders, asylum, immigration and judicial cooperation on civil matters into the first pillar. For the first five years after the entry into force of the Treaty, the Council will take decisions by unanimity in these areas, following proposals by either the Commission or a Member State. After that the Council will decide, on proposals from the Commission, by unanimity to apply the co-decision procedure and QMV when adopting measures under Title IIIa.

The third pillar is an emaciated one following the communitarization of these areas, leaving only 'police and judicial cooperation in criminal matters' (Title VI TEU) within its remit. Decision-making procedures here are streamlined. The Treaty also brings about the incorporation of the Schengen *acquis* into the framework of the EU, though establishing a legal basis for Schengen measures will be a complex process lacking in transparency. As Monar has noted, internal security matters in the EU are fragmented, given the opt-outs granted to the UK, Ireland and Denmark on border controls and/or Schengen measures. Matters falling within both Title IIIa and Title VI will be subject to the jurisdiction of the ECJ but there is no direct citizen access to the Court in these areas while the maintenance of law and order plus internal security are excluded from the Court's remit.

The Amsterdam Treaty includes a new employment title and makes the objective of 'a high level of employment' a 'matter of common concern' for Member States. As Kenner has noted, this marks an important change of direction in Community social policy and the election of centre-left governments in key Member States has raised expectations of further action in this field. The Labour government in Britain accepted the Agreement on Social Policy, allowing its incorporation into the EC Treaty and the repeal of the Social Protocol. But the social dimension itself is not significantly extended. Anti-discrimination and human rights provisions are strengthened; and new measures on the equal treatment of men and women are also included. Only limited improvements have been made to provisions on citizenship.

The Treaty has been particularly criticized for failing to provide concrete institutional reforms ahead of the anticipated enlargement of the Union. The re-weighting of votes in the Council and the size of the Commission in an enlarged Europe proved intractable issues, opening up new divisions over the appropriate balance between large and small Member States. Large states sought a new voting formula to replace the simple arithmetical calculations under which a coalition of small states might in future be able to outvote their more powerful neighbours. Proposals on re-weighting were rejected, leaving the much maligned 'Ioannina Compromise' in force. Crucial decisions were postponed, a Protocol appended to the Treaty stating that another IGC must be held 'to carry out a comprehensive review of the provisions of the Treaties on the composition and functioning of the institutions' at least a year before EU membership exceeds 20. The weighting of votes and size of the Commission are linked: after the next enlargement, the College of Commissioners will comprise one national from each Member State, provided that votes in the Council have been satisfactorily re-weighted. The EP is restricted to a maximum of 700 MEPs.

The EU's legislative process has, however, been simplified and the role of the European Parliament enhanced. The number of legislative routes is reduced to three main procedures, namely co-decision, assent and consultation. The cooperation procedure is only retained for four monetary policy provisions. The co-decision procedure is extended and simplified. A third reading will no longer be possible; if the Council and EP cannot reach agreement, the proposal will fail. The approval of the EP will be required for the appointment of the Commission President and the President-elect will have a greater say in the appointment of his or her fellow Commissioners. The use of qualified majority voting is extended, provisions on transparency added and the flow of information to national parliaments improved. Rules regarding the application of subsidiarity are set out in a Protocol. However, this does not amount to the extension of the principle of subsidiarity which had been hoped for and may have limited practical effect.

The jurisdiction of the ECJ is extended but the principle that it must be uniform has been abandoned so that in future differentiated case law will be the rule. The judicial protection of the citizen remains incomplete, particularly in areas relating to the third pillar and the area of 'freedom, security and justice'.

A general clause on closer cooperation, allowing a majority of Member States to push ahead with further integration subject to the unanimous approval of all Member States, is included in the new Treaty. Additional conditions are set out in specific clauses in the EC Treaty and TEU. However, the strict conditions and inclusion of a 'Luxembourg Compromise' arrangement (allowing a Member State to effectively veto closer cooperation if it declares such a move prejudicial to its national interests) are likely to limit the possibility of states pursuing flexible integration within the framework of the EU.

The Treaty effects little more than marginal improvements to the CFSP, enhancing its visibility through a new post of High Representative and a planning unit. 'Constructive abstention' allows dissenting states to avoid participation in a common policy without having to block the proposal. In defence terms, Amsterdam represents the maintenance of the status quo, due in large part to the fact that NATO's process of adaptation had eclipsed the demands for a stronger European defence identity. The EU and WEU are only likely to act in a future crisis if NATO has declined to take the lead.

Taken as a whole, the complex and fragmented nature of the Treaty of Amsterdam reflects its status as a deal born from compromise, limited ambition and an inability to solve some of the central problems facing the Union. Its positive points reflect an incremental development of the EU rather than a giant stride forward. Some eagerly anticipated changes, notably institutional reform, failed to materialize, while progress in other areas (e.g. Schengen and closer cooperation) brought the danger of further fragmentation. Although decisions on institutional reform were postponed, Westlake has argued that the IGC took some steps towards mapping out the parameters of a future reform package by promoting discussion of possible scenarios. Away from the IGC, internal reform processes are under way in the Council and Commission, promising significant improvements in their working methods.

Key challenges at the millennium

The Amsterdam Treaty failed to get to grips with one of the central dilemmas facing the EU at the millennium, namely institutional reform. In accordance with the Amsterdam Protocol on institutions, the June 1999 Cologne European Council decreed that another IGC will be held in 2000 to 'resolve the institutional issues left open in Amsterdam that need to be settled before enlargement'. In particular, the new IGC will focus on the size and composition of the Commission; the weighting of votes in the Council and the possible extension of QMV. The resignation of the disgraced Santer Commission in March 1999 following the First Report of the Committee of Independent Experts, which presented damning evidence of serious irregularities and fraud, increased the urgency for reform. New Commission President Romano Prodi has pledged to 'transform the Commission into a modern, efficient administration which has learnt the lessons of recent experience and put its house in order' and take seriously any demand by the European Parliament to remove a Commissioner who fell foul of a stricter code of conduct. The further development of effective policies, enhanced legitimacy of the Union and the management of diversity, all of which were central themes in the IGC, remain key issues. Despite these shortcomings, progress on two of the most significant issues facing the Union – EMU and eastward enlargement – accelerated in the late 1990s. A brief assessment of these challenges follows.

1. 'A Europe closer to its citizens'

In the post-Maastricht period, questions about the legitimacy of the EU and its perceived 'democratic deficit' have been raised by both Europhiles and Euro-sceptics. Democracy, efficiency and the relationship between the Union and its citizens were highlighted as key themes for the IGC by the Reflection Group and Turin European Council. However, norms of legitimacy and democracy are primarily associated with the liberal democractic nation state and cannot be automatically applied to the EU, given the lack of consent for majoritarian democracy and the limits of European identity. In the EU, legitimacy and democracy have both supranational aspects (e.g. a directly elected Parliament, a Court upholding the rule of law and a Commission acting in a regulatory capacity in the Single Market) and intergovernmental aspects (ministers are elected by national electorates and accountable to national parliaments).[20]

Supranational legitimacy is enhanced by the Amsterdam Treaty's provisions granting an increased legislative role for the EP, changes to the process of appointing Commissioners and the extension of the ECJ's jurisdiction in justice and home affairs matters. The EU's commitment to justice and rights is further clarified. Provisions on the role of national parliaments in EU decision-making and greater transparency strengthen democratic accountability in a national context. The IGC negotiations recognized that the legitimacy of the EU also depends in part on the effectiveness and efficiency of its policies, a utilitarian outlook which produced further action on employment.[21] Concerns about the accountability of the ECB illustrate that debates about legitimacy, democracy, transparency and efficiency remain potent.

The Amsterdam Treaty did not mark a giant stride towards a European constitution which delineates EU, national and sub-national competences and provides a 'Bill of Rights' enshrining citizens' rights. The term 'constitution' refers to the basic framework of (written or uncodified) rules of a society regarding the relationship between its constituent elements. For a number of reasons, it is too early to speak of a constitution for Europe existing in the late 1990s. Firstly, it is unclear whether the putative constitution would be that of the EU for, unlike the European Communities, the EU is not endowed with legal personality. Secondly, neither the European Union nor the European Communities are involved in the process of identification of citizens of the Union. This remains the prerogative of the Member States, which not only results in unequal access to citizenship but also inequality of influence over the process. Another limitation is that European citizens do not have democratic influence over either EU law-making or the basic norms governing the Union or Communities. As such, they are largely detached from constitution-making and from the application and interpretation of the constitution. Enhancing the legislative role of the EP does not by itself adequately close the democratic deficit.

The rights derived from the Treaty cannot be uniformly enforced by those subject to it by direct recourse to a constitutional court. The jurisdiction of the ECJ is subject to limitations in the form of Article 46 (ex Article L) TEU, especially in relation to the third pillar where its jurisdiction is at best partial and seemingly subject to the discretion of the Member States (Article 68 TEU). In addition, where there is conflict between the basic Treaties and norms of justice, there is no guarantee that the latter will prevail or that the outcome of such a conflict will be the same across the Union. The protection of human rights is also imperfectly guaranteed. Access to justice may become a real problem in the Union of the future, both because of deficiencies in the legal protection of the individidual inherent in the new Treaty and because impending enlargement may exacerbate existing difficulties regarding the Court's functioning. Finally, the EU lacks an independent power of taxation, limiting its capacity to develop new policies and take effective action in existing spheres of competence.

The Communities have clear legal personality and, owing to the effect of legal norms as derived by the ECJ from the Treaties, are frequently referred to as supranational entities. Here, 'supranational' denotes that the law enforceable within a Member State can be made without the express agreement of that state's government. Supranationality is an intrinsically negative concept, concerned with the loss of decision-making power rather than the creation of a fully fledged constitution. It does not cater for the creative aspects of a society, which one would expect to be present in a framework for a constitution.

Given the developments of the 1990s, is the EU moving closer towards a constitution? The influence of the EP has certainly expanded, especially within the EC, where the co-decision procedure is now the rule rather than the exception, but this has not significantly closed the democratic deficit. Overall, the Amsterdam Treaty does not mark a decisive move closer to a European constitution. Its provisions on citizenship do not add much in terms of qualitative rights or the circle of recipients. Citizenship of the Union is still predicated upon citizenship of a Member State and is incapable of addressing the plight of non-EC nationals lawfully resident in the Union who, while forming part of European society, are denied citizenship. Indeed, the provisions for closer cooperation mean that progress in some policy areas may be achieved at the expense of unity, without sufficient legal guarantees of equality between citizens of the Union should some but not all states proceed with closer cooperation. The greater scope for flexibility may well work against the development of a European constitution.

2. Effective policies

The onus is on the EU and its Member States to ensure that the apparatus put in place by the Maastricht and Amsterdam Treaties for dealing with problems such as unemployment, illegal immigration, organized crime and threats to European security work effectively. The Single Market and EMU are crucial to the economic prosperity of the Union. The Single Market is the EU's major success story of the 1990s, yet a handful of problems continue to frustrate business leaders. The Commission's 1996 report on 'The Impact and Effectiveness of the Single Market' concluded that it was working effectively, but additional efforts were required for the benefits to be fully enjoyed.[22] The report estimated that the Single Market had resulted in up to 900,000 extra jobs being created in the Union, had increased EU GDP by up to 1.5 per cent and intra-EU trade by 20 per cent. It also found evidence of greater competition; accelerated industrial restructuring and sectoral specialization; a wider range of products being available at lower prices, and greater mobility of goods and persons.

The Commission's 1997 first Single Market Scoreboard indicated that 359 of the 1,339 Single Market directives, some 25 per cent, had not yet been implemented in all Member States.[23] At the Amsterdam European Council, Member States endorsed the Single Market Action Plan.[24] This set four strategic targets: (i) making Single Market rules more effective through proper enforcement; (ii) dealing with major distortions such as tax barriers and anti-competitive behaviour; (iii) removing sectoral obstacles to market integration, including further progress towards the liberalization of the gas, telecommunications and electricity sectors; and (iv) increasing citizen awareness of the benefits of the Single Market.

EMU is the centrepiece of European integration and the future development of the Union. In May 1998 a special European Council meeting confirmed that 11 Member States – Austria, Belgium, Finland, France, Germany, Ireland Italy, Luxembourg, the Netherlands, Spain and Portugal – would form the 'first wave' of states joining the single currency, even though only four of these states (Finland, France, Luxembourg and Portugal) unequivocally met all of the convergence criteria.[25] Stage III of EMU duly began on 1 January 1999 as the euro became a currency in its own right, exchange rates of the 11 participating Member States became irrevocable conversion rates and the ECB began conducting monetary policy for the euro zone.[26] Citizens will continue to use national banknotes, which survive as denominations of the euro until 1 January 2002 when euro banknotes and coins will be introduced into circulation.

A successful EMU promises a number of benefits – an end to exchange rate uncertainty in intra-EU trade, the elimination of transaction costs on cross-border trade. However, as Healey has noted, a number of potential economic costs and political risks exist. The ECB sets interest rates for the euro zone as a whole, acting as though convergence was sufficient and that 'one monetary policy fits all'. Economic and political difficulties will arise in the event of an asymmetric shock adversely affecting only some states or regions in the euro zone. The Stability and Growth Pact curtails the extent to which governments can resort to fiscal policy to stabilize their economies. Given this limited leeway, the less economically integrated states may endure persistent high unemployment, fuelling social unrest and creating political pressure targeted at the ECB, ultimately destabilizing the Union.

Other areas of concern include the political tensions between Member States on the economic governance of EMU and the relationship between EMU 'ins' and 'outs'. The post-Maastricht negotiations on the governance of EMU saw disputes between France and Germany. At Amsterdam, Member States confirmed their commitment to budgetary discipline by finalizing agreement on a Stability and Growth Pact which provides for public surveillance of national economic performance and possible sanctions against euro zone states which fail to reduce excessive deficits.[27] The creation of an ERM II linking the currencies of Member States outside the euro area with the euro was also confirmed, though membership of the new mechanism will be voluntary. The French government was keen for national finance ministers (via the Euro-11 group) to play an active role in the governance of EMU, but this has been resisted by Germany, which is unwilling to undermine the primary role of the independent ECB. A Franco–German dispute over the nomination of Wim Duisenberg as first President of the European Central Bank also overshadowed the May 1998 special European Council on EMU.[28]

Finally, the management of an EMU of 'ins' and 'outs' has already provoked disputes concerning the role of the Euro-11 group in which the finance ministers of the 'first-wave' states discuss EMU-related issues. Britain, which feared being excluded from decision-making, won an undertaking that decisions on broader economic policy would only be formally taken in Ecofin meetings, but it seems likely that the euro zone states will cooperate more closely on matters of common interest. Some 'first-wave' states are also eager to forge ahead with cooperation on flanking policies such as social protection and taxation. Given the political costs of exclusion from a successful euro zone, Greece and Britain can be expected to seek entry early in the next millennium, placing further pressure on Denmark and Sweden to join.

3. *Eastward enlargement*

In order to absorb new members successfully while maintaining the momentum of European integration, the Union will need to adapt its institutions and policies, and decide how to manage a more diverse organization. It must also ensure that enlargement proceeds smoothly, assisting applicant states to meet clearly established criteria for membership. Although the EU remains committed to eastward enlargement, the enthusiasm for enlargement has waned somewhat as the scale of the challenge became apparent.[29]

The 1994 Copenhagen European Council offered east and central European states the prospect of full membership of the EU provided that they met membership criteria including stable democratic institutions, a functioning market economy, the capacity to cope with competitive pressures inside the EU and the ability to adopt the *acquis*, including the goals of political union and EMU. A 'pre-accession strategy' was mapped out at the 1994 Essen European Council. 'Europe Agreements' with applicant states would develop market access, establish free trade in industrial goods, provide economic and cultural cooperation, and assist the approximation of legislation. The focus of the Phare programme, originally created to support economic restructuring, was extended to include assistance in managing the market economy and reforming administrative systems. A 'structured relationship' of regular meetings between ministers from the EU and applicant states was also established. A 1995 White Paper set out a detailed series of measures which applicant states would have to introduce in order to participate in the Single European Market. Following reports and discussions on the suitability of each applicant state, accession negotiations with Cyprus, the Czech Republic, Estonia, Hungary, Poland and Slovenia were formally opened in 1998. The other east European applicant states – Bulgaria, Latvia, Lithuania, Romania and Slovakia – must wait. The deterioration of Turkey's relationship with the EU as its chances of membership have receded provides a salutary warning of the dangers of artificially raising then dashing expectations.

The Commission set out its proposals for the substantial reform of the Common Agricultural Policy (CAP) and the Structural Funds in its 1997 Agenda 2000 Communication, concrete legislative proposals following thereafter.[30] A target of reaching agreement on the Agenda 2000 proposals in 1999 has been set, but given the vested interests many states have in EC regional funding and agricultural price support, difficult negotiations lay ahead at the time of writing. Negotiations on the Community's financial framework, in which Germany is pressing for a reduction in its net budget contributions, may also prove difficult. As for institutional reform, the Amsterdam negotiations illustrated the difficulties of ensuring effective EU institutions which reflect the importance of the large states while also protecting the interests of small states and maintaining formal equality amongst Member States.

The diversity of capacity and political will already apparent within a Union of 15 Member States will be exacerbated by enlargement. The provisions on differentiated integration in the Maastricht and Amsterdam Treaties testify to the problems the EU already faces in managing diversity. Yet the Treaties do little to ease the accession of east and central European states. The Accession Strategy seeks to adapt to eastward enlargement the traditional technocratic mode of enlargement, in which new Member States accept the existing *acquis* in full but are granted transition periods. The EU is thus playing an active role in encouraging applicant states to adapt to the *acquis*. New members will also have to accept the goal of EMU membership and the associated convergence criteria, plus the newly incorporated Schengen *acquis*, while existing opt-outs will not be open to new Member States.

Over the next decade or so, the EU will undergo significant change as EMU brings deeper integration and the Union expands to encompass some 27 Member States. The next enlargement presents an unprecedented challenge, bringing into the Union states with an average real GDP per person of only 40 per cent of the EU average[31] and, particularly in the case of Poland, substantial agricultural sectors. Market economies, civil society and democratic political cultures are also still at a relatively early stage of their development in east and central Europe.

The EU's existing institutional arrangements and decision-making procedures are in need of overhaul. The political, economic and social diversity already evident in the EU will become more pronounced with differentiated integration becoming an operating code of an enlarged Union. The eastward and southern extension of the EU's external border will also bring the new 'hard' and 'soft' security challenges of the post-Cold War era into sharper focus (e.g. relations with Russia, ethnic conflict, organized crime and migration).

Whither the European Union?

The development of the EU has neither resulted in a federal polity with clearly demarcated competences, nor an intergovernmental union of states in which national governments enjoy a monopoly over decision-making. Its day-to-day functioning instead suggests a multi-level polity in which a range of actors are involved in European governance across distinct policy sectors. Though internal reforms are under way within the EU institutions, national governments are still the most important actors in the EU's reform process. Indeed, the elite-driven nature of European integration to date has been a factor in the Union's recent legitimacy problems. The reforms brought about by the Maastricht and Amsterdam Treaties have been important but insufficient steps along the EU's road to reform. The Union's success in the early years of the twenty-first century will be judged by the effectiveness of its policies, the progress made towards developing a 'Europe closer to its citizens', and the ability of its leaders to forge a consensus on the direction of the road to reform and the measures which need to be taken *en route*.

Endnotes

1. H. Wallace, 'The Challenge of Governance', in H. Wallace and W. Wallace (eds), *Policy-Making in*

the European Union, Oxford: Oxford University Press, 1996, p. 12 uses the metaphor of a pendulum to describe movements in the integration process. See also D. Corbey, 'Dialectical Functionalism: Stagnation as a Booster of European Integration', *International Organization*, Vol. 49, 1995, pp. 253–84.

2. See, for example, W. Sandholtz and J. Zysman, '1992: Recasting the European Bargain', *World Politics*, Vol. 42, 1989, pp. 95–128.
3. A. Moravcsik, 'Preferences and Power in the European Community: A Liberal Intergovernmentalist Approach', *Journal of Common Market Studies*, Vol. 31, 1993, pp. 473–524.
4. J. Pinder, 'European Community and Nation-State: A Case for a Neo-Federalism?', *International Affairs*, Vol. 62, 1986, pp. 41–54.
5. Case 294/83, *Les Verts* v. *European Parliament*, [1986] ECR 1339.
6. J. H. H. Weiler, 'The Transformation of Europe', *Yale Law Review*, Vol. 100, 1991, pp. 2403–83; J. H. H. Weiler, 'The Reformation of European Constitutionalism', *Journal of Common Market Studies*, Vol. 35, 1997, pp. 267–99.
7. J. Peterson, 'Decision-Making in the European Union: Towards a Framework for Analysis', *Journal of European Public Policy*, Vol. 2, 1995, pp. 69–93.
8. S. Bulmer, 'The Governance of the European Union: A New Institutionalist Approach', *Journal of Public Policy*, Vol. 13, 1994, pp. 351–80.
9. G. Marks, L. Hooghe and K. Blank, 'European Integration from the 1980s: State-Centric versus Multi-Level Governance', *Journal of Common Market Studies*, Vol. 34, 1996, pp. 341–78.
10. See G. Majone, *Regulating Europe*, London: Routledge, 1996.
11. See S. Bulmer, 'Domestic Politics and European Community Policy-Making', *Journal of Common Market Studies*, Vol. 21, 1983, pp. 351–80.
12. K. Dyson, *Elusive Union: The Process of Economic and Monetary Union in Europe*, London: Longman, 1994, Chs 9 and 10.
13. G. Ross, *Jacques Delors and European Integration*, Oxford: Polity Press, 1995, emphasizes Delors's role in the EMU policy process.
14. *The Reflection Group Report*, 1995. SN 520/95 (REFLEX 21), Brussels, p. iii.
15. The referendum results were, however, as much a reflection of domestic factors as concern about the Maastricht Treaty. See M. Franklin, M. Marsh and L. McLaren, 'Uncorking the Bottle: Popular Opposition to European Unification in the Wake of Maastricht', *Journal of Common Market Studies*, Vol. 32, 1994, pp. 455–72.
16. Governments also resorted to more suspect short-term measures to meet the convergence criteria, such as a one-off tax in Italy, the partial privatization of the telecommunications industry in France and an attempted revaluation of gold reserves in Germany.
17. See B. Laffan, 'The Politics of Identity and Political Order in Europe', *Journal of Common Market Studies*, Vol. 34, 1996, pp. 81–102.
18. A. Szukala and W. Wessels, 'The Franco-German Tandem', in G. Edwards and A. Pijpers (eds), *The Politics of European Treaty Reform*, London: Pinter, 1997, pp. 74–99.
19. I. Davidson, 'Fault-Lines Appear', *The Financial Times*, 25 June 1998.
20. See D. Beetham and C. Lord, *Legitimacy and the European Union*, London: Longman, 1998.
21. See R. Dehousse, 'European Institutional Architecture after Amsterdam: Parliamentary System or Regulatory Structure?', *Common Market Law Review*, Vol. 35, 1998, pp. 595–627.
22. European Commission, *The Impact and Effectiveness of the Single Market*, Communication from the Commission to the European Parliament and Council, 30 October 1996. COM(96)250. See also, A. Caiger and D. Floudas, *1996 Onwards: Lowering the Barriers Further*, London: John Wiley, 1996.
23. European Commission Press Release 19 November 1997, 'Single Market first Scoreboard highlights Strengths and Weaknesses', IP/97/1017. By late 1998, the figure for non-implementation had fallen to 14.9 per cent.
24. European Commission, *Action Plan for the Single Market*, Communication of the Commission to the European Council, 1997, (CSE(97)1).
25. Council decision of 2 May 1998 in accordance with Article 109j(4) EC.
26. Further information is available from the EU's euro website at: http://www.europa.eu.int/euro/html/home.5html?lang=5
27. Amsterdam European Council Presidency Conclusions of 16 June 1997. CONF4001/97.
28. *Agence Europe*, No. 7213 (special edition), 3 May 1998.
29. See K. Hughes, 'A Most Exclusive Club', *The Financial Times*, 26 August 1998; Q. Peel and S. Wagstyl, 'Journey into the Unknown', *The Financial Times*, 9 November 1998. For a more detailed

assessment, see M. Maresceau (ed.), *Enlarging the European Union: Relations between the EU and Central and Eastern Europe*, London: Longman, 1997.

30. Commission Communication 'Agenda 2000: For a Stronger and Wider Europe', COM(97) 2000.
31. Eurostat Statistics in Focus, *Economy and Finance*, No. 28/98, 'The GDP of Candidate Countries of Central and Eastern Europe and Cyprus'. Slovenia (68 per cent of EU average) had the highest real GDP of the five 'first wave' eastern and central European states, Estonia the lowest (37 per cent).

Index